NEW YORK

JAN

ACKNOWLEDGMENTS

We gratefully acknowledge the help of our representatives for their efficient and perceptive inspections of the lodgings listed. Forbes Travel Guide is also grateful to the talented writers who contributed to this book.

ISBN: 9-780841-61420-8   Manufactured in the USA

10 9 8 7 6 5 4 3 2 1

TABLE OF CONTENTS

NEW YORK
★★★★★

STAR ATTRACTIONS

If you've been a reader of Mobil Travel Guide, you will have heard that this historic brand partnered with another storied media name, Forbes, in 2009 to create a new entity, Forbes Travel Guide. For more than 50 years, Mobil Travel Guide assisted travelers in making smart decisions about where to stay and dine when traveling. With this new partnership, our mission has not changed: We're committed to the same rigorous inspections of hotels, restaurants and spas—the most comprehensive in the industry with more than 500 standards tested at each property we visit—to help you cut through the clutter and make easy and informed decisions on where to spend your time and travel budget. Our team of anonymous inspectors are constantly on the road, sleeping in hotels, eating in restaurants and making spa appointments, evaluating those exacting standards to determine a property's rating.

What kind of standards are we looking for when we visit a proprety? We're looking for more than just high-thread count sheets, pristine spa treatment rooms and white linen-topped tables. We look for service that's attentive, in-dividualized and unforgettable. We note how long it takes to be greeted when you sit down at your table, or to be served when you order room service, or whether the hotel staff can confidently help you when you've forgotten that one essential item that will make or break your trip. Unlike other travel ratings entities, we visit the places we rate, testing hundreds of attributes to compile our ratings, and our ratings cannot be bought or influenced. The Forbes Five Star rating is the most prestigious achievement in hospitality—while we rate more than 8,000 properties in the U.S., Canada, Hong Kong, Macau and Beijing, for 2010, we have awarded Five Star designations to only 53 hotels, 21 restaurants and 18 spas. When you travel with Forbes, you can travel with confidence, knowing that you'll get the very best experience, no matter who you are.

We understand the importance of making the most of your time. That's why the most trusted name in travel is now Forbes Travel Guide.

STAR RATED HOTELS

Whether you're looking for the ultimate in luxury or the best value for your travel budget, we have a hotel recommendation for you. To help you pinpoint properties that meet your needs, Forbes Travel Guide classifies each lodging by type according to the following characteristics:

★★★★★These exceptional properties provide a memorable experience through virtually flawless service and the finest of amenities. Staff are intuitive, engaging and passionate, and eagerly deliver service above and beyond the guests' expectations. The hotel was designed with the guest's comfort in mind, with particular attention paid to craftsmanship and quality of product. A Five-Star property is a destination unto itself.

★★★★These properties provide a distinctive setting, and a guest will find many interesting and inviting elements to enjoy throughout the property. Attention to detail is prominent throughout the property, from design concept to quality of products provided. Staff are accommodating and take pride in catering to the guest's specific needs throughout their stay.

★★★These well-appointed establishments have enhanced amenities that provide travelers with a strong sense of location, whether for style or function. They may have a distinguishing style and ambience in both the public spaces and guest rooms; or they may be more focused on functionality, providing guests with easy access to local events, meetings or tourism highlights.

★★The Two Star hotel is considered a clean, comfortable and reliable establishment that has expanded amenities, such as a full-service restaurant.

★The One Star lodging is a limited-service hotel or inn that is considered a clean, comfortable and reliable establishment.

For every property, we also provide pricing information. All prices quoted are accurate at the time of publication; however, prices cannot be guaranteed.

STAR RATED RESTAURANTS

Every restaurant in this book comes highly recommended as an outstanding dining experience.

★★★★★Forbes Five-Star restaurants deliver a truly unique and distinctive dining experience. A Five-Star restaurant consistently provides exceptional food, superlative service and elegant décor. An emphasis is placed on originality and personalized, attentive and discreet service. Every detail that surrounds the experience is attended to by a warm and gracious dining room team.

★★★★These are exciting restaurants with often well-known chefs that feature creative and complex foods and emphasize various culinary techniques and a focus on seasonality. A highly-trained dining room staff provides refined personal service and attention.

★★★Three Star restaurants offer skillfully-prepared food with a focus on a specific style or cuisine. The dining room staff provides warm and professional service in a comfortable atmosphere. The décor is well-coordinated with quality fixtures and decorative items, and promotes a comfortable ambience.

★★The Two Star restaurant serves fresh food in a clean setting with efficient service. Value is considered in this category, as is family friendliness.

★The One Star restaurant provides a distinctive experience through culinary specialty, local flair or individual atmosphere.

Because menu prices can fluctuate, we list a pricing range rather than specific prices. The pricing ranges are per diner, and assume that you order an appetizer or dessert, an entrée and one drink.

STAR RATED SPAS

Forbes Travel Guide's spa ratings are based on objective evaluations of more than 450 attributes. About half of these criteria assess basic expectations, such as staff courtesy, the technical proficiency and skill of the employees and whether the facility is clean and maintained properly. Several standards address issues that impact a guest's physical comfort and convenience, as well as the staff's ability to impart a sense of personalized service. Additional criteria measure the spa's ability to create a completely calming ambience.

★★★★★Stepping foot in a Five Star Spa will result in an exceptional experience with no detail overlooked. These properties wow their guests with extraordinary design and facilities, and uncompromising service. Expert staff cater to your every whim and pamper you with the most advanced treatments and skin care lines available. These spas often offer exclusive treatments and may emphasize local elements.

★★★★Four Star spas provide a wonderful experience in an inviting and serene environment. A sense of personalized service is evident from the moment you check in and receive your robe and slippers. The guest's comfort is always of utmost concern to the well-trained staff.

★★★These spas offer well-appointed facilities with a full complement of staff to ensure that guests' needs are met. The spa facilities include clean and appealing treatment rooms, changing areas and a welcoming reception desk.

NEW YORK

THE LARGEST OF THE NORTHEASTERN STATES, NEW YORK STRETCHES FROM THE GREAT Lakes to the Atlantic. The glitter and glamour of New York City—from the skyscrapers in Midtown to the beaches of Coney Island—make America's most populous city a world capital. But New York State has much more to offer than just Gotham. Niagara Falls, Genesee Gorge, the Finger Lakes, the Thousand Islands of the St. Lawrence, the Catskills (where Rip Van Winkle is said to have slept for 20 years), the white-sand beaches of the Hamptons, the lakes and forested peaks of the Adirondacks and the stately bluffs along the Hudson are just a few of the features that attract millions of tourists every year.

When Giovanni da Verrazano entered New York Harbor in 1524, the Native Americans who inhabited the area were at constant war with one another. Around 1570, under Dekanawidah and Hiawatha, they formed the Iroquois Confederacy (the first League of Nations) and began to live in peace. They were known as the Five Nations and called themselves the "Men of Men."

In 1609, Samuel de Champlain explored the valley of the lake that now holds his name, and Henry Hudson sailed up the river that also bears his name. New Amsterdam (later called New York City) was founded in 1625. Wars with the Native Americans and the French kept the area in turmoil until after 1763. During the Revolution, eastern New York was a seesaw of military action and occupation. After the war, George Washington was inaugurated as president in 1789 in the federal government's new capital, New York City.

Governor DeWitt Clinton later envisioned a canal extending from the Hudson River in Albany to the city of Buffalo in order to develop the state and offer aid to its Western farmers. Constructed from 1817 to 1825, the Erie Canal became the gateway to the West and was one of the greatest engineering feats of its time, reducing the cost of freight between Buffalo and New York City from $100 to $5 a ton. Enlarged and rerouted, it is now part of the New York State Canal system, 527 miles of waterways used predominately today for recreational boating.

New York is a center for modern advancement, from industry to politics to finance. Industry commenced in New York due to its waterpower; trade and farming flourished of the far-reaching Erie Canal. Optimistic immigrants flooded the eastern shores offering the labor that helped provoke an Industrial Revolution. Four New York natives served as United States presidents (Van Buren, Fillmore and both Roosevelts) and two more built their careers there (Cleveland and Arthur). New York City's Wall Street is central to world economics. There are few states as influential New York.

From the Big Apple to Niagara Falls, from the rolling hills near the Canadian border to the picturesque stretch of Long Island, New York has something for every traveler.

ALBANY

See also Howes Cave, Schenectady, Troy

Albany is situated on the Hudson River where Henry Hudson ended the voyage of the Half Moon in 1609. It was settled by immigrants from Holland,

Norway, Denmark, Germany and Scotland during the patronship of Kiliaen Van Rensselaer and was named in honor of the Duke of Kent and Albany when the British took over the city in 1664. Despite the French and Indian War, Albany was a thriving fur-trading center in 1754. Albany's General Philip Schuyler commanded the northern defenses during the Revolution and, according to Daniel Webster, was "second only to Washington in the services he performed for his country."

Albany has been a transportation hub since American Indian trail days. Robert Fulton's first commercial steamboat, the Clermont, ferried passengers here from New York City in 1807. The Erie Canal opened in 1825, and by 1831, 15,000 canal boats and 500 ocean-going ships crowded Albany's docks.

Politics is a colorful part of the business in New York's capital city. Located on the western bank of the Hudson River and at the crossroads of several major state highways, Albany is a center for democracy, transportation, business, industry and culture.

WHAT TO SEE
ALBANY INSTITUTE OF HISTORY & ART
125 Washington Ave., Albany, 518-463-4478; www.albanyinstitute.org

Founded in 1791, the Albany Institute is the second oldest museum in the United States, and specializes in the history and art of the Upper Hudson Valley spanning the last four centuries. The curatorial collection is extensive with more than 30,000 pieces including paintings, prints, sculptures, furnishings, textiles, silver and more. If you're traveling with kids, check the Web site for the many family-friendly activities.

Admission: adults $10, seniors and students $8, children under 13 $6, children under 6 free. Wednesday-Saturday 10 a.m.-5 p.m., Sunday noon-5 p.m., Tuesday registered groups only. Closed Monday.

ADIRONDACK PARK

From Albany, take Route 9 north to Glens Falls and Lake George Village. Described as "the most queenly of American lakes," Lake George is long and slim extending 32 miles to the north, yet averaging less than 2 miles in width. It is dotted with exactly 395 islands. Opportunities for water recreation abound in this vacation mecca while fresh powder awaits winter travelers north on Route 28 at the Gore Mountain Ski Area in North Creek.

Farther north on Route 28 is Adirondack Park, which is bordered by Lake Champlain to the east, the Black River to the west, the St. Lawrence River in the north and the Mohawk River valley in the south. At six million acres, Adirondack State Park is the largest U.S. park outside of Alaska (9,000 square miles—that's the size of New Jersey and Rhode Island combined). You could spend days here and not even scratch the surface of all that there is to see and do. Whitewater raft the Hudson, Moose or Black rivers. Climb one of the 46 peaks in the Adirondack Range. Feeling exceptionally adventurous? Have a go at Mount Marcy, also known as Cloud Splitter, which is the highest peak in the range at 5,344 feet. If you're not a climber, try canoeing, fishing or mountain biking instead.

The next stop north is Blue Mountain Lake. Take the three-mile trail to the summit for spectacular views of Adirondack Park. Then head to the Adirondack Museum for insight into Adirondack history and modes of life. Housed in 20 buildings on 30 acres, the museum also showcases one of the best boat collections in the world, including sail canoes, steamboats and the famous Adirondack guide boat.

AUSABLE CHASM

2144 Route 9, Ausable Chasm, 518-834-7454; www.ausablechasm.com

Located in the beautiful Champlain Valley, this sandstone gorge often referred to as the "Little Grand Canyon of the East" plummets 150 feet to the Au Sable River. Stroll through the Adirondack Forest, float along the river in a raft or tube or follow a guide into the chasm at dusk on a "lantern tour." Admission: adults $16, children 5-13 $9, children under 5 free. Mid-May-October, daily.

CRAILO STATE HISTORIC SITE

9 1/2 Riverside Ave., Rensselaer, 518-463-8738; http://www.nysparks.state.ny.us

This 18th-century Dutch house is now a museum of Dutch culture in the Hudson Valley. Exhibits highlight the history and development of Dutch settlements in America.

Admission: adults $5, seniors and students $4, children under 13 free. Mid-April-May and September-October, Wednesday-Sunday 11 a.m.-5 p.m.; June-August, Tuesday-Sunday 11 a.m.-5 p.m.; November-March, Monday-Friday 11 a.m.-4 p.m.

NEW YORK STATE MUSEUM

Cultural Education Center of the Empire State Plaza, Madison and State streets, Albany, 518-474-5877; www.nysm.nysed.gov

The scientific fields of geology, biology and anthropology are promoted at this educational center. Life-size dioramas, photomurals and thousands of artifacts illustrate the past, present and future relationship between people and nature in New York State. Three major halls detail life in metropolitan New York, the Adirondacks and upstate New York. Be sure to visit the working carousel and the memorial to the World Trade Center.
Daily 9:30 a.m.-5 p.m.

SCHUYLER MANSION STATE HISTORIC SITE

32 Catherine St., Albany, 518-434-0834; www.nysparks.state.ny.us

This Georgian mansion, built in 1761, was the home of Philip Schuyler, a general of the Revolutionary War and U.S. Senator. Alexander Hamilton married Schuyler's daughter Elizabeth here in 1780, and other prominent early leaders visited the estate.

Admission: adults $4, seniors and students $3, children under 12 free. Mid-May-October, Wednesday-Sunday 11 a.m.-5 p.m.; November-mid-May, by appointment only.

SHAKER HERITAGE SOCIETY

875 Watervliet Shaker Road, Albany, 518-456-7890; www.shakerheritage.org

As the first Shaker settlement in America, the site includes a museum, located in the original 1848 Shaker Meeting House, a barnyard, an orchard and an herb garden. Stroll around the Ann Lee Pond nature preserve and the Shaker Cemetery where founder Mother Ann Lee is buried.

Free (donations accepted). February-October, Tuesday-Saturday 9:30 a.m.-4 p.m.; November-December, Monday-Saturday 10 a.m.-4 p.m.

STATE CAPITOL
Empire State Plaza, State and Swan streets, Albany, 518-474-2418;
www.assembly.state.ny.us

The New York State capitol took four decades to construct and is a $25,000,000 granite "French" chateau. Legislative session begins on the Wednesday after the first Monday in January.

WHERE TO STAY
★★★ALBANY MARRIOTT
189 Wolf Road, Albany, 518-458-8444, 800-443-8952; www.marriott.com

Convenience is king at this seven-story brick hotel: It is within two miles of the Albany International Airport; downtown Albany is approximately 10 miles away; and Sarasota Springs is a 30-minute drive to the north. If you're looking to stay put, there is an indoor and outdoor pool, a sizeable fitness center and a patio that receives great afternoon sun.

359 rooms. Restaurant, bar. Business center. Fitness center. Pool. $151-250

★★BEST WESTERN SOVEREIGN HOTEL-ALBANY
1228 Western Ave., Albany, 518-489-2981, 888-963-7666; www.bestwestern.com

Located next to the State University of New York and only minutes from the State Capitol and the New York Giants training camp, this full-service hotel is ideal for visiting parents, history buffs and football fans alike. The rooms are clean and updated with useful amenities including refrigerators, satellite TVs and high-speed Internet access. The complimentary breakfast is exceptionally good with a wide spread of options.

192 rooms. Restaurant, bar. Complimentary breakfast. Fitness center. Pool. Pets accepted. $61-150

★★CENTURY HOUSE HOTEL
997 New Loudon Road (Route 9), Latham, 518-785-0931, 888-674-6873;
www.thecenturyhouse.com

This Clarion Hotel is rich with history, originally purchased by the Rensselaer family in 1790. Today, the property offers modern, basic accommodations and a convenient location near the Albany airport and the Capital District. Feast on the complimentary country breakfast, and you will be reminded that you are far from Manhattan. If the weather permits, enjoy the outdoor pool and seasonal tennis courts. If you're looking for extended stay accommodations, this is one of the best options in Albany.

68 rooms. Restaurant, bar. Complimentary breakfast. Fitness center. Pool. Pets accepted. Tennis. $151-250

★★COURTYARD BY MARRIOTT ALBANY AIRPORT
168 Wolf Road, Albany, 518-482-8800, 866-541-6400; www.marriott.com/albca

Business travelers in for a quick visit to the state capital will find this hotel convenient and reliable with complimentary Internet access, two-line phones and well-appointed conference rooms. The indoor pool and hot tub are relaxing year round and the fitness center, though small, is an added perk. The hotel offers free shuttle service to the Albany International Airport and an onsite convenience market for any forgotten necessities.

78 rooms. Restaurant, bar. Business center. Fitness center. Pool. $151-250

★★★CROWNE PLAZA HOTEL ALBANY-CITY CENTER

40 Lodge St., Albany, 518-462-6611, 877-227-6963; www.ichotelsgroup.com

Catering to business travelers and politicos, this hotel is located in historic downtown Albany, across from the Capitol Building and near the Empire State Plaza and Pepsi Arena, it is within walking distance of the city's top attractions. Guest rooms feature Crowne Plaza Sleep Advantage bedding replete with triple-sheeted pillow-top mattresses and the pillow of your choice. Book a room on the club floor for access to executive lounge services including a business center, complimentary snacks and happy hour cocktails.

386 rooms. Restaurant, bar. Business center. Fitness center. Pool. $151-250

★★★DESMOND HOTEL AND CONFERENCE CENTER

660 Albany Shaker Road, Albany, 518-869-8100, 800-448-3500;
www.desmondhotels.com

With indoor courtyards and elegantly decorated rooms, the Desmond feels more like an 18th century village than a hotel. The location is within minutes of downtown and Albany International Airport. Guest rooms are full of Old World charm with large fireplaces, original oil paintings and classic furnishings. Business travelers are equally catered to with writing desks in the rooms and a large conference center and amphitheater with state-of-the-art digital technology.

324 rooms. Restaurant, bar. Business center. Fitness center. Pool. $151-250

★★★GREGORY HOUSE COUNTRY INN

3016 Highway 43, Averill Park, 518-674-3774; www.gregoryhouse.com

This country inn, located near Albany and Troy, offers 12 rooms and a restaurant that specializes in high-end Italian fare. Each guest room is decorated differently with antique furniture, French doors and original artwork. The inn is the perfect accommodation for those planning to visit nearby Tanglewood in Lenox, Massachusetts, the summer home of the Boston Symphony.

12 rooms. Restaurant, bar. Complimentary breakfast. $61-150

★★HOLIDAY INN ALBANY

205 Wolf Road, Albany, 518-458-7250, 888-465-4329; www.hialbanywolf.com

For business travelers visiting General Electric, IBM, Verizon or one of the other big Tech Valley businesses, this suburban Albany hotel is as convenient as it gets, especially since it is equipped with a 24-hour business center with printing and fax capabilities. If you find yourself with downtime, all guest rooms are outfitted with flat-screen TVs. There is also an outdoor pool and sauna, as well as a 24-hour fitness center.

312 rooms. Restaurant, bar. Business center. Fitness center. Pool. Pets accepted. $151-250

WHERE TO EAT
★BONGIORNO'S RESTAURANT

23 Dove St., Albany, 518-462-9176; www.bongiornositalianrestaurant.com

Family-owned and -operated since 1978, locals flock to Bongiorno's for the authentic Southern Italian cuisine made from fresh local ingredients. Don't let the aging country décor fool you; the dishes are inventive and tasty.

Italian. Lunch, dinner. Closed Sunday. Outdoor seating. Bar. $16-35

★★★JACK'S OYSTER HOUSE
42 State St., Albany, 518-465-8854; www.jacksoysterhouse.com

This downtown landmark—a two-block walk from the State Capitol and just across from the city's former 19th-century train station—has been dishing seafood to local politicians, businessmen and families since 1913. Enormous photos of historic Albany hang above elegant black-leather booths and table-tops adorned with flowers and candles. Renowned for its impressive oyster selection, Jack's also serves superb steaks.

American. Lunch, dinner. Reservations recommended. Children's menu. Bar. $16-35

★★★LA SERRE
14 Green St., Albany, 518-463-6056; www.laserrealbany.com

Located in a historic building that dates to the 1840s, La Serre, "the green-house" in French, features vintage-looking light fixtures and a gas fireplace that add to its cultivated décor. The continental-style menu features standouts such as Angus beef and New Zealand lamb. This is a great choice if you're following dinner with a show at the Palace or Capital Repertory theaters, which are only a short walk from La Serre.

Continental. Lunch, dinner. Closed Sunday. Reservations recommended. Outdoor seating. Bar. $16-35

★★★MANSION HILL
115 Philip St., Albany, 518-465-2038, 888-299-0455; www.mansionhill.com

This charming inn bills itself as Albany's best-kept secret, and indeed meals at this downtown bed and breakfast are top notch. The menu, which might include homemade ravioli, pan-roasted half duckling or chicken tenderloins, emulates the traditionally elegant décor—with hardwood furnishings and bouquets of fresh flowers. In warmer weather, a spot at one of the outdoor tables is perfect for laid-back people-watching.

American. Breakfast, dinner. Closed Sunday. Reservations recommended. Outdoor seating. $16-35

★★★SCRIMSHAW
660 Albany Shaker Road, Albany, 518-452-5801, 800-448-3500;
www.desmondhotels.com

Elegance is paramount at this 18th-century-style eatery within the Desmond Hotel where the fish—brought in daily from Boston—takes the spotlight. Specialties include oysters on the half-shell, cedar-plank salmon, several surf-and-turf dishes and the signature Scrimshaw Potato, whipped potatoes served within a puff pastry shell. American. Dinner. Closed Sunday. Reservations recommended. Children's menu. Bar. $16-35

ALEXANDRIA BAY
See also Clayton

The resort center of the Thousand Islands, Alexandria Bay overlooks a cluster of almost 1,800 green islands divided by intricate waterways. The islands range in size from a few square inches (a handful of rocks with a single tree) to several miles in length.

WHAT TO SEE
BOLDT CASTLE
Collins Landing, Alexandria Bay, 315-482-9724, 800-847-5263; www.boldtcastle.com

George C. Boldt arrived from Prussia in the 1860s and became the most successful hotel magnate in America by managing the Waldorf-Astoria in New York City and owning the Bellevue-Stratford in Philadelphia. The Boldt Castle on Heart Island was a $2.5-million gift from Boldt to his wife Louise, who died in 1904, unfortunately prior to the building's completion. After undergoing an extensive restoration, the castle has reclaimed its grandeur. Admission: adults $6.50, children 6-12 $4. May-October, daily 10 a.m.-5:30 p.m.; July-August, daily 10 a.m.-7:30 p.m.

WELLESLEY ISLAND STATE PARK
44927 Cross Island Road, Fine View, 315-482-2722, 800-456-2427; www.wellesleyisland.net

Wellesley Island State Park is 2600-plus acres of family fun. There is a marina with boat rentals, four boat launch sites, a natural sand beach, picnic area, concession and a beautiful ongoing shoreline. There are also more than 430 campsites.
Free. Daily.

WHERE TO STAY
★★BONNIE CASTLE RESORT
Holland Street, Alexandria Bay, 315-482-4511, 800-955-4511; www.bonniecastle.com

This hotel takes full advantage of its waterfront location on the St. Lawrence River. From the indoor and outdoor pools to the riverside bar and grill to the alfresco live entertainment on weekends, there is little reason to stay indoors. 128 rooms. Restaurant, bar. Pool. $61-150

★★EDGEWOOD RESORT
Edgewood Park Road, Alexandria Bay, 315-482-9923; www.theedgewoodresort.com

In the heart of the Thousand Island Resort area, the Edgewood is all about the water. Most rooms include balconies overlooking the St. Lawrence River, and the full-service onsite marina allows for you to come by sea, or land. Opt for a suite if you plan to stay awhile, as they include Jacuzzis and full kitchens. 110 rooms. Restaurant, bar. Pool. $151-250

★★PINE TREE POINT RESORT
70 Anthony St., Alexandria Bay, 315-482-9911; www.pinetreepointresort.com

This rustic resort is surrounded by the natural beauty of the Thousand Islands area. The cozy cottage-style rooms offer country furnishings and spectacular views of the river. You can be as active or as relaxed as you'd like with offered activities including biking, scuba diving, hiking and lazing by the pool. 96 rooms. Restaurant, bar. Pool. Closed November-April. $151-250

★★★RIVEREDGE RESORT HOTEL
17 Holland St., Alexandria Bay, 315-482-9917, 800-365-6987; www.riveredge.com

Situated on the St. Lawrence River, this resort offers rooms that are spacious, though somewhat dated—outfitted with floral wallpaper and country-style wooden furnishings—and have scenic views of either the channel or Alexandria Bay. The sunny channel-view deck is a great spot to watch the boats in the onsite marina while dining on fresh seafood from the Windows on the Bay Restaurant.

129 rooms. Restaurant, bar. Pool. $151-250

WHERE TO EAT
★★CAVALLARIO'S STEAK & SEAFOOD HOUSE
24 Church St., Alexandria Bay, 315-482-9867; www.thousandislands.com/cavallarios
Don't be put off by the faux-castle exterior. Once inside, the medieval knight theme recedes and is replaced by friendly service and reliably good American fare. The roasted rack of lamb is flavorful and the kids may enjoy picking out their lobster themselves. American. Dinner. Closed November-April. Bar. Children's menu. $16-35

★★★THE CRYSTAL DINING ROOM
31 Holland St., Alexandria Bay, 315-482-4511; www.bonniecastle.com
Located in the Bonnie Castle Resort and overlooking the St. Lawrence River, the Crystal Dining Room serves a basic menu heavy with seafood options. The mirrored baby grand piano and tuxedo-clad waitstaff accentuate the Vegas-like atmosphere of this elaborately adorned (think fountains and chandeliers) restaurant. Ask for a table by the window for views of the St. Lawrence River and the Boldt Castle.
American. Breakfast, lunch, dinner. Outdoor seating. Children's menu. Bar. No handicapped accessibility. $16-35

AMAGANSETT
See also Bridgehampton, East Hampton, Montauk, Sag Harbor
This small village, or hamlet, in the Hamptons dates back to the 1680s and offers all the natural beauty of the region. Adore its bays, natural beaches and rolling dunes, as well as its charming seaside cafes and boutiques. Keep your eyes peeled for celebrities; Amagansett is a favorite promenade for Billy Joel, Jerry Seinfeld, Gwyneth Paltrow, Sarah Jessica Parker and Matthew Broderick, among others.

WHAT TO SEE
MISS AMELIA'S COTTAGE MUSEUM
Montauk Highway 27A and Windmill Lane, Amagansett, 631-267-3020
This original home, built in 1725, is part of Amagansett history. Mary Amelia Schellinger was a descendant of Jacob Schellinger, the founder of Amagansett. As the last of her family to live in the house, she went without electricity and running water for years, passing away in 1930. The cottage features its original furnishings and depicts life in Amagansett through the colonial period. Throughout the summer, there are weekend pony rides and a bi-seasonal antique sale.
Admission: $2. Pony ride $5. June-September, Friday-Sunday 10 a.m.-4 p.m.

TOWN MARINE MUSEUM
301 Bluff Road, Amagansett, 631-267-6544; www.easthamptonhistory.org
Offering a history lesson on Long Island's East End community, this museum includes three floors of exhibits on commercial and sports fishing, local ship-

wrecks and underwater archaeology. The permanent collection of artifacts, photographs and displays on the offshore whaling industry from colonial times to the present is a highlight.

Admission: adults $4, seniors $3, students $2. June-mid-October, Saturday 10 a.m.-5 p.m., Sunday noon-5 p.m.; also July-August, Friday and Monday 10 a.m.-5 p.m.

WHERE TO STAY
★SEA CREST ON THE OCEAN
2166 Montauk Highway, Amagansett, 631-267-3159, 800-732-3297
This family-friendly resort offers direct beach access and spacious one- and two-bedroom units, many with in-suite kitchens. While the décor is basic, the rooms are airy and bright. There are barbecue pits near the dunes for evening bonfires.
66 rooms. Pool. Beach. Tennis. $151-250

WHERE TO EAT
★LOBSTER ROLL
1980 Montauk Highway, Amagansett, 631-267-3740; www.lobsterroll.com
This local dive is little more than a shack by the sea, but few seem to mind once they taste the creamy New England clam chowder and fresh lobster rolls. The booths and outdoor picnic tables are packed all summer with hungry locals and tourists taking breaks from the beach.
Seafood. Lunch, dinner. Closed November-April. Outdoor seating. Children's menu. $15 and under

AUBURN
See also Finger Lakes, Seneca Falls, Skaneateles, Syracuse
On Owasco Lake, Auburn is one of the largest cities in the Finger Lakes region. Harriet Tubman, whose home was a link in the Underground Railroad, lived here. Auburn has been a key industrial center since the early 1800s, producing everything from diesel engines and aviation spark plugs to bottles and air conditioners.

WHAT TO SEE
CAYUGA MUSEUM/CASE RESEARCH LAB
203 Genesee St., Auburn, 315-253-8051; www.cayuganet.org/cayugamuseum
The Cayuga Museum is housed in a Greek Revival Willard-Case Mansion built in 1836 and explores the industrial history of Cayuga County. A large emphasis is given to the Auburn Correctional Facility, the oldest continually operating prison in the nation. Other highlights include original 19th-century furnishings and a Civil War exhibit. Behind the museum is the Case Research Lab where T.W. Case and E.I. Sponable invented sound film in 1926, putting an end to the silent-movie era.
Admission: $3 suggested donation. Cayuga Museum: Tuesday-Sunday noon-5 p.m. Case Research Lab: Tuesday-Sunday noon-4:30 p.m. Closed January.

FORT HILL CEMETERY
19 Fort St., Auburn, 315-253-8132
Fort Hill Cemetery was incorporated on May 15, 1851 under its official name:

"Trustees of the Fort Hill Cemetery Association of Auburn." but had been used by Native Americans for burial mounds as early as AD 1100. Today the cemetery consists of 83 acres, more than 10,000 burial sites and remains one of the most beautiful landscapes in Auburn. Many famous historical Auburn residents including William H. Seward and Harriet Tubman rest here.
Admission: Dailysunrise-sunset.

HARRIET TUBMAN HOME
180 South St., Auburn, 315-252-2081
Born as a slave, Harriet Tubman escaped in 1849 and rescued more than 300 slaves via the Underground Railroad. She assisted the Union Army during the Civil War and, after settling in Auburn after the war, continued to pursue other humanitarian endeavors.
Admission: $4. Tuesday-Friday 11 a.m.-4 p.m.

SEWARD HOUSE
33 South St., Auburn, 315-252-1283; www.sewardhouse.org
This building was the home of William Henry Seward, governor of New York, U.S. Senator, and Abraham Lincoln and Andrew Johnson's secretary of state. Seward was instrumental in bringing California into the Union as a free state and later in purchasing Alaska. The house is stocked with antique furniture, decorative arts, photographs and family documents.
Admission: adults $7, seniors $6, students $2, children under 10 free. Tuesday-Saturday 10 a.m.-4 p.m.

WILLARD MEMORIAL CHAPEL AND WELCH MEMORIAL BUILDING
17 Nelson St., Auburn, 315-252-0339; www.willardchapel.org
A National Historic Landmark, these gray-and-red stone Romanesque Revival buildings were once part of the Auburn Theological Seminary in the early 1800s. The chapel's interior was designed and handcrafted by the Tiffany Glass and Decoration Company and is the only complete and unaltered Tiffany chapel known to exist. Tiffany Concert Series in the chapel take place every summer at lunchtime.
Admission: $3 suggested donation. Tuesday-Friday 10 a.m.-4 p.m.

WHERE TO STAY
★★★AURORA INN
391 Main St., Aurora, 315-364-8888, 866-364-8808; www.aurora-inn.com
A perfectly charming 1833 Federal-style structure perched on the banks of Cayuga Lake, this Finger Lakes-area inn offers recently renovated rooms with beds in Frette linens and contemporary touches such as flat-screen TVs and whirlpool baths. Public rooms are cozy and inviting with Oriental rugs and antique furnishings. The onsite restaurant is a local favorite and features a large outdoor patio with views of the lake for memorable dining in warm weather.
10 rooms. Restaurant. Complimentary breakfast. $251-350

★★HOLIDAY INN
75 North St., Auburn, 315-253-4531; www.hiauburn.com
Catering primarily to business travelers, this large hotel is situated in the

heart of Auburn and includes spacious desks, high-speed Internet, and two-line telephones in all guest rooms. The Cayuga and Seneca lakes wine trails are nearby, as is the Waterloo Premium Outlets and Bass Pro Shop. Request a room facing the courtyard to avoid a view of the parking lot.

165 rooms. Restaurant, bar. Business center. Fitness center. Pool. Pets accepted. $61-150

★★SPRINGSIDE INN
6141 W. Lake Road, Auburn, 315-252-7247; www.springsideinn.com
This country clapboard inn dating back to 1851 is charming and well managed. Each room is unique, but all include private baths, Victorian antiques and views of the pond, outdoor fountain or gazebo. Locals come for the lavish Sunday brunch, which includes a heavenly cheese soufflé.

7 rooms. Complimentary breakfast. Restaurant, bar. $151-250

WHERE TO EAT
★★★AURORA INN DINING ROOM
391 Main St., Aurora, 315-364-8888, 866-364-8808; www.aurora-inn.com
Located in the recently renovated Aurora Inn, this comfortable restaurant offers perfectly prepared versions of American classics with a lakefront setting. Dishes include traditional recipes such as lobster Newburg, Waldorf salad and a traditional pot roast, slow-cooked and served with roasted fingerling potatoes and vegetables. Pair your meal with one of the many local Finger Lakes wines on offer for an added indulgence.

American. Breakfast, lunch, dinner. $16-35

★★LASCA'S
252-258 Grant Ave. (Route 5), Auburn, 315-253-4885; www.lascas.com
A local staple for 20 years, this casual eatery serves up consistently good American fare at reasonably low prices. House specialties include the veal piccata and filet n' tail which comprises Australian lobster tail and mushroom-topped filet mignon.

Italian, American. Dinner. Closed Monday, first two weeks in February. Children's menu. Bar. $16-35

BINGHAMTON
See also Ithaca
Largest of the Triple Cities (Johnson City and Endicott branched off later), Binghamton lies at the junction of the Chenango and Susquehanna rivers. Completion of the Chenango Canal in 1837 made it an important link between the coal regions of Pennsylvania and the Erie Canal. Greater Binghamton is home to Binghamton University, which brings a youthful academic energy to the city. Other claims to fame include the fifth oldest zoo in the nation and the world's largest collection of functioning antique carousels (which explains the nickname "Carousel Capital of the World").

WHAT TO SEE
BINGHAMTON ZOO AT ROSS PARK
60 Morgan Road, Binghamton, 607-724-5461; www.rossparkzoo.com
Officially opened in 1875, the Binghamton Zoo is the fifth oldest zoological

institution in the country behind those in Philadelphia, Chicago, Cincinnati and Buffalo. The 90-acre plot was donated to the city of Binghamton by a wealthy businessman, Erastus Ross. The zoo includes several botanical gardens and a new outdoor exhibit featuring snow leopards and cougars.

Admission: adults $7, seniors, students, military $6, children 3-11 $4.50, children under 3 free. April-November, daily 10 a.m.-5 p.m.

DAY OF A PLAYWRIGHT
The Forum, 236 Washington St., Binghamton, 607-778-2480;
"Day of a Playwright" is a permanent exhibit at the Forum Theatre for the Performing Arts. This theater has an exhibit honoring Syracuse-born Rod Serling, who grew up in Binghamton and created The Twilight Zone TV series. It includes photos and documents highlighting his career in TV and film.

Admission: donation accepted. September-May, Monday-Friday 8 a.m.-4 p.m.

DISCOVERY CENTER OF THE SOUTHERN TIER
60 Morgan Road, Binghamton, 607-773-8661; www.thediscoverycenter.org
Kids love this hands-on museum that includes a life-sized fire truck (with dress-up fireman uniforms), a simulated news television studio with video monitor, and imitation hospital and dentist offices. The interactive educational opportunities are endless. Exhibits change regularly.

Admission: adults $5, children 1-16 $6, children under 1 free. Tuesday-Friday 10 a.m.-4 p.m., Saturday 10 a.m.-5 p.m., Sunday noon-5 p.m.

WHERE TO STAY
★★CLARION COLLECTION GRAND ROYALE HOTEL
80 State St., Binghamton, 607-722-0000, 888-242-0323; www.grandroyalehotel.com
Formerly a city hall, this historic Beaux Arts building boasts 20-foot ceilings and a beautiful lobby fireplace. This hotel is conveniently located near the Binghamton Zoo, Binghamton University and the Discovery Center. Complimentary Internet access and an onsite business center make this a good choice for business travelers. A fitness center is offered free of charge at the nearby YMCA.

61 rooms. Restaurant, bar. Complimentary breakfast. Business center. Pets accepted. $61-150

★DAYS INN
65 Front St., Binghamton, 607-724-2412, 800-329-7466; www.daysinn.com
Located in downtown Binghamton, this hotel offers basic accommodations with free outdoor parking, available meeting spaces and a complimentary continental breakfast.

106 rooms. Complimentary breakfast. $61-150

★★HOLIDAY INN
2-8 Hawley St., Binghamton, 607-722-1212; www.holidayinnbinghamton.com
Recently renovated rooms at this riverfront hotel provide ample space for relaxation with available valet laundry service and cable TV. The fitness center includes a large indoor heated pool and sauna. Request a room on one of the higher floors for a nicer view.

240 rooms. Restaurant, bar. Fitness center. Pool. $61-150

WHERE TO EAT
★ THE NEW ARGO
117 Court St., Binghamton, 607-724-4692; www.thenewargo.com

After two years of renovation, this restaurant maintained its classic Greek diner atmosphere, though with a cleaner, brighter appeal. The menu is extensive and the portions are hefty. Be sure to save room for dessert—it's made fresh daily by the owner's mother.

Greek, Italian. Breakfast, lunch, dinner. Children's menu. $15 and under.

★★NUMBER FIVE
33 S. Washington St., Binghamton, 607-723-0555; www.number5restaurant.com

Operating in a fire station built in 1897, this American steak and seafood house has been open since 1978. Located on the south side of downtown Binghamton and convenient to hotels, the antique-filled, fine dining atmosphere is warm and romantic. Try the stuffed Greek tenderloin or the jumbo crab cakes, both local favorites. They also offer an awarded wine list and live music on weekends.

American, seafood. Dinner. Children's menu. Bar. $16-35

BOLTON LANDING
See also Glens Falls, Lake George, Warrensburg

Bolton Landing, on the shores of Lake George, has been home to musicians, artists and authors. It earned the nickname "Millionaires Row" after an influx of wealthy urbanites chose to summer here in the 1800s. Today, most of the waterfront mansions have been converted into resorts, but the cultural atmosphere lives on. While Bolton Landing attracts fewer tourists than nearby Lake George village, summers can still be quite crowded.

WHAT TO SEE
BOLTON HISTORICAL MUSEUM
4924 Main St., Bolton Landing, 518-644-9960; www.boltonhistorical.org

Housed in a former church, this small museum explores the historical past of the Lake George region with collections of boats, including ice boats, a Smith-Granger rowboat built in Bolton around 1900, antique photographs of lakeside mansions and antique farming equipment.

Admission: adults $10, seniors and students $5. July-August, daily 9 a.m.-2 p.m., 7-9 p.m. Closed Sunday evening. Spring and Fall, Saturday-Sunday 9 a.m.-2 p.m.

MARCELLA SEMBRICH OPERA MUSEUM
4800 Lake Shore Dr., Bolton Landing, 518-644-9839; www.operamuseum.com

Metropolitan Opera diva Marcella Sembrich used this studio in the early 20th century to teach piano, violin and vocals to promising pupils from Juilliard and the Curtis Institute. The studio was part of her summer lakeside mansion, named Bay View. Today, the museum displays operatic memorabilia from throughout Sembrich's career including opera costumes, paintings and sculptures, and autographed photographs from her contemporaries such as Brahms and Puccini. Be sure to explore the grounds, which exhibit great views of Lake George.

Admission: $2 suggested donation. Mid-June-mid-September, daily 10 a.m.-12:30 p.m., 2-5:30 p.m.

WHERE TO STAY

★★MELODY MANOR RESORT

4610 Lakeshore Drive, Bolton Landing, 518-644-9750; www.melodymanor.com

On the shores of Lake George amidst the Adirondack Mountains, the Melody Manor certainly has a winning locale. The rooms are bland apart from their scenic lake views, but with amenities including a beach with rowboats and paddleboats, a swimming pool and clay tennis courts, there is no reason to stay inside. The onsite Italian restaurant serves simple hearty cuisine.

40 rooms. Restaurant, bar. Pool. Beach. Tennis. Closed November-April. $151-250

★★★THE SAGAMORE

110 Sagamore Road, Bolton Landing, 518-644-9400, 866-385-6221; www.thesagamore.com

This historic resort reigns over its own private 72-acre island in Lake George. From golf, tennis and water sports to myriad winter activities, this resort is a year-round destination. Two types of accommodations offer you the choice of comfortable rooms at the historic hotel or cabin retreats in spacious lodges. Dining always comes with a view at any of the six restaurants; meals are even served aboard the resort's own replica of a 19th-century touring vessel.

350 rooms. Restaurant, bar. Fitness center. Pool. Spa. Beach. Golf. Tennis. $251-350

WHERE TO EAT

★FREDERICK'S RESTAURANT

4970 Lake Shore Drive, Bolton Landing, 518-644-3484; www.fredericksrestaurant.com

This casual hot spot draws locals and tourists year-round with live music and a stellar raw bar on Sundays in summer and cozy fireside dining during the winter.

Seafood. Lunch, dinner. Outdoor seating. Bar. $16-35

★★★TRILLIUM

110 Sagamore Road, Bolton Landing, 518-644-9400; www.thesagamore.com

This restaurant boasts some of the most majestic views of Lake George in the area and is pleasantly paired with a casual, stylish atmosphere and a professional staff that provides unsurpassed service. Organic and local ingredients fill the imaginative menu, including Kobe steak sandwiches and honey and paprika glazed duck. The wine list is also impressive.

American. Dinner. Reservations recommended. $16-35

★★VILLA NAPOLI

4608 Lakeside Drive, Bolton Landing, 518-644-9047; www.melodymanor.com

Located within the Melody Manor Resort, the main dining room is inspired by Italy with a hand-carved Carrera marble fireplace, Venetian plaster walls and original hand-painted murals. The fare is equally authentic and includes wild boar sausage over slow-cooked peperonata and stuffed eggplant in a red pepper sauce.

Italian. Breakfast, dinner. Closed mid-October-mid-May. Reservations recommended. Outdoor seating. Children's menu. Bar. $16-35

BREWSTER

See also Mount Kisco, White Plains

Sixty miles north of Manhattan, Brewster and the surrounding villages are home to a number of important historic buildings, including the Walter Brewster House, former home of the town's namesake.

WHAT TO SEE
SOUTHEAST MUSEUM
67 Main St., Brewster, 845-279-7500; www.southeastmuseum.org
Step back in time to the early years of the American Circus, the Harlem Line Railroad and the birth of the Town of Southeast at this museum established in 1963. Even the location is historic: It is in the 1896 Old Town Hall of Southeast. The museum presents various changing exhibits, drawing on its extensive collection of antique farm and household implements, quilts, clothing and assorted Americana reflecting 19th-century material culture.
April-December, Tuesday-Saturday 10 a.m.-4 p.m.

THUNDER RIDGE SKI AREA
137 Birch Hill Road, Patterson, 845-878-4100; www.thunderridgeski.com
Located in the rolling hills of Patterson, Thunder Ridge offers acres of skiing and snowboarding for all ages and skill levels. The facilities include ski schools, night skiing and equipment rentals. The longest run is one mile.
Admission: Lift ticket: Full Day: Adult $50 weekend, $40 weekday, children under 13 $37 weekend, $25 weekday; Half Day: Adult $45 weekend, $35 weekday, children under 13 $32 weekend, $20 weekday. December-March, daily.

WHERE TO EAT
★★★ARCH
Route 22, Brewster, 845-279-5011; www.archrestaurant.com
Named for its windows—which overlook lush, manicured gardens—Arch offers an extensive, four-course prix fixe dinner of classic European cuisine and savory game entrées. There is also a substantial à la carte menu (available Monday through Friday) that includes winning dishes such as foie gras with raspberries, apples and cassis and sautéed veal scaloppini with fresh mint and potato pancakes. Service is attentive and friendly.
French. Lunch, dinner, Sunday brunch. Closed Monday-Tuesday. Outdoor seating. Children's menu. Bar. $16-35

BRIDGEHAMPTON

See also Amagansett, East Hampton, Sag Harbor, Southampton, Montauk

This a small community in the Hamptons hosts the Hampton Classic, an annual summer horse show, and the Mercedes-Benz Polo Challenge. It's also home to several palatial estates situated along the sandy coastline. The village of Bridgehampton is clustered with antique shops, art galleries and upscale restaurants. Wine is a burgeoning business in this region with boutique wineries arriving on nearly every corner.

WHAT TO SEE
BRIDGEHAMPTON COMMONS
Montauk Highway, Bridgehampton, 631-537-2174

Get out the credit cards and do a little damage. Actually, prices aren't as bad as you'd think at this retail outpost, with brand name stores like Banana Republic, Victoria's Secret and Williams-Sonoma.
Free. Daily.

CHANNING DAUGHTERS WINERY
1927 Scuttlehole Road, Bridgehampton, 631-537-7224; www.channingdaughters.com

This 28-acre winery produces a host of hand-picked varieties, such as pinot grigio, chardonnay, pinot noir and merlot. Although small, Channing Daughters poses special offerings like a discounted wine club and a wood sculpture garden that showcases the art of owner Walter Channing. The winery offers wine tastings from May to October.
Admission: Tasting: $5. May-September, daily 11 a.m.-5 p.m.; October-April, Thursday-Monday 11 a.m.-5 p.m.

WÖLFFER ESTATE VINEYARD
139 Sagg Pond Road, Sagaponack, 631-537-5106; www.wolffer.com

This Tuscan-style winery is more reminiscent of an enchanted European estate than a vineyard in the Hamptons, but the harvests are decidedly American. The local soil acts as the perfect host for Wölffer's slow-growing vines, and the cool climate, thanks in part to the close proximity of the Atlantic, allows for late harvests and strong, natural acidity. A visit to the estate is a special affair: immaculately manicured grounds and a trickling, circular fountain greet you as you make your way into the impressive 12,000-square-foot winery. While the winemaking facilities make their home on the lower level, the main floor impresses with terracotta tiling, antique stained-glass windows and massive French doors that open onto the vineyards. Sit, imbibe on a glass of crisp chardonnay and take in the spectacular view and you'll forget that you're farther from Italy than it seems.
November-March, Sunday-Wednesday 11 a.m.-5 p.m., Thursday 11 a.m.-7:30 p.m., Friday-Saturday 11 a.m.-6 p.m.; April-October, Sunday-Wednesday 11 a.m.-6 p.m., Thursday 11 a.m.-7:30 p.m., Friday-Saturday 11 a.m.-7 p.m.

SPECIAL EVENT
HAMPTON CLASSIC HORSE SHOW
240 Snake Hollow Road, Bridgehampton, 631-537-3177; www.hamptonclassic.com

Every August, Bridgehampton crowds with horse trailers, jockeys and garrulous spectators. The Hampton Classic equestrian competition draws the best competitors from around the globe for a week of jumping, racing and high-society socializing.
Admission: adults $10, children under 6 free. Last week in August.

WHERE TO EAT
★★★ALISON
95 School St., Bridgehampton, 631-324-5440; www.alisonrestaurant.com

Special emphasis is placed on local, coastal cuisine and the wines of the Hamptons at this always-hopping spot. Fresh seafood dishes are the menu's topliners, with entrees such as sautéed striped bass and Atlantic salmon making frequent appearances. The frozen lemon meringue pie with a pecan crust is a great finish to any meal.

American, seafood. Dinner. Bar. $36-85

★★BOBBY VAN'S STEAKHOUSE

2393 Montauk Highway, Bridgehampton, 631-537-0590; www.bobbyvans.com

Named after Bobby Van, a local piano player and actor who entertained his well-heeled friends at his area Hamptons home, this restaurant continues to attract a monied crowd of Manhattanites enjoying an escape in the Hamptons. French doors and polished wood paneling give the space a masterful look and the waitstaff is without flaw. Seafood is king here with dishes like miso-steamed black sea bass and crispy skin-on salmon with morel mushrooms and fava beans. Steak-seekers should also bring their appetites.

Seafood, steak. Lunch, dinner. Bar. $16-35

BUFFALO

See also East Aurora, Niagara Falls

Buffalo, at the eastern end of Lake Erie, is New York's second-largest city and one of the largest railroad centers in America. Fifteen freight depots and one passenger terminal handle more than 25,000 trains annually. The city is as well known for its brutal winters, namesake chicken wings and tenacious NFL team, the Buffalo Bills.

Planned by Joseph Ellicott in 1803, the city was modeled after Washington, D.C., which was laid out by his brother, Major Andrew Ellicott. Buffalo radiates from Niagara Square, dominated by a monument to President William McKinley, who was assassinated here while attending the Pan-American Exposition in 1901.

Historically, in 1679, when Buffalo was claimed by the French, Robert de La Salle embarked on the first boat to sail the Great Lakes, the wooden Griffon. During the War of 1812, Buffalo was set ablaze by the British, but its 500 citizens returned a few months later and rebuilt. In 1816, Walk-on-the-Water, the first steamboat to ply the Great Lakes, was launched here. The opening of the Erie Canal in 1825 made Buffalo the major transportation hub between the East and West and brought trade and prosperity. Joseph Dart's 1843 invention of a steam-powered grain elevator caused Buffalo's grain-processing industry to boom. Since completion of the St. Lawrence Seaway in 1959, Buffalo has been one of the top Great Lakes ports in import-export tonnage.

Current-day Buffalo is attractive for its architectural stunners, such as its $7 million art deco City Hall, its 1895 Prudential Building, recognized as the world's first skyscraper, and several Frank Lloyd Wright houses. Public parks also appeal throughout the city, many of which were designed by Frederick Law Olmsted, father of American landscape architecture. The Buffalo Philharmonic Orchestra, Albright-Knox Art Gallery and many cultural nightclubs cater to the varied interests of residents and visitors, and the six colleges and universities in the area inspire a youthful vibe.

WHAT TO SEE
ALBRIGHT-KNOX ART GALLERY
1285 Elmwood Ave., Buffalo, 716-882-8700; www.albrightknox.org

One of the oldest arts organizations in the United States, the gallery has a varied collection, including extensive works from 18th-century English, 19th-century French and 20th-century American and European painters. Works by Picasso, Matisse, Monet, Renoir and Van Gogh are on display, as well as sculpture from 3000 B.C. to present.

Admission: adults $12, seniors and students $8, children under 12 free. Wednesday 10 a.m.-5 p.m., Thursday-Friday 10 a.m.-10 p.m., Saturday-Sunday 10 a.m.-5 p.m. Closed Monday-Tuesday.

BUFFALO AND ERIE COUNTY BOTANICAL GARDENS
Olmsted's South Park, 2655 S. Park Ave., Buffalo, 716-827-1584;
www.buffalogardens.com

Boasting a Victorian conservatory and gardens, this 156-acre park is teeming with plants in its 11 greenhouses and desert, rainforest and Mediterranean collections.

Admission: adults $6, seniors and students $5, children 6-13 $3, children under 6 free. Daily 10 a.m.-5 p.m.

BUFFALO AND ERIE COUNTY NAVAL & MILITARY PARK
One Naval Park Cove, Buffalo, 716-847-1773; www.buffalonavalpark.org

This is the largest inland naval park in the nation and displays multiple ships, aircraft and tanks, including cruiser USS Little Rock, destroyer USS The Sullivans and submarine USS Croaker. There are also exhibits on women in the military, Vietnam veterans and Marine Corps memorabilia from WWI to the present.

Admission: adults $9, seniors and children 6-16 $6. April-October, daily 10 a.m.-5 p.m., November, Saturday-Sunday 10 a.m.-4 p.m. Closed December-March.

BUFFALO MUSEUM OF SCIENCE
1020 Humboldt Parkway, Buffalo, 716-896-5200, 866-291-6660;
www.buffalomuseumofscience.org

Explore exhibits on astronomy, botany, geology, zoology, anthropology and natural sciences in one of the region's premier museums, which also contains a research library. Kids will love Camp-In, a program that lets them spend a night in the museum.

Admission: adults $7, seniors $6, military and students $5, children 3-18 $5, children under 3 free. July-August, Monday-Saturday 10 a.m.-5 p.m.; September-July, Wednesday-Saturday 10 a.m.-5 p.m., Sunday noon-5 p.m.

BUFFALO ZOOLOGICAL GARDENS
Delaware Park, 300 Parkside Ave., Buffalo, 716-837-3900; www.buffalozoo.org

More than 2,200 animals roam in this 23 1/2-acre park. It features indoor and outdoor exhibits, a gallery of Boehm wildlife porcelains, a tropical gorilla habitat, outdoor lion and tiger exhibits and a children's zoo. Be sure to visit the newest member of the Buffalo Zoo, a baby Indian Rhinoceros named Clover.

Admission: adults $9.50, seniors and students $7, children 2-14 $6, children under 2 free. July-August, daily 10 a.m.-5 p.m.; September-June, 10 a.m.-4 p.m. Closed January-February, Monday-Tuesday.

CITY HALL/OBSERVATION TOWER
65 Niagara Square, Buffalo, 716-851-4200; www.ci.buffalo.ny.us
City Hall is an exceptional example of art deco architecture. Enjoy panoramic views of western New York, Lake Erie, and Ontario, Canada from the observation deck.
Admission: free. Monday-Friday 8 a.m.-4 p.m.

FRANK LLOYD WRIGHT HOUSES
Buffalo, 716-856-3858; www.darwinmartinhouse.org
The famed American architect designed several buildings in Buffalo. They include the Darwin D. Martin house (125 Jewett Parkway); George Barton House (118 Summit); Gardener's Cottage (285 Woodward); Walter V. Davidson House (57 Tillinghast Place) and the William Heath House (76 Soldiers Place). The Martin House is perhaps the best example of Wright's famed Prairie House style, characterized by horizontally oriented structures, prominent foundations and organic materials.
Admission: varies by location. Hours vary.

PRUDENTIAL BUILDING
28 Church St., Buffalo, 716-854-0003
Designed by Dankmar Adler and Louis Sullivan and completed in 1896, the Prudential (formerly Guaranty) Building is an outstanding example of Sullivan's famed functional design and terracotta ornament, and is proclaimed as America's first skyscraper. It was declared a National Historic Landmark in 1975.
Admission: free. Daily.

SHEA'S PERFORMING ARTS CENTER
646 Main St., Buffalo, 716-847-1410; www.sheas.org
Two theaters comprise Buffalo's premier performing arts center. Shea's Buffalo Theatre and Shea's Smith Theatre (right next door) both showcase a constant influx of Broadway shows, dance performances, operas, musical acts and family programs.
Admission: prices vary. Ticket Office: Monday-Friday 10 a.m.-5 p.m., Saturday 10 a.m.-2 p.m.

STUDIO ARENA THEATRE
710 Main St., Buffalo, 716-856-8025, 800-777-8243; www.studioarena.org
This regional professional theater presents world premieres, musicals, classic dramas and contemporary works. It's a great spot to scout fresh talent; Kelsey Grammer graced the Studio Arena stage before making it big with Cheers and Frasier.
Admission: prices vary. Showtimes vary

WILCOX MANSION: THEODORE ROOSEVELT INAUGURAL
NATIONAL HISTORIC SITE

641 Delaware Ave., Buffalo, 716-884-0095; www.nps.gov/thri

Theodore Roosevelt was inaugurated in this classic Greek Revival mansion in 1901 following the assassination of President McKinley. The site recently underwent massive renovations to upgrade the aging mansion and create a reconstructed carriage house addition.

Admission: adults $5, seniors and students $3, children 6-14 $1, children under 5 free. Monday-Friday 9 a.m.-5 p.m., Saturday-Sunday noon-5 p.m.

SPECIAL EVENT
TASTE OF BUFFALO

Main Street, Buffalo, 716-831-9376; www.tasteofbuffalo.com

Hosting more than 50 local restaurants, this annual event dating back to 1984 represents some 15 ethnic and regional varieties of food, including Greek, Italian, Indian, Chinese, Middle Eastern, Mexican and Southwestern. You'll be able to sample traditional American favorites and local specialties, as well as all manners of desserts. More than 450,000 people attend annually. Mid-July.

WHERE TO STAY
★★★ASA RANSOM HOUSE

10529 Main St., Clarence, 716-759-2315, 800-841-2340; www.asaransom.com

This charming bed and breakfast is surrounded by gardens and offers nine rooms, each with a distinct character and charm. Rooms are furnished with antiques and period reproductions, and several have both fireplace and private balconies. Don't miss the full country breakfast served at your leisure every morning.

9 rooms. Restaurant. Complimentary breakfast. Closed January. $151-250

★BEST WESTERN INN-ON THE AVENUE

510 Delaware Ave., Buffalo, 716-886-8333, 888-868-3033; www.bestwestern.com

The Best Western Inn–On The Avenue puts the many sights and attractions of Buffalo right at your fingertips. Comfortable and attractive guest rooms feature basics like hair dryers, ironing boards, and coffee/tea makers, while the lobby features something you most likely won't find anywhere else: a talking and whistling African grey parrot.

61 rooms. Complimentary breakfast. Pets accepted. $61-150

★★★BUFFALO MARRIOTT NIAGARA

1340 Millersport Highway, Amherst, 716-689-6900, 800-334-4040;
www.buffaloniagaramarriott.com

Although situated in a quiet suburban location, the Buffalo Marriott Niagara is close to the Buffalo Airport, downtown Buffalo and Niagara Falls. Rooms are bright, elegant and spacious. Amenities include a complimentary airport shuttle, indoor/outdoor pool and a 24-hour health club. There are also numerous golf courses nearby.

356 rooms. Restaurant, bar. Business center. Fitness center. Pool. $151-250

★★COMFORT SUITES DOWNTOWN
601 Main St., Buffalo, 716-854-5500, 877-424-6423; www.comfortsuites.com

Business travelers come for the convenience this hotel provides, including a location within walking distance of the Buffalo Niagara Convention Center and downtown business district, free airport transportation and copy and fax machine access.

146 rooms. Restaurant, bar. Complimentary breakfast. $61-150

★★★HYATT REGENCY BUFFALO
Two Fountain Plaza, Buffalo, 716-856-1234; www.buffalo.hyatt.com

This hotel is located downtown and connected to the Buffalo Convention Center. It is also on the metro rail and within walking distance of shopping, restaurants, theaters, cultural and sports entertainment and other attractions. Guest rooms are spacious and include Hyatt Grand beds and work desks with dataports. Request a room with a view of Lake Erie and the Peace Bridge to Canada.

396 rooms. Restaurant, bar. Business center. Fitness center. Pool. $151-250

WHERE TO EAT
★★★ASA RANSOM HOUSE
10529 Main St., Clarence, 716-759-2315, 800-841-2340; www.asaransom.com

Sample fare like the Asa chicken potpie loaded with homegrown vegetables or the grilled apple butter salmon at this romantic, country-style retreat. Choose your ambience: enjoy the formal Ransom Room or head for the more casual Clarence Hollow Room should you wish to leave the sport coat behind. The same menu is offered in all dining areas.

American. Breakfast, lunch, dinner. Closed January-mid-February. Outdoor seating. Children's menu. $36-85

★★★SALVATORE'S ITALIAN GARDENS
6461 Transit Road, Buffalo, 716-683-7990, 800-999-8082; www.salvatores.net

One of Buffalo's finest Italian eateries, Salvatore's is renowned for its "dinner for two" meals as well as its seafood medley and several varieties of veal. The house garlic bread is buttery and delicious and the steak Joseph, a tender filet topped with lump crab meat and finished in sherry lobster sauce, will have you coming back next time you're in town.

American, Italian. Dinner. Children's menu. Bar. $36-85

CAMILLUS
See also Syracuse

A 20-minute drive from Syracuse, this town is a center of outdoor recreation and rich in history, with five museums in its vicinity.

WHERE TO EAT
★★★INN BETWEEN
2290 State Route 5, Camillus, 315-672-3166; www.inn-between.com

Located outside Syracuse, this 1880 country house sits on the outskirts of central New York wine country and boasts standout dishes such as crispy roast duckling with an herb-filled stuffing. Day trips to local wineries and special wine festivals in the fall are among the unique activities offered.

American. Lunch, dinner. Closed Monday. Children's menu. Bar. $16-35

CAZENOVIA

See also Hamilton, Oneida, Syracuse

Located in central New York on the shores of Cazenovia Lake, this town has worked to preserve its historical buildings and the stories that go with them. Apart from great outdoor activities year round, Cazenovia offers cozy country inns for rest between activities.

WHAT TO SEE
CHITTENANGO FALLS STATE PARK

2300 Rathbun Road, Cazenovia, 315-655-9620; www.nysparks.com/parks

Glaciers carved out this picturesque area millions of years ago, sculpting a landscape filled with hiking trails, rivers for fishing and a 167-foot waterfall. The park grounds include a picnic area, playground and tent and trailer sites. Free. Daily.

LORENZO STATE HISTORIC SITE

17 Rippleton Road, Cazenovia, 315-655-3200; www.lorenzony.org

This elegant 1807 Federal-period mansion built by John Lincklaen has retained its original furnishings. The last addition to the estate was the historic Rippleton schoolhouse circa 1814 that was moved onto the property in two pieces in 1997.

Admission: adults $5, seniors and students $4, children under 12 free. May 13-October 26, Tuesday-Sunday 10 a.m.-4:30 p.m.

TOGGENBURG SKI CENTER

Toggenburg Road, Fabius, 315-683-5842, 800-720-8644; www.skitog.com

This family-owned and -operated ski center offers 24 trails, serviced by five lifts. There is a ski school for kids new to the sport and a well-run terrain park with rails, boxes and jumps for those looking for an added challenge.

Admission: Lift ticket: adults: $15-$45, seniors $15-20, children 6-18 $10-35, children under 6 free. December-March, daily.

WHERE TO STAY
★★★BREWSTER INN

6 Ledyard Ave., Cazenovia, 315-655-9232; www.thebrewsterinn.com

Built in 1890 as the summer home of financier Benjamin B. Brewster, the inn overlooks the calming waters of Cazenovia Lake and offers a carefree and relaxed setting. You can choose to stay in a room in the main house or in the renovated carriage house. All rooms are tastefully furnished with period antiques, and many have Jacuzzi tubs, fireplaces, and views of the lake. Massage therapists are on hand to offer relaxation.

17 rooms. Restaurant, bar. Complimentary breakfast. $61-150

★★★LINCKLAEN HOUSE

79 Albany St., Cazenovia, 315-655-3461; www.lincklaenhouse.com

Since the turn of the 20th century, this property has provided fine dining and lodging for luminaries like former president Grover Cleveland and John D. Rockefeller. Rooms are elegantly decorated. Modern amenities like free wireless Internet access, air conditioning and cable TV bring this historic residence into the 21st century.

23 rooms. Complimentary breakfast, lunch and dinner. $61-150

WHERE TO EAT
★★BRAE LOCH INN
5 Albany St., Cazenovia, 315-655-3431; www.braelochinn.com

Though the dark dining room makes reading the menu challenging at times, the polished wood paneling, tartan carpeting and open grill brighten the scene to create an enjoyable, country atmosphere. Stick to the signature Scottish dishes like Haggis purse, a plate of homemade haggis (oats, ground lamb, liver and scotch) baked in a pastry and drizzled with whisky cream. American. Dinner, Sunday brunch (September-June). Children's menu. Bar. $16-35

★★★BREWSTER INN
6 Ledyard Ave., Cazenovia, 315-655-9232; www.thebrewsterinn.com

This gourmet restaurant at the historic Brewster Inn offers an elegant atmosphere and house specialties such as New Zealand rack of lamb, crispy boneless duck and the Brewster Inn veal "Atlantis"—lightly sautéed veal topped with lobster served on a bed of tender greens and finished with a tarragon beurre blanc. American, French. Dinner, Sunday brunch. Outdoor seating. Bar. $16-35

CHAUTAUQUA

See also Jamestown

On the shores of Chautauqua Lake, this small resort community is best known as being the birthplace of the New York Chautauqua Assembly, later renamed the Chautauqua Institution. Chautauqua is an adult education movement that became popular in the late 19th and early 20th centuries and strives to bring arts, education, religion and recreation to an entire community. Programs at the Chautauqua Institution are offered to adults and children, and the summer population often swells to more than 10,000. The community began as a Sunday school teachers' training camp and developed into a cultural center that started nationwide book clubs and correspondence schools. It has provided a platform for presidents, as well as artists and entertainers.

WHAT TO SEE
CHAUTAUQUA AMPHITHEATER
Bowman Street and Roberts Avenue, Chautauqua, 716-357-6200, 800-836-2787; www.ciweb.org

This 5,000-seat amphitheater built in 1893 is the home of the Chautauqua Symphony Orchestra. It also hosts recitals, ballet, opera, lectures and special popular musical events.

Prices and showtimes vary.

CHAUTAUQUA BELLE
78 Water St., Mayville, 716-269-2355; www.269belle.com

A replica of a 19th-century paddlewheel steamboat, the Chautauqua Belle cruises around the lake on various trips and themed cruises, including wine tasting events and fall foliage tours.

Admission: adults $15, children $10. May-October, daily.

THE CHAUTAUQUA INSTITUTION

1 Ames St., Chautauqua, 716-357-6200, 800-836-2787; www.ciweb.org

Often described as a place for renewal and self-exploration, this famous center for arts, education, religion and recreation offers relaxing and revitalizing summer programs that touch on everything from pop culture to politics. The nine-week season features a lecture platform as well as performing arts events. Admission: prices vary. Mid-June-August.

WHERE TO STAY
★★WEBB'S LAKE RESORT

115 West Lake Road Route 394, Mayville, 716-753-2161; www.webbsworld.com

Guest rooms are a step up from basic with mahogany furniture and floral prints, but the staff is friendly and attentive and the resort includes an onsite miniature golf course, indoor pool and candy factory. You're only minutes from Chautauqua Lake and The Chautauqua Institution.

51 rooms. Restaurant, bar. Complimentary breakfast. Fitness center. Pool. $61-150

★★★WILLIAM SEWARD INN

6645 S. Portage Road, Westfield, 716-326-4151; www.williamsewardinn.com

Southwest Chautauqua County is the perfect setting for this 1837 country inn with its nearby attractions such as ski areas, Chautauqua Lake and the well-known Chautauqua Institution. Rooms are quaint, if a tad busy, with rich fabrics and comfortable furnishings. Many rooms have four-poster beds and cozy reading nooks. Sample the black olive-crusted salmon or apricot-stuffed quail in the two dining rooms.

12 rooms. Restaurant. Complimentary breakfast. No children under 10 years. $151-250

WHERE TO EAT
★★★ATHENAEUM

South Lake Drive, Chautauqua, 716-357-4444, 800-821-1881;
www.athenaeum-hotel.com

This grand Victorian hotel has been serving guests since 1881 and is now listed on the National Historic Register. Head here for the formal, five-course dinner or stellar Sunday brunch. If space is available, ask for a table on the bright lakefront verandah.

American. Breakfast, lunch, dinner, Sunday brunch. Closed September-May. Reservations recommended. Outdoor seating. Jacket required. Children's menu. $16-35

CLAYTON

See also Alexandria Bay, Kingston, Thousand Islands, Watertown

Clayton juts into the St. Lawrence River in the midst of the Thousand Islands resort region and serves as the home for numerous pleasure boats that line the waterfront docks. In the early 19th century, Clayton was one of the major shipbuilding and steamship ports. Today, the museums that capture the town's nautical history are a major draw for tourists. Although there are a plethora of activities in Clayton, there are far fewer accommodations. Your best bet is to head back to Alexandria Bay for the night.

WHAT TO SEE
ANTIQUE BOAT MUSEUM

750 Mary St., Clayton, 315-686-4104; www.abm.org

This nautical museum showcases more than 200 antique boats, including canoes, sailboats, hydroplanes and cruisers, as well as artifacts related to boating. Be sure to check out the 65-foot yacht in the collection, as well as the 1903 historic houseboat La Duchesse.

Admission: adults $12, seniors $11, students, military and children 7-12 $6, children under 7 free. Mid-May-mid-October, daily 9 a.m.-5 p.m.

CEDAR POINT STATE PARK

36661 Cedar Point State Park Drive, Clayton, 315-654-2522; www.nysparks.state.ny.us

One of the oldest state parks in New York, Cedar Point State Park offers everything from swimming and fishing in the St. Lawrence River to camping and picnicking at one of the many campsites. Boat rentals are also available in the marina.

Admission: free. Mid-May-mid-October, daily.

THOUSAND ISLANDS MUSEUM

312 James St., Clayton, 315-686-5794; www.timuseum.org

The rich history of the Thousand Islands is reflected inside this town hall museum, which, despite being founded in the 1960s, has become the driving force behind numerous annual events, including the Decoy Show and Christmas Festival of Trees. An extensive research library is housed on the second floor and includes maps, photographs and scrapbooks recounting local histories.

Admission: adults $3, seniors and children $2. May-mid-October, daily 9 a.m.-5 p.m.; Mid-October-December, Monday-Friday 10 a.m.-4 p.m.; December-April, Monday-Friday 10 a.m.-4 p.m. by appointment.

SPECIAL EVENT
ANTIQUE BOAT SHOW

Antique Boat Museum, 750 Mary St., Clayton, 315-686-4104; www.abm.org

This is the oldest antique boat show in the country, celebrating 45 years in 2009. The show features more than 125 restored antique crafts in addition to the museum's 200 antique boats. There are sailing skiff races, a boat parade and an auction of boats.

Admission: adults $15, children 5-17 $10, military and children under 5 free. Mid-August.

WHERE TO EAT
★★THOUSAND ISLANDS INN

335 Riverside Drive, Clayton, 315-686-3030, 800-544-4241; www.1000-islands.com

Built in 1897, the Thousand Islands Inn is the last remaining original full-service hotel in the area. Among its claims-to-fame, the Inn's restaurant is credited with introducing Thousand Island salad dressing to the public and serving such celebrities as Johnny Cash and Loretta Lynn. Try the local wall-eye or Thousand Island yellow perch if you're in the mood for seafood.

American, seafood. Breakfast, lunch, dinner. Closed October-mid-May. Children's menu. Bar. $16-35

COLD SPRING

See also West Point

If you're searching for the quintessential small-town atmosphere, Cold Spring on the Hudson River is a good choice. The Main Street shopping district attracts shoppers and visitors who just want to stroll the charming streets. The surrounding area offers opportunities for outdoor recreation, including hiking, boating and kayaking. Don't miss the unique Hudson Fjord.

WHAT TO SEE
FOUNDRY SCHOOL MUSEUM

63 Chestnut St., Cold Spring, 845-265-4010; www.pchs-fsm.org

You can learn a lot from this old-fashioned schoolroom, which contains West Point Foundry memorabilia, paintings, Native American artifacts and antiques. Maintained by the Putnam County Historical Society, the museum contains a genealogy and historical research library and rotating exhibits.
Admission: adults $5, seniors and children 7-12 $2, children under 7 free. Wednesday-Sunday 11 a.m.-5 p.m.

RIVERFRONT DOCK AND BANDSTAND

Lower Main Street and the Hudson River, Cold Spring This 100-foot dock offers views of the Hudson Highlands as well as Bear Mountain and Crow's Nest. Fishing draws locals and visitors to the area. You're in for a special experience on Sunday nights in July and August when free concerts are put on at the bandstand.
Free. July-August, Sunday.

WHERE TO STAY
★★★HUDSON HOUSE INN

2 Main St., Cold Spring, 845-265-9355; www.hudsonhouseinn.com

This circa-1832 country inn on the banks of the Hudson River offers 11 guest rooms and two suites. Guest rooms are charming, brimming with French-country furnishings and antiques. Be sure to ask for a room with a private balcony or terrace for exceptional views of the Hudson. After settling in, head downstairs to dine in the country-styled restaurant or sup alfresco on the front porch with its terrific river vistas.
13 rooms. Restaurant, bar. Complimentary breakfast. $151-250

WHERE TO EAT
★★★BRASSERIE LE BOUCHON

76 Main St., Cold Spring, 845-265-7676

This adorable French restaurant is as authentic as it gets in the Hudson Valley. The menu reads like a greatest hits of classic French cooking, from escargot kissed with garlic butter to hearty cassoulet. Don't leave without ordering the profiteroles.
French. Dinner. Reservations recommended. Outdoor seating. Bar. $16-35

★★HUDSON HOUSE INN

2 Main St., Cold Spring, 845-265-9355; www.hudsonhouseinn.com

Set in the picturesque Hudson House Inn, this restaurant provides a win-win combination of inventive contemporary cuisine and outstanding alfresco dining on the riverside veranda. Locals pack the place on Sunday for the generous prix fixe brunch.

American. Lunch, dinner, Sunday brunch. Reservations recommended. Outdoor seating. Children's menu. Bar. $36-85

★★★PLUMBUSH INN
1656 Route 9D, Cold Spring, 845-265-3904; www.plumbushinn.net

Just across the Hudson River from West Point, this Victorian inn offers elegant dinners in a romantic waterfront setting. Take your pick between eating in one of the oak-paneled dining rooms, the bright airy garden room or on the terrace overlooking the manicured grounds.

American. Lunch, dinner, Sunday brunch. Closed Monday-Tuesday. Bar. $36-85

CONGERS
Who would guess that you could enjoy the pastoral Hudson River Valley only 16 miles from Manhattan? Leisure activities here range from golf and boating to shopping and dining. If you need a respite from urban life, this is a fantastic daytrip option.

WHERE TO EAT
★★★RESTAURANT X AND BULLY BOY BAR
117 N. Route 303, Congers, 845-268-6555; www.xaviars.com

Chef/owner Peter Kelly started off strong, opening the nationally praised Xavier's at Garrison at the young age of 23. Now, more than 15 years and three restaurants later, he wins kudos at this contemporary American restaurant in the woods of Rockland County. Attached to the rustic Bully Boy Bar, the country atmosphere complements the menu, which includes dishes like Hudson Valley mushroom bisque with black pepper biscotti and the medallions of Millbrook venison with chive spaetzle, Brussels sprouts and bacon.

American. Lunch, dinner, Sunday brunch. Closed Monday. Reservations recommended. Bar. $36-85

COOPERSTOWN
See also Oneonta

Founded by James Fenimore Cooper's father, Judge William Cooper, Cooperstown is in the center of "Leatherstocking" country. Here in 1839, on the south end of Otsego Lake, legend has it that Abner Doubleday devised modern baseball. By the late 19th century, wealthy New Yorkers started snatching up land for summer vacation homes, many of which were well preserved and remain in the area today. The National Baseball Hall of Fame and Museum is located on Main Street and draws more than 300,000 avid baseball fans each year.

WHAT TO SEE
THE FARMERS' MUSEUM AND VILLAGE CROSSROADS
5775 State Highway 80, Cooperstown, 607-547-1450, www.farmersmuseum.org

An outdoor museum of rural life, this sprawling 10-acre site showcases craftspeople presenting printing, weaving and blacksmithing in an historic setting. The famous "Cardiff Giant," a 10-foot statue presented to the public

A BASEBALL KIND OF TOWN

Cooperstown is best known as the home of the Baseball Hall of Fame, and anyone who has an affinity for the game will love being immersed in it here. Not a baseball fan? Don't worry—the town also offers a variety of entertaining historic sites, activities, shops and restaurants.

Start by picking up a copy of the self-guided walking tour at the information kiosk in the **Chamber of Commerce** *(31 Chestnut Street)*. From there, turn right and walk into the heart of town. At the corner of Chestnut and Main is the Cooper Inn, which was built in 1813 and is surrounded by its own pocket park. Peek at the entrance hall and lobby, highlighted by paintings from the Fenimore Art Museum. Return to Main Street and walk east. On the right is Doubleday Field where, if your timing is right, a baseball game might be in progress.

Both sides of Main Street are lined with shops, many of which have baseball themes. Among these are **Cooperstown Bat Company** *(66 Main Street)*, **America's Game** *(75 Main Street)*, **National Pastime** *(81 Main Street)*, **Third Base** *(83 Main Street)*, **Where It All Began Bat Company** *(87 Main Street)*, **The Cap Company** *(108 Main Street)*, **Collector's World** *(139 Main Street)* and **Grand Slam Collectibles** *(134 Main Street)*. Other Main Street shops of note are the **Cooperstown General Store** *(45 Main Street)* and **Cooperstown Kid Co.** *(131 Main Street)*. Take a left onto alley-like Hoffman Lane, and visit the **Cooperstown Book Nook** *(1 Hoffman Lane)*. Stop in next door for a meal at Hoffman Lane Bistro, a modern café with outdoor dining.

Return to Main Street, turn left and visit the **National Baseball Hall of Fame** *(25 Main Street)*. The nearby **Doubleday Café** *(93 Main Street)* serves up good home-made food in a real small-town atmosphere. After lunch, head north on First Street and follow it to the end for nice views of Otsego Lake.

Go west on Lake Street for two blocks to Lake Front Park at the foot of Pioneer Street—a good spot for a picnic. From there, walk about two more blocks to the Otesaga Resort Hotel—it's the huge building on your right with the three-story columns guarding the entry portico. The lobby is immense and filled with fine art. Peek into the ballroom, decorated with circa-1910 murals by Blendon Campbell and a lounge on the back veranda overlooking the lake. The food here is excellent, too.

in 1869 as a petrified prehistoric man, is here. Kids will love the Empire State Carousel that boasts 25 hand-carved animals .

Admission: Mid-May-mid-October: adults $11, seniors $9.50, children 7-12 and students $5, children under 7 and military free. April-mid-May, mid-October-late-October: adults $9, seniors $8, students $5, children 7-12 $4, children under 7 and military free. April-mid-May, Tuesday-Sunday 10 a.m.-4 p.m.; Mid-May-mid-October, daily 10 a.m.-5 p.m.; Mid-October-late-October, Tuesday-Sunday 10 a.m.-4 p.m. Closed November-March.

FENIMORE ART MUSEUM

5798 State Highway 80, Cooperstown, 607-547-1400, www.fenimoreartmuseum.org

This museum doubles as the headquarters of the New York State Historical Association and is filled with exhibits of Native American art and artifacts, academic and decorative arts of the Romantic Era, a research library and a large American folk art collection. The permanent exhibit on the Cooper family is particularly interesting.

Admission: adults $11, seniors $9.50, students and children 7-12 $5, children under 7 and military free. April-mid-May, Tuesday-Sunday 10 a.m.-4 p.m.; Mid-May-mid-October, daily 10 a.m.-5 p.m.; Mid-October-December, Tuesday-Sunday 10 a.m.-4 p.m.

GLIMMERGLASS STATE PARK

1527 County Highway 31, Cooperstown, 607-547-8662; www.nysparks.com/parks

The same Glimmerglass mentioned in James Fenimore Cooper's Leatherstocking Tales, this park overlooks Ostego Lake. Plenty of outdoor activities are available, including swimming, fishing, hiking, biking, cross-country skiing and picnicking.

Free. Daily.

NATIONAL BASEBALL HALL OF FAME AND MUSEUM

25 Main St., Cooperstown, 607-547-7200, 888-425-5633; www.baseballhalloffame.org

This nationally known museum is dedicated to the game and its players. The Hall of Fame Gallery contains plaques honoring the game's all-time greats. The museum also features displays on baseball's greatest moments, the World Series, All-Star Games, ballparks and a complete history of the game. New Hall of Famers are inducted annually (between June and August), and if you're in the area or a baseball junkie, the event is worth the stop, and it's free.

Admission: adults $16.50, seniors $11, children 7-12 $6, military and children under 7 free. September-May, daily 9 a.m.-5 p.m.; June-August, daily 9 a.m.-9 p.m.

SPECIAL EVENT
GLIMMERGLASS OPERA

Alice Busch Opera Theater, 7300 State Highway 80, Cooperstown, 607-547-2255; www.glimmerglass.org

A non-profit summer opera company, the Glimmerglass Opera started in 1975 when a handful of community opera fans staged a performance of La Boheme at the local high school. Today, the company performs four operas during the summer season and offers educational internships in production and artistic administration, giving aspiring talent the experience of working with a true repertory opera.

Prices and showtimes vary.

WHERE TO STAY
★BEST WESTERN INN AND SUITES AT THE COMMONS

50 Commons Drive, Cooperstown, 607-547-7100; www.bestwestern.com

Only four miles from the National Baseball Hall of Fame and Doubleday Field, this hotel is all about convenience for baseball fans. Guest rooms are thin on personality, but include king or queen beds, work desks and a refrigerator and microwave.

99 rooms. Complimentary breakfast. Fitness center. Pool. $61-150

★★LAKE FRONT MOTEL

10 Fair St., Cooperstown, 607-547-9511; www.lakefrontmotelandrestaurant.com

Guest rooms are basic, but spacious and offer either park or lake views. Some even include private balconies and porches. But the real reason to stay here is the one block proximity to the Baseball Hall of Fame and Main Street shops. If you're grabbing a meal at the onsite restaurant, try to get a table on the outdoor patio.

45 rooms. Restaurant, bar. $61-150

★★★OTESAGA RESORT

60 Lake St., Cooperstown, 607-547-9931, 800-348-6222; www.otesaga.com

The elegant accommodations and lovely surroundings of this grand lakeside resort have been a draw for visitors since 1909. The Federalist-style building, with its large wood-columned portico and stunning veranda that overlooks Lake Otsego, is part of the Historic Hotels of America. Spacious guest rooms feature a charming, antique feel, yet include amenities such as wireless Internet access. The championship 18-hole Leatherstocking Golf Course is adjacent, and tennis, fishing, jogging, biking and horseback riding are also available.

135 rooms. Restaurant, bar. Complimentary breakfast. Closed December-mid-April. $250-350

CORNING

See also Finger Lakes, Watkins Glen

This world glassmaking center began to grow when completion of the Chemung Canal brought in shipments of Pennsylvania anthracite, a type of coal. In 1868, lower fuel and materials costs attracted the Brooklyn Flint Glass Works, incorporated in 1875 as the Corning Glass Works. Mass production of bulbs for Thomas A. Edison's electric light soon began, lending the city the nickname Crystal City. The central shopping district has been restored to its 1890s appearance and has some worthwhile restaurants and shops to visit.

WHAT TO SEE

BENJAMIN PATTERSON INN MUSEUM COMPLEX

59 W. Pulteney St., Corning, 607-937-5281; www.pattersoninnmuseum.org

The central attraction at this complex is a restored and furnished 1796 inn, originally built to encourage settlement in Genesee Country. The two-story structure includes a public room and kitchen on the first floor and a ballroom and two bedrooms on the second floor. The DeMonstoy Log Cabin, Browntown one-room schoolhouse, Starr Barn with agricultural exhibit and blacksmith shop are also onsite.

Admission: adults $4, seniors $3.50, students $2, families $12. Monday-Friday 10 a.m.-4 p.m.

CORNING MUSEUM OF GLASS

One Museum Way, Corning, 607-937-5371, 800-732-6845; www.cmog.org

More than 25,000 objects are on display in this real-life glass menagerie, including outstanding pieces of both antique and modern Steuben glass and an 11-foot-high leaded glass window designed by Tiffany Studios in 1905. The library has the most complete collection of materials on glass in the world. The Steuben Factory, the only factory in the world that produces Steuben crystal, features skilled craftsmen transforming hot molten glass into fine crystal.

Admission: adults $12.50, seniors and students $11.25, local residents $5, children under 19 free. June-August, daily 9 a.m.-8 p.m.; September-May, daily 9 a.m.-5 p.m.

ROCKWELL MUSEUM OF WESTERN ART

111 Cedar St., Corning, 607-937-5386; www.rockwellmuseum.org

Along with antique firearms and changing exhibits, this museum contains the largest collection of American Western art in the East, including paintings by Remington, Russell, Bierstadt, Catlin and others. The museum also offers a combination ticket in conjunction with the Corning Glass Museum. If all this art gets you hungry, grab a bite at the onsite Southwestern restaurant Catalina.

Admission: adults $6.50, seniors and students $5.50, children under 19 free. June-August, daily 9 a.m.-8 p.m.; September-May, daily 9 a.m.-5 p.m.

WHERE TO STAY
★COMFORT INN

66 W. Pulteney St., Corning, 607-962-1515, 877-424-6423; www.comfortinn.com

The hotel is within walking distance of Market Street, the Rockwell Museum and the Benjamin Patterson Inn Museum complex. Guest rooms are plain, but roomy and your stay includes complimentary wireless Internet and an above-average complimentary breakfast.

62 rooms. Complimentary breakfast. Fitness center. Pool. $61-105

★★DAYS INN

23 Riverside Drive, Corning, 607-936-9370, 800-329-7466; www.daysinn.com

Whether you're in Corning for a visit or just passing through, this ideally located motel has everything to make your stay comfortable and enjoyable. Set next to the Museum of Glass among the shops and restaurants of charming downtown Corning, you have no excuse to stay in your basic and outdated room.

56 rooms. Restaurant. Complimentary breakfast. Pool. $61-150

★★RADISSON HOTEL CORNING

125 Denison Parkway E, Corning, 607-962-5000, 800-333-3333; www.radisson.com

This hotel is all about location. The Rockwell Museum of Art is next door, while the Museum of Glass and area shopping and dining are also steps away. The lobby has a spacious, natural feel, with many trees and foliage, and the calming sound of running water coming from an impressive waterfall fountain. Guest rooms are updated and bright with exclusive Sleep Number beds and luxurious down comforters.

177 rooms. Restaurant, bar. Fitness center. Pool. Pets accepted $61-150

WHERE TO EAT
★★LONDON UNDERGROUND CAFE

69 E. Market St., Corning

If the name doesn't tip you off, this eatery is all about British influence. The décor is dominated by artwork depicting London's subway, and the three-level space does gives a sense of being underground at times. The menu includes great salads and pasta dishes. If the signature fish and chips is on the menu, it's light and tasty. All desserts are made in house.

American. Lunch, dinner. Closed Sunday. Children's menu. $16-35

CORTLAND

See also Finger Lakes, Ithaca

Cortland lies in the midst of rich farm country and is the home of the State University College at Cortland. Settled in 1791, the village earned the nickname Crown City because of its location on a high plain surrounded by seven valleys.

WHAT TO SEE

1890 HOUSE MUSEUM

37 Tompkins St., Cortland, 607-756-7551; www.1890house.org

Built in a style known as Victorian chateauesque, the former mansion of industrialist Chester F. Wickwire has four stories and 30 rooms adorned with hand-carved cherry and oak woodwork, stained- and painted-glass windows, parquet floors and elaborate stenciling. The house remained in the Wickwire family until 1973. Exhibits explore typical recreation activities in the 19th century as well as Victorian-era building techniques. Many of the original furnishings still remain in place.

Admission: adults $5, seniors and students $3, children under 12 free. Friday-Saturday 1-4 p.m.

CORTLAND COUNTRY MUSIC PARK

1804 Route 13, Cortland, 607-753-0377; www.cortlandcountrymusicpark.com

Self-proclaimed as the "Nashville of the Northeast," this non-profit Hall of Fame museum and park was created to honor country western musicians from New York. The park has an Opry Barn with a large dance floor, an outdoor stage and a memorial garden. It hosts concerts, dinner theater, dance classes and bingo.

Prices vary. Showtimes and hours vary.

FILLMORE GLEN STATE PARK

1686 Highway 38, Cortland, 315-497-0130; www.nysparks.com/parks

This park is home to a replica of President Millard Fillmore's birthplace cabin. The park itself offers a full-service cottage located on the shore of Cayuga Lake at Long Point. Cottage amenities include a full kitchen and bath, hot water, electricity, sleeping arrangements, a wood stove, boat dock, picnic table and a fire ring and grill. The park offers numerous hiking trails that afford spectacular views of the surrounding lakes and dense forest. Take a dip in the stream-fed natural pool or go fishing in the Owaso Lake inlet. In winter, cross-country skiing and snowmobiling are popular with locals.

Admission: free. Campgrounds and trails: mid-May-mid-October, daily.

GREEK PEAK MOUNTAIN RESORT

2000 Highway 392, Cortland, 607-835-6111, 800-995-2754; www.greekpeak.net

It's not the Alps, but Greek Peaks provides family-friendly skiing in the heart of New York's famous Snow Belt with 32 trails that range in difficulty and terrain. There is a half pipe and terrain park for seasoned skiers and snowboarders, as well as a Progressive Park for those just starting out. If skiing isn't your thing, there are also runs reserved exclusively for tubing. Labrador Mountain and Song Mountain are nearby ski alternatives.

Admission: Full day: adults $58, children under 15 $49, tubing $21. December-April, daily.

SUGGETT HOUSE MUSEUM AND KELLOGG MEMORIAL
RESEARCH LIBRARY

25 Homer Ave., Cortland, 607-756-6071; www.cortland.org/ent/museums

Headquarters of the Cortland County Historical Society, the museum houses vignettes of home arts from 1825 to 1900, including an 1882 kitchen. The circa 1880 building also contains military memorabilia, local art, a children's room and changing exhibits. The library has local history and genealogy material. Admission: $3. Museum: Tuesday-Saturday 1-4 p.m. Library: Tuesday-Saturday 1-5 p.m.

SPECIAL EVENTS
CENTRAL NEW YORK MAPLE FESTIVAL

42 Front St., Marathon, 607-849-3812; www.maplefest.org

It's all about syrup at this family-friendly festival in the heart of Central New York. There are a variety of events showing the process of making maple syrup, as well as a pancake contest, arts and crafts, hay rides and a Maple Queen beauty contest.
Early April.

CORTLAND REPERTORY THEATRE

Dwyer Memorial County Park Pavilion Theatre, 37 Franklin St., Cortland, 607-753-6161,
800-427-6160; www.cortlandrep.org

The Cortland Repertory Theatre performs musicals, comedies and dramas in the Edward Jones Playhouse of the Little York Pavilion, a former trolley park pavilion now listed on the National Historic Register. The pavilion overlooks Little York Lake and offers picnic facilities.
Tickets: evenings $25-27, matinees $20-22. Mid-June-early-September, Tuesday-Saturday 7:30 p.m., Sunday 2 p.m.

WHERE TO STAY
★★★BENN CONGER INN

206 W. Cortland St., Groton, 607-898-5817; www.benncongerinn.com

This property is located near downtown Ithaca, wineries, antique shops, horseback riding and more. The inn, a Greek Revival mansion and former home of Benn Conger, the founder of Smith Corona, features large rooms with custom mattresses and imported linens. There is also a Victorian cottage with six rooms that boast fireplaces and whirlpools. A five-course breakfast is included.
9 rooms. Restaurant, bar. Complimentary breakfast. $151-250

★COMFORT INN

2 ½ Locust Ave., Cortland, 607-753-7721; www.comfortinn.com

If you're coming to the area to hit the slopes, this hotel offers a central location for Greek Peak, Labrador Mountain and Song Mountain. It's also only minutes from SUNY Cortland, and a half hour from Cornell University in Ithaca. The guest rooms are basic and small, but the hotel does offer a fitness room and a free continental breakfast.
66 rooms. Restaurant. Complimentary breakfast. Fitness center. $61-150

★HAMPTON INN

26 River St., Cortland, 607-662-0007; www.hampton-inn.com

Updated rooms are spacious and bright and include lap desks and free Internet access. The hotel also provides a complimentary beverage and breakfast area in case you get thirsty between meals.

111 rooms. Complimentary breakfast. Business center. Fitness center. $61-150

WHERE TO EAT
★★★BENN CONGER INN

206 W. Cortland St., Groton, 607-898-5817; www.benncongerinn.com

This elegant restaurant in the Benn Conger Inn offers a wide selection of Mediterranean-inspired cuisine accompanied by an award-winning wine list. The inn's signature prime rib is generous and delicious, as is the chicken mushroom casserole.

Mediterranean. Dinner. Closed Monday-Tuesday. Reservations recommended. Children's menu. Bar. $36-85

CROWN POINT

See also Ticonderoga

Located on a peninsula that forms the northernmost narrows of Lake Champlain, the Point was a strong position from which to control the trade route between New York and Canada during the French and Indian War. In the early 19th century, iron ore was discovered here which quickly transformed the town into a booming industrial center, particularly for the use of shipbuilding by the U.S. Navy.

WHAT TO SEE
CROWN POINT STATE HISTORIC SITE

739 Bridge Road, Crown Point, 518-597-4666; www.nysparks.com/sites

During the French and Indian and Revolutionary wars, both French and English troops built forts along the shores of Lake Champlain. Today, those forts can be viewed as ruins, including those of Fort St. Frederic, dating back to 1734, and Fort Crown Point. The onsite museum also houses exhibits examining Crown Point's turbulent history.

Admission: Museum: adults $3, seniors and students $2, children under 13 free. Wednesday-Monday, 9 a.m.-5 p.m. Grounds: free. May-October, daily 9 a.m.-sunset.

PENFIELD HOMESTEAD MUSEUM

703 Creek Road, Crown Point, 518-597-3804; www.penfieldmuseum.org

A museum of local history built around the Adirondack iron industry and industrialist Allen Penfield, this museum marks the site of the first industrial use of electricity in the United States. The site encompasses 550-acres and includes a carriage barn, a church and a monument honoring Penfield's war horse, Billy.

Admission: adults $4, children $2. June-mid-October, Thursday-Sunday 11 a.m.-4 p.m.

WHERE TO STAY
★★CANOE ISLAND LODGE
3820 Lakeshore Drive, Diamond Point, 518-668-5592; www.canoeislandlodge.com

Guests return to the family vacations of their youths at this 50-year-old, knotty-pine-filled resort on Lake George in the Adirondack Mountains. The namesake island is actually one mile offshore, providing a peaceful spot to connect with nature, go swimming, sailing or water skiing, or just relax on the beach with a book. Accommodations are rustic but spacious and comfortable with views of the lake.

65 rooms. Restaurant, bar. Complimentary breakfast, dinner. Closed mid-October-mid-May. Beach. $151-250

DUNKIRK
See also Buffalo

A pleasant city southwest of Buffalo on the shores of Lake Erie about 35 miles from the Pennsylvania border, Dunkirk was the birthplace of author-historian Samuel Hopkins Adams. Due to relatively mild winters and rich soil, the region is well-suited for wine-making. The historic lighthouse built in 1875 is worth a visit.

WHAT TO SEE
DUNKIRK LIGHTHOUSE
1 Lighthouse Point Drive, Dunkirk, 716-366-5050; www.dunkirklighthouse.com

While the stone tower and attached residence weren't constructed until 1875, the light was established long before that, on Point Gratiot in 1827, where it performed double duty with a pier head beacon to steer ships safely into Dunkirk Harbor. Today, the light shines a 27-mile radius, making it one of the most prominent beacons on Lake Erie. The residence has been transformed into a museum displaying military artifacts.

Admission: adults $6, children 4-12 $2.50, children under 4 free. September-October, May-June, Monday-Tuesday, Thursday-Saturday 10 a.m.-2 p.m.; July-August, Monday-Tuesday, Thursday-Saturday 10 a.m.-4 p.m.

EVANGOLA STATE PARK
10191 Old Lake Shore Road, Irving, 716-549-1802; www.evangolastatepark.com

This 733-acre park opened in 1954. It was formerly farmland, used to grow tomatoes, beans and corn. Since the very beginning, Evangola's attraction has been its arc-shaped shoreline and natural sand beach. The park has a variety of habitats (including lakeshore, woodland, meadow and wetlands); and varied wildlife call Evangola home.

Admission: June-August $7 per vehicle, September-May free. Daily.

LAKE ERIE STATE PARK
5905 Lake Road., Brockton, 716-792-9214; www.nysparks.state.ny.us

Views of Lake Erie can be seen from almost anywhere within the park thanks to its bluff-top location. Enjoy swimming, fishing and hiking in the summer, and cross-country skiing and snowmobiling in winter. There are more than 100 campsites, as well as cabins for those who aren't the outdoorsy type.

Admission: June-August $7 per vehicle; September-May free. Daily.

SPECIAL EVENT
CHAUTAUQUA COUNTY FAIR
1089 Central Ave., Dunkirk, 716-366-4752; www.chautauquacountyfair.org
The Chautauqua County Fair has been going for more than 127 years. Expect rides, games and food in the fair's midway. Children will love the petting zoo and kids' tractor pull.
Admission: prices vary. Last week in July.

WHERE TO STAY
★★DAYS INN
10455 Bennett Road, Fredonia, 716-673-1351; www.daysinn.com
The guest rooms could use an update, but the hotel is centrally located in the Dunkirk wine region and includes amenities such as a heated indoor pool.
135 rooms. Restaurant, bar. Complimentary breakfast. Pets accepted. $61-150

★★★THE WHITE INN
52 E. Main St., Fredonia, 716-672-2103, 888-373-3664; www.whiteinn.com
This inn has all the comfort and charm of a country manor and offers eloquently decorated rooms and suites and fine dining, as well as a location close to cultural, historical and recreational attractions. Dating back to 1868, the inn boasts a lovely collection of Victorian antiques. The onsite restaurant is popular with locals.
23 rooms. Restaurant, bar. Complimentary breakfast. $151-250

WHERE TO EAT
★★★THE WHITE INN
52 E. Main St., Fredonia, 716-672-2103, 888-373-3664; www.whiteinn.com
This stately country manor with an impressive columned portico and authentic Victorian décor serves a delectable rack of lamb rubbed with Dijon mustard and bone-in chicken breast pan roasted and seared in olive oil. Nothing starts a day better than a serving of White Inn crepes with sautéed apples, sausage and fruit.
American. Breakfast, lunch, dinner. Outdoor seating. Bar. $16-36

EAST AURORA
See also Buffalo
East Aurora lies very close to the large industrial center of Buffalo. In the early 1900s, Elbert Hubbard, author of A Message to Garcia, lived here and made it the home of the Roycroft, a handicraft community known for making fine books, copper and leather ware and furniture. The Roycroft campus is still operating, and it is the only continuous operation of its kind in America today. East Aurora is also the headquarters of Fisher-Price toys. The Baker Memorial Methodist Church, which has hand-signed Tiffany windows, is located here.

WHAT TO SEE
THE ELBERT HUBBARD ROYCROFT MUSEUM
363 Oakwood Ave., East Aurora, 716-652-4735; www.roycrofter.com/museum.htm
This five-bedroom, 1910 Craftsman period home built by and for the Roy-

crofters is a testament to their handiwork. It contains Roycroft furniture, modeled leather, hammered metal, leaded glass, books, pamphlets and other artifacts from 1895 to 1938. There's also material on Elbert Hubbard, author of the famous essay A Message to Garcia.

Admission: $5. June-October, Wednesday, Saturday-Sunday 1-4 p.m.

KISSING BRIDGE SKI AREA

10296 State Road, Glenwood, 716-592-4963; www.kbski.com

With 700 acres of terrain at its disposal, Kissing Bridge offers some of the best ski runs in the Colden Snowbelt of western New York. The trails run from beginner to expert, and most are lit for night skiing. There are also rail and terrain parks to practice your latest tricks.

Admission: adults $16-52, children under 14 $16-42. December-March, daily.

MILLARD FILLMORE MUSEUM

24 Shearer Ave., East Aurora, 716-652-8875

This is the house President Millard Fillmore built for his wife in 1825, though he only lived here for four years. It contains memorabilia, furnishings and a 1830s herb and rose garden. The Carriage house, built in 1830 of lumber from the former Nathaniel Fillmore farm, contains antique tools and a Fillmore sleigh.

Admission: adults $5. June-October, Wednesday, Saturday-Sunday 1-4 p.m.

SPECIAL EVENT
TOYFEST

636 Girard Ave., East Aurora, 716-687-5151; www.toytownusa.com

This annual celebration commemorates Fisher-Price Toy Company's establishment here in the 1930s. Antique toys from various periods in history are on display, and there is an antique car show and a town parade.

Admission: prices vary. Last weekend in August.

WHERE TO STAY
★★★ROYCROFT INN

40 S. Grove St., East Aurora, 716-652-5552, 800-267-0525; www.roycroftinn.com

Visit this birthplace of the New York Arts and Crafts movement, located just 30 minutes from Buffalo. The grounds, called the Roycroft Campus, originally housed 500 craftsmen and their shops and now are a national landmark. Rooms are breathtaking showcases of original furniture and fixtures.

28 rooms. Restaurant, bar. Complimentary breakfast. $151-250

WHERE TO EAT
★★OLD ORCHARD INN

2095 Blakeley Corners Road, East Aurora, 716-652-4664; www.oldorchardny.com

A century-old rustic country inn, this former hunting lodge offers hearty food in a warm atmosphere. During the summer months, enjoy its covered patio seating or wander through the property's 25 wooded acres. The Macadamia sea bass topped with a warm wildberry sauce is fantastic.

American. Lunch, dinner. Closed Monday-Tuesday; also January-April. Outdoor seating. Bar. $36-85

★★★ROYCROFT INN
40 S. Grove St., East Aurora, 716-652-5552; www.roycroftinn.com

This inn originally opened in 1905 to accommodate the thousands of visitors to the thriving Roycroft Arts and Crafts Community, a large, self-contained group of writers and craftspeople. Today, the restaurant is a popular gathering place for locals and serves creative and fresh cuisine with continental influences, including French onion soup au gratin, rack of lamb and sesame-encrusted tuna.

American. Lunch, dinner, Sunday brunch. Reservations recommended. Outdoor seating. Children's menu. Bar. $16-35

EAST HAMPTON
See also Amagansett, Montauk, Sag Harbor, Shelter Island, Southampton

East Hampton is an old village founded in 1648 by a group of farmers. Agriculture was the main livelihood until the mid-1800s, when the town began to develop into a fashionable resort. Today, the town glitters in the summer months when celebrities and wealthy Manhattanites escape to their palaces by the sea.

WHAT TO SEE
GUILD HALL MUSEUM
158 Main St., East Hampton, 631-324-0806; www.guildhall.org

This small museum features regional art exhibits and seasonally changing shows. There are also interesting art and poetry lectures and classes. Film festivals and concerts often take place at the John Drew Theater.

Free. June-August, Monday-Saturday 11 a.m.-5 p.m., Sunday noon-5 p.m.; September-May, Friday-Saturday 11 a.m.-5 p.m., Sunday noon-5 p.m.

HISTORIC CLINTON ACADEMY
151 Main St., East Hampton, 631-324-6850; www.easthamptonhistory.org

The first preparatory school in New York is now a museum housing a collection of Eastern Long Island artifacts. The Georgian-style building was restored in 1921 and boasts beautiful gardens throughout the property.

Admission: adults $4, seniors $3, students $2. June-mid-October, Saturday 10 a.m.-5 p.m., Sunday noon-5 p.m.; July-August, Friday 10 a.m.-5 p.m.

HISTORIC MULFORD FARM
10 James Lane, East Hampton, 631-324-6850; www.easthamptonhistory.org

This living history museum and farm features 18th-century New England architecture, colonial history, period rooms and costumed interpretation. The property includes the Mulford House, constructed in 1680, and the Mulford Barn, which was built in 1721 and remains one of the best examples of an early 18th century English barn plan. Admission: adults $4, seniors $3, students $2. June-mid-October, Saturday 10 a.m.-5 p.m., Sunday noon-5 p.m.; July-August, Friday 10 a.m.-5 p.m.

"HOME SWEET HOME" HOUSE
14 James Lane, East Hampton, 631-324-0713;
www.easthampton.com/homesweethome

Named after the popular 19th-century song, Home, Sweet Home, written by

John Howard Payne, this house was originally owned by Payne's grandfather, Aaron Isaacs (the first Jewish person to settle in the area). The historic lean-to house features a stunning collection of antiques and china and is dedicated to Payne, who was also an actor, playwright and diplomat.

Admission: adults $4, seniors $3, students $2. May-September, Monday-Saturday 10 a.m.-4 p.m., Sunday 2-4 p.m.; April, October-November, Friday-Saturday 10 a.m.-4 p.m., Sunday 2-4 p.m.

POLLOCK-KRASNER HOUSE AND STUDY CENTER
830 Fireplace Road, East Hampton, 631-324-4929;
http://naples.cc.sunysb.edu/CAS/pkhouse.nsf

Abstract Expressionist Jackson Pollock's studio and house, plus a reference library on 20th-century American art, are open to the public and worth a trip. Inside the unassuming house circa 1879, remains much of the furniture used by Pollock, as well as a collection of jazz records and a personal library. Don't miss Pollock's paint-covered studio floor.

Admission: $5. May, September-October, Thursday-Saturday 11 a.m.-4 p.m.; June-August, Thursday-Saturday noon-4 p.m.

WHERE TO STAY
★★★THE 1770 HOUSE
143 Main St., East Hampton, 631-324-1770; www.1770house.com

This restored 18th-century house proffers antique furnishings and a prime location near East Hampton's top-notch shopping and dining. The rooms are sumptuous and elegant with Frette linens and flat-screen televisions. Some of

ART IN THE HAMPTONS

The history of art in the Hamptons can be traced back to the Montauket and Shinnecock Indians, who transformed seashells into wonderful wampum they traded with 17th-century colonists. By the 1870s, the area's luminous light, fertile farmlands and sandy shores lured painters to a rural countryside that reminded them of Europe. The artists—Winslow Homer, Edwin Austin Abbey, John Twachtman and William Merritt Chase—called themselves "The Tile Club" and created what became the second-oldest art colony in America.

As time passed, artists continued to move eastward. Childe Hassam arrived in the 1920s. In the 1940s, Jackson Pollock and Lee Krasner, Willem and Elaine de Kooning and Robert Motherwell reinterpreted the landscape according to their individual sensitivities. Abstract Expressionism attracted more artists and the first of dozens of art galleries opened. (This first gallery is now known as the Elaine **Benson Gallery and Sculpture Garden,** *2317 Montauk Highway, Bridgehampton; 631-537-3233.*) Artists from the New York School displayed their work and exhibitions, including pop artist Larry Rivers, cubist Fernand Leger, abstract painter Harry Kramer, glass artist Dale Chihuly, sculptor Louise Nevelson, ceramist Toshiko Takaezu and jeweler David Yurman.

Most of the art galleries are found in the villages of Southampton, Westhampton Beach and East Hampton. On just one tiny passageway between Main Street and the public parking lot in East Hampton, art lovers can stop in to **Vered** *(68 Park Place, 631-324-3303)* and see work by Marc Chagall, Pablo Picasso, Henri Matisse, Ben Shahn, David Hockney and Louise Nevelson. The **Wallace Gallery,** across the Passage *(37A Main Street, 631-329-4516),* displays a retrospective of local landscapes and seascapes that reflect the authentic history of the region, including work by east-end artists Edward Lamson Henry, Thomas Moran and Childe Hassam.

the rooms also have fireplaces.

7 rooms. Restaurant, bar. Complimentary breakfast. Children over 12 years only. $151-250

★★★THE MAIDSTONE
207 Main St., East Hampton, 631-324-5006; www.maidstonearms.com

The Osborne family built this estate as a private residence in the 1750s, and the terrifically situated property has been operating as an inn since the 1870s. Enjoy the bustle of the Hamptons during the summer months or settle in by the fireplaces during cozy winter stays. The recently refurbished property is adorned with classic furnishings and sophisticated touches. The back garden becomes vibrant with flowers in spring.

19 rooms. Restaurant, bar. Complimentary breakfast. $151-250

WHERE TO EAT

★★★ALISON AT THE MAIDSTONE
207 Main St., East Hampton, 631-324-5440; www.alisonrestaurant.com

Alison is frequently visited by celebrities such as Scarlett Johannson, Christy Turlington, Julianne Moore and Shirley MacLaine. Housed inside a charming white clapboard inn with striped awnings, the real attraction is on the plates. Wrap up dinner with a cigar in in the Water Room Lounge.

American. Breakfast, lunch, dinner. Bar. $36-85

★★★DELLA FEMINA
99 N. Main St., East Hampton, 631-329-6666; www.dellafemina.com

The celebrity caricatures that line the walls of this New American eatery hint at the see-and-be-seen reputation that it carries during summer months. The off-season welcomes a more mellow atmosphere where good food and reasonable prix fixe menus dominate the scene.

American. Dinner, Sunday brunch (November-April). Closed Wednesday (November-April). Outdoor seating. Bar. $36-85

★★★EAST HAMPTON POINT
295 Three Mile Harbor Road, East Hampton, 631-329-2800;
www.easthamptonpoint.com

With stunning waterfront and sunset vistas overlooking Three Mile Harbor, East Hampton Point has a subtle nautical décor. The skilled kitchen turns out dishes such as roasted Scottish salmon with asparagus, morel risotto with a truffle-leek sauce and Maine halibut with black olives, tomatoes, fennel and baby artichokes.

American. Lunch, dinner. Closed September-March. Reservations recommended. Outdoor seating. Children's menu. Bar. $36-85

★★NICK & TONI'S
136 N. Main St., East Hampton, 631-324-3550; www.nickandtonis.com

The décor of the dining room is simple, bright and colorful with a mosaic wood-burning brick oven and an open-air patio. The wood-roasted chicken is a good bet, as are any of the oven-charred pizzas. Arrive early in summer and be prepared to wait.

Mediterranean. Dinner, Sunday brunch. Bar. $36-85

★★PALM

94 Main St., East Hampton, 631-324-0411; www.thepalm.com

Though not the cheapest option in East Hampton, this restaurant serves consistently delicious American fare in a charming old-fashioned setting. The prime rib is fantastic, as is the lobster.

Seafood, steak. Dinner. Bar. $36-85

ELMIRA

See also Corning, Finger Lakes, Oswego, Watkins Glen

Elmira resides on both shores of the Chemung River—it's located on a site where, in 1779, the Sullivan-Clinton expedition found an American Indian village. By the mid-19th century, railroads and canals were opening new fields of industry here; first lumber, later metalworking and textiles. Samuel Clemens (Mark Twain) spent more than 20 summers at Quarry Farm, the Elmira country home of his wife's sister, Susan Crane. Elmira also is the birthplace of noted filmmaker Hal Roach, fashion designer Tommy Hilfiger and astronaut Eileen Collins, the first woman to pilot a space shuttle.

WHAT TO SEE
ARNOT ART MUSEUM

235 Lake St., Elmira, 607-734-3697; www.arnotartmuseum.org

Named for a 19th-century local banker, Mathias Arnot, whose art collection represents the majority of the work on display, the museum specializes in European and American paintings from the 17th to the 19th centuries. The museum is set inside an 1833 three-story mansion.

Admission: $5. Tuesday-Saturday 10 a.m.-5 p.m.

CHEMUNG VALLEY HISTORY MUSEUM

415 E. Water St., Elmira, 607-734-4167; www.chemungvalleymuseum.org

The Chemung Valley History Museum examines the history of the Chemung River Valley region by showcasing a collection of artifacts that focuses on the Southern Tier of New York State and neighboring northern Pennsylvania. Exhibits include a fascinating display on Mark Twain.

Admission: adults $3, seniors $2, students $1, children under 5 free. Tuesday-Saturday 10 a.m.-5 p.m.

ELMIRA COLLEGE

1 Park Place, Elmira, 607-735-1800; www.elmira.edu

Coeducational since 1969, Elmira College was the first to grant women degrees equal to those of men in 1855. Mark Twain did much of his writing here, including The Adventures of Huckleberry Finn. The Mark Twain Study was presented to the college by the Langdon Family in 1952, and there is also a Mark Twain exhibit in Hamilton Hall with memorabilia.

Free. Daily.

NATIONAL SOARING MUSEUM

51 Soaring Hill Drive, Elmira, 607-734-3128; www.soaringmuseum.org

This museum features a large collection of soaring planes that depict the history of this type of motorless flight. There are also exhibits on meteorology, aerodynamics and aviation. The simulator is a good place to test what soaring feels like before signing up for the real thing.

Admission: adults $6.50, senior $5.50, children 5-17 $4, children under 5 free. Monday-Friday 10 a.m.-5 p.m.

WHERE TO STAY
★BEST WESTERN MARSHALL MANOR

3527 Watkins Road, Horseheads, 607-739-3891, 800-780-7234; www.bestwestern.com

A charming red brick building with white pillars, this comfortable motel is set on the rolling countryside and is convenient to local wineries and a large shopping mall.

40 rooms. Restaurants. Complimentary breakfast. Pool. $61-150

★★HOLIDAY INN

760 E. Water St., Elmira, 607-734-4211; www.holidayinn.com

Situated just off the highway, this well-maintained, family-friendly motel features a large outdoor pool and a wading pool for kids. The hotel also has a fitness room.

149 rooms. Restaurant, bar. Fitness center. Pool. $61-150

WHERE TO EAT
★★HILL TOP INN

171 Jerusalem Hill Road, Elmira, 607-732-6728, 888-444-5586; www.hill-top-inn.com

Serving country favorites since 1933, the Hill Top Inn is the oldest licensed restaurant in New York State. Try the spring lamb chops with mint jelly or the Chesapeake chicken stuffed with homemade crabmeat and served over couscous—you won't be disappointed.

American. Dinner. Closed Sunday; also November-February. Reservations recommended. Outdoor seating. Children's menu. Bar. $16-35

FINGER LAKES

49

See also Auburn, Corning, Cortland, Elmira, Geneva, Hammondsport, Ithaca, Oswego, Rochester, Skaneateles, Syracuse, Watkins Glen

Scientists say glaciers scooped out the Finger Lakes, resulting in one of the most delightful landscaping jobs in America. There are 11 lakes in all, and Canandaigua, Keuka, Seneca, Cayuga, Owasco and Skaneateles are the largest. The smaller lakes also have the characteristic finger shape. Seneca is the deepest at 630 feet and Cayuga the longest at 40 miles. The region has many glens and gorges with plunging streams. Hundreds of recreation spots dot the shores, offering every imaginable sport. The famous New York State wine grapes grow in the many miles of vineyards in the area.

FISHKILL

See also Newburgh, Poughkeepsie

In the Hudson River Valley, a great place to commune with Mother Nature, brush up on your American history and enjoy a day strolling along its historic streets. In the 19th century factories and mills dominated the landscape, and Fishkill enjoyed an industrial boom until the Great Depression. Today, technology is the industry of choice, but visitors still flock to the area for a glimpse back at Hudson Valley history.

WHAT TO SEE
MADAM BRETT HOMESTEAD
50 Van Nydeck Ave., Beacon, 845-831-6533

The oldest standing structure in Dutchess County, this 1709 house has period furnishings dating back seven generations, from Dutch Colonial through the Federal and Victorian eras. The homestead was used to stock military supplies during the Revolutionary War. Don't miss the delicately manicured garden on the grounds.

Admission: adults $4, students $2. April-December, second Saturday of every month 1-4 p.m., and by appointment.

MOUNT GULIAN HISTORIC SITE
145 Sterling St., Beacon, 845-831-8172; www.mountgulian.org

This is the headquarters of Baron von Steuben during the final period of the Revolutionary War. It's also the birthplace of the Order of the Society of Cincinnati, the first veteran's organization. There's a Dutch barn and restored garden on the grounds.

Admission: adults $8, seniors $6, children 6-18 $4. Mid-April-October, Wednesday-Friday, Sunday 1-5 p.m.

VAN WYCK HOMESTEAD MUSEUM
504 Route 9, Fishkill, 845-896-9560

During the revolution, the Continental Army requisitioned this house as headquarters and issued orders from here. It was also the site of court-martials, including that of Enoch Crosby, counterspy for the American forces. Washington, Lafayette and Baron von Steuben all visited here. The museum has a nice collection of Hudson Valley Folk Art.

Admission: donation accepted. June-October, Saturday-Sunday 1-4 p.m.

WHERE TO STAY
★RAMADA FISHKILL-POUGHKEEPSIE
20 Schuyler Blvd., Fishkill, 845-896-4995, 800-272-6232; www.ramada.com

This hotel is only minutes from the Interstate, as well as sites like Dutchess Stadium and Splash Down Beach. Guest rooms are short on charm, but big on space and microwaves and refrigerators come standard with each room. Free passes to the nearby All Sport Fishkill Health and Fitness Center is an added perk.

81 rooms. Bar. Complimentary breakfast. $61-150

WHERE TO EAT
★★HUDSON'S RIBS & FISH
1099 Route 9, Fishkill, 845-297-5002, www.hudsonsribsandfish.com

This casual upscale restaurant serves some of the freshest seafood in the Hudson Valley. The homemade New England clam chowder hits the spot on a chilly night, and Hudson's famous "fish box" will have you stuffed for days. Steaks are also a good bet here, and include the restaurant's signature hot popover with strawberry butter.

Seafood. Dinner. Children's menu. Bar. $16-35

FREEPORT

See also Long Island

This Long Island village has a prime waterfront spot, so anglers, boaters and swimmers will enjoy its easy access to the water. Residents of the Big Apple come here in the summer for the beaches, great seafood and lively ambiance.

WHAT TO SEE
NAUTICAL MILE

Woodcleft Ave., Freeport

A stroll along Freeport's Nautical Mile on a warm, summer afternoon cannot be beat. This revitalized stretch of walkway in the seaport village offers a mix of restaurants, clam bars, knickknack shops, ice cream parlors, a seaport museum and boats for sale. Start off by eating shrimp or clams outdoor at one of the many ultra-causal restaurants (some have live bands on the weekends in summer), stroll nearby and enjoy Ralph's Ices (the best around), admire the boats and take in the atmosphere. Finish off the day by sitting on the scenic pier at the end of the avenue to enjoy the waterfront view.

WHERE TO EAT
★★SCHOONER

435 Woodcleft Ave., Freeport, 516-378-7575; www.theschooner.com

With a prime waterfront patio, this restaurant offers some of the best alfresco dining on Long Island. In addition to a generous prix fixe option, the menu offers such seafood favorites as crispy calamari, pecan-crusted halibut and Maryland crab cakes.

Seafood, steak. Lunch, dinner. Closed mid-January. Outdoor seating. $16-35

GARDEN CITY

See also Long Island

Established in 1869 by merchant millionaire Alexander Turney Stewart, Garden City was one of the country's first planned communities. Wide streets, lots of vegetation and handsome buildings still distinguish this town.

WHAT TO SEE
CRADLE OF AVIATION MUSEUM

Charles Lindbergh Blvd., Garden City, 516-572-4111; www.cradleofaviation.org

With an emphasis on Long Island's important and colorful history in the field of aviation, the museum offers exhibits on World War I, World War II, the Jet Age and Space Travel, to name a few. There also is an IMAX Theater.

Admission: adults $9, seniors and children 2-12 $8. Tuesday-Sunday 9:30 a.m.-5 p.m.

LONG ISLAND CHILDREN'S MUSEUM

Mitchell Center, 11 Davis Blvd., Garden City, 516-224-5800; www.licm.org

This popular museum located in a former military base offers many hands-on interactive exhibits. Some include a bubble machine, climbing ramps and a beach exhibit that lets kids shape their own sand dunes. There are performances on weekends and programs held during the week.

Admission: adults and children 2-18 $10, seniors $9, children under 1 free.

September-June, 10 a.m.-5 p.m. Closed Monday. July-August, daily 10 a.m.-5 p.m.

WHERE TO STAY
★★★THE GARDEN CITY HOTEL
45 Seventh St., Garden City, 516-747-3000; www.gardencityhotel.com
This hotel, which was built in 1874, features sophisticated accommodations and service that have attracted notable families such as the Kennedys and Vanderbilts. Spacious guest rooms feature antique desks, wireless Internet access, fully stocked bars and luxury bath amenities. Room service is available 24 hours a day, but the hotel offers a number of other dining options, including the Polo Restaurant, Rein Bar and Bistro and the Atrium Café.
300 rooms. Restaurant, bar. Business center. Fitness center. Pool. $250-350

WHERE TO EAT
★★AKBAR
2 South St., Garden City, 516-357-8300; www.theakbar.com
For an authentic Indian meal, this is a great choice. The tandoori dishes cooked in a clay oven are particularly tasty and the spicy Bengal fish curry will certainly tickle your tastebuds.
Indian. Lunch, dinner, Sunday brunch. Reservations recommended. $16-35

★★ORCHID
730 Franklin Ave., Garden City, 516-742-1116
The bronze mirrored ceiling, marble bar, and large Chinese vases give a pronounced glitz to this local Chinese restaurant; the food does the rest. Specialty dishes such as honey spare ribs, Peking duck and orange-flavored beef come out of the kitchen in top form, plated alongside intricate carvings of birds and flowers made of fruits and vegetables.
Chinese. Lunch, dinner. Reservations recommended. Bar. $16-35

GENEVA
See also Finger Lakes, Seneca Falls, Waterloo
In the 19th century, Geneva attracted large numbers of retired ministers and spinsters and became known as "the saints' retreat and old maids' paradise." Located at the foot of Seneca Lake, the deepest of the Finger Lakes, the town is surrounded by rich farmland, which explains why Cornell University's Agricultural Experiment Station is here.

WHAT TO SEE
GENEVA HISTORICAL SOCIETY MUSEUM
543 S. Main St., Geneva, 315-789-5151; www.genevahistoricalsociety.com
Prouty-Chew House, built in 1829, is a Federal-style home with items of local history and changing exhibits. The collections contain 30,000 historical photographs, as well as furniture, decorative art, costumes, textiles, fine art, tools and equipment.
Admission: donation accepted. July-August, Tuesday-Friday 9:30 a.m.-4:30 p.m., Saturday-Sunday 1:30-4:30 p.m.; September-June, Tuesday-Friday 9:30 a.m.-4:30 p.m., Saturday 1:30-4:30 p.m.

ROSE HILL MANSION

Route 96A, Geneva, 315-789-3848; www.genevahistoricalsociety.com

This elegant 1839 country estate has Greek Revival architecture and Empire furnishings adorning the 21 rooms that are open to the public. The property includes a carriage house, outbuildings and a beautiful boxwood garden. Admission: adults $6, seniors and students $4, children under 10 free. May-October, Monday-Saturday 10 a.m.-4 p.m., Sunday 1-5 p.m.

SENECA LAKE STATE PARK

1 Lakefront Drive, Geneva, 315-789-2331; www.nysparks.state.ny.us/parks

This state park provides the longest strip of public lakeshore in the entire Finger Lakes region, ideal for swimming, fishing and boating. Kids will love the Sprayground (the first in the New York State Park system) that sprays water with more than 100 water jets. There is also a playground and picnic site; and boat slips are available.

Free. Daily.

SMITH OPERA HOUSE FOR THE PERFORMING ARTS

82 Seneca St., Geneva, 315-781-5483; www.thesmith.org

One of the oldest operating theaters in the United States, the Smith hosts concerts, films, children's programs, and of course operas. The Richardsonian Romanesque building was constructed in 1894 by local philanthropist William Smith. The interior was completely renovated in 1930 in the art-deco style that was so popular at the time. The Smith stage has seen performances by such talents as Isadora Duncan, Wynton Marsalis, Jay Leno and Billy Joel.

Prices vary. Showtimes vary.

WHERE TO STAY

★★★GENEVA ON THE LAKE

1001 Lochland Road, Geneva, 315-789-7190, 800-343-6382;
www.genevaonthelake.com

Situated in the Finger Lakes wine district on Seneca Lake, this hotel was built as a private home in 1914. Resembling an Italian villa, the property boasts Italian marble fireplaces, wood-coffered ceilings and Ionic columns. Activities include a 70-foot pool, volleyball, 9- and 18-hole golf courses within a mile and romantic dining overlooking the scenic formal gardens and waterfront.

29 rooms. Restaurant. Complimentary breakfast. Pool. $151-250

ALSO RECOMMENDED

BELHURST CASTLE

4069 Route 14 S., Lochland Road, Geneva, 315-781-0201; www.belhurst.com

The 1889 stone castle offers a unique stay thanks to its dramatic architecture and views of Seneca Lake. There are multiple cottages and buildings within the Belhurst property. If possible, ask for a room in the original castle, where you'll be treated to four-poster beds, fireplaces, oriental rugs and breathtaking lake views. Choose from one of the six dining rooms or eat alfresco at Edgar's - the in house elegant dining option.

47 rooms. Restaurant, bar. Continental breakfast. $151-250

GREENPORT

See also Long Island, Riverhead, Shelter Island, Southold

Greenport is a bit of New England on Long Island's North Fork. This nautical, artsy, harborside village exudes charm, offering a mix of beaches, wineries, craft shops, art galleries, antique stores, restaurants, ice cream parlors and candy shops. Stroll by the water and stop for clams or buy some one-of-a-kind nautical knickknacks. Take your time and appreciate the old world atmosphere, especially on a warm, sunny day. Walk a little bit off Main Street and you can admire some of the old Victorian houses.

WHAT TO SEE
EAST END SEAPORT AND MARITIME MUSEUM
North Ferry Dock, Third Street, Greenport, 631-477-2100; www.eastendseaport.org
The maritime history of Long Island's East End is depicted through exhibits that include actual yachts used during World War II, a small aquarium and submarine mock-ups. There also is a maritime festival held in late September.
Admission: $2. Mid-May-June, Saturday-Sunday 11 a.m.-5 p.m.; July-August, Monday, Wednesday-Friday 11 a.m.-5 p.m., Saturday-Sunday 9:30 a.m.-5 p.m.; September, Saturday-Sunday 11 a.m.-5 p.m.

MITCHELL PARK CAROUSEL
Front Street, near the post office, Greenport
This four-acre waterfront park is often considered the "jewel of Greenport." At its heart is a 1920s carousel housed in an airy glass atrium.
Admission: $1. June-August, daily 10 a.m.-10 p.m.; September-May, Saturday-Sunday.

WHERE TO STAY
★★SOUND VIEW INN
58775 Route 48, Greenport, 631-477-1910; www.soundviewinn.com
While it may not look impressive from the street, the view from the waterfront deck onto the sprawling private beach is sure to change your mind. All guest rooms are updated and airy with views of Long Island Sound from beachside decks.
45 rooms. Restaurant, bar. Fitness center. Pool. Closed January-mid-March. $61-150

WHERE TO EAT
★★CLAUDIO'S
111 Main St., Greenport, 631-477-0627; www.claudios.com
Claiming to be the oldest same family run restaurant in the United States, dating back to 1870, this harborside spot serves up some of the freshest seafood in Greenport. The New England clam chowder is rich and delicious and the outdoor clam bar is a smart spot to position yourself for straight-off-the-boat oysters and views of the harbor.
Seafood, steak. Lunch, dinner. Outdoor seating. Bar. Closed December-mid-April. $16-35

HAMILTON

See also Cazenovia, Oneida

Colgate University, one of the country's celebrated liberal arts colleges, is in Hamilton. This college town also offers great biking and running—if you consider hills great—and in the winter, visitors and locals ski in the nearby Adirondacks.

WHAT TO SEE
COLGATE UNIVERSITY

13 Oak Drive, Hamilton, 315-228-1000; www.colgate.edu

This handsome campus has buildings dating from 1827. The Charles A. Dana Arts Center, designed by Paul Rudolph, houses the Picker Art Gallery. Fall is a beautiful time to visit the campus as the surrounding foliage bursts into vibrant color.

Admission: free. Daily.

ROGERS ENVIRONMENTAL EDUCATION CENTER

2721 Highway 80, Sherburne, 607-674-4017; www.dec.ny.gov/education/1831.html

Set on 600 rural acres, the Roger Center is ideal for snowshoeing, bird watching and hiking. There is also an observation tower providing views of the Chenango Valley.

Admission: free. Daily, sunrise-sunset.

WHERE TO STAY
★★COLGATE INN

1 Payne St., Hamilton, 315-824-2300; www.colgateinn.com

Ideal for parents and visiting students, this hotel is only minutes from the Colgate campus in the village of Hamilton. Rooms are simply decorated with floral curtains and dark wood furnishings. The recently renovated parlor is a good spot to relax.

45 rooms. Restaurant, bar. Complimentary breakfast. $61-150

WHERE TO EAT
★★THE TAP ROOM

1 Payne St., Hamilton, 315-824-2300; www.colgateinn.com

Housed inside the Colgate Inn, this pub-style restaurant serves American comfort food such as chicken wings, burgers and fish-n-chips. Live jazz is performed on Tuesdays.

American. Lunch, dinner, Sunday brunch. Outdoor seating. Children's menu. Bar. $15 and under

HAMMONDSPORT

See also Finger Lakes

Located at the southern tip of Keuka Lake, this is the center of the New York State wine industry. The grape growers are mainly of German and Swiss origin and have more than a century of viticulture in New York State behind them, dating from 1829, when the Reverend William Bostwick planted the first vineyard. Further, Glenn H. Curtiss, a pioneer aviator, was born here, and most of his early experimental flights took place in this area. The town is also known for its antique shops.

WHAT TO SEE
GLENN H. CURTISS MUSEUM
8419 State Route 54, Hammondsport, 607-569-2160; www.glennhcurtissmuseum.org

Like the Wright brothers, local aviator Glenn H. Curtiss owned a bicycle shop. His invention of the first flying boat, which took off over Lake Keuka, gave him the nickname "the father of naval aviation." The museum displays the Curtiss bicycle shop and a Dawn of Aviation Gallery.

Admission: adults $7.50, seniors $6, children 7-18 $4.50, children under 7 free. May-October, Monday-Saturday 9 a.m.-5 p.m., Sunday 10 a.m.-5 p.m.; November-April, Monday-Saturday 10 a.m.-4 p.m., Sunday 10 a.m.-4 p.m.

WINE AND GRAPE MUSEUM OF GREYTON H. TAYLOR/BULLY HILL VINEYARDS
8843 Greyton H. Taylor Memorial Drive, Hammondsport, 607-868-3610; www.bullyhill.com

Learn about the wine-making techniques of the 18th century at this museum as well as the equipment that was used at the time. There are also exhibits on early champagne and brandy production. Be sure to see the presidential wine glass collection.

Admission: Tour: free. Tasting: $2. May-October, Monday-Saturday 9 a.m.-4 p.m., Sunday 11:30 a.m.-4 p.m. Visitor Center: May-October, Monday-Thursday 9 a.m.-6 p.m., Friday-Saturday, 9 a.m.-8 p.m., Sunday 10 a.m.-6 p.m.; November-April, Monday-Saturday 9 a.m.-5 p.m., Sunday 10 a.m.-5 p.m.

HILLSDALE
See also Hudson

Hillsdale's Columbia County is a stretch of land from the Berkshire foothills to the Hudson River, and only five miles from the Massachusetts border. If you're here to spend a little quality time with Mother Nature, you'll find plenty of places to hike, boat, fish, snow ski and golf. If you're searching for a quiet place to spend an afternoon, consider visiting the local boutiques or one of the area's wineries.

WHAT TO SEE
CATAMOUNT SKI AREA
3200 State Highway 23, Hillsdale, 518-325-3200, 800-342-1840; www.catamountski.com

Opening in 1939, Catamount remains one of the oldest operating ski areas in the Northeast. There are more than 30 trails on the mountain designed for all skill levels. Visit the terrain park to test your ability on the half pipe or boardercross.

Admission: adults $20-56, seniors and children 7-13 $20-45, children under 7 $10-25. December-March, daily.

TACONIC STATE PARK
Route 344, Hillsdale, 518-329-3993, 800-456-2267; www.nysparks.com/parks

This park occupies more than 4,800 acres and offers everything from hiking and biking to swimming and snowshoeing. Bash Bish Stream and Ore Pit Pond are in the park, as is the old Copake Iron Works site. In winter, there is ice skating on Rudd Pond.

Admission: free. Daily sunrise-sunset.

WHERE TO STAY
★★★SIMMONS' WAY VILLAGE INN
Main Street, Route 44, Millerton, 518-789-6235; www.simmonsway.com

This inn offers Victorian elegance near the Berkshire Foothills. Guest rooms include down pillows, luxury linens and antique furnishings. Some also have fireplaces, canopy beds and private porches. There is also a wonderful dining room.

9 rooms. Restaurant. Complimentary breakfast. $151-250

★★SWISS HUTTE
Route 23, Hillsdale, 518-325-3333; www.swisshutte.com

Originating as an old farmhouse from the mid-1800s, this chalet-style inn is within walking distance of the Catamount ski area. Rooms have been recently renovated with large picture windows, and private balconies.

14 rooms. Restaurant, bar. Pool. Pets accepted. Tennis. $61-150

WHERE TO EAT
★★★MARTHA'S
Main Street, Route 44, Millerton, 518-789-6235; www.simmonsway.com

Guests travel many miles for the elegant country fare found at this restored Victorian inn. The formal dining room—complete with a cathedral ceiling and Oriental rugs—is the perfect setting for connoisseurs to sample the restaurant's fine wines and complex dishes. Standout dishes include the coriander-infused salmon filet and the roasted rack of spring lamb with lavender honey and herbs de provence.

International. Dinner, Sunday brunch. Closed Monday-Tuesday. Outdoor seating. Bar. $36-85

HOWES CAVE
See also Albany, Schenectady

This community west of Albany in upstate New York got its name from Lester Howe, the man who discovered the caverns that attract visitors today.

WHAT TO SEE
HOWE CAVERNS
255 Discovery Drive, Howes Cave, 518-296-8990; www.howecaverns.com

Discovered in 1842, this elaborately developed series of caverns with an underground river and lake, and unique rock formations sit nearly 200 feet below ground. The caverns are reached by elevator, and tours include a boat ride on underground Lake of Venus. Dress warmly for your visit as the caverns remain at a chilly 52 degrees.

Admission: adults $18, seniors and children 12-15 $15, children 5-11 $10, children under 5 free. April-October, daily 9 a.m.-6 p.m.; November-March, daily 9 a.m.-5 p.m.

OLD STONE FORT MUSEUM COMPLEX
Highway 7, Schoharie, 518-295-7192; www.schohariehistory.net/OSF.htm

Built as a church in 1772, this old stone complex was fortified against raids by Tories and American Indians during the Revolutionary War and became known as Lower Fort. Today, the fort houses a museum with exhibits on the

Revolutionary War and Schoharie Valley history.
Admission: adults $5, seniors $4.50, children 5-17 $1.50, children under 5 free. May-October, Tuesday-Saturday 10 a.m.-5 p.m., Sunday noon-5 p.m.; July-August, also Monday 10 a.m.-5 p.m.

WHERE TO STAY
★★BEST WESTERN INN OF COBLESKILL
121 Burgin Drive, Cobleskill, 518-234-4321; www.bestwestern.com
Tucked between the Catskill and Adirondack mountains, this hotel offers a convenient location with added amenities such as a game room, indoor pool and fitness center.
76 rooms. Restaurant, bar. Business center. Fitness center. Pool. $61-150

HUDSON
See also Hillsdale, Saugerties
Green pastures, meandering trails, fresh air—this area has it all. It's the gateway to the scenic Hudson Valley and has seen an influx of wealthy New York urbanites coming up for weekends in recent years. Antique shops are king in this charming town, but trendy restaurants and art galleries are quickly catching up.

WHAT TO SEE
AMERICAN MUSEUM OF FIREFIGHTING
117 Harry Howard Ave., Hudson, 518-828-7695, 877-347-3687; www.fasnyfiremuseum.com
This museum harbors an elaborate collection of antique firefighting equipment including a 1725 Newsham fire engine and a pair of horse-drawn trucks. There is also a moving exhibit on the firefighters who lost their lives in the September 11th attacks.
Admission: adults $5, children 12-18 $2, children under 12 free. Daily 10 a.m.-5 p.m.

CLERMONT STATE HISTORIC SITE
1 Clermont Ave., Germantown, 518-537-4240; www.nysparks.com/sites
This site marks the ancestral home of Robert R. Livingston, one of five men elected to draft the Declaration of Independence, who later as chancellor of New York administered the oath of office to George Washington. The house was lived in by seven generations of the Livingston family and both the mansion and the grounds retain their 1930s appearance, illustrating 200 years of changing design.
Admission: free. Mid-April-October, Tuesday-Sunday 11 a.m.-5 p.m.; November-March, Saturday-Sunday 11 a.m.-4 p.m.

MARTIN VAN BUREN NATIONAL HISTORIC SITE
1013 Old Post Road, Kinderhook, 518-758-9689; www.nps.gov/mava
This is the retirement house of America's eighth president. The estate, Lindenwald, was purchased by Van Buren from General William Paulding in 1839. The house contains 36 rooms and a museum with a variety of artifacts.
Admission: individual $5, family $12. Mid-May-October, daily 9 a.m.-4 p.m.

OLANA STATE HISTORIC SITE

5720 Highway 9G, Hudson, 518-828-0135; www.nysparks.state.ny.us/sites

Some of the best views in the Hudson Valley are from this 250-acre 1870 hilltop estate which includes a Moorish mansion and grounds landscaped in the Romantic style, all designed by Hudson River School artist Frederic Edwin Church as a multidimensional work of art. There are five miles of carriage roads for walking with views planned by the artist. The interior of the mansion is breathtaking with carved screens, Persian rugs and intricate tile detailing. The house is only accessible by popular guided tours, so make reservations if possible.

Admission: adults $9, seniors and students $7, children under 12 free. April-October, Tuesday-Sunday 10 a.m.-4 p.m.; November-March, Friday-Sunday, 11 a.m.-3 p.m.

WHERE TO STAY
★★ST. CHARLES HOTEL

16-18 Park Place, Hudson, 518-822-9900; www.stcharleshotel.com

This 139-year-old brick Victorian hotel has been completely renovated, but still retains its historic charm. Warren Street and the heart of downtown Hudson is only a short walk from the hotel, as is the American Museum of Firefighting. Rooms are modest in décor, but include sitting areas and a complimentary breakfast.

34 rooms. Restaurant, bar. Complimentary breakfast. $61-150

WHERE TO EAT
★★MEXICAN RADIO

537 Warren St., Hudson, 518-828-7770; www.mexrad.com

The bright orange two-story interior, complete with wrought-iron crucifixes and Mexican artwork, sets the tone at this upbeat outpost. The menu has all of the Mexican staples you'd expect and some that you wouldn't, including Mexican macaroni and cheese and Mexican spring rolls with raspberry chipotle peanut sauce. Many consider Mexican Radio to serve the best margaritas in the Hudson Valley.

Mexican. Lunch, dinner. Reservations recommended. Bar. $16-35

HUNTER

See also Shandaken

Hunter is in the area known as "the mountaintop"—a stretch of land in the picturesque northern Catskills. Hunter Mountain is the second tallest peak in the Catskills and boasts the oldest ski resort in the range. There is plenty to do off the mountain as well thanks to the thriving art scene and seasonal festivals.

WHAT TO SEE
HUNTER MOUNTAIN SKI RESORT

Highway 23A, Hunter, 518-263-4223, 800-486-8376; www.huntermtn.com

Once winter strikes, Hunter Mountain becomes the go-to spot for skiing and snowboarding in the Catskills. There are more than 52 trails, a well-established ski-school and rental outfitters.

Admission: adults $35-63, children 13-18 $35-57, seniors and children 7-12 $35-43, children under 7 free-$10. November-mid-April, daily.

WHERE TO STAY
★★★SCRIBNER HOLLOW LODGE
Route 23A, Hunter, 518-263-4211, 800-395-4683; www.scribnerhollow.com

This resort has a classical mountain lodge atmosphere with modern hotel conveniences. The lodge has custom-decorated guest rooms, many with exposed wood beams, river-stone fireplaces and balconies with mountain views. Be sure to check out the unique cave-like underground pool and hot tub with seven waterfalls.

37 rooms. Restaurant, bar. Pool. Tennis. Closed April-mid May. $151-250

HUNTINGTON

See also Long Island, Oyster Bay, Smithtown

Although the expanding suburban population of New York City has reached Huntington, 37 miles east on Long Island, the town still retains its rural character. Huntington is a township of 17 communities, in which there are more than 100 industrial plants. The area has five navigable harbors and 51 miles of shoreline.

WHAT TO SEE
HECKSCHER MUSEUM OF ART
2 Prime Ave., Huntington, 631-351-3250; www.heckscher.org

The museum opened in 1920 under the care of German-American industrialist August Heckscher with a collection of 150 works. Today, the collection has grown to more than 2,100, representing American and European masters such as Georgia O'Keeffe, Gustave Courbet, Charles Sheeler and Thomas Moran.

Admission: adults $8, seniors $6, students $5, children under 10 free. Tuesday-Friday 10 a.m.-5 p.m. Saturday-Sunday 1-5 p.m.

TARGET ROCK NATIONAL WILDLIFE REFUGE
12 Target Rock Road, Huntington, 631-286-0485; www.fws.gov

An 80-acre refuge filled with a hardwood forest, pond and beach. Birdwatching is very popular here, as the environment attracts a large variety of song and shorebirds.

Admission: $2. Daily.

WALT WHITMAN BIRTHPLACE STATE HISTORIC SITE
246 Old Walt Whitman Road, West Hills, 631-427-5240;
www.waltwhitmanbirthplace.org

Streets and malls are named for this famous American author; now you can see where he grew up. This simple home, which features 19th-century furnishings (including Whitman's schoolmaster's desk), offers a tour, as well as an exhibit that tells the story of Whitman's life. There is also a recording available of the author himself reading one of his poems.

Admission: adults $5, seniors and students $4, children under 6 free. Mid-June-August, Monday-Friday 11 a.m.-4 p.m., Saturday-Sunday 11 a.m.-5 p.m.; September-mid-June, Wednesday-Friday 1-4 p.m., Saturday-Sunday 11 a.m.-4 p.m.

WHERE TO STAY
★★★HILTON LONG ISLAND/HUNTINGTON
598 Broad Hollow Road, Huntington, 631-845-1000; www.hiltonlongisland.com
Guests enter the Hilton to find an atrium lobby with running waterfalls and a tropical setting. Rooms are comfortable, and the location is perfect for exploring Long Island's so-called "Gold Coast" and its numerous attractions.
305 rooms. Restaurant, bar. Fitness center. Pool. Tennis. $251-250

★HUNTINGTON COUNTRY INN
270 W. Jericho Turnpike, Huntington Station, 631-421-3900, 800-739-5777; www.huntingtoncountryinn.com
Conveniently located off a major thoroughfare, this country inn offers affordable accommodations with a subtle country charm. All rooms come equipped with jetted tubs, refrigerators, microwaves and CD players.
63 rooms. Complimentary breakfast. Business center. Fitness center. Pool. $61-150

HYDE PARK
See also New Paltz, Poughkeepsie, Rhinebeck
Hyde Park was named for Edward Hyde, Lord Cornbury, provincial governor of New York, who in 1705 presented a parcel of land along the river to his secretary. Hyde's name was given to an estate on that property and later to the town itself. The area, noted for the varying scenery—from rock outcroppings to scenic water views—is best known as the site of Springwood, the country estate of Franklin Roosevelt.

WHAT TO SEE
ELEANOR ROOSEVELT NATIONAL HISTORIC SITE AT VAL-KILL
56 Val-Kill Park Drive, Hyde Park, 845-229-9115, 800-967-2283; www.nps.gov/elro
Dedicated as a memorial to Eleanor Roosevelt on October 11, 1984, the 100th anniversary of her birth, Val-Kill was her country residence from the 1920s until her death. The original house on the property, Stone Cottage, is now a conference center. Her second house at Val-Kill was originally a furniture and crafts factory that Roosevelt sponsored in an effort to stimulate rural economic development. After closing Val-Kill Industries, she had the factory remodeled to reflect her tastes and humanitarian concerns. She used the space to entertain family, friends and heads of state from around the world.
Admission: adults $8, children under 16 free. May-October, daily 9 a.m.-5 p.m.; November-April, Thursday-Monday 9 a.m.-5 p.m.

FRANKLIN D. ROOSEVELT PRESIDENTIAL LIBRARY AND MUSEUM
4079 Albany Post Road, Hyde Park, 845-486-7770, 800-337-8474; www.fdrlibrary.marist.edu
First of the public presidential libraries, it has exhibits covering the private lives and public careers of Franklin and Eleanor Roosevelt. Research library contains family artifacts and documents and presidential archives.
Admission: adults $7, children under 16 free. November-April, daily 9 a.m.-5 p.m.; May-October, daily 9 a.m.-6 p.m.

HOME OF FRANKLIN D. ROOSEVELT NATIONAL HISTORIC SITE

4097 Albany Post Road, Hyde Park, 845-229-9115; www.nps.gov/hofr

This Hyde Park estate, Springwood, was President Roosevelt's birthplace and lifelong residence. The central part of the building and oldest section dates from about 1826. The house was bought in 1867 by FDR's father and was extensively remodeled and expanded in 1915 by FDR and his mother, Sara Delano Roosevelt. At that time, the frame Victorian house took on its present brick and stone, neo-Georgian form. The interior is furnished exactly as it was when FDR died. Roosevelt and his wife's graves are in the rose garden.
Admission: adults $14, children under 16 free. Daily 9 a.m.-5 p.m.

MILLS MANSION STATE HISTORIC SITE

Highway 9 and Old Post Road, Staatsburg, 845-889-8851; www.staatsburgh.org

Built for Ogden Mills in 1895-1896 by prominent architect Stanford White, this Greek Revival mansion includes 65 rooms furnished in Louis XIV, Louis XV and Louis XVI styles, with tapestries, art objects, marble fireplaces and gilded plasterwork. The surrounding park affords beautiful views of the Hudson River.
Admission: adults $5, seniors and students $4, children under 13 free. January-March, Saturday-Sunday 11 a.m.-4 p.m.; April-October, Tuesday-Saturday 10 a.m.-5 p.m., Sunday noon-5 p.m.

VANDERBILT MANSION NATIONAL HISTORIC SITE

Highway 9, Hyde Park, 845-229-9115; www.nps.gov/vama

This 1898 Beaux-Arts mansion designed by McKim, Mead & White for Frederick W. Vanderbilt is a prime example of the mansions typical of the period. The interior retains most of the original furnishings as designed by turn-of-the-century decorators. The grounds offer superb views up and down the Hudson River.
Admission: adults $8, children under 16 free. Daily 9 a.m.-5 p.m.

WHERE TO EAT

★★AMERICAN BOUNTY

433 Albany Post Road, Hyde Park, 845-471-6608; www.ciachef.edu/restaurants/bounty

Run by the Culinary Institute of America, this student-run restaurant occupies a stunning room in Roth Hall, once part of an old Jesuit seminary. Everything on this regional American menu is fresh and tasty.
American. Lunch, dinner. Closed Sunday-Monday; also three weeks in July, two weeks in December. Bar. $16-35

★★★THE ESCOFFIER

433 Albany Post Road, Hyde Park, 845-471-6608;
www.ciachef.edu/restaurants/escoffier

Student chefs of the Culinary Institute of America prepare dishes that their peers serve in this classic French eatery that presents a lighter, more contemporary take on the cooking of Auguste Escoffier (think Asian-style braised veal cheeks with gratin potatoes). The seared sea scallops are exceptional.
French. Lunch, dinner. Closed Sunday-Monday; also three weeks in July, two weeks in December. $16-35

★★★RISTORANTE CATERINA DE MEDICI
433 Albany Post Road, Hyde Park, 845-471-6608;
www.ciachef.edu/restaurants/caterina

With its five distinct dining areas—from the more casual to the formal—the Culinary Institute of America's flagship restaurant will carry you to Tuscany thanks to dishes like branzino con guazza verde, a Mediterranean sea bass shallow poached in an herb broth with fingerling potatoes.
American. Lunch, dinner. Closed Saturday-Sunday. Reservations recommended. Bar. $36-85

ITHACA
See also Binghamton, Cortland, Finger Lakes, Watkins Glen

Ithaca climbs from the plain at the head of Cayuga Lake up the steep slopes of the surrounding hills. Creeks flow through town and cut picturesque gorges with cascading waterfalls. Named for Grecian Ithaca by Simeon De Witt, surveyor general under Washington, Ithaca is a center of inland water transportation and an educational nexus of New York State.

WHAT TO SEE
BUTTERMILK FALLS
105 Enfield Falls Road, Ithaca, 607-273-5761; www.nysparks.state.ny.us/parks

Located on Ithaca's south border, Buttermilk Falls State Park is divided into an upper park with hiking trails along the rim of the gorge, and lower park with a natural swimming hole, campgrounds and a meadow. Ten waterfalls flow through the gorge
Admission: $7 per vehicle, Mid-June-August, daily; September-mid-June, weekends.

CORNELL UNIVERSITY
159 Sapsucker Woods Road, Ithaca, 607-254-4636; www.cornell.edu

This 745-acre campus of 20,000 students overlooks Cayuga Lake and includes Beebe Lake, gorges and waterfalls. Historic buildings pepper the hilly campus. The educational center, made up of 13 colleges, was founded both as a land grant and privately endowed college by Ezra Cornell and Andrew Dickson White. Don't miss the Herbert F. Johnson Museum of Art, designed by I.M. Pei; while the collection of more than 30,000 works is impressive, the views from the top floor may trump it all.
Free. Campus: daily. Museum: Tuesday-Sunday 10 a.m.-5 p.m.

THE HISTORY CENTER
401 E. State St., Ithaca, 607-273-8284; www.thehistorycenter.net

This small museum explores the local history of Tompkins County through the eyes of women, African-Americans, agriculturalists and children through time. An on-going quilt preservation project is one of the popular exhibits on display.
Free. Tuesday, Thursday, Saturday 11 a.m.-5 p.m.

SCIENCENTER

601 First St., Ithaca, 607-272-0600; www.sciencenter.org

There are 200 hands-on interactive science exhibits and an outdoor science park here. A highlight is the Sagan Planet Walk, a scale model of the solar system built in remembrance of Ithaca resident and Cornell Professor Carl Sagan. Kids will particularly love the hands-on exhibits like Watergates and the Slap Organ that allow them to learn scientific theory through touch and sensation. Galaxy Golf is also an attraction.

Admission: adults $7, seniors $6, children 3-17 $5, children under 3 free. Tuesday-Saturday 10 a.m.-5 p.m., Sunday noon-5 p.m.

TAUGHANNOCK FALLS

Taughannock State Park, 2221 Taughannock Park Road, 607-387-6739; www.taughannock.com

The falls have a drop of 215 feet, one of the highest east of the Rockies. The park also features swimming, a bathhouse, fishing, boating, nature trails, hiking trails, cross-country skiing, ice skating, picnicking and a playground. Monday-Friday 8 a.m.-4:30 p.m.

SMALL-TOWN NEW YORK

Ithaca combines the best of small-town America with college-town sophistication, as well as the spectacular natural sites of Cayuga Lake and a variety of gorges and waterfalls. This walk explores Ithaca's center with a stroll to the nearby falls. For those who really love to hoof it, other options include the Cornell University Plantations, an arboretum and botanical gardens, and, on the other end of town, Stewart Park along Cayuga Lakes shoreline.

Start on Green Street and walk west to Cayuga Street. City Hall is on the right. Turn right and walk a half block to the Commons, home to a wide variety of shops, restaurants, cafés and a gallery. Duck into the Susan Titus Gallery and ask about the Ithaca Arts guide to galleries and artists' studios throughout the region. Other shops of interest at the Commons are Autumn Leaves, Ithaca Books, Angelheart Designs, Hand Block and Harold's Army Navy and The Outdoor Store. The Home Dairy Bakery is a great place to grab a snack. Here, too, begins the Sagan Planet Walk. Named after astronomer Carl Sagan, this is an outdoor, scale model of the solar system that stretches 3/4 mile from the Commons to the Sciencenter on Second Street.

Leaving the west end of the Commons, turn right on Cayuga. The Clinton House Art Space is located at 116 Cayuga, and DeWitt Mall is on the next block on the right. More shopping and eating await here. Highlights include the famous Moosewood Restaurant, Calhoun's Antiques and the Sola Gallery. Continue up Cayuga past DeWitt Park and turn left on Cascadilla Street. Go four blocks and turn right onto First Street. After two more blocks, you will reach the Sciencenter, an imaginative hands-on science exploratorium. Return along First Street and go left on Adams, which eventually merges to the right with East Lewis Street. Follow East Lewis three blocks to Tioga and turn left. The walk travels here through a pleasant residential neighborhood. After three blocks, turn right onto Falls Street, and walk two blocks to Lake Street to arrive at Ithaca Falls and Fall Creek Gorge.

These falls stand almost as high as Niagara. Pause for a picnic, play on the rocks in the stream or just admire the view. The energetic can follow the hiking trail into the upper areas of Fall Creek Gorge and onto the Cornell University campus, where a variety of trails lead to several waterfalls and Beebe Lake.

SPECIAL EVENTS
APPLE HARVEST FESTIVAL
Downtown Ithaca Commons, 171 E. State St., Ithaca, 607-277-8679;
www.downtownithaca.com
This annual event features apples, cider, a craft fair and entertainment. There is also a farmers market and amusement park rides. Last weekend in September.

HANGAR THEATRE
116 N. Cayuga St., Ithaca, 607-273-8588; www.hangartheatre.org
Summer in Ithaca gets people out and about, and one popular destination is the Hangar Theatre, a professional summer theater in a park setting adjacent to Treman Marina. There are five main stage productions including dramas, comedies and musicals.
Admission: adults $16-32, seniors and students $14, children under 19 $16. June-August, Tuesday-Sunday.

ITHACA FESTIVAL
215 N. Cayuga Street, Ithaca, 607-273-3646; www.ithacafestival.org
This four-day event features food, a parade and more than 1,000 local musicians and performers. Last weekend in May.

WHERE TO STAY
★BEST WESTERN UNIVERSITY INN
1020 Ellis Hollow Road, Ithaca, 607-272-6100, 800-937-8376;
www.bestwesternuniversityinnithaca.com
Just outside the Cornell University campus, this spacious motel has the feel of a lodge with vaulted ceilings in both the lobby and guest rooms. Located within walking distance of shopping and a short drive to the airport, the hotel is ideal for a visit to the university or local attractions.
101 rooms. Complimentary breakfast. Pets accepted. $61-150

★★★LA TOURELLE RESORT & SPA
1150 Danby Road, Ithaca, 607-273-2734, 800-765-1492; www.latourelle.com
Offering guests a beautiful countryside setting and panoramic views of Cayuga Lake and its surrounding hill country, this inn is adjacent to state park lands with hiking trails and fishing ponds. Perfect for a romantic getaway, the inn evokes the feel of a far-flung French country estate. The inn is convenient to Ithaca College and Cornell University.
54 rooms. Restaurant. Fitness center. Spa. Tennis. $151-250

★★★STATLER HOTEL AT CORNELL UNIVERSITY
130 Statler Drive, Ithaca, 607-257-2500, 800-541-2501; www.statlerhotel.cornell.edu
Because this well-appointed hotel serves as the main teaching facility for Cornell's prestigious School of Hotel Administration, no detail here has been overlooked. Boasting breathtaking views of the hills and dells of the campus's picturesque Finger Lakes location, each luxurious guest room features pillow-top mattresses and turndown service. Fresh flowers and rich wood floors are found throughout the hotel's open spaces.
153 rooms. Restaurant, bar. Business center. Fitness center. $151-250

WHERE TO EAT
★★★JOHN THOMAS STEAKHOUSE
1152 Danby Road, Ithaca, 607-273-3464; www.johnthomassteakhouse.com

John Thomas Steak House, an 1850s-era former farmhouse with lamp-lit white-clad tables beside a blazing fire, serves sophisticated cuts of meat like a porterhouse for two and a 25-ounce T-bone steak paired with German fried potatoes and creamed spinach.

Steak. Dinner. Reservations recommended. Bar. $36-85

★★MAHOGANY GRILL
112 N. Aurora St., Ithaca, 607-272-1438; www.mahoganygrill.com

A charming older building with tin ceilings and brass railings serves as the home of Mahogany Grill. The American menu offers standards like steak and seafood.

American. Lunch, dinner, Sunday brunch. Reservations recommended. Outdoor seating. Children's menu. Bar. $16-35

★MOOSEWOOD RESTAURANT
215 N. Cayuga St., Ithaca, 607-273-9610; www.moosewoodrestaurant.com

This is the famous vegetarian restaurant, which has produced several cookbooks. If you're a carnivore, never fear—you may enjoy the food so much you won't realize it's meat-free. The menu changes daily and a vegan option is always available.

Vegetarian. Lunch, dinner. Outdoor seating. Children's menu. $16-35

JAMESTOWN
See also Chautauqua

Jamestown made its mark early in the 19th century with the manufacturing of metal products and furniture. These industries still flourish in this city located at the southern end of Chautauqua Lake. Tourism and farming are important to the economy as well.

WHAT TO SEE
FENTON HISTORY CENTER
67 Washington St., Jamestown, 716-664-6256; www.fentonhistorycenter.org

Home of post-Civil War governor, Reuben Fenton, this brick mansion built in 1863 retains many of its original Victorian interior details. There is a fascinating exhibit on Lucille Ball, focusing on her early years in Jamestown.

Admission: adults $5, children 4-12 $4, children under 4 free. Monday-Saturday 10 a.m.-4 p.m.; Mid-November-mid-January, also Sunday 1-4 p.m.

LUCILLE BALL-DESI ARNAZ CENTER
10 W. Third St., Jamestown, 716-484-0800; www.lucydesi.com

Fans of "I Love Lucy" will swoon at the sizeable collection of Lucy and Desi's personal effects including costumes, photographs and family scrapbooks. Interactive exhibits provide a look into the lives and careers of this comedy duo.

Admission: adults $10, seniors $9, children 6-18 $7. Monday-Saturday 10 a.m.-4 p.m.

PANAMA ROCKS PARK

11 Rock Hill Road, Panama, 716-782-2845; www.panamarocks.com

This private park contains a massive rock outcrop of a primeval seashore formation dating back more than 300 million years. These 25-acres are filled with vegetation..

Admission: adults $6, seniors, students and children 13-17 $5, children 6-12 $4, children under 6 free. May-mid-October, daily 10 a.m.-5 p.m.

WHERE TO STAY
★COMFORT INN

2800 N. Main St. Extension, Jamestown, 716-664-5920, 800-453-7155; www.comfortinn.com

The guest rooms at this chain aren't big on charm, but they are clean and the price is right. Some even have in-room jet tubs.

99 rooms. Restaurant. Business center. Fitness center. Complimentary breakfast. Pets accepted. $61-150

WHERE TO EAT
★★IRONSTONE

516 W. Fourth St., Jamestown, 716-487-1516; www.ironstonerestaurant.net

Housed in an 1884 building with Victorian décor, this Italian restaurant serves generous portions of steak, seafood and, of course, pasta. The flat breads are particularly good, as is the Chautauqua cheesecake. There is a lounge attached.

Italian. Lunch, dinner. Closed Sunday. Reservations recommended. Children's menu. Casual attire. Bar. $16-35

JOHNSTOWN

See also Saratoga Springs, Schenectady

A center of leather tanning and related industries, Johnstown often is called a twin city to Gloversville, which it adjoins. A Revolutionary War battle was fought here six days after Cornwallis surrendered at Yorktown. Women's rights pioneer Elizabeth Cady Stanton was born here in 1815.

WHAT TO SEE
JOHNSON HALL STATE HISTORIC SITE

Highway 29 West and Hall Avenue, Johnstown, 518-762-8712; www.nysparks.state.ny.us/sites

This house was the residence of Sir William Johnson, first baronet of New York colony and the largest single landowner in the establishment of the Mohawk Valley. American Indians and colonists held meetings here. The site includes a hall with period furnishings, a stone blockhouse, an interpretation center and dioramas depicting the history of the estate.

Admission: adults $4, resident seniors $3, children under 13 free. May-October, Wednesday-Monday 10 a.m.-5 p.m.

WHERE TO STAY
★★HOLIDAY INN

308 N. Comrie Ave., Johnstown, 518-762-4686, 800-465-4329; www.holiday-inn.com

Only minutes from Johnson Hall, this chain hotel offers updated rooms with

large windows. There is also an outdoor pool to enjoy.
99 rooms. Restaurant, bar. Fitness center. Pool. $61-150

WHERE TO EAT
★★UNION HALL INN
2 Union Place, Johnstown, 518-762-3210; www.unionhallinnrestaurant.com
History and folklore surround this post-Revolutionary tavern dating back to 1798 and the interior retains that cozy country atmosphere. Menu highlights include barbequed duck breast with hominy grits and pan-seared Atlantic salmon with roasted fennel.
American. Lunch, dinner. Closed Sunday-Monday. Bar. $16-35

KINGSTON
See also Clayton, New Paltz, Rhinebeck, Saugerties, Shandaken, Woodstock
In more than 300 years, Kingston has had several names, including Esopus and Wiltwyck, and has been raided, burned and fought over by Native Americans, Dutch, British and Americans. It was the first capital of New York. The Delaware River and Hudson Canal and then the railroads brought prosperity. A huge cement industry prospered and then ceased on Rondout Creek harbor in the 19th century. Today, the downtown area has been revitalized with a thriving art scene and popular river cruises.

WHAT TO SEE
HUDSON RIVER MARITIME MUSEUM
50 Rondout Landing, Kingston, 845-338-0071; www.hrmm.org
Models, photographs and paintings depict an era of river commerce with changing exhibits featuring steam tugboats and a variety of antique and modern pleasure boats. Guided tours of the old Kingston Lighthouse depart from the museum's dock and you can take a ride on an authentic 1925 trolley to Kingston Point.
Admission: adults $5, seniors and children 6-12 $4, children under 6 free. May-October, Thursday-Monday 11 a.m.-5 p.m.

OLD DUTCH CHURCH
272 Wall St., Kingston, 845-338-6759; www.olddutchchurch.org
Though the congregation was established in 1659 and a small structure was built, it was burned down shortly thereafter; the church that resides at the site today was built in the mid-1800s, and has a Tiffany Studio window. Buried on the grounds is George Clinton, first governor of New York and vice president under Madison and Jefferson.
Free. Monday-Friday 10 a.m.-4 p.m. by appointment.

SENATE HOUSE STATE HISTORIC SITE
296 Fair St., Kingston, 845-338-2786; www.nysparks.state.ny.us/sites
This stone residence held the first New York State Senate meeting in 1777. The interior is furnished in an 18th-century Dutch style, and includes delft tiles, Hudson Valley furniture and paintings by John Vanderlyn and others in the adjacent museum. There is also a boxwood garden.
Admission: adults $4, seniors $3, children under 12 free. Mid-April-October, Monday, Wednesday, Saturday 10 a.m.-5 p.m., Sunday 11 a.m.-5 p.m.

ULSTER PERFORMING ARTS CENTER

601 Broadway, Kingston, 845-339-6088; www.upac.org

This historic Vaudeville theater presents professional Broadway touring companies, dance, contemporary music, comedy and children's productions. The Hudson Valley Philharmonic performs here frequently.

Prices and showtimes vary.

WHERE TO STAY

★★HOLIDAY INN

503 Washington Ave., Kingston, 845-338-0400, 800-465-4329; www.hikingston.com

With standard rooms and a convenient off-the-highway location, the Holidome indoor recreation center is what sets this hotel apart from other chain properties. The Holidome is ideal for families as it offers a heated indoor pool, sauna, Jacuzzi, game room and relaxation patio.

212 rooms. Restaurant, bar. Pool. $61-150

WHERE TO EAT

★HICKORY BBQ AND SMOKEHOUSE

743 Highway 28, Kingston, 845-338-2424; www.hickoryrestaurant.com

This award-winning casual smokehouse has some of the best chili, ribs and pulled pork in the Hudson Valley. There is no hope keeping clean at this joint; just roll up your sleeves, slide into a booth and ask for extra napkins.

American. Lunch, dinner. Closed Wednesday. Reservations recommended. Outdoor seating. Children's menu. Bar. $16-35

★★LE CANARD ENCHAINÉ

276 Fair St., Kingston, 845-339-2003; www.le-canardenchaine.com

This charming French bistro is popular with locals for its prix fixe menus and life music on Saturday night. The New Zealand rack of lamb is phenomenal if you're looking to splurge.

French. Lunch, dinner. Bar. $36-85

LAKE GEORGE

See also Bolton Landing, Glens Falls, Lake Luzerne, Ticonderoga, Warrensburg

This area near the Adirondack Mountains is a traveler's dream: you'll find everything from lakeside fun to quiet mountain retreats. Early explorers and settlers knew Lake George as Lac du St. Sacrement—the name it was given when it was a Jesuit mission. In the foothills of the Adirondacks, the area is a center for winter as well as summer sports; there are many miles of snowmobile trails.

WHAT TO SEE

FORT WILLIAM HENRY MUSEUM

48 Canada St., Lake George, 518-668-5471; www.fwhmuseum.com

A 1755 fort rebuilt from original plans, the complex includes dungeons, army barracks and an example of an Iroquois longhouse. The onsite museum hosts exhibits involving relics from the French and Indian War. Get a taste of battle in the 18th century as costumed guides provide demonstrations of typical military drills, musket firings, bullet molding and cannon demonstrations. A replica of the fort was used in the filming of the movie The Last of the Mohicans.

Admission: adults $14.95, seniors and military $12.95, children 3-11 $7.95, children under 3 free. May-mid-October, daily 9 a.m.-6 p.m.

THE GREAT ESCAPE AND SPLASHWATER KINGDOM FUN PARK
1172 State Route 9, Queensbury, 518-792-3500; www.sixflags.com/parks/greatescape
New York's largest theme park has more than 120 rides, live shows and attractions, including numerous roller coasters, Raging River Raft Ride, All-American High-Dive Show and a Storytown-themed children's area. Splashwater Kingdom water park features a giant wave pool, water slides, Adventure River and kiddie pools.
Admission: prices vary. Mid-May-mid-September, daily 11 a.m.-6 p.m.

LAKE GEORGE BATTLEFIELD PICNIC AREA
139 Beach Road, Lake George Village, 518-668-3352
Grab a blanket and bring a picnic to the site of the Battle of Lake George. There are ruins of the original Fort William Henry as well as a monument to French missionary Isaac Jogues.
Admission: $7 per vehicle. Mid-June-August, daily.

SPECIAL EVENT
AMERICADE
Canada Street, Lake George; www.tourexpo.com
This annual motorcycle touring rally includes seminars, exhibits, shows, social events and guided scenic tours. The event attracts 50,000 motorcycle enthusiasts each year. First week in June.

WHERE TO STAY
★BEST WESTERN OF LAKE GEORGE
Exit 21 and I-H 87 Lake George, 518-668-5701, 800-582-5540; www.bestwestern.com
An Adirondack style brings this chain motel up a notch, as some of the rooms offer sloped wood ceilings and fireplaces. Request a room with scenic mountain views (as opposed to poolside). Lake George beaches are just a mile down the road.
87 rooms. Complimentary breakfast. Pool. $151-250

★COLONEL WILLIAMS MOTOR INN
Highway 9, Lake George, 518-668-5727, 800-334-5727;
www.colonelwilliamsresort.com
There is something surprisingly charming about this canary yellow motel, complete with a clock tower and naturally manicured grounds. A dream come true for kids, this inn has two playgrounds, a game room, badminton, basketball and volleyball courts and heated pools. Guest rooms could use a make-over, but large picture windows seem to make up for the outdated furnishings and matching floral bedspreads and curtains.
40 rooms. Fitness center. Pool. $61-150

★★★FORT WILLIAM HENRY RESORT
48 Canada St., Lake George, 518-668-3081, 800-234-0267; www.fortwilliamhenry.com
With a spectacular setting in the Adirondacks—along with courteous service and elegant accommodations—visitors are easily attracted to this Lake

George resort, the oldest in the area. Guest rooms vary by size and, depending on type, include king beds, full-size sleeper sofas, microwaves, refrigerators, whirlpool tubs and executive desks with workstations. Nosh at the resort's onsite restaurants, the White Lion, where breakfast is served with a spectacular lake view, and J.T. Kelly's Steak and Seafood, a casually elegant haven serving classic American and Italian cuisines.

193 rooms. Restaurant, bar. Business center. Fitness center. Pool. Spa. $151-250

★★THE GEORGIAN

384 Canada St., Lake George, 518-668-5401, 800-525-3436; www.georgianresort.com

The rooms are in need of a face-lift, but the views of Lake George and the Adirondacks from the lakeside property make up for it. There is a private beach and marina. Ask for a room with a private balcony.

162 rooms. Restaurant, bar. Pool. Beach. $61-150

★★HOWARD JOHNSON TIKI RESORT

2 Canada St., Lake George, 518-668-5744, 800-446-4656; www.tikiresort.com

If you've never bathed in a red heart-shaped bathtub, now is your chance (in the Honeymoon Suite). This resort with views of Lake George is a tad cheesy with its Polynesian-themed dinner theater, but the rooms are updated with large picture windows and many have balconies overlooking the Adirondacks.

110 rooms. Restaurant, bar. Fitness center. Pool. Closed November-April. $151-250

★★ROARING BROOK RANCH & TENNIS RESORT

Route 9N South, Lake George, 518-668-5767, 800-882-7665;
www.roaringbrookranch.com

Two miles from Lake George, this resort offers three pools, five tennis courts with tennis pros, 25 horses for wilderness riding, golf nearby, and so much more. The resort's conference center makes it attractive for meetings and special events. Guest rooms are plain, but roomy and a stay here includes two meals a day.

142 rooms. Restaurant, bar. Business center. Fitness center. Pool. Tennis. Closed March-mid-May, November-December. $61-150

WHERE TO EAT

★★LOG JAM

1484 Highway 9, Lake George Village, 518-798-1155; www.logjamrestaurant.com

You may feel like you're stepping back in time at this log cabin-like eatery with heavy wood furniture and fireplaces galore. Rest assured that the seafood is some of the freshest around. The maple syrup glazed salmon is a signature dish.

American. Lunch, dinner. Bar. Reservations recommended. Children's menu. $16-35

★★★MONTCALM

1415 Highway 9, Lake George Village, 518-793-6601

Rich American classics such as roast rack of lamb and veal Oscar are the mainstay of this resort-town restaurant where the reasonable prices attract a loyal following. Salads are prepared tableside by an attentive waitstaff.

American. Lunch, dinner. Reservations recommended. Children's menu. Bar. $16-35

LAKE LUZERNE
See also Glens Falls, Lake George
Lumber and papermaking formed the economic background of Lake Luzerne, now an all-year resort. In addition to its location on the small lake for which it is named, this town is near Great Sacandaga Lake, another popular area for summer and winter sports.

WHAT TO SEE
BOW BRIDGE
Lake Luzerne, 518-696-3500
This parabolic bridge spans the Hudson and Sacandaga rivers. It is the only remaining semideck lenticular iron truss bridge, typical of the late 19th-century iron bridges, in New York State.
Admission: free. Daily.

WHERE TO EAT
★CIRO'S
1439 Lake Ave., Lake Luzerne, 518-696-2556; www.cirosrestaurantlakeluzerne.com
This no-fuss Italian restaurant is popular with locals for its dependable fare and generous portions. House specialties include veal parmigiana and linguini with clam sauce.
Italian, American. Dinner. Children's menu. Bar. $16-35

LAKE PLACID
See also Saranac Lake, Tupper Lake, Wilmington
Mount Marcy, the highest mountain in New York State (5,344 feet), rises from the Adirondack peaks that surround this town. On Lake Placid, the village also partly surrounds Mirror Lake. This is one of the most famous all-year vacation centers in the East and the site of the 1932 and 1980 Winter Olympics. The Intervale Olympic Ski Jump Complex has 229-foot and 296-foot ski jumps constructed for the 1980 games, now open to the public and used for training and competition.

WHAT TO SEE
JOHN BROWN FARM HISTORIC SITE
115 John Brown Road, Lake Placid, 518-523-3900; www.nysparks.state.ny.us/sites/
This historic site marks abolitionist John Brown's final home and burial place. In 1859, Brown attempted to lead a slave revolt at Harper's Ferry. Two of his sons and ten others died in the struggle. Brown was tried and executed. There are nice hiking trails throughout the 244-acre grounds.
Admission: adults $2, seniors and children 13-18 $1, children under 12 free. May-October, Wednesday-Monday 10 a.m.-5 p.m.

LAKE PLACID CENTER FOR THE ARTS
17 Algonquin Drive, Lake Placid, 518-523-2512; www.lakeplacidarts.org
Concerts, films, dance performances and art exhibits come through this large

art center year round. It is home to the Lake Placid School of Ballet and the LPCA Children's Theatre.

Prices and showtimes vary.

MACKENZIE-INTERVALE SKI JUMPING COMPLEX

Route 73, Lake Placid, 518-523-2202; www.orda.org

Though these towering structures may seem awkward against the landscape, the view from the top is extraordinary. Take a glass elevator up the 26-stories for vistas of Lake Placid and the surrounding mountains, and a sense of what these skiers experience before every jump.

Admission: adults $10, children and seniors $7. Mid-October-mid-December, Thursday-Sunday 9 a.m.-4 p.m. Mid-December-mid-March, Wednesday-Sunday 9 a.m.-4 p.m.

OLYMPIC CENTER

218 Main St., Lake Placid, 518-523-1655; www.orda.org

Built for the 1932 Winter Olympics and renovated for the 1980 winter games, this arena hosts winter and summer skating shows, hockey games and concerts. It was made famous in the 1980 Olympics as the place where the United States hockey team beat the seemingly invincible Soviets, an account reenacted in the Hollywood movie Miracle. The center also includes a museum with Olympic paraphernalia.

Admission: Rink: adults $7, seniors and children $5. Museum: adults $5, seniors and children $3. Rink: daily 7 p.m.-9 p.m. Museum: daily 10 a.m.-5 p.m.

WHERE TO STAY

★★ADIRONDACK INN BY THE LAKE

2625 Main St., Lake Placid, 518-523-2424, 800-556-2424; www.adirondack-inn.com

Situated across the street from the Olympic Arena and Mirror Lake, this hotel is within walking distance to all that Lake Placid has to offer. Guests can find a nice spot to relax at the back of the property, where a lovely lily pond and brick patio can be found. Guest rooms are basic and most have exterior entries.

49 rooms. Restaurant. Complimentary breakfast. Business center. Fitness center. Pool. Beach. $61-150

★ART DEVLIN'S OLYMPIC MOTOR INN

2764 Main St., Lake Placid, 518-523-3700; www.artdevlins.com

This budget-friendly property is located three blocks from the Olympic Arena and a short drive to town. The lobby has an interesting and unique display case holding hundreds of medals and trophies acquired by Art Devlin Sr., a former Olympic ski jumper. His son Art Devlin Jr. still owns and manages the motel.

44 rooms. Pool. Pets accepted. $61-150

★★CROWNE PLAZA RESORT AND GOLF CLUB LAKE PLACID

101 Olympic Drive, Lake Placid, 518-523-2556, 877-570-5891; www.lakeplacidcp.com

Situated on a hilltop, this resort offers an incredible view of the town of Lake Placid and Mirror Lake. Guest rooms in the Adirondack wing of the hotel are full of luxurious amenities such as granite countertops, full kitchens, antler light fixtures, mission-style furniture and white bed linens and duvets.

The beach is a few blocks away, and complimentary paddle and rowboats are available to guests.

245 rooms. Restaurant, bar. Fitness center. Pool. Pets accepted. Beach. Golf. Ski in/ski out. Tennis. $61-150

★★GOLDEN ARROW LAKESIDE RESORT
2559 Main St., Lake Placid, 518-523-3353, 800-582-5540; www.golden-arrow.com

The lobby of this lakeside resort is a large A-frame building with a magnificent view of Mirror Lake and a wood-burning fireplace. Each guest room is decorated in gold tones with Broyhill or Thomasville furniture. You can enjoy the hotel's beach, complete with paddleboats, rowboats, kayaks, canoes, and a swimming area.

150 rooms. Restaurant, bar. Fitness center. Pool. Pets accepted. Beach. $151-250

LAKE PLACID LODGE
144 Lodge Way, Lake Placid, 877-523-2700; www.lakeplacidlodge.com

This charming resort, situated on the edge of Lake Placid in the heart of the Adirondacks, has reopened after a 2005 fire destroyed the original, historic main lodge. Though the structure is now new, its arts and craft style remains true to the original rustic spirit of the lodge. The interior is a luxurious take on rustic Americana, with warm colors and traditional furnishings dressed up with proper plaids, animal prints and florals. The lodge now features two restaurants: a casual pub where you can sip a hot toddy while playing a game of chess, and an upscale dining room, Artisans, which serves masterfully presented takes on fresh, organic American cuisine.

30 rooms. Restaurant, bar. Complimentary breakfast.

★★★MIRROR LAKE INN RESORT AND SPA
77 Mirror Lake Drive, Lake Placid, 518-523-2544; www.mirrorlakeinn.com

Located on a hilltop at the edge of Lake Placid's downtown, this resort overlooks Mirror Lake as well as a stunning mountain range on the horizon. The lake can be seen from many of the guest rooms and the resort's restaurants, where the décor mixes a mission-style sensibility with walnut floors, marble, antiques and stone fireplaces.

129 rooms. Restaurant, bar. Fitness center. Pool. Spa. Beach. Tennis. $250-350

WHERE TO EAT
★★★ARTISANS, LAKE PLACID LODGE
Whiteface Inn Road, Lake Placid, 518-523-2700; www.lakeplacidlodge.com

At this much-lauded restaurant located in the cozy Lake Placid Lodge, you will find anything from duck consommé to lobster and sweetbread ravioli paired with stunning lake vistas. There are also three- and four-course prix fixe menus to choose from. Guests are required to be over age 12.

American. Dinner. Reservations recommended. Outdoor seating. Bar. $36-85

LETCHWORTH STATE PARK

Within this 14,344-acre park are 17 miles of the Genesee River Gorge, sometimes called the Grand Canyon of the East. Sheer cliffs rise 600 feet at some points, and the river roars over three major falls, one of them 107 feet high. The park has a variety of accommodations, including an inn and a motel, a

270-site tent and trailer camping area and 82 camping cabins ranging from one room to family size.

The park offers plenty of amenities and activities, including swimming pools with bathhouses, fishing, whitewater rafting, hot air balloon rides, nature and hiking trails and outstanding fall foliage. The William Pryor Letchworth Museum, the grave of Mary Jemison and a restored Seneca Indian Council House are also in the park.

WHERE TO EAT
★★GLEN IRIS INN
7 Letchworth State Park, Castile, 585-493-2622; www.glenirisinn.com

Housed in an old lumber mill with spectacular views of the neighboring waterfalls, the Glen Iris Inn's fine dining restaurant offers traditional fare and reasonable prices. Try one of the fresh seafood dishes such as cedar-plank salmon in a barbecue maple glaze or shrimp genesee stuffed with feta cheese and wrapped in bacon.

American. Breakfast, lunch, dinner. Children's menu. Closed November-April. $16-35

LOCKPORT
See also Niagara Falls

The town was originally settled around a series of locks of the Erie Canal, now the New York State Barge Canal. The historic downtown district sits right on the canal and affords great views of the action.

WHAT TO SEE
CANAL BRIDGE
Cottage Street, Lockport

Claimed to be one of the widest single-span bridges in the world at 399 1/2 feet, this bridge offers unparalleled views of the locks' operation, raising and lowering barges and pleasure crafts more than 60 feet.

Free. Daily.

COLONEL WILLIAM BOND HOUSE
143 Ontario St., Lockport, 716-434-7433; www.niagarahistory.org

This pre-Victorian home was built with bricks made onsite. Dating back to 1824, the restored house has 12 furnished rooms open to the public. The kitchen and children's garret are particularly interesting.

Free. May-December, Thursday, Saturday-Sunday 1-5 p.m.

KENAN CENTER
433 Locust St., Lockport, 716-433-2617; www.kenancenter.org

Occupying 25 acres, the center encompasses a sports arena, converted carriage house theater, recreation fields, a community meeting space and the Kenan house, a 19th-century Victorian mansion with an art gallery and formal gardens. Exhibits change frequently in the gallery, but showcase painting, sculpture, photography and textiles, all set against the backdrop of carved mahogany entrances, Italian marble floors and stunning Victorian fireplaces.

Free. September-May, Monday-Friday noon-5 p.m., Saturday-Sunday 2-5 p.m.; June-August, Monday-Friday noon-5 p.m., Sunday 2-5 p.m.

NIAGARA COUNTY HISTORICAL CENTER

215 Niagara St., Lockport, 716-434-7433; www.niagarahistory.org

The historical center occupies an 1860 brick house filled with antiques, Erie Canal artifacts and 19th century farming equipment. Also on display is the Niagara Fire Company No. 1 fire engine with pumpers from 1834 and 1836, and 19th-century farming equipment.

Free. Monday-Saturday 9 a.m.-5 p.m.

WHERE TO STAY
★LOCKPORT MOTEL

315 S. Transit Road, Lockport, 716-434-5595; www.lockportmotel.com

This family-owned motel has clean rooms, some with fireplaces and Jacuzzi tubs, and a large courtyard with a swimming pool. The staff is friendly and available.

90 rooms. Pool. $61-150

WHERE TO EAT
★GARLOCK'S

35 S. Transit Road, Lockport, 716-433-5595; www.garlocksrestaurant.com

Originally constructed to house canal laborers, this 1821 building is packed with antiques. Simple American dishes are served with loads of taste. Steak is a specialty. Seafood, steak. Dinner. Children's menu. Bar. $16-35

LONG ISLAND

See also Freeport, Garden City, Greenport, Huntington, Montauk, Oyster Bay

Long Island stretches 118 miles east by northeast from the edge of Manhattan to the lonely dunes of Montauk. Much of the island is ideal resort country, with vast white beaches, quiet bays, vineyard coves and woods. A mix of city sophistication and rural simplicity, Long Island is a playground for New Yorkers, who find the state parks, wildlife sanctuaries and small towns refreshing.

At the eastern tip, Montauk Light stands on its headland. On the southwestern shore is Coney Island. New York City sprawls over the whole of Long Island's two westernmost counties—Queens and Kings (the boroughs of Queens and Brooklyn).

Nassau County, adjoining the city, is made up of suburbs filled with residential communities. Eastward in Suffolk County, city influence eases. Potatoes and the famous Long Island duck are still raised here alongside farms for horse breeding and the vineyards producing Long Island wines.

Long Island has many miles of sandy barrier beaches along the south shore, with swimming and surf-casting. The bays behind these make natural small-boat harbors. On the more tranquil waters of the north shore is a series of deeper harbors along Long Island Sound, many of them with beaches and offering good sailing opportunities.

The island has played a major role in U.S. history from the early 17th century, and the record of this role is carefully preserved in many buildings, some 300 years old. Few regions offer such varied interests in so small an area. The Long Island Railroad conducts tours to points of interest on the island from late May to early November.

LONG ISLAND WINERIES

When Moses Fournier planted his French grapes during the pre-colonial period, he couldn't have imagined that vintners and visitors would be drawn to the region hundreds of years later for the same qualities that lured him: sunshine and fertile soil. Today, wine tastings and winery tours are popular in the Hamptons, particularly in the fall and on rainy weekends. Winemaking dates back almost 30 years on Long Island, and the region received a special designation as an American Viticultural Area on July 16, 2001. This assures that the grape-growing region has specific, ideal winemaking characteristics, including the right climate and soil conditions. Though there are fewer South Fork wineries than North Fork ones, visiting these wineries is always a pleasant way to spend an afternoon. Channing Daughters Winery (1927 Scuttle Hole Road, Bridgehampton, 631-537-7224) opened its tasting room in 1998. A large chateau is the home of Duck Walk Vineyards (231 Montauk Highway, Water Mill, 631-726-555) where Dr. Herodotus Damianos of Pindar Vineyards grows local grapes and produces wine. Wölffer Estate Vineyard (139 Sagg Road, Sagaponack, 631-537-5106), formerly known as Sagpond Vineyards, was the first winery to produce estate-bottled wines. The estate's owner, Christian Wölffer, has built a stunning winery where tasting and sales take place under soaring ceilings.

Visitors willing to spend an extra hour (each way) traveling to Long Island's Wine Country on the North Fork will find the experience more than worthwhile. (Of course, this trip can take much longer on busy summer days.) The North Fork's two main roads run for 30 miles west to east, but there are a number of wineries near Greenport. Follow the grape cluster signs on Main Road (Route 25) and on Sound Avenue (North Road/Route 48). Among the top Main Road wineries are Bedell Cellars, Bidwell Vineyards, Corey Creek Vineyards, Gristina Vineyards, Lenz Winery, Paumonok Vineyards, Pellegrini Vineyards and Pindar Vineyards. Pugliese Vineyards is on Bridge Lane in Cutchogue, one of the many short north/south roads that connect the two east/west arteries. On Sound Avenue, Hargrave Vineyards and Palmer Vineyards offer award-winning selections.

MANHASSET

A suburb of New York City, Manhasset is a community of family homes along tree-lined streets and a chic shopping district.

WHAT TO SEE
MIRACLE MILE
2060 Northern Blvd., Manhasset, 516-627-2277; www.americanamanhasset.com
This high-end stretch of stores in Nassau County features names such as Hermès, Tiffany & Co. and Brooks Brothers. It's a pleasant, outdoor area to shop—with ample parking. Just don't come expecting to find any bargains. Free. Monday-Saturday 10 a.m.-6 p.m., Sunday noon-6 p.m., Thursday 10 a.m.-8 p.m.

WHERE TO EAT
★★★LA COQUILLE
1669 Northern Blvd., Manhasset, 516-365-8422; www.la-coquille-manhasset.com
Dinner at this restaurant enchants with an array of French cuisine such as Long Island duck with a hazelnut and rice stuffing. Impeccable service—along with delectable homemade desserts—makes the experience unforgettable. French. Dinner. Reservations recommended. Jacket required. $36-85

MONTAUK

See also Amagansett, Bridgehampton, East Hampton, Long Island

This is a lively, somewhat honky-tonk fishing town at the far eastern end of Long Island, with a big business in deep-sea fishing (tuna, shark, marlin, striped bass and other varieties). Boats can be rented, and there are miles of uncrowded sandy beaches for sunning and surfing. Of course, there is also a glittering summer community here, too, but residents like Ralph Lauren tend to be more low-key than the denizens of other nearby Hamptons communities.

WHAT TO SEE
HITHER HILLS STATE PARK
50 S. Fairview Ave., Montauk, 631-668-2554

If you're looking to camp next to the Atlantic, this is the place to pitch your tent. The 1,755-acre park has hiking and biking trails, pine forests and some of the best beachside camping in the country. The "walking dunes" are located on the eastern boundary of the park, so named because powerful northwest winds cause the mammoth dunes to shift nearly three feet every year. Admission: $8 per vehicle. Daily sunrise-sunset.

MONTAUK LIGHTHOUSE
Montauk Point, Montauk, 631-668-2544; www.montauklighthouse.com

You've come as far east as you can on Long Island. In fact, Montauk Point is called "The End" by locals. What better way to end a trip on Long Island than with a visit to this historic lighthouse that was commissioned by George Washington and completed in 1796? It's the oldest lighthouse in the state, featuring 137 winding narrow steps to the top and views of the ocean from any angle. The lighthouse beacon still rotates and can be seen for 19 nautical miles. Admission: adults $8, seniors $7, children under 13 $4. May-October, daily 10:30 a.m.-4:30 p.m.; closing and off-season times vary.

MONTAUK POINT STATE PARK
50 S. Fairview Ave., Montauk, 631-668-3781; www.nysparks.state.ny.us/parks

Surrounding Montauk Lighthouse, this park is filled with barren moors and grassy dunes. Rip tides prevent swimming, but surf-casting (fishing near the shoreline) is popular here. Beachcombing and bird-watching are also favored pastimes at this park. Admission: $6 per vehicle. Daily sunrise-sunset.

WHERE TO STAY
★★★GURNEY'S INN RESORT AND SPA
290 Old Montauk Highway, Montauk, 631-668-2345, 800-445-8062; www.gurneys-inn.com

This sprawling resort facing the Atlantic Ocean provides a peaceful escape. Once here, head to the beautiful beach, take a sunrise walk or participate in activities like volleyball or yoga. The Seawater Spa offers body wraps and scrubs, massage therapy, facials and salon services. The indoor heated pool, which features seawater drawn from the resorts own wells, has views of the Atlantic from its floor-to-ceiling windows. Contemporary elegance is the theme of guest rooms.
109 rooms. Restaurant, bar. Spa. Beach. $251-350

★★★MONTAUK YACHT CLUB
32 Star Island Road, Montauk, 631-668-3100, 888-692-8668;
www.montaukyachtclub.com

The resort's 60-foot lighthouse replica, built in 1928, is still a focal point at this elegant retreat overlooking Lake Montauk. The numerous activities include volleyball, charter fishing, the La Bella Vita Spa and a fitness center with saunas. Recently renovated guest rooms have floor-to-ceiling windows and private balconies.

107 rooms. Restaurant, bar. Fitness center. Pool. Spa. Beach. Tennis. Closed December-March. $151-250

WHERE TO EAT

★★CROW'S NEST RESTAURANT & INN
4 Old West Lake Drive, Montauk, 631-668-2077; www.crowsnestinn.com

Though the nautical décor is a slightly kitschy, the fresh seafood is anything but. The clam chowder is worth the calories and the lobsters are sweet and delicious. Kids will love the 14-foot aquarium filled with exotic tropical fish and the shark tank.

Seafood. Lunch, dinner. Children's menu. Bar. $16-35

★★DAVE'S GRILL
468 W. Lake Drive, Montauk, 631-668-9190; www.davesgrill.com

This no-nonsense spot on the Montauk fishing docks serves fresh seafood including clams casino, stuffed lobster and Dave's famous fish stew. Don't leave without indulging in the signature chocolate bag dessert, a playful take on a sundae.

Seafood. Dinner. Closed Wedneday; also November-April. Outdoor seating. Bar. $16-35

★★GOSMAN'S RESTAURANT
500 W. Lake Drive, Montauk, 631-668-5330; www.gosmans.com

A dockside hangout popular with locals, Gosman's is a good spot for anything seafood. The Montauk lobsters are brought in daily, of course.

Seafood. Lunch, dinner. Closed mid-October-mid-April. Outdoor seating. Children's menu. Bar. $16-35

★★HARVEST ON FORT POND
11 S. Emery St., Montauk, 631-668-5574; www.harvest2000.com/hfp/

Family-style portions and breathtaking sunset views are the draw at this waterfront restaurant. In warm weather, ask to dine in the herb garden.

Mediterranean. Dinner. Closed February. Outdoor seating. Bar. $36-85

★★SECOND HOUSE TAVERN
161 Second House Road, Montauk, 631-668-2877; www.secondhousetavern.com

Situated on Fort Pond, this large airy restaurant keeps a casual atmosphere with farmstand tables and lofted ceilings. The grilled Australian lamb chops with mustard spaetzle and the seared sea scallops are specialties of the house.

Dinner. Outdoor seating. Children's menu. Bar. $16-35

MOUNT KISCO

See also Brewster, White Plains

About 35 miles north of New York City, Mount Kisco is an affluent community and the hub of Westchester County.

WHAT TO SEE
CARAMOOR CENTER FOR MUSIC AND THE ARTS
149 Girdle Ridge Road, Katonah, 914-232-5035; www.caramoor.org

The grounds at Caramoor are exquisite and include a European-style villa, the Rosen House, built during 1930s and surrounding formal gardens. Martha Stewart's farm is just across the street. The house contains a collection of Chinese art, Italian Renaissance furniture, and European paintings, sculptures and tapestries dating from the Middle Ages through the 19th century. The center is also host to many concerts and festivals throughout the years.
Admission: adults $10, children under 16 free. Daily.

JOHN JAY HOMESTEAD STATE HISTORIC SITE
400 Jay St., Katonah, 914-232-5651; www.johnjayhomestead.org

The estate that housed the first chief justice of the United States and four generations of his descendants contains period furnishings and an American portrait collection. The grounds have nice gardens and various farm buildings. Visits by guided tour only.
Admission: adults $7, seniors and students $5, children under 13 free. April-October, Tuesday-Saturday 10 a.m.-5 p.m., Sunday 11 a.m.-5 p.m.; November-March, Wednesday-Saturday 10 a.m.-4 p.m., Sunday 11 a.m.-4 p.m.

WHERE TO STAY
★★HOLIDAY INN
1 Holiday Inn Drive, Mount Kisco, 914-241-2600, 888-452-5771; www.himtkisco.com

More like a country inn than a chain hotel, this property has a welcoming lobby with a huge stone fireplace and mural of the Hudson River. Guest rooms have large picture windows and ergonomic armchairs and spacious work desks in case business calls. There is even a nightclub on the premises.
122 rooms. Restaurant, bar. Fitness center. Pool. $61-150

WHERE TO EAT
★★★CRABTREE'S KITTLE HOUSE
11 Kittle Road, Chappaqua, 914-666-8044; www.kittlehouse.com

This impressive historic restaurant serves the likes of slow-cooked wild Alaskan salmon with Jerusalem artichokes as well as acorn and butternut squash risotto with toasted pumpkin seeds in a romantic, country-style setting. The Artisanal cheese tray is a great finish to your meal.
American. Lunch, dinner. Reservations recommended. Outdoor seating. Bar. $36-85

★★★LA CAMELIA
234 N. Bedford Road, Mount Kisco, 914-666-2466

This Spanish gem is located high upon a hilltop and is the perfect spot for a romantic dinner date. Share any of the wonderful tapas selections—like the piquillo peppers stuffed with cod or the traditional gazpacho Andaluz—

paired with a bottle of rioja.

Spanish. Lunch, dinner, Sunday brunch. Closed Monday. Reservations recommended. Outdoor seating. Bar $16-35

★★LE JARDIN DU ROI
95 King St., Chappaqua, 914-238-1368; www.lejardinchappaqua.com

Candlelight and rich leather booths create a welcoming atmosphere at this cozy French bistro. Omelet fans will rejoice at the breakfast options served until 4 p.m. daily. The quiche du jour is always light and flavorful.

French. Breakfast, lunch, dinner, brunch. Outdoor seating. $16-35

★★★TRAVELER'S REST
Route 100, Ossining, 914-941-7744; www.thetravelersrest.com

Serving continental-German food since the 1800s, this restaurant prepares seafood, beef and poultry specialties such as beef Wellington and baked stuffed fillet of sole in an old-world setting surrounded by formal gardens.

Continental, German. Dinner, brunch. Closed Monday-Tuesday. Reservations recommended. Outdoor seating. Children's menu. Bar. $36-85

MOUNT TREMPER

See also Woodstock

This getaway in the Catskills is not far from the free love and artists' haven of Woodstock. Anglers often try their luck in the nearby Esopus Creek.

WHERE TO STAY

★★★EMERSON RESORT & SPA
5340 Route 28, Mount Tremper, 877-688-2828; www.emersonresort.com

A country retreat with a Zen feel, rooms at this resort are available in the rustic lodge or the adults-only inn, which has 25 luxury suites with fireplaces and whirlpool tubs. The Phoenix restaurant serves sophisticated dishes with an Asian flair, while the Spa Café delivers food as soothing and delicious as a day at the resort's onsite spa.

53 rooms. Restaurant, bar. Complimentary breakfast. Fitness center. Pool. Spa. Pets accepted. No children allowed. $251-350

★★KATE'S LAZY MEADOW MOTEL
5191 Highway 28, Mount Tremper, 845-688-7200; www.lazymeadow.com

Owned by Kate Pierson of B-52s fame, this small single story motel offers far more than what meets the eye upon seeing the exterior. The décor is funky to say the least, with mini kitchenettes, custom wallpaper and vintage furnishings. Family cabins, lodges and airstream trailers are also available.

10 rooms. No children under 14. $151-250

WHERE TO EAT

★SWEET SUE
49 Route 28, Main St., Phoenicia, 845-688-7852

The pancakes are the thing to order at this low-key diner. Unfortunately, you won't be the only one in town who wants them; lines can be brutally long on weekends.

American. Breakfast, lunch, brunch. Closed Tuesday. Outdoor seating. Children's menu. $15 and under.

SPA

★★★★THE EMERSON SPA

5340 Route 28, Mount Tremper, 877-688-2828; www.emersonresort.com

This Indian-influenced upstate spa features 10 treatment rooms perfect for sampling a variety of eastern-inspired treatments. Indian head massages, Dosha balancing massages and Abhyanga massages, involving two therapists in unison, are some of the bodywork offerings, while shirodhara and bindi herbal body treatments round out the Ayurvedic menu. From aromatherapy facials and sea salt body scrubs to warm mud wraps, many of the treatments use natural ingredients for cleansing, detoxifying, and healing the skin.

NAPLES

At the south end of Canandaigua Lake, one of the Finger Lakes, Naples is the center of a grape-growing, winemaking area. Many of its residents are descendants of Swiss and German winemakers. Artists also flock to this picturesque village, especially in fall when the foliage is at its peak.

WHAT TO SEE

CUMMING NATURE CENTER OF THE ROCHESTER MUSEUM & SCIENCE CENTER

6472 Gulick Road, Naples, 585-374-6160; www.rmsc.org

A 900-acre living museum, the center has nature trails, natural history programs and conservation trail with an operating sawmill. In winter, there are 15 miles of groomed trails for cross-country skiing and snowshoeing.
Admission: $3 suggested donation. Late December-mid-November, Wednesday-Friday 9 a.m.-3:30 p.m., Saturday-Sunday 9 a.m.-4:30 p.m.

WIDMER'S WINE CELLARS

1 Lake Niagara Lane, Naples, 585-374-6311; www.widmerwine.com

If the name Widmer doesn't ring a bell, how about Brickstone Cellars or Manischewitz? Widmer's is one of the largest wineries on the East Coast, and produces wines under many label titles. Tours take you though the wine-making process from start to finish, and free tastings are available in the gift shop. Rabbis are also onsite to explain the process of making Kosher wine.
Tours: $2. Tasting: free. May-December, daily 10 a.m.-5 p.m.; January-April, daily noon-4 p.m.

WHERE TO EAT

★★NAPLES HOTEL

111 S. Main St., Naples, 585-374-5630

Housed in an 1895 Federal-style building, this restaurant is full of antiques and Victorian flare, including lace curtains and plush furnishings. German dishes are their focus. If you're looking for a more casual atmosphere, head to the taproom next door.
German. Lunch, dinner. Children's menu. Bar. $16-35

NEW PALTZ

See also Hyde Park, Kingston, Newburgh, Poughkeepsie

New Paltz was founded by a dozen Huguenots who were granted land by the colonial governor of New York. The town is surrounded by the fertile farmlands of the Wallkill River Valley, with apple orchards and vineyards. Rock climbers come to New Paltz for the "Gunks," cliffs of the Shawangunk Mountains that border the town and offer challenging steep facades.

WHAT TO SEE
HUGUENOT STREET OLD STONE HOUSES
New Paltz, 914-255-1660; www.huguenotstreet.org

Six original stone dwellings dating between 1692 and 1712 line this historic street. There is also a reconstructed French church nearby. If you're in New Paltz in August, check for the Colonial Street Festival, a one-day celebration where all of the stone houses are opened to the public.

Admission: adults $9-12, seniors and students $8-11, children 6-17 $4-6, children under 6 free. May-October, Thursday-Tuesday 10 a.m.-5 p.m.; November-December, Saturday-Sunday 10 a.m.-5 p.m.

LOCUST LAWN
400 Highway 32 S., New Paltz, 845-255-1660; www.huguenotstreet.org

Visit this Federal mansion built in 1814 by Josiah Hasbrouck, a U.S. congressman under Jefferson, Madison and Monroe. The property includes a smokehouse and a farmers' museum with an original ox cart on display.

Admission: adults $8, seniors $7, students and children 6-17 $4, children under 6 free. June-October, Saturday-Sunday 11 a.m.-4 p.m.

WHERE TO STAY
★★ROCKING HORSE RANCH RESORT
600 Highway 44-55, Highland, 845-691-2927, 800-647-2624; www.rhranch.com

If you've always dreamed of spending time on a dude ranch, this is your opportunity. Guest rooms are spacious and decorated in a western style.

119 rooms. Bar. Pool. Spa. Tennis. $151-250

WHERE TO EAT
★★★DEPUY CANAL HOUSE
Route 213, High Falls, 845-687-7700; www.depuycanalhouse.net

Located in a charming, 18th-century stone house, the DePuy Canal House creates culinary wonders like quarter-braised duck with pierogies and quail and duck sfogliatelle on a whole button mushroom sauce. There is also a handful of charming guest rooms.

American. Dinner, brunch. Closed Monday-Wednesday. Reservations recommended. Outdoor seating. Bar $36-85

★MAIN STREET BISTRO
59 Main St., New Paltz, 845-255-7766; www.mainstreetbistro.com

This casual eatery serves everything from buttermilk flapjacks to Waldorf salads to tofu stirfrys. The frittatas are particularly hearty.

American, Vegetarian. Breakfast, lunch, dinner, brunch. Outdoor seating. $16-35

★★ROSENDALE CAFE

434 Main St., Rosendale, 845-658-9048; www.rosendalecafe.com

Veggies rejoice. This hip, local joint serves inventive vegetarian fare with a healthy serving of live music on the side. Weekend concerts feature all genres. Vegetarian. Lunch, dinner. Reservations recommended. Outdoor seating. $16-35

NEW ROCHELLE

See also Mamaroneck, New York, White Plains

New Rochelle was founded in 1688 by a group of Huguenot families. Prior to European settlement, the area was home to the Siwanoys, a tribe of Mohegans stemming from the Algonquins. Boat building was the trade of most early settlers, who used these boats to carry goods to and from New York City and other coastal ports.

WHAT TO SEE
THOMAS PAINE COTTAGE

20 Sicard Ave., New Rochelle; www.thomaspainecottage.org

Located on the last two acres of the original 320 given to Thomas Paine by New York State in 1784, you will find Thomas Paine's second cottage (rebuilt after a fire claimed the first in 1793), and the Sophia Brewster one-room schoolhouse. The cottage contains original artifacts including a cast-iron Franklin Stove gifted by Benjamin Franklin.

Tuesday, Thursday, Saturday-Sunday 10 a.m.-5 p.m., Friday 2-5 p.m.

NEW YORK CITY

New York is the nation's most populous city, the capital of finance, dining, business, communications, theater, fashion, beauty—and the list goes on. It may or may not be the center of the universe—native New Yorkers swear it is—but the metropolis does occupy a central place in the global community.

Giovanni da Verrazano was the first European to take a glimpse at Manhattan Island in 1524, but the area was not explored until 1609, when Henry Hudson sailed up the river that was later named after him in search for a passage to India (he was clearly amiss). The Dutch West Indian Company established the first trading post in 1615. Peter Minuit is said to have bought the island from American Indians for $24 worth of beads and trinkets in 1626, and New Amsterdam was founded—the greatest real estate bargain in history.

In 1664, the Dutch surrendered to a British fleet and the town was renamed New York in honor of the Duke of York. One of the earliest trials of independence occurred here in 1734 when John Peter Zenger, publisher and editor of the New York Weekly Journal, was charged with seditious libel and jailed for making anti-government remarks. Following the Battle of Long Island in 1776, the British occupied the city through the Revolution until 1783.

On the balcony of Federal Hall at Wall Street, April 30, 1789, George Washington was inaugurated as the first president of the United States, and for a time New York was the country's capital.

When the Erie Canal opened in 1825, New York City expanded as a port. In 1898, Manhattan merged with Brooklyn, the Bronx, Queens and Staten Island. In the next half-century, several million immigrants entered the United States through New York, providing the city with the supply of labor needed for its growth. Each wave of immigrants has brought new customs, culture and lifestyles, which make New York City the diverse metropolis it is today.

The city was changed permanently on September 11, 2001 when terrorists hijacked two commercial airliners and flew them into the World Trade Center towers, which later collapsed. Nearly 3,000 people were killed in the towers, planes and on the ground. The emotional and physical scars left by these attacks were universally profound. The area where the World Trade Center and many of its surrounding buildings once existed has since been cleared, and plans for a memorial and rebuilding in the area are under way. Many visitors now make the pilgrimage to the Lower Manhattan site to better understand the events and implications of this tragic event.

Since 2001, New York has revitalized its image as the Big Apple, attracting more than 47 million visitors each year. Most of its many attractions are centered in Manhattan; however, do not overlook the wealth of sights and activities the outlying boroughs have to offer. In Brooklyn there is Coney Island, the New York Aquarium, the superb Brooklyn History Museum, Brooklyn Botanic Garden, Brooklyn Children's Museum and the famous Brooklyn Bridge. The Bronx is noted for its excellent Botanical Garden and Zoo and the New Yankee Stadium. Flushing Meadows-Corona Park, in Queens, was the site of two World's Fairs; nearby is Citi Field, home of the New York Mets. Uncrowded Staten Island has Richmond Town Restoration, a re-creation of 18th-century New York, rural farmland, beaches, salt marshes and wildlife preserves.

NEIGHBORHOODS
CHELSEA/HELL'S KITCHEN/GARMENT DISTRICT

There's something for everyone in Chelsea, which lies to the north of Greenwich Village on Manhattan's west side. Long known as a home to both art galleries and gay culture, the neighborhood is also loved by foodies who frequent the gourmet stalls and restaurants at Chelsea Market, and fitness-minded types who come to Chelsea Piers, a riverfront sports complex containing batting cages, volleyball courts and an ice rink. To the north, hugging the Hudson River, Hell's Kitchen once had a reputation as a crime-ridden, decaying part of the city. But gentrification means that these days, strollers line the sidewalks and brunch at one of the many bistros lining Ninth Avenue is the most common sight. Unfortunately, you won't find ateliers and couture shops in the Garment District, which sits in Midtown between the Javits Convention Center and Empire State Building—just the warehouses used by garment manufacturers and offices of big and small names in the world of fashion.

CHINATOWN/LITTLE ITALY/NOLITA

Your senses will be on high alert when you head downtown and hit Chinatown. The visual and aural assault of crowds haggling for deals on knock-off designer handbags and tchotchkes in crammed retail stalls on Canal Street is only overshadowed by the aromas wafting from the fresh seafood shops. But it's your taste buds that reap the real reward, thanks to what seems like an endless array of dim sum and noodle restaurants. If you prefer prosciutto to Peking duck, Little Italy is literally just steps away. It may be more tourist-trap than true Italian nowadays, except during the Feast of San Gennaro festival each September (www.sangennaro.org), when it's worth a squeeze through the crowds for a paper bag full of warm zeppoles (fried dough balls with powdered sugar). Nolita (just north of Little Italy, like its name suggests) mixes independent (and often tiny) bars and restaurants with one-of-a-kind boutiques.

EAST VILLAGE/LOWER EAST SIDE

Long associated with the immigrants and working class who occupied the tenements here (especially Eastern European Jews), the Lower East Side's landscape changed in the 1990s to one with more art galleries, alt-rock venues, and hipster-haunt restaurants and bars than cheap apartments and kosher delis. The East Village was once considered a part of this low-income neighborhood, but the area east of the Bowery from Houston to 14th streets eventually developed a counter-culture vibe where artists and activists like Andy Warhol, Keith Haring, Abbie Hoffman and The Velvet Underground made names for themselves. Gentrification—most notably by ever-expanding New York University—has led to a shift in the arts scene to the Williamsburg section of Brooklyn and other parts of the city.

FINANCIAL DISTRICT/BATTERY PARK CITY

There's more to the downtown Financial District than the New York Stock Exchange and a bunch of stiff suits. Even if it's a bear market, the bronze Charging Bull sculpture on Wall Street inspires optimism, and if things are looking up, you can drop a pretty penny at South Street Seaport's touristy shops and restaurants. The area is also a somber stop for visitors who want a look at Ground Zero—and surrounding street vendors are at the ready, hawking everything from commemorative snow globes to t-shirts. A good place to escape them is adjacent Battery Park City, a planned community on the southern tip of Manhattan where you'll find sweeping views of New York Harbor and the Statue of Liberty.

GREENWICH VILLAGE/SOHO/WEST VILLAGE

Once the center of New York's hippie scene, Greenwich Village is a little less counter-culture these days, but no less colorful. It's anchored at the southern tip of Fifth Avenue by Washington Square Park, where street performers intermingle with protestors and chess players. The giant arch at its center is one of New York City's most recognizable symbols. Soho is the neighborhood south of Houston (pronounced "HOW-ston," not like the city in Texas) Street, which can be summed up in one word: shopping. Designers such as Anna Sui and John Varvatos mix it up with the likes of the Apple Store and Bloomingdale's here, and the crowds never cease. Things are a little more diverse between Sixth Avenue and the Hudson River in the West Village, where the cobblestone streets are lined with bars, bistros and boutiques. The neighborhood has long been famous as a home for artists and writers both real (Dylan Thomas, Charlie Parker) and fictional.

MIDTOWN/MIDTOWN EAST

Midtown Manhattan is just that—the middle of the island (from 34th to 59th streets), and with all this bit of prime real estate has going on, it may as well be the center of the universe. This is where you'll find the Empire State Building, Chrysler Building, Rockefeller Center and Madison Square Garden. The business district—from the 40s up and along the Avenue of the Americas, a.k.a. Sixth Avenue—is where some of the world's most influ-ential advertising, financial and media companies have their headquarters. Midtown East, between the East River and Madison Avenue, is home to the United Nations and Grand Central Terminal.

THEATER DISTRICT/TIMES SQUARE

Hundreds of thousands of people descend upon Times Square—an area between 42nd and 47th streets, where Broadway and Seventh Avenue con-verge—every December 31st to watch an LED ball drop from the top of One Times Square and ring in the new year. Once a seedy, crime-plagued pock-et of peep-shows and adult movie theaters, the neighborhood is now more family friendly than down-and-out, catering to mobs of tourists visiting the G-rated retail flagships of Hershey, Toys "R" Us and the like. The adjacent Theater District is where the lights of Broadway theater marquees illuminate what's affectionately known as the Great White Way.

TRIBECA/MEATPACKING DISTRICT

Tribeca—an acronym for Triangle Below Canal (Street)—is a downtown neighborhood where industrial warehouses have been converted into pricey loft apartments. The influential Tribeca Film Festival was co-founded by longtime resident Robert De Niro to spur the neighborhood's economy fol-lowing the September 11 terrorist attacks at the nearby World Trade Center. Just to the north, the animal carcasses and butchers that once defined the Meatpacking District—which spans from the Hudson River to Hudson Street to the north—have made way in the last decade for pretty people who like to see and be seen at velvet-rope clubs and restaurants.

UNION SQUARE/FLATIRON DISTRICT/GRAMERCY PARK/ MURRAY HILL

Union Square is the entry to Greenwich Village and downtown, and is an-chored by Union Square Park—a mammoth four-square block plaza that never stops bustling. The park is a popular meeting spot and home to the city's best-known farmers market, a dog run and one of the city's largest subway stations. To the north, the Flatiron District is named for the Flatiron Building, a striking, triangular building at 23rd Street where Broadway and Fifth Avenue converge that was one of the earliest steel structures built. Gramercy Park is a nearby residential neighborhood lauded for a residents-only private park. Murray Hill is a quiet, no-nonsense eastside neighborhood that lies between 29th and 42nd streets, known for its solidly middle-class inhabitants.

UPPER WEST SIDE/COLUMBUS CIRCLE

Cultural bastions including Lincoln Center and the American Museum of Natural History make their home on the Upper West Side, along with thou-sands of New Yorkers who love the neighborhood's proximity to their Mid-town jobs and plethora of shops, restaurants and accessibility to Central Park. Come hungry: New York's legendary H&H Bagels and Zabar's gourmet deli are both here. Columbus Circle, at 59th Street and the southern opening to

Central Park, was long-known as nothing more than a super-congested traffic circle before the Time Warner Center—a mixed-use building containing shops, fancy restaurants, a hotel and music halls—opened here in 2003.

OUTER BOROUGHS
BROOKLYN
With 2.6 million residents, Brooklyn is New York City's most populous borough and has a distinct culture all its own. Thanks to its proximity to downtown Manhattan, there's a vibrant arts and cultural scene—writers, painters, designers and restaurateurs migrate to Brooklyn for its less expensive rents and neighborhood-centric way of life. The borough is home to some of the city's most recognized institutions, including the Brooklyn Academy of Music, Brooklyn Botanic Garden, Prospect Park and Coney Island.

THE BRONX
The Bronx is the northernmost of New York City's five boroughs and the only part attached to North American mainland. It is most famous as the home of the New York Yankees (a.k.a., Bronx Bombers, who have a brand new stadium here, since 2009, just like the Mets) and the Bronx Zoo, the largest nature preserve in the United states, spanning 265 acres and containing more than 4,500 animals.

HARLEM
Harlem is arguably the cultural epicenter of African-American arts and culture. The landmark Apollo Theater is credited with launching the careers of James Brown, Michael Jackson, Stevie Wonder and countless other singer and musicians, while Sylvia's Soul Food has long attracted a mix of locals and visiting celebs—especially politicians on the stump. The historic brownstones that line many of the neighborhood's residential streets have become some of the city's most coveted real estate in recent years.

QUEENS
Most visitors to New York City know Queens as the part of the city they fly into—it's where John F. Kennedy and LaGuardia airports are located. But the borough is also one of the most diverse places in all of the United States—it's home to New York's Greektown (in Astoria), the city's second Chinatown (in Flushing) a "Little Guyana" (Richmond Hill) and a bevy of other ethnic pockets. The New York Mets play in brand-new Citi Field in Flushing Meadows, and right next door you can check out the unofficial symbol of Queens, the 12-story high Unisphere—a massive globe structure commissioned for the 1964-1965 World's Fair, which took place here.

STATEN ISLAND
Staten Island feels more like a suburb than one of the five boroughs with its wealth of (by New York City standards) sprawling homes with backyards and pools, as well as strip malls and chain restaurants. Separated from the other boroughs by New York Bay, Staten Island is the only part of the city not serviced by its subway system. One of the best tourist attractions in town is a round-trip ride between here and Manhattan on the free (yes, free) Staten Island Ferry, which offers breath-taking views of New York Harbor and the Statue of Liberty.

BRONX (NEW YORK)
WHAT TO SEE
BARTOW-PELL MANSION MUSEUM
895 Shore Road, Bronx, 718-885-1461; www.bartowpellmansionmuseum.org

This Greek Revival stone mansion, built between 1836 and 1842, has been functioning as a museum since 1946 and exemplifies the type of country living that existed in the Pelham Bay Park area in the early 19th century. Educational programs are run year-round for children and adults and include lectures, environmental walks, art exhibitions and musical concerts.

Admission: adults $5, seniors and students $3, children under 6 free. Wednesday, Saturday-Sunday noon-4 p.m.

BRONX MUSEUM OF THE ARTS
1040 Grand Concourse, Bronx, 718-681-6000; www.bxma.org

This often overlooked museum houses more than 800 works of art from all mediums representing the ethnically diverse make-up of the Bronx. Changing exhibits focus on contemporary art and current subjects pertaining to the communities in the borough.

Admission: adults $5, seniors and students $3. Free Friday. Thursday-Sunday 11 a.m.-6 p.m., Friday 11 a.m.-8 p.m.

BRONX ZOO
Fordham Road and Bronx River Parkway, Bronx, 718-367-1010; www.bronxzoo.com

The largest urban wildlife conservation park in the country, the Bronx Zoo boasts 265-acres for more than 4,000 animals to roam. Much of the zoo's land has been made into special habitats suited for its diverse variety of animals, including gorillas, lions, gibbons and grizzly bears. Take a 20-minute monorail ride along the Bronx River and take in the surroundings of the Wild Asia portion of the zoo with tigers, elephants and rhinos roaming nearby. And an interactive children's zoo lets kids check out animal homes, try on simulated claws and paws, and get their picture taken with chickens. There are also several indoor exhibits to explore, including the Butterfly Garden, Monkey House and World of Birds.

Admission: adults $15, seniors $13, children 3-12 $11. April-October, Monday-Friday 10 a.m.-5 p.m., Saturday-Sunday 10 a.m.-5:30 p.m.; November-March, daily 10 a.m.-4:30 p.m.

CITY ISLAND
Off the southeast coast of the mainland, Bronx, 718-829-4111; www.cityisland.com

Considered a slice of New England in the city, City Island is devoted to shipping and shipbuilding. The City Island Historical Nautical Museum is also located here.

Free. Daily.

EDGAR ALLAN POE COTTAGE
East Kingsbridge Road and Grand Concourse, Bronx, 718-881-8900;
www.bronxhistoricalsociety.org/poecottage.html

The last years of Edgar Allan Poe's life, 1846 to 1849, were spent in the Bronx at Poe Cottage. Poe picked this bucolic setting in the hopes that the fresh country air would cure his ailing wife Virginia. Many of Poe's greatest works were penned here including Annabel Lee, The Bells and Eureka. Admission: adults $5, seniors, students and children $3. Monday-Friday 9 a.m.-5 p.m., Saturday 10 a.m.-4 p.m., Sunday 1-5 p.m.

ARTHUR AVENUE

Pay a visit to the real Little Italy of New York. Italians made the area of Belmont their home at the turn of the century, and many made their living by selling food items from pushcarts on Arthur Avenue. In 1940, Mayor Fiorello LaGuardia greenlighted construction of an indoor market where they could sell their goods. Seventy years later, the passion for artisanal foods and wines continues. Visit the European market (2344 Arthur Ave.) and you'll be overtaken by the smell of freshly baked breads, aromatic cheeses and house-cured meats. Beyond the market, there is also an abundance of restaurants, pizza parlors and pastry shops—some dating to the 1920s. At Roberto's (632 E. 186th St., 718-733-9503), everyone orders from the blackboard list of specials and waiters spoon heaps of fresh pasta on your plate. Calandra Cheese (2314 Arthur Ave., 718-365-7572) sells fresh mozarella and other cheeses, while the bread sold at Terranova Bakery (691 E. 187th St., 718-733-3827) is a feast in itself. .

FORDHAM UNIVERSITY
Rose Hill Campus, Bronx, 718-817-1000; www.fordham.edu

All four original Gothic structures of the Rose Hill campus are designated landmarks: University Chapel (St. John's Church), St. John's Residence Hall, the Administration Building and the Alumni House. A second campus is at 60th and Columbus Avenue, across from the Lincoln Center for the Performing Arts. Free. Daily.

THE HALL OF FAME FOR GREAT AMERICANS
University Avenue and West 181st Street, Bronx, 718-289-5161; www.bcc.cuny.edu/hallofFame/

Located on the Bronx Community College campus, this 630-foot open-air Neo-Classical colonnade provides the framework for bronze busts of great Americans that have had a profound impact on the nation's history. Busts on exhibit include Alexander Graham Bell, Eli Whitney and George Westinghouse. Daily10 a.m-5 p.m.

THE NEW YORK BOTANICAL GARDEN
200th Street and Kazimiroff Boulevard, Bronx, 718-817-8700; www.nybg.org

With more than one million plants, this is one of the largest and oldest (founded in 1891) botanical gardens in the country. It consists of 250 landscaped acres and 50 curated gardens. The property also contains the last 50 acres of native forest that once covered New York City. The Enid A. Haupt Conservatory has 11 distinct plant environments with changing exhibits and permanent displays, including the Fern Forest, Palm Court and Rose Garden. There is a great emphasis on education, with programs on horticulture and science. For the kids, there is the Everett Children's Adventure Garden, a 12-acre space that offers a boulder maze and giant animal topiaries. The botanical garden is one of the best ways to "get out of the city" without leaving its borders.

Admission: adults $6, seniors and students $3, children 2-12 $1, children under 2 free. Free Wednesday, 10 a.m.-noon Saturday. April-mid-January, Tuesday-Sunday 10 a.m.-6 p.m., mid-January-March 10 a.m.-5 p.m.

NEW YORK YANKEES

Yankee Stadium, 161st Street and River Avenue, Bronx, 718-293-6000; www.yankees.com

If you're a baseball fan visiting New York City in-season, you owe it to yourself to catch a Yankees game. Watching the Bronx Bombers is the quintessential New York experience. Get tickets as early as possible, because these legendary pinstripers are popular with locals and tourists alike. The annual subway series games between the Yankees and the New York Mets sell out quickly. The 2009 season was the first to be held in the new stadium, a block away from the historic original.

Prices vary. March-October, hours vary.

PELHAM BAY PARK

East of the Hutchinson River, Bronx, 718-430-1832; www.nycgovparks.org

Stretching out over 2,700 acres (more than three times the size of Manhattan's Central Park), Pelham Bay Park is New York City's largest park and takes advantage of the sprawling space. The expansive public park includes Orchard Beach, 13 miles of shoreline along Long Island Sound, an 18-hole and miniature golf course, a wildlife refuge, an environmental center, nature trails, a visitor center, tennis courts, ball fields, a running track, riding stables and bridle paths and picnicking.

Free. Daily.

VAN CORTLANDT GOLF COURSE

Van Cortlandt Park South and Bailey Avenue, Bronx, 718-543-4595; www.nycgovparks.org

The Van Cortlandt Golf Course was the nation's first public course when it opened in 1895. The Golf Clubhouse, built in 1902, is situated on the lake and contains equipment rental facilities, lockers and a snack shop. Former New York mayor Rudy Giuliani appropriated some $4 million in the late 1990s, which helped create 20 new tee boxes and contributed to the overall renovation of the course, which was run down from years of heavy play. With two par-fives of more than 600 yards each, today it's one of the best urban golf courses in the nation.

Admission: $60 weekend, $57 weekday, $33 twilight. Daily, sunrise-sunset.

WAVE HILL

West 249th Street and Independence Avenue, Bronx, 718-549-3200; www.wavehill.org

This Hudson River estate was, at various times, home to notables such as Mark Twain, Teddy Roosevelt and Arturo Toscanini. It's now a public garden and cultural center featuring Wave Hill House built in 1843, gardens, four greenhouses, nature trails, woods and meadows. The grounds consist of 28 acres overlooking the Hudson. Special events include concerts, dance programs, art exhibits, and education and nature workshops.

Admission: adults $6, seniors and students $3, children 6-18 $2, children under 6 free. Free Tuesday, Saturday morning. Mid-April-mid-October,

Tuesday-Sunday 9 a.m.-5:30 p.m.; Mid-October-mid-April, Tuesday-Sunday 9 a.m.-4:30 p.m.

WHERE TO STAY

★★★LE REFUGE INN

586 City Island Ave., Bronx, 718-885-2478; www.lerefugeinn.com

Le Refuge Inn, as its name suggests, is a splendid escape. Surrounded by the waters of the Long Island Sound, this 19th-century Victorian manor house on historic City Island is a cozy retreat of warmth, peace and romance—perfect for unwinding. The rooms are individually decorated with numerous antiques.

7 rooms. Restaurant, bar. Complimentary breakfast. $61-150

WHERE TO EAT

★★EMILIA'S

2331 Arthur Ave., Bronx, 718-367-5915; www.emiliasrestaurant.com

The Bronx is certainly not short on Italian food, but Emilia's Southern Italian dishes are wholesome and hearty standouts. Lunch specials are the reason many locals flock here, but dinner is also a sure thing with generous portions of pasta, fish and meat. Emilia's serves an alcohol-soaked tiramisu that will likely prompt a return trip.

Italian. Lunch, dinner. Closed Monday. Bar. $16-35

★FEEDING TREE

892 Gerard Ave., Bronx, 718-293-5025

Feeding Tree is one of New York's most beloved Jamaican restaurants, located within a home run's distance of Yankee Stadium. At this friendly and lively joint, steel drums echo against the walls, and you will definitely feel the Caribbean vibe. Tuck a napkin into your collar and fill up on jerk chicken, stewed kingfish, oxtails, curried goat and crisp golden patties filled with spiced meat—the perfect pre-game snack.

Caribbean. Breakfast, lunch, dinner. Children's menu. $15 and under.

★★★LE REFUGE INN

586 City Island Ave., Bronx, 718-885-2478; www.lerefugeinn.com

You'll immediately be transported to the French countryside once you step inside this elegant antique-filled dining room with arched windows and crystal chandeliers. The sophisticated menu offers classic dishes such as bouillabaisse and duck a l'orange. No meal is compete without an order of the decadent profiteroles.

French. Dinner. Closed Monday. Reservations recommended. Outdoor seating. Jacket required. Children's menu. Bar. $16-35

★★LOBSTER BOX

34 City Island Ave., Bronx, 718-885-1952; www.lobsterboxrestaurant.com

The Lobster Box is a historic City Island landmark that, true to its name, offers its specialty, fresh lobster, any way you like it. Choices include broiled, steamed, stuffed Fra Diavolo (tomato and garlic) or marinara, and every preparation is delicious. Pasta is also on the menu, many laden with meaty bits of lobster, such as the lobster-stuffed ravioli tossed in a sage lemon butter cream sauce.

Seafood. Lunch, dinner. Bar. Casual attire. Valet parking. $16-35

★★ROBERTO RESTAURANT
603 Crescent Ave., Bronx, 718-733-9503; www.roberto089.com

Set in the Italian enclave of the Bronx, Roberto's restaurant is not high on décor or elegant atmosphere, but it is filled with terrific food prepared in the Positano style. The sure-handed kitchen sends out home-style dishes like grilled calamari and assorted pastas. For a real treat, ask for the house specialty, a four-course meal with dishes from Roberto's native Amalfi coast that will induce rounds of applause.

Italian. Lunch, dinner. Closed Sunday. Outdoor seating. $16-35

★VENICE RESTAURANT AND PIZZERIA
772 E. 149th St., Bronx, 718-585-5164; www.venicerestaurant149.com

Old-school pizza and pasta are what you'll find at Venice. Though the décor is lacking, the attraction should be the honest and modestly-priced Italian-American food. Founded more than 50 years ago, Venice's menu focuses on seafood, but stick to the steaming thin-crust pizza for your best bet.

Italian, pizza. Lunch, dinner. Children's menu. $15 and under.

BROOKLYN (NEW YORK)
WHAT TO SEE
ATLANTIC AVENUE
Atlantic Avenue, Brooklyn

Imagine a colorful shopping bazaar in downtown Cairo, and you've just pictured Atlantic Avenue. This area has a mix of more than 30 antiques and gift shops, ethnic food and bread stores, and savory Middle Eastern restaurants. If you crave real falafel, kebabs and hummus at value prices, this is the neighborhood to visit.

BROOKLYN ACADEMY OF MUSIC (BAM)
30 Lafayette Ave., Brooklyn, 718-636-4100; www.bam.org

Founded in 1859, BAM is the oldest performing arts center in America, presenting original productions in offbeat and contemporary styles and adaptations. In the Next Wave Festival each fall, BAM opens its stage to noted national and international theater, dance and opera companies, and classical and contemporary music programs. There is also a movie theater that shows limited-release art films and blockbusters.

Prices and showtimes vary.

BROOKLYN BOTANIC GARDEN
Prospect Park, 1000 Washington Ave., Brooklyn, 718-623-7200; www.bbg.org

For a peaceful respite away from Manhattan, hop the 1 or 2 subway to Eastern Parkway in Brooklyn and enjoy a natural wonder: the 52-acre Brooklyn Botanic Garden. It features a gorgeous Japanese garden; the Steinhardt Conservatory, which has several greenhouses filled with a variety of plants; and the Fragrance Garden, designed specifically for the blind. There are rose gardens, an annual cherry blossom festival, a terrific alfresco café and many other beautiful sights.

Admission: adults $8, seniors and students $4, children under 12 free. Tuesday-Friday 8 a.m.-6 p.m., Saturday-Sunday 10 a.m.-6 p.m.

BROOKLYN BRIDGE
Lower Manhattan/Downtown Brooklyn
One of four bridges spanning the East River (the others are the Williamsburg, Manhattan and Queensboro bridges), this 6,016-foot-long wonder connects the boroughs of Manhattan and Brooklyn and was the longest suspension bridge in the world at the time of its completion in 1883. More than 150,000 people paid one cent to walk across the bridge on opening day (bringing a hog or sheep cost an additional two cents). Today, more than 126,000 vehicles cross the bridge each day, in addition to a steady stream of foot traffic from commuters and tourists looking to get a bit of exercise while enjoying the spectacular views of the river and the Statue of Liberty.

BROOKLYN CHILDREN'S MUSEUM
145 Brooklyn Ave., Brooklyn, 718-735-4400; www.bchildmus.org
Founded in 1899, this is the world's oldest children's museum, featuring interactive exhibits, workshops and special events. One of the museums newest exhibits, World Brooklyn, brings global diversity to a kid-friendly scale with a cityscape that includes a Chinese stationary store for kids to practice Chinese calligraphy, a Mexican bakery with a giant mixer and pretend dough, and a West African import store filled with African instruments, beauty products and textiles, among other ethnic storefronts.
Admission: $7.50, children under 1 free. Wednesday-Friday noon-5 p.m., Saturday-Sunday 10 a.m.-5 p.m.

BROOKLYN HEIGHTS PROMENADE
Columbia Heights and Middagh Street, Brooklyn, 718-965-8900
If it's the perfect view you're after, you'll find it at this well-manicured pedestrian walkway above the hum of the Brooklyn-Queens Expressway. Overlooking lower Manhattan, the East River and the Brooklyn Bridge, the esplanade is a popular spot for joggers, Rollerbladers, sightseers, locals looking to relax and film crews coveting the picturesque skyline. (And in case you're wondering, the traffic noise from below won't kill the mood.)
Daily 24 hours.

BROOKLYN HISTORICAL SOCIETY
128 Pierrepont St., Brooklyn Heights, 718-222-4111; www.brooklynhistory.org
Brooklyn was originally the commercial and cultural center of Long Island, which explains why this society was originally founded in 1863 as the Long Island Historical Society. But since 1881, the terracotta and pressed-brick building designed by noted architect George Post has marked the headquarters for the Brooklyn Historical Society. During World War I, the BHS contributed to the war effort by transforming its 600-seat auditorium into a Red Cross headquarters. Today, both temporary and permanent exhibits like It Happened in Brooklyn expose Brooklyn history.
Admission: adults $6, seniors and students $4, children under 12 free. Wednesday-Friday, Sunday noon-5 p.m., Saturday 10 a.m.-5 p.m.

BROOKLYN MUSEUM OF ART
Prospect Park, 200 Eastern Parkway, Brooklyn, 718-638-5000

Housed in a 560,000-square-foot Beaux-Arts building, this is one of the oldest and largest art museums in the country. The permanent collections represent a wide range of mediums and cultures, with everything from ancient Egyptian masterpieces and Andean textiles to Rodin sculptures and Winslow Homer paintings. The "First Saturday" series (the first Saturday of every month, 5-11 p.m.) featuring free concerts, performances, films, dances and dance lessons.

Admission: adults $8 suggested, seniors and students $4 suggested, children under 12 free. Wednesday-Friday 10 a.m.-5 p.m., Saturday-Sunday 11 a.m.-6 p.m

CONEY ISLAND
1208 Surf Ave., Brooklyn, 718-372-5159; www.coneyisland.com

Boardwalks, hot dogs and roller coasters: You'll find them all here. One of the most popular amusement areas of the early 20th century, the south Brooklyn neighborhood (which is actually a peninsula and not an island) feels stuck in a bit of a time warp, with its rickety boardwalks and old-school theme parks. The fate of these amusement parks—most notably the recently shuttered Astroland—has been up in the air for years, but for now some remain open, allowing a new generation to experience vintage rides such as the Cyclone, one of the oldest (and coolest) wooden roller coasters still in operation. Recent additions, including KeySpan Park (home of the minor-league Brooklyn Cyclones) have helped breathe new life into the stagnant neighborhood. But Coney Island is more than just fun in the sun. Indoor entertainment is also available in the form of the New York Aquarium and Coney Island Museum.

Open year-round; amusement parks open Easter-Labor Day.

GATEWAY NATIONAL RECREATION AREA
Kings Highway and Flatbush Avenue, Brooklyn, 718-354-4606; www.nps.gov/gate

This sprawling collection of urban recreation areas consists of approximately 26,000 acres of land and water covering areas of two states, New York and New Jersey. Jamaica Bay Wildlife Refuge in Broad Channel, Queens wildlife observation and hiking trails, and Floyd Bennett Field in Brooklyn offer attractive nature observation opportunities. Jacob Riis Park in Queens, with a mile-long boardwalk, offers beach and waterfront activities and practice your angling skills at Fort Tilden in Queens. The free summer weekend concert series on Canarsie Pier in Brooklyn is a hit with locals.

Free. Daily.

NEW YORK AQUARIUM
West Eighth Street and Surf Avenue, Brooklyn, 718-265-3474; www.nyaquarium.org

A varied collection of marine life that includes sharks, beluga whales, seals, seahorses, jellyfish, penguins, sea otters and walruses resides here. This home to more than 8,000 animals is New York's only aquarium, as well as the nation's oldest. If you visit between April and October, you might see dolphin feedings and sea lion shows.

Admission: adults $13, seniors $10, children 3-12 $9, children under 3 free. April-May, September-October, Monday-Friday 10 a.m.-5 p.m., Saturday-

Sunday 10 a.m.-5:30 p.m.; June-August, Monday-Friday 10 a.m.-6 p.m., Saturday-Sunday 10 a.m.-7 p.m.; November-March, daily 10 a.m.-4:30 p.m.

PROSPECT PARK

95 Prospect Park West, Brooklyn, 718-965-8951; www.prospectpark.org

Central Park may be New York's most famous, but ask any Brooklynite about their favorite green space, and they'll be quick to sing the praises of this 585-acre park in the heart of their beloved borough. Designed by Central Park architects Frederick Law Olmsted and Calvert Vaux, Prospect Park features a 90-acre spread of grass aptly name the Long Meadow, plus Brooklyn's only forest and a zoo with nearly 400 animals. In the park's boathouse, you can visit the first urban Audubon Center for hands-on nature exhibits. The park is also home to an antique carousel, frequent concerts and performances. Daily 5 a.m.-1 a.m.

WHERE TO STAY

★★★NEW YORK MARRIOTT AT THE BROOKLYN BRIDGE

333 Adams St., Brooklyn, 718-246-7000, 888-436-3759; www.brooklynmarriott.com

Located in downtown Brooklyn, this hotel features spacious guest accommodations with wonderful amenities—luxurious bedding, massaging showerheads, plush bathrobes and in-room video games. A large indoor lap pool with a whirlpool and Jacuzzi, and complimentary guest access to Eastern Athletic Club provide ways to stay fit while on the road.

665 rooms. Restaurant, bar. Business center. Fitness center. Pool. $151-250

WHERE TO EAT

★★AL DI LA

248 Fifth Ave., Brooklyn, 718-636-8888; www.aldilatrattoria.com

Past the crush of hungry waiting diners and thick velvet drapes at the door lies a cozy dining room where a glassy chandelier suspends from the ceiling. You'll think you can hear gondoliers singing outside when you tuck into the authentic Northern Italian dishes like creamy cuttlefish risotto, braised rabbit and pillowy squash ravioli sautéed in brown butter and sage. Years of positive reviews and a no-reservations policy create painfully long waits on weekends, but the restaurant's wine bar around the corner is a colorful and comfortable spot to happily spend your wait.

Northern Italian. Dinner. Closed Tuesday. $36-85

★★ALMA

187 Columbia St., Brooklyn, 718-643-5400; www.almarestaurant.com

After many years as chef at Zarela, one of Manhattan's most popular authentic Mexican restaurants, chef Gary Jacobson decided to take his soulful chile-laden fare to Brooklyn. At Alma, a bi-level restaurant and bar with a stunning lantern-lit roof deck with skyline views, you will find that the food has remained as good as it was on Second Avenue. Guacamole; tortillas filled with braised duck; sweet, warm tamales; and tender seafood ceviche make up some of the best appetizers. Generous entrées include ancho chile rellenos stuffed with shredded pork, raisins, and green olives.

Mexican. Dinner, Saturday-Sunday brunch. Reservations recommended. Outdoor seating. Bar. $16-35

★★BLUE RIBBON BRASSERIE

280 Fifth Ave., Brooklyn, 718-840-0404; www.blueribbonrestaurants.com

Blue Ribbon is everything a good brasserie should be—woody and warm, with a menu that leans heavily on upgraded comfort classics like strip steak and fried chicken but expertly folds in worldly touches like paella. The candlelit eatery (the crown jewel of the local empire that includes Blue Ribbon Sushi and Blue Ribbon Bakery) excels with its always-fresh raw bar and juicy bomb of a burger. Tip for the chef-obsessed: With a kitchen that serves until 4 a.m. (at the Soho location), Blue Ribbon has long been a favorite late-night hangout for the toqued set after they finish shifts at nearby restaurants. Contemporary American. Dinner. $36-85

★★BLUE RIBBON SUSHI

278 Fifth Ave., Brooklyn, 718-840-0408; www.blueribbonrestaurants.com

Blue Ribbon Sushi is the beloved Brooklyn sibling of the Bromberg brothers' Blue Ribbon Sushi in Manhattan. Located on a thriving strip of Fifth Avenue in Park Slope, this lively wood-accented restaurant and sushi bar offers the same winning formula the Brombergs offer in Manhattan. Expect the best raw fish in town, receptive and knowledgeable service, and a tremendous selection of sake—but there won't be a table after 7 p.m. without a wait. Japanese, sushi. Dinner, late-night. Closed Monday. Children's menu. $16-35

★★CHESTNUT

271 Smith St., Brooklyn, 718-243-0049; www.chestnutonsmith.com

Chestnut, a cozy spot on Cobble Hill's restaurant row (Smith Street), attracts fans from both the neighborhood and Manhattan. With its wide French doors, high blond chestnut-beamed ceilings and raw slate-tiled walls, the restaurant is a warm, lively gathering place that will make you feel like staying a while. The menu features rustic dishes like chicken liver and apple toast as well as more elegant dishes like tea-smoked scallops with fingerling potatoes and sweet-hot mustard, and comforting plates like roasted organic chicken with artichokes and soft polenta.

American. Dinner, Sunday brunch. Closed Monday. Reservations recommended. Outdoor seating. Bar. $16-35

★★CONVIVIUM OSTERIA

68 Fifth Ave., Brooklyn, 718-857-1833; www.convivium-osteria.com

Convivium Osteria is a local gem serving some of the most soul-satisfying Mediterranean fare in the borough, if not all of New York City. With a setting straight out of a hillside in Tuscany, the restaurant is all aglow in candlelight and a rustic, distressed vintage design that makes you feel like it's been here forever. The menu is stocked with country-style dishes from Spain, Portugal and Italy that focus on robust flavors in casseroles, as well as earthy pastas, slow-cooked meats and plentiful amounts of preserved, cured, and smoked ingredients—think salt cod and lots of delicious pig parts. Mediterranean. Dinner. Outdoor seating. $16-35

★DINER

85 Broadway, Brooklyn, 718-486-3077; www.dinernyc.com

Williamsburg hipsters march in masses to Diner like ants to a picnic. Indeed, this place often feels like a zoo for young, thrift-shop clad locals. The menu is as fun as the setting —a loungy, refurbished dining car—with contemporary American dishes including juicy burgers, fresh salads and crispy golden fries. American. Lunch, dinner, late-night, Saturday-Sunday brunch. $15 and under.

★GRIMALDI'S PIZZERIA
19 Old Fulton St., Brooklyn, 718-858-4300; www.grimaldis.com/brooklyn.htm
If the line snaking down the sidewalk for a red-and-white-checkered-table cloth-topped table doesn't tip you off, then we'll spell it out: The coal-oven pizzas here are sublime, from the creamy ricotta cheese topping down to the blistered crust underneath. A large pie is just $15 and toppings add a few dollars more, so if you can't get a table, order one to go—this pizza tastes just as good when you're eating it sitting on the stoop outside. Grimaldi's is near the base of the Brooklyn Bridge, in fashionable Dumbo, making the walk over the bridge and back to Manhattan easy as pie..
Pizza. Lunch, dinner. $15 and under..

★★★THE GROCERY
288 Smith St., Brooklyn, 718-596-3335; www.thegroceryrestaurant.com
Located about 20 minutes from Manhattan in this pretty Brooklyn neighborhood, the Grocery is an unassuming-yet-overachieving eatery specializing in exceptional farmers market fare (roasted beets with goat cheese ravioli, slow-rendered duck breast with kasha) churned out by chefs Charles Kiely and Sharon Pachter, a low-key husband-and-wife team. The 30-seat restaurant feels quaint—with the chefs sometimes even serving the food. There's a positively lovely garden out back and sage-green walls inside, so anywhere you dine is a delight. But the prices ($130 for a six-course tasting menu with wine) remind you that Brooklyn is just a stone's throw from Manhattan. Contemporary American. Dinner. Closed Sunday-Monday. $16-35

★★M SHANGHAI BISTRO & DEN
129 Havenmeyer St., Brooklyn, 718-384-9300; www.mshanghaiden.com
Decorated in slinky style, with chocolate brown banquet tables, brick walls, and a moody soundtrack, M Shanghai is a lovely den of design and food, and graciously presided over by owner May Liu. The menu skirts from the fray with vibrant dishes of steamed dumplings and puffy pork buns, with deliciously flavored main courses such as shredded pork with bean curd and salmon with well-seasoned tofu sauce.
Chinese. Lunch, dinner, late-night. Closed Monday. Bar. $16-35

★★★PETER LUGER STEAK HOUSE
178 Broadway, Brooklyn, 718-387-7400; www.peterluger.com
Just over the East River in a somewhat-sketchy part of Brooklyn near the Williamsburg Bridge is the legendary Peter Luger's, whose dining room can only be described as beer-hall chic—weathered wooden tables, a few beer steins on the shelves and somewhat surly servers who seem like they've been here since the restaurant opened in 1887. The Forman family, which owns the venerable steakhouse, personally selects the prime beef and then dry ages it onsite, resulting in tasty cuts that go unrivaled by other steakhouses. Our advice: Skip the menu and simply explain whether you want steak for one,

for two and so on. Sides are simple classics, like German fried potatoes and creamed spinach, intended to keep the buttery broiled porterhouse the deserved star of the meal. Unless you have a Peter Luger credit card (apply online at the restaurant's Web site), you must pay cash or risk the wrath of a crusty, bow-tied waiter.

Steak. Lunch, dinner. $36-85

★★RELISH

225 Wythe Ave., Brooklyn, 718-963-4546; www.relish.com

At Relish, a sleek, refurbished railcar diner, you can dig into contemporary Southern American fare in style. This former dining car is now a bright, stylish, windowed hang, offering regional comfort food like macaroni and cheese, hearty cheeseburgers, and rich, smoked pork loin with spiced mango chutney. Relish is quite the popular spot on weekends, when the crowds line up for the eggs with Serrano ham and cheddar grits.

American. Lunch, dinner, Saturday-Sunday brunch. Bar. $16-35

★★★RIVER CAFÉ

1 Water St., Brooklyn, 718-522-5200; www.rivercafe.com

Located on the Brooklyn waterfront with an unmatched view of the East River and the twinkling Manhattan skyline, this elegant old timer has always been a favorite for celebrating special occasions. The kitchen prepares sophisticated, artistically plated new American fare such as lobster, rack of lamb and duck. The wine list is award winning, and the service is unobtrusive.

American. Lunch, dinner. Reservations recommended. Outdoor seating. Jacket required. Bar. $36-85

★★SAUL

140 Smith St., Brooklyn, 718-935-9844; www.saulrestaurant.com

Known for its terrific contemporary American menu—courtesy of chef/owner Saul Bolton—Saul is urbane in décor, with warm, sandy tones and exposed brick walls. The modest menu reflects Bolton's training at Le Bernardin; expect plates adorned with stunning seasonal ingredients and simple, flavorful preparations of everything from diver scallops to leg of lamb and foie gras. Order with dessert in mind; Saul is known for its sweets, especially the classic baked Alaska.

American. Dinner, Sunday brunch. Bar. $16-35

★★SEA

114 N. Sixth St., Brooklyn, 718-384-8850; www.seathairestaurant.com

Sea is known just as much for its wild Zen-inspired disco décor (complete with an in-ground pool watched over by a golden Buddha) as it is for its fiery Thai food. Often crowded and loud, with fast servers interested in turning tables, Sea may not be a peaceful place to dine, but it sure is a tasty one. The menu includes dishes like whole red snapper, rice paper-wrapped spring rolls, and a fun list of desserts like the crispy banana with green tea ice cream.

Thai. Lunch, dinner, late-night. Reservations recommended. Bar. $16-35

★★SUPERFINE
126 Front St., Brooklyn, 718-243-9005

Located in DUMBO, Superfine is a casual neighborhood eatery with a warm, earthy vibe marked by brick walls, high ceilings and views of the Manhattan Bridge. The kitchen boasts some serious skills, turning out robust Texas-style fare like seared duck breast with rutabaga and sliced shiitake mushrooms, and grilled pork chops with mashed potatoes and bitter greens. On Sunday, brunch is entertained by a bluegrass band and burritos laced with eggs, refried beans and zesty salsa.

American. Lunch, dinner, Sunday brunch. Closed Monday. Bar. $16-35

MANHATTAN (NEW YORK)
WHAT TO SEE
AMERICAN FOLK ART MUSEUM

45 W. 53rd St., New York, 212-265-1040; www.folkartmuseum.org

This museum houses an impressive collection of folk art of all types, including paintings, sculptures, quilts, needlework, toys, weather vanes and furniture. Be sure to check out the collection of Henry Darger manuscripts, paintings and watercolors.

Admission: adults $9, students and seniors $7, children under 12 free. Tuesday-Thursday, Saturday-Sunday 10:30 a.m.-5:30 p.m., Friday 10:30 a.m.-7:30 p.m

AMERICAN MUSEUM OF NATURAL HISTORY

79th Street and Central Park West, New York, 212-769-5100; www.amnh.org

One of the largest natural history institutions in the world, this enormous Upper West Side museum is famous for its fossil halls, including two dinosaur halls that are home to more than one million specimens (about 600 are actually on display). Throughout the museum you'll also find life-like dioramas with taxidermied animals like bears, elephants and jaguars in their natural habitats. A few of the stuffed elephants on display in the Hall of African Mammals came courtesy of famous folks like Theodore Roosevelt, who often sent the museum animals he collected during safaris. The Rose Center for Earth and Space, which was completed in 2000, features a renovated planetarium and exhibit halls covering the 13-billion year history of the universe.

Admission: adults $15, students and seniors $11, children 2-12 $8.50. Daily 10 a.m.-5:45 p.m.

ANGELIKA FILM CENTER

18 W. Houston St., New York, 212-995-2000; www.angelikafilmcenter.com

Visit this Soho arthouse that has attracted lovers of independent film for years. You'll find a generally urbane crowd at the diverse films shown in the theater. The Angelika Cafe in the lobby area is a great place to grab a latte and a scone before a flick or a soda and a sandwich after the movie. On Sunday mornings, the cafe is a popular spot for locals to relax and enjoy a coffee and The New York Times.

Admission: adults $12.50, seniors and children $9. Showtimes vary.

ASIA SOCIETY AND MUSEUM

725 Park Ave., New York, 212-288-6400; www.asiasociety.org

Masterpieces of Asian art, donated by founder John Rockefeller, make up most of this museum's permanent collection. Its works include sculptures, ceramics and paintings from places such as China, Korea, Japan and India. In addition, the museum offers a schedule of films, performances and lectures. The Asia Society also has a lovely indoor sculpture garden and cafe, which make for a nice stop on a hectic day of sightseeing.

Admission: adults $10, seniors $7, students $5, children under 16 free. Tuesday-Thursday, Saturday-Sunday 11 a.m.-6 p.m., Friday 11 a.m.-9 p.m.

BERGDORF GOODMAN

754 Fifth Ave., New York, 212-753-7300; www.bergdorfgoodman.com

With designer handbags that can set you back as much as $4,000, $700 swimsuits and nightgowns that cost $500, Bergdorf Goodman is one of the city's most posh department stores. Ladies who lunch, yuppie professionals and stylish hipsters with trust funds are equally at home in this shopping mecca. The store's windows are attractions themselves.

Monday-Wednesday, Friday-Saturday 10 a.m.-7 p.m., Thursday 10 a.m-8 p.m., Sunday noon-6 p.m.

BLOOMINGDALE'S

1000 Third Ave., 212-705-2000; www.bloomingdales.com

Everyone in New York knows the name Bloomingdale's and the sight of its famous brown shopping bags. This world-renowned department store loved by locals and tourists alike, sells a mix of merchandise in a modern setting. You can find designer clothing for men and women, high-quality housewares, jewelry, cosmetics and just about everything else. A newer Soho location (504 Broadway) focuses on contemporary collections.

Free. Monday-Friday 10 a.m.-8:30 p.m., Saturday-Sunday 10 a.m.-7 p.m.

BLUE NOTE

131 W. Third St., New York, 212-475-8592; www.bluenote.net

For some of the world's best names in jazz, head downtown to Greenwich Village and the Blue Note. This nightclub has played host to many well-known jazz performers, as well as rising stars. Although the cover charge is higher here than at many other venues, the acts are worth it. Monday night, when the record companies promote new releases, costs $10. The club also serves a variety of food and drinks.

Admission: prices vary. Daily 8 p.m., 10:30 p.m.

BOWLING GREEN

Broadway and Whitehall Street, New York

This small, wedge-shaped plaza has at least two claims to historical fame. In 1626 it was the spot where Dutch governor Peter Minuit purchased Manhattan for $24 worth of goods, leading some to call this grassy parcel the birthplace of New York. It also happens to be NYC's first official park. Today, most visitors know it as the home of the bronze sculpture Charging Bull, a 7,000-pound bronze statue that stock market investors often rub for good luck.

Free. Daily.

BOWLMOR LANES

110 University Place, New York, 212-255-8188; www.bowlmor.com

A New York landmark since 1938, this 42-lane, two-level bowling alley features a retro bar and lounge. Richard Nixon, Cameron Diaz and the Rolling Stones have all bowled these lanes, where a colorful Village crowd stays until all hours. Snack on anything from nachos and hamburgers to fried calamari and grilled filet mignon in the restaurant or have your meal brought straight to your lane. It's a funky, fun hangout, even if you don't bowl. No one under 18 is permitted after 7 p.m. Monday-Thursday and Sunday, and no one under 21 is admitted after 7 p.m. Friday and Saturday.

Admission: prices vary. Monday, Thursday 2 p.m.-2 a.m., Tuesday-Wednesday 2 p.m.-1 a.m., Friday noon-3:30 a.m., Saturday 11 a.m.-3:30 a.m., Sunday 11 a.m.-midnight.

BRYANT PARK

Between 40th and 42nd streets and 5th and 6th avenues, Mid-town

The park's central location just one block from Times Square, free entertainment all summer long and free wire-less Internet access makes it very popular with office workers and tourists alike. Entertainment includes concerts and movies on Monday nights after dusk. Bring a blanket and picnic and come early—the lawn starts filling up quickly after 5 p.m. The park also includes four 'wichcraft kiosks, where you can sample some of Top Chef judge Tom Colicchio's yummy food. These include a coffee kiosk, where you can also buy Greek yogurt and granola for breakfast; a creamery for ice cream, floats and milkshakes, or hot chocolate in winter; a soup and salad kiosk; and a sandwich kiosk near the north fountain. A fa-vorite spot in the park is the Reading Room, an open-air library where you can sit and read books and magazines.

CARNEGIE HALL

57th Street and Broadway, 212-247-7800; www.carnegiehall.org

This famous Midtown concert hall has played host to some of the most well-practiced classical, pop and jazz musicians of the last century, including Maria Callas, Sergei Rachmaninoff, Bob Dylan, Judy Garland, Frank Sinatra and Billie Holiday. Built by and named after wealthy businessman and philanthropist Andrew Carnegie, this six-story structure with an Italian Renaissance façade of terracotta and brick boasts not one, but three performance spaces. The Hall faced demolition in 1960 before the city bought it for $5 million.

Prices and showtimes vary. Tours: October-June by appointment. September-June, Monday-Friday 11:30 a.m., 2 p.m., 3 p.m

CASTLE CLINTON NATIONAL MONUMENT

Battery Park, New York, 212-344-7220; www.nps.gov/cacl

Built as a fort in 1811, this later was a place of public entertainment called Castle Garden where Jenny Lind sang in 1850 under P.T. Barnum's management. In 1855, it was taken over by the state of New York for use as an immigrant receiving station. More than eight million people entered the United States here between 1855 and 1890; Ellis Island was opened in 1892. The castle became the New York City Aquarium in 1896, which closed in 1941 and reopened at Coney Island in Brooklyn. The site has undergone modifications to serve as the visitor orientation/ferry departure center for the Statue of Liberty and Ellis Island.

Daily 9 a.m.-5 p.m.

CATHEDRAL CHURCH OF ST. JOHN THE DIVINE

1047 Amsterdam Ave., New York, 212-316-7540; www.stjohndivine.org

Under construction since 1892, when completed, this will be the largest Gothic cathedral in the world at 601 feet long and 124 feet high. Bronze doors of the central portal represent scenes from the Old and New Testaments. The great rose window, 40 feet in diameter, is made up of more than 10,000 pieces of glass. A tapestry, painting and sculpture collection is also housed here. The cathedral and five other buildings are on 13 acres with a park and garden areas, including the Biblical Garden.

Free. Monday-Saturday, 7 a.m.-6 p.m., Sunday 7 a.m.-7 p.m.

CENTRAL PARK

59th St. and Fifth Ave., New York, 212-360-3444; www.centralpark.org

Central Park was reclaimed in 1858 as 843 acres of swampland that was used as a garbage dump and occupied by the homeless. Landscape designer Frederick Law Olmsted fulfilled his dream to bring city dwellers the kind of refreshment found only in nature. A century-and-a-half later, the park still offers just that; today, it's a source of varied outdoor entertainment. Stop at the visitors' center, called the Dairy—mid-park at 65th Street—for a map and a calendar of events. Jog around the Reservoir or rent ice skates at Wollman Rink or at Lasker Rink, which becomes a swimming pool in the summer. Rent a rowboat at Loeb Boathouse or a kite from Big City Kites at Lexington and 82nd Street and walk over to the park to catch the breeze on the Great Lawn. If you have kids, visit one of the 19 themed playgrounds, the petting zoo, the Carousel, the raucous storytelling hour at the Hans Christian Andersen statue or the Model Boat Pond, where serious modelers race their tiny remote-controlled boats on weekends. In summer, something is going on every night, and it's free! See Shakespeare in the Park at the Delacorte Theater. Get comfortable on the Great Lawn to hear the New York Philharmonic or the Metropolitan Opera under the stars. SummerStage brings well-known artists to Rumsey Playfield for jazz, dance, traditional and contemporary musical performances. The Band Shell is the venue for classical concerts. Amble through the forested Ramble. Stroll down the venerable, elm-lined Mall and past the bronze statues of Balto the dog, Alice in Wonderland and famous poets.

Free. Daily.

CENTURY 21

22 Cortlandt St., New York, 212-227-9092; www.c21stores.com

This is a can't-miss store if you want designer merchandise at rock-bottom prices and have time to scavenge through aisles of items. The three-story department store sells men's, women's and children's clothing, cosmetics, housewares and electronics. The store's extended morning hours are a benefit for both New Yorkers who want to make purchases before work and early-bird tourists.

Free. Monday-Wednesday 7:45 a.m.-9 p.m., Thursday-Friday 7:45 a.m.-9:30 p.m., Saturday 10 a.m.-9 p.m., Sunday 11 a.m.- 8 p.m.

CHELSEA MARKET

75 Ninth Ave., Chelsea, 212-243-6005; www.chelseamarket.com
This sprawling urban marketplace has the stuff to make die-hard foodies take notice and picky eaters cry uncle. Once home to the Oreo cookie factory (they also made Fig Newtons and Saltines), Chelsea Market encompasses an entire city block and houses gourmet-goody shops, drool-worthy restaurants and even a few TV studios (Food Network and Oxygen most notably). You better come hungry if you're even going to scratch the surface of this gastronomical playland.
Monday-Friday 7 a.m.-9 p.m., Saturday-Sunday 10 a.m.-8 p.m.

CHELSEA PIERS SPORTS AND ENTERTAINMENT COMPLEX

24th Street and West Side Highway, New York, 212-336-6666; www.chelseapiers.com
Long a mooring point for luxury liners (the Titanic was bound for Chelsea Piers when it struck its fateful iceberg in April 1912), the Hudson River docks fell into a slow but steady decline as the jet-setting lifestyle sank nautical travel. Thanks to a $100 million renovation in the 1990s, Piers 59 through 62 were transformed into a 28-acre sports and entertainment complex boasting a 40-lane bowling alley, golf club (where swingers can tee off on 51 simulated championship courses), an ice skating rink, sports training facility and more. Athletes can soothe sore muscles with a hot-stone massage or clean up with a manicure at The Spa at Chelsea Piers.
Prices vary. Monday-Friday 6 a.m.-11 p.m., Saturday-Sunday 8 a.m.-9 p.m.

CHRISTIE'S

20 Rockefeller Plaza, New York, 212-636-2000; www.christies.com
Get a taste of high society at a Christie's auction. Whether you're just a spectator or you have lots of spare cash to purchase something wonderful, attending an auction at this institution is a thrilling, fast-paced experience. Items sold at auction at Christie's have included the "Master of Your Domain" script from the television show Seinfeld, gowns worn by the late Princess Diana and a Honus Wagner baseball card (the most expensive card ever sold).
Monday-Friday 9:30 a.m.-5:30 p.m.

CHRYSLER BUILDING

405 Lexington Ave., New York, 212-682-3070
One of the most iconic examples of Art Deco architecture, the Chrysler Building rises more than 1,000 feet (77 stories) above Lexington Avenue and 42nd Street. Designed to house the motorcar company's offices, architect William Van Alen added automotive accents like metal hubcaps, car fenders and radiator-cap gargoyles to the structure's façade. Briefly the tallest skyscraper in the world, it was soon eclipsed by the taller Empire State Building. Though there are no guided tours of the edifice, the lobby is open to visitors who wish to gaze at the ceiling's fresco depicting buildings, airplanes and the Chrysler assembly line.
Daily.

CIRCLE LINE CRUISES

Pier 83, W. 42nd Street and 12th Avenue, New York, 212-563-3200;
www.circleline42.com

Grab a seat on the port (left) side for a spectacular view of the skyline. Narrated by knowledgeable, personable guides, these tours take you past the Statue of Liberty and under the Brooklyn Bridge; if you opt for the three-hour cruise, you'll also see the New Jersey Palisades, a glorious sight in autumn. Food and drinks are available on board.
Admission: $19-34. April-December, daily; January-February, daily. Closed Tuesday-Wednesday; March-April, daily. Closed Tuesday.

CITY CENTER

131 W. 55th St., New York, 212-581-1212, 877-581-1212; www.citycenter.org

This landmark theater hosts world-renowned dance companies, including the Alvin Ailey American Dance Theater, the Paul Taylor Dance Company and Merce Cunningham Dance Company. It also presents American music and theater events. Downstairs, City Center Stages I and II host the Manhattan Theatre Club.
Prices vary. Showtimes vary.

THE CLOISTERS

99 Margaret Corbin Drive, Fort Tryon Park, New York, 212-923-3700;
www.metmuseum.org/cloisters

An extension of the Metropolitan Museum of Art, the Cloisters house approximately 5,000 pieces of medieval European art dating back to 800 A.D. with emphasis on works from the 12th through 15th centuries. This castle-like edifice incorporates elements from five medieval French cloisters and is a piece of art itself. Inside, you'll find one of The Cloisters' best-known works: seven wool-and-silk woven tapestries depicting The Hunt of the Unicorn. Many additional tapestries, sculptures, manuscripts and stained glass windows are also on display.
Admission: adults $20, seniors $15, students $10, children under 12 free. March-October, 9:30 a.m.-5:15 p.m.; November-February, 9:30 a.m.-4:45 p.m.

COLUMBIA UNIVERSITY

2960 Broadway, New York, 212-854-1754; www.columbia.edu

This Ivy League university was originally King's College; classes were conducted in the vestry room of Trinity Church. King's College still exists as Columbia College, with 3,000 students. The campus has more than 62 buildings, including the Low Memorial Library and the administration building (which has the Rotunda and the Sackler Collection of Chinese Ceramics and Butler Library, with more than five million volumes). The university numbers Alexander Hamilton, Gouverneur Morris and John Jay among its early graduates and Nicholas Murray Butler, Dwight D. Eisenhower and Andrew W. Cordier among its former presidents.
Daily.

COLUMBUS CIRCLE

Broadway and Central Park South, Columbus Circle

Once nothing more than a traffic nightmare—New York architecture critic

Paul Goldberger described Columbus Circle as "a chaotic jumble of streets that can be crossed in about 50 different ways, all of them wrong"—the historic plaza is now a destination for shopping, top-notch dining and general lounging, with traffic thankfully not so much an issue any longer. In the heart of the circle stands a 77-foot granite column topped with a marble sculpture of explorer Christopher Columbus, a gift from the Italian-American community to commemorate the 400-year anniversary of his historic voyage, surrounded by a large fountain where locals and visitors relax. Standing behind this is the Time Warner Center, home to more than 50 shops, the Mandarin Oriental Hotel, an enormous Whole Foods Market that locals love (and a great place to pick up a picnic before heading into the park), Jazz at Lincoln Center (where some of the best names perform on a regular basis), and CNN's New York studio.

THE DAKOTA

1 W. 72nd St., New York

The first and most famous of the lavish apartment houses on Central Park West, the Dakota got its name because it was considered so far north that New Yorkers joked that it might as well be in the Dakotas. Planned as a turreted, chateau-like structure, it was then embellished with Wild West ornamentation. It has been the home of many celebrities, including Judy Garland, Boris Karloff, John Lennon and Yoko Ono. On December 8, 1980, Lennon was shot and killed by a crazed fan at its gate. Five years later, Yoko Ono—who still resides here—had a section of Central Park visible from the Dakota landscaped with foliage and a mosaic with the title of Lennon's song Imagine. Today, that area is known as Strawberry Fields.

Admission: Entrance is not permitted, but the structure is viewable from the street or Central Park West. Daily.

EL MUSEO DEL BARRIO

1230 Fifth Ave., New York, 212-831-7272; www.elmuseo.org

Dedicated to Puerto Rican, Caribbean and other Latin American art, this museum features changing exhibits on both contemporary and historic subjects and houses a superb permanent collection of santos de palo or carved wooden saints. The museum also hosts films, theater, concerts and educational programs.

Admission: adults $6, students and seniors $4, children under 12 free. Wednesday-Sunday 11 a.m.-5 p.m.

ELLIS ISLAND IMMIGRATION MUSEUM

Ellis Island, New York, 212-344-0996; www.ellisisland.org

More than 40 percent of Americans can trace their ancestors' first steps on U.S. soil to the country's first federal immigration station, which opened shortly after the arrival of the Statue of Liberty in 1892. In search of the American dream, roughly 12 million immigrants passed through here before the station closed in 1954. Now it's open to visitors as an interactive museum, where you can take a self-guided tour, check out photographs, artifacts and even search records to locate family members.

Admission: Museum: free. Ferry transport: adults $12, seniors $10, children 4-12 $5, children under 4 free. Mid-April-October, 8:30 a.m.-6 p.m.; November-mid-April 9 a.m.-5 p.m.

EMPIRE STATE BUILDING

350 Fifth Ave., New York, 212-736-3100; www.esbnyc.com

King Kong perched atop its lofty spire. Cary Grant and Deborah Kerr made the observation deck a quintessential spot for romantics in 1957's An Affair to Remember. As New York's tallest—and most famous—skyscraper, it's no wonder many a movie moment have transpired atop this majestic marvel. Constructed shortly after its Art Deco cousin the Chrysler Building, the Empire State Building stands 1,224 feet tall—that's 1,860 steps to the top if you are thinking about climbing it by foot—with a design inspired by a simple pencil. Observatories on the 86th and 102nd floors, open year-round, promise an unparalleled view of the Big Apple.

Admission: adults $18.45, seniors $16.61, children $12.92. Daily 8 a.m.-2 a.m.

FAO SCHWARZ

767 Fifth Ave., New York, 212-644-9400; www.fao.com

Kids big and small will have a blast at the 50,000-square-foot playland that serves as the flagship for this famous high-end toy giant. (And yes, you can dance on the huge floor piano like Tom Hanks did in the movie Big.) The oldest and swankiest toy store in the country moved to its current Fifth Avenue location in 1986, where three floors are stuffed to the rafters. Kids can even create their own playthings at toy factories dedicated to Hot Wheels, Madame Alexander Dolls and Barbie.

Monday-Wednesday 10 a.m.-6 p.m., Thursday-Saturday 10 a.m.-7 p.m., Sunday 11 a.m.-5 p.m.

FEDERAL HALL NATIONAL MEMORIAL

26 Wall St., New York, 212-825-6888; www.nps.gov/feha

Greek Revival 1842 building on the site of the original Federal Hall, where the Stamp Act Congress met in 1765, George Washington was inaugurated April 30, 1789 and the first Congress met from 1789-1790. Originally a customs house, the building was for many years the sub-treasury of the United States. The John Quincy Adams Ward statue of Washington is on the Wall Street steps.

Free. Monday-Friday 9 a.m.-5 p.m.

FEDERAL RESERVE BANK OF NEW YORK

33 Liberty St., New York, 212-720-6130; www.ny.frb.org

Approximately one-third of the world's supply of gold bullion is stored here in a vault 80 feet below ground level. Marvel at cash handling operations and an historical exhibit of bank notes and coins. Tour reservations are required at least one week in advance.

Monday-Friday 9:30 a.m.-3:30 p.m.

FLATIRON BUILDING

175 Fifth Ave. (between 22nd and 23rd streets), Flatiron District

It's been said that when this laundry iron-shaped wonder was completed in 1902, it caused such irregular wind patterns that women's skirts would blow up as they walked down 23rd Street. Throngs of men crowded the street hoping to catch a glimpse of the show, but they were shooed away by police officers giving them what became known as the "23 Skidoo" (a derivative of skedaddle). The structure may not cause such a ruckus nowadays, but it is still considered a jewel of New York's skyline Designed by famed Chicago architect Daniel Burnham, this Beaux Arts beauty made of limestone and terracotta measures an amazingly slim six-and-a-half feet wide at its apex.

FRAUNCES TAVERN MUSEUM

54 Pearl St., New York, 212-425-1778; www.frauncestavernmuseum.org
The museum is housed in the historic Fraunces Tavern and four adjacent 19th-century buildings. It interprets the history and culture of early America through permanent collections of prints, paintings, decorative arts and artifacts, changing exhibitions and period rooms, one of which, the Long Room, is the site of George Washington's farewell to his officers at the end of the Revolutionary War.
Admission: adults $10, seniors and children 7-18 $5, children under 7 free. Monday-Saturday noon-5 p.m.

THE FRICK COLLECTION

1 E. 70th St., New York, 212-288-0700; www.frick.org
The mansion of Henry Clay Frick, wealthy tycoon, infamous strikebreaker and avid collector of art, contains a remarkably diverse assemblage of paintings. The walls of one room are covered with large, frothy Fragonard depicting the Progress of Love. In other rooms are masterworks by Bellini, Titian, Holbein, Rembrandt, El Greco, Turner, Degas and many others.
Admission: adults $15, seniors $10, students $5. Tuesday-Saturday 10 a.m.-6 p.m., Sunday 11 a.m.-5 p.m. No children under 10; under 16 must be accompanied by an adult.

GENERAL GRANT NATIONAL MEMORIAL

122nd Street and Riverside Drive, New York, 212-666-1640; www.nps.gov/gegr
The largest mausoleum in North America, the General Grant National Monument is the home of Ulysses S. Grant's tomb, along with that of his wife. When Grant died in 1885, he had led the North to victory in the Civil War and served two consecutive terms as President of the United States before retiring to New York City. General Grant was so popular that upon his death, more than 90,000 private citizens donated a total of $600,000 (the equivalent of over $11.5 million in today's dollars) to help in the building of his tomb. The tomb was dedicated on April 27, 1897, on the 75th anniversary of Grant's birth. Located near picturesque Columbia University, the monument draws more than 75,000 visitors annually.
Daily 9 a.m.-5 p.m.

GRAND CENTRAL TERMINAL

87 E. 42nd Street, New York, 212-532-4900; www.grandcentralterminal.com
This Beaux Arts-style behemoth is more than just a place to hop a train. Originally constructed in 1871 at the behest of Cornelius Vanderbilt, then rebuilt between 1903 and 1913, Grand Central Terminal is an architectural gem, a bustling transportation center, and a lively retail and dining district. The station's expansive main concourse—with its celestial ceiling (keep your eyes peeled for backwards constellations) and acorn and oak-leaf dec-

orations (symbols of the Vanderbilt family)—is by far the building's most iconic section.

Daily 5:30 a.m.-1:30 a.m.

GROUND ZERO
Lower Manhattan, New York

Nearly a decade after the horrific attacks of September 11, 2001, the old World Trade Center site is alive with the sound of jackhammers and bulldozers as new buildings begin to take shape against lower Manhattan's skyline. The first completed building, the office complex at 7 World Trade Center, opened its doors in May 2006. But for the most part, the site is still shrouded by chain link fences and barricades. The National September 11 Memorial and Museum is scheduled for a 2011 opening, but in the meantime, there are a variety of ways to pay tribute and recognize the events of September 11. Pedestrian bridges across West Street, located on both Liberty and Vesey streets, provide a view of the site, as does the PATH train station and the World Financial Center in nearby Battery Park. The Tribute WTC Visitor Center *(120 Liberty St., 866-737-1184)* and Ground Zero Museum Workshop *(420 W. 14th Street, 646-509-0456)* exhibit artifacts, photographs and highlight the stories of those we lost.

Admission: prices vary. Daily. Ground Zero Museum Workshop: Closed Wednesday.

INTERNATIONAL CENTER OF PHOTOGRAPHY
1133 Avenue of the Americas, New York, 212-857-0000; www.icp.org

Photography buffs won't want to miss the International Center for Photography, recently relocated from the Upper East Side to Midtown. In these spacious galleries, you'll find changing exhibits featuring everyone from Weegee to Annie Leibovitz.

Admission: adults $12, students and seniors $8, children under 12 free. Tuesday-Thursday, Saturday-Sunday 10 a.m.-6 p.m., Friday 10 a.m.-8 p.m.

JACOB K. JAVITS CONVENTION CENTER
655 W. 34th St., New York, 212-216-2000; www.javitscenter.com

This exposition hall has 900,000 square feet of exhibit space and more than 100 meeting rooms. Designed by I.M. Pei, the center is easily recognized by its thousands of glass cubes that reflect the skyline by day.

Admission: prices vary. Daily.

LIBERTY HELICOPTER TOURS
Downtown Manhattan Heliport, West 30th Street and 12th Avenue, New York, 212-967-6464, 800-542-9933; www.libertyhelicopters.com

See the grand sights of the city—from the Empire State Building to Yankee Stadium to the Chrysler Building—all from magnificent heights. Liberty offers six different tours on its seven-passenger helicopters, which last from six minutes to as long as 25 minutes. Inclusive helicopter and cruise packages also available. A photo ID is required, and your bags will be screened. No carry-ons are allowed, except for cameras and video equipment.

Admission: prices vary. Daily.

LINCOLN CENTER FOR THE PERFORMING ARTS

70 Lincoln Center Plaza, New York, 212-875-5456; www.lincolncenter.org

Some of the Big Apple's most renowned performance groups, including the New York Philharmonic, the New York City Ballet and The Metropolitan Opera make this Upper West Side cultural destination their home. Rising stars frequent the 16-acre complex, too, because it's also the site of the revered Juilliard School (alumni include Robin Williams, Kelsey Grammer and Patti LuPone). The surrounding area, known as Lincoln Square, is a bustling restaurant and retail district and the nearby Time Warner Center contains a 1,200-seat theater designed specifically for jazz performances, if you need more of a culture fix.

Prices and showtimes vary.

LOWER EAST SIDE TENEMENT MUSEUM

108 Orchard St., New York, 212-431-0233; www.tenement.org

Looking to profit from the rising number of immigrants flooding New York in the mid-1800s, Lukas Glockner opened a cheap tenement at 97 Orchard Street to house them. Between 1863 and 1935, more than 7,000 tenants—primarily the poor and working class—occupied his sparse Lower East Side apartment building. It later fell into disrepair but was refurbished and opened as a museum in 1988—the first of its kind. Guided tours are required to learn about the immigrant experience and the traditions they brought with them from all over the world.

Admission: adults $17, students and seniors $13. Daily 11 a.m.-5 p.m.

MACY'S HERALD SQUARE

151 W. 34th St., New York, 212-695-4400; www.macys.com

They don't call Macy's flagship the "World's Largest Store" without reason. Boasting more than one million square feet of retail space, the shopping mecca might better be described as a small city. Nine floors hold an expansive inventory of designer perfumes, handbags, clothing and housewares, plus eateries like Au Bon Pain and Starbucks for famished fashionistas. The behemoth also sponsors several holiday extravaganzas every year, most famously the Macy's Thanksgiving Day Parade, when crowds cram the streets to catch glimpses of celebrity-studded floats and balloons as they glide down Broadway to Macy's storefront.

Monday-Saturday 10 a.m.-9:30 p.m., Sunday 11 a.m.-8:30 p.m.

MADISON SQUARE GARDEN

4 Pennsylvania Plaza, New York, 212-465-6741; www.thegarden.com

The Garden has been the site of major sporting events, concerts and other special events for more than a century. The present Garden, the fourth building bearing that name, opened in 1968. (The original Garden was actually on Madison Square.) It is the home of the New York Knicks and Liberty basketball teams, and New York Rangers hockey club. The Garden complex includes a 20,000-seat arena and a theater at Madison Square Garden, which features performances of the holiday classic A Christmas Carol every year as well as innumerable big-ticket concerts.

Prices and showtimes vary.

METROPOLITAN MUSEUM OF ART

1000 Fifth Ave., New York, 212-535-7710; www.metmuseum.org

Monet, da Vinci, Picasso, van Gogh and Degas—they're all part of the two-million-plus piece collection at this enormous Gothic-Revival building. Founded in 1870, the museum moved into this building on the eastern edge of Central Park along what's known as Museum Mile. The works here span more than 5,000 years and include the most definitive collection of American art in the world. Arguably the finest Egyptian art collection outside of Cairo is also here, and the collections from Europe and Asia are equally impressive. Those art history classes will pay off when you recognize such works as van Gogh's *Cypresses*, Gauguin's *la Orana Maria* and Degas's *The Dancing Class*.

Admission: adults $20, seniors $15, students $10, children under 12 free. Tuesday-Thursday, Sunday 9:30 a.m.-5:30 p.m., Friday-Saturday 9:30 a.m.-9 p.m.

METROPOLITAN OPERA COMPANY

Metropolitan Opera House, Lincoln Center, Broadway and 64th St., New York,
212-362-6000; www.metoperafamily.org

This is arguably the most well-known opera company in the world, historically showcasing orchestral and vocal talent with an international following. Maria Callas, Leontyne Price and the Met's most notable diva, Beverly Sills, have graced the stage here. Offstage, conductors such as Andre Previn and directors like Julie Taymor add their dash of star power. Even artists like Marc Chagall and David Hockney have showcased their talents here, creating high-concept set designs. The Met focuses on opera's canon but it doesn't shy away from premieres or new technology. Recent initiatives to further expand the Met's presence—perhaps as an effort to draw younger fans—include the broadcast of live Met shows in high-definition movie theaters around the world, public dress rehearsals (free) and reduced ticket prices (the cheapest go for as low as $15).

Prices and showtimes vary. September-May.

MORRIS-JUMEL MANSION

Roger Morris Park, 65 Jumel Terrace, New York, 212-923-8008; www.morrisjumel.org

Built in 1765 by Colonel Roger and Mary Philipse Morris, this mansion was George Washington's headquarters in 1776 and later became a British command post and Hessian headquarters. Purchased by French merchant Stephen Jumel in 1810, the house was the scene of the marriage of his widow, Madame Eliza Jumel, to former Vice President Aaron Burr in 1833. The mansion is the only remaining colonial residence in Manhattan.

Admission: adults $4, students and seniors $3, children under 12 free. Wednesday-Sunday 10 a.m.-4 p.m. Tuesday-Wednesday by appointment only.

MURRAY'S CHEESE

254 Bleecker St., New York, 212-243-3289, 888-692-4339; www.murrayscheese.com

For the best gourmet cheese selection in the city, pop into this 69-year-old New York institution in the Village. The shop will entice any discerning palate with its 250 varieties of domestic and imported cheeses.

Free. Monday-Saturday 8 a.m-8 p.m., Sunday 10 a.m-7 p.m.

MUSEUM OF CHINESE IN THE AMERICAS (MOCA)

215 Centre St., New York, 212-619-4785; www.mocanyc.org

This recently relocated cultural and historical museum in Chinatown, also known as MoCA, is a small but fascinating place filled with photographs, mementos and poetry culled from nearly two decades of research in the community. Women's roles, religion and Chinese laundries are among the subjects covered on exhibit.

Admission: adults $3, seniors and students $1. Tuesday-Saturday noon-6 p.m.

MUSEUM OF JEWISH HERITAGE-A LIVING MEMORIAL TO THE HOLOCAUST

Battery Park City, 36 Battery Place, New York, 646-437-4200; www.mjhnyc.org

Opened in 1997, this museum features thousands of moving photographs, cultural artifacts and archival films documenting the Holocaust and the resilience of the Jewish community. It's housed in a building the shape of a hexagon, symbolic of the Star of David. The East Wing houses a theater, special-exhibit galleries, a memorial garden and a café.

Admission: adults $12, seniors $10, students $7, children under 12 free. Sunday-Tuesday, Thursday 10 a.m.-5:45 p.m., Wednesday 10 a.m.-8 p.m., Friday 10 a.m.-3 p.m. Mid-March-October, also Friday 10 a.m.-5 p.m.

MUSEUM OF MODERN ART

11 W. 53rd St., New York, 212-397-6980; www.moma.org

The Museum of Modern Art, often referred to as "MoMA," contains one of the most impressive contemporary art collections in the world and has been recognized as a key player in the advancement of modern art in today's society. Within MoMA, there are over 150,000 works including Monet's Water Lilies and Van Gogh's Starry Night. MoMA also offers academic programs, film viewings (of the approximately 22,000 films in house), and an archive of more than 300,000 books and periodicals, which is open to the public. Though it is nearly impossible to avoid swooning at the artwork alone, be sure to admire the building itself since its $425 million facelift.

Admission: adults $20, seniors $16, students $12, children under 17 free. Sunday-Monday, Wednesday-Thursday, Saturday 10:30 a.m.-5:30 p.m., Friday 10:30 a.m.-8 p.m.

MUSEUM OF THE CITY OF NEW YORK

1220 Fifth Ave., New York, 212-534-1672; www.mcny.org

Explore unique aspects of the city in this Upper East Side mansion dating to 1930. Displays include a toy gallery; collections of decorative arts, prints and photographs; and an exhibit on Broadway, complete with costumes and set designs. Other exhibits feature slide shows, paintings, memorabilia and sculptures, all dedicated to the fascinating history of the city up to the present day.

Admission: adults $9, seniors and students $5, children under 12 free. Tuesday-Sunday 10 a.m.-5 p.m.

THE PALEY CENTER FOR MEDIA

25 W. 52nd St., New York, 212-621-6800; www.paleycenter.org

William Paley, the former head of CBS, founded this museum to collect, preserve and make available to the public the best of broadcasting. View special screenings or, at a private console, hear and see selections of your own choosing from the vast archive of more than 100,000 programs. From the comedy of Burns and Allen to the Beatles in America, and from a teary-eyed Walter Cronkite reporting on President Kennedy's assassination to a tireless Peter Jennings persevering through an endless 9/11, it's there for the asking. Admission: adults $10, seniors and students $8, children under 14 $5. Tuesday-Sunday noon-6 p.m., Thursday noon-8 p.m.

NEW YORK CITY FIRE MUSEUM

278 Spring St., New York, 212-691-1303; www.nycfiremuseum.org
Although it isn't really a children's museum, the New York City Fire Museum has great appeal for kids. Housed in an actual firehouse that was used until 1959, the museum is filled with new and old fire engines, helmets and uniforms, hoses and lifesaving nets. Retired firefighters take visitors through the museum, reciting fascinating tidbits of firefighting history along the way. Admission: adults $5, seniors and students $2, children under 12 $1. Tuesday-Saturday 10 a.m.-5 p.m., Sunday 10-a.m.-4 p.m.

NEW YORK HISTORICAL SOCIETY

170 Central Park West, New York, 212-873-3400; www.nyhistory.org
This monument to the history of the city recently reawakened after years of inactivity due to financial trouble. Spread out over many high-ceilinged rooms, the society presents temporary exhibits on everything from the legendary Stork Club—frequented by everyone from Frank Sinatra to JFK—to the small African-American communities that once dotted Central Park. The Henry Luce III Center for the Study of American culture features 40,000 objects, including George Washington's camp bed at Valley Forge and the world's largest collection of Tiffany lamps, as well as a nice collection of paintings, sculptures, furniture and decorative objects. Admission: adults $10, seniors $7, students $6, children under 13 free. Tuesday-Saturday 10 a.m.-6 p.m., Sunday 11 a.m.-5:45 p.m.

NEW YORK PUBLIC LIBRARY

Fifth Avenue and 42nd Street, New York, 212-930-0501; www.nypl.org
It took 500 workers two years to dismantle Fifth Avenue's Croton Reservoir (New York City's main water source), but once they were finished in 1902, the coast was clear for New York's first truly public library. This majestic Beaux Arts-style building (and the largest marble structure constructed in the U.S.) is also known as the Humanities and Social Sciences Library. Guarded by marble lions Patience and Fortitude, the library's initial collections were a conglomerate of materials from John Jacob Astor and James Lenox's failing libraries. The NYPL now has four major research libraries and 86 branches spread throughout the city. Most of the library's materials are free to use onsite. Free. Monday 11 a.m.-6 p.m., Tuesday-Wednesday 11 a.m.-7:30 p.m., Thursday-Saturday 11 a.m.-6 p.m., Sunday 1-5 p.m.

NEW YORK UNIVERSITY

22 Washington Square N., New York, 212-998-4524; www.nyu.edu
One of the largest private universities in the country, NYU is known for its

undergraduate and graduate business, medical and law schools, school of performing arts and fine arts programs. Most programs, including the Graduate Business Center, are located on the main campus surrounding Washington Square Park; the medical and dental schools are on the East Side.
Free. Daily.

RADIO CITY MUSIC HALL

1260 Avenue of the Americas, Midtown, 212-307-7171; www.radiocity.com

This venue drips with stardom, thanks to the many lumi-naries that have graced the Great Stage (among them the Dalai Lama, Bill Cosby and Frank Sinatra), not to mention those leggy bastions of Americana, the Radio City Rock-ettes. Some stars show up to perform, others to receive ac-colades at the Grammys, the Tonys or the MTV Video Mu-sic Awards, which have all been held here. The Christmas Spectacular is indeed spectacular, so if you're in town for the holidays and like traditional celebrations in that vein, make sure you check it out (but get tickets far in advance). Check the Web site for performance information.

Tour tickets: adults $17, seniors $14, children 12 and under $10. Tours: Daily 11 a.m.-3 p.m. Box office: Mon-day-Saturday 11:30 a.m.-6 p.m.

RIVERSIDE PARK

475 Riverside Drive, New York, 212-639-9675; www.nycgovparks.org

Hugging the banks of the Hudson River, this nearly 270-acre park stretches four solid miles. Yet another Frederick Law Olmsted-designed recreational area, the park has basketball courts, baseball and soccer fields, playgrounds, a skate park and even a public marina. You'll also find several monuments within the park's borders, including Grant's Tomb—the burial site of President Ulysses S. Grant and his wife Julia, and the largest in North America.
Free. Daily.

ROCKEFELLER CENTER

30 Rockefeller Plaza, New York, 212-632-3975; www.rockefellercenter.com

John D. Rockefeller leased this space in the heart of Midtown from Columbia University in 1928 hoping to create a new home for The Metropolitan Opera. Though his plans were derailed by the Great Depression, today Rockefeller Center is a bustling 19-building complex full of shops, restaurants and offices. Many well-known tenants are housed in the center, including Radio City Music Hall, NBC studios and the famous Rockefeller Center Christmas tree, for which an elaborate lighting ceremony is televised to kick off the holiday season each year. (Insider tip: The Top of the Rock observation decks at 30 Rockefeller Center on the 67th, 69th and 70th floors offer expansive views of Manhattan and are often less crowded than the Empire State Building observation deck.) Other popular activities include the NBC Studio Tour (peek backstage at Saturday Night Live, Late Night with Conan O'Brien and more), Today show tapings and wintertime skating in the plaza's rink.
Free. Daily.

SMITHSONIAN COOPER-HEWITT, NATIONAL DESIGN MUSEUM

2 E. 91st St., New York, 212-849-8400; www.ndm.si.edu

Once home to 19th-century industrialist Andrew Carnegie, this 64-room 1901 Georgian mansion is now a branch of the Smithsonian Institution dedicated to design and the decorative arts. The exhibits are temporary and focus on mediums such as ceramics, furniture, textiles and metalwork. Out back is a romantic garden, where concerts are sometimes presented.

Admission: adults $15, seniors and students $10, children under 12 free. Monday-Friday 10 a.m.-5 p.m., Saturday 10 a.m.-6 p.m., Sunday noon-6 p.m.

SOLOMON R. GUGGENHEIM MUSEUM

1071 Fifth Ave., New York, 212-423-3500; www.guggenheim.org

Critics the world over weren't sure what to make of this coiling ivory-colored tower rising from Manhattan's Upper East Side when it was unveiled in 1959. One heralded it "the most beautiful building in America," while another dubbed it "an indigestible hot cross bun." Many argued that its grandiose design overshadowed the art housed within its walls, though its famed architect Frank Lloyd Wright insisted that it perfectly complimented the works, creating an "uninterrupted, beautiful symphony." The building's design seems to bother few nowadays, as thousands flock to this contemporary and modern art museum for both its permanent collection (including works by Pablo Picasso, Marc Chagall, Salvador Dalí and Henri Matisse) and to take in Wright's awesome creation.

Admission: adults $18, seniors and students $15, children under 12 free. Saturday-Wednesday 10 a.m.-5:45 p.m., Friday 10 a.m.-7:45 p.m.

SOTHEBY'S

1334 York Ave., New York, 212-606-7000; www.sothebys.com

Attending an auction at this institution is a thrilling, fast-paced experience. Sotheby's has held auctions for items belonging to the Duke and Duchess of Windsor and innumerable other celebrities and jet-setters. It has fashion, book and manuscript, and vintage car departments, just to name a few. Publications such as New York magazine and The New York Times contain listings of upcoming events. Two forms of I.D. required to register for a paddle.

Free. Hours vary.

SOUTH STREET SEAPORT

19 Fulton St., New York, 212-732-7678; www.southstreetseaport.com

Part mall, part historic landmark, Lower Manhattan's South Street Seaport has a little something for everyone. In the shopping center you'll find all of the usual shops plus a TKTS discount ticket booth, in addition to restaurants like the Pan Asian Pacific Grill and food-court fare including Subway sandwiches and New York-style pizza. It's the South Street Seaport Museum, however, that really captures the spirit of the former commercial and transportation hub. The museum boasts an extensive collection of luxury liner memorabilia; visitors can feast their eyes on a scale model of the Titanic and a vast collection of cigarette cards, china, medals and tea sets.

Free. Daily. Museum: adults $10, seniors and students $8, children 5-12 $5, children under 5 free. Daily 10 a.m.-5 p.m.

ST. PATRICK'S CATHEDRAL

460 Madison Ave., New York, 212-753-2261; www.saintpatrickscathedral.org

Opened in 1879, St. Patrick's Cathedral is the largest gothic style Catholic cathedral in the United States and the seat of the Archbishop of New York. Though a popular tourist attraction, this ornate place of worship still hosts weekly mass services. Located in Midtown and facing Rockefeller Center, the cathedral is well known for its stunning architecture—including its beautiful rose window, a pieta which is three times the size of Michelangelo's, and altars designed by Tiffany & Co.

Daily 6:30 a.m.-8:45 p.m.

STATEN ISLAND FERRY

1 Whitehall St., New York, 718-815-2628; www.nyc.gov

Commutes aren't supposed to be romantic. But that's the best way to describe the 5.2-mile run between St. George Terminal in Staten Island and the White-hall Terminal in lower Manhattan. Sure, pragmatists would point out that the ferries provide Staten Islanders with free (you read that right—free!) transportation to their Manhattan day jobs. But those with a little imagination know the 25-minute ride is a tourist treasure, too, far more a sightseeing pleasure cruise than weary work trip. From the decks, passengers can take in picturesque views of the Statue of Liberty, Ellis Island and Manhattan's skyline.

Free. Monday-Friday midnight-11:30 p.m., Saturday-Sunday midnight-11 p.m.

STATUE OF LIBERTY NATIONAL MONUMENT

Liberty Island, New York, 212-363-3200; www.nps.gov/stli

Perhaps the most enduring symbol of America's promise of freedom and democracy, the Liberty Enlightening the World statue (its formal name) has served as a beacon welcoming immigrants and visitors for more than 120 years. A gift of friendship from the French, the monument was dedicated on October 28, 1886, and stands more than 305 feet from the ground to the top of the torch. Designer Frederic-Auguste Bartholdi placed several symbolic touches throughout the monument: The seven rays of Lady Liberty's crown represent the seven seas and continents of the world, and the tablet she holds in her left hand reads in Roman numerals "July 4th, 1776." The lady was restored for her centennial on July 2, 1986. Visitors are allowed onto the Statue's observation deck and can also get an inside view through a glass ceiling.

Free. Ferry transport: adults $12, seniors $10, children 4-12 $5, children under 4 free. Mid-April-October, 8:30 a.m.-6 p.m.; November-mid-April 9 a.m.-5 p.m.

STRAND BOOKSTORE

828 Broadway, Greenwich Village, 212-473-1452; www.strandbooks.com

Named after the famous London street, this independent bookstore was just one of 48 booksellers occupying New York's famous "Book Row" in the late 1920s. Today, the Strand is the only one left. The shop, which moved to its current location from Fourth Avenue in the 1950s, contains 18 miles of shelves stocked with new and used books, in addition to NYC's largest collection of rare books (think the first American edition of Alexis de Tocqueville's *Democracy in America*). The expansive store also hosts author signings and events.

Monday-Saturday 9:30 a.m.-10:30 p.m., Sunday 11 a.m.-10:30 p.m.

STUDIO MUSEUM IN HARLEM

144 W. 125th St., New York, 212-864-4500; www.studiomuseum.org

Founded in 1968, this museum is dedicated to black artists and culture in America and is spread out over several well-lit floors in a turn-of-the-century building. The permanent exhibit features works by masters such as Romare Bearden, James VanDerZee and Jacob Lawrence; temporary exhibits present a mixture of both world-renowned and emerging artists. The Studio is also known for its lively lecture and concert series, presented September through May.

Admission: adults $7, seniors and students $3, children under 12 free. Wednesday-Friday, Sunday noon-6 p.m., Saturday 10 a.m.-6 p.m.

TIMES SQUARE

Broadway and Seventh Avenue, New York, 212-768-1560; www.timessquare.com

More than one million people flock to the "crossroads of the world" each year to ring in the New Year after watching the ball drop. But there's plenty to see and do in this bustling neighborhood the other 364 days of the year. Named in honor of The New York Times (the iconic newspaper's offices were once located at the intersection of Seventh Avenue, Broadway and 42nd Street), Times Square is a 24-hour tourist's haven, overflowing with shopping, dining and cultural activities—a sharp contrast to the depressed, crime-ridden row of X-rated movie houses it was in the 1970s. You'll find mostly Mall of America-type shopping, including Hershey's Time Square and Sephora, but Restaurant Row (West 46th Street between Broadway and Ninth Avenue) will satisfy your grumbling stomach with eclectic options from Thai to tapas. Then it's just a short walk to one of the dozens of Broadway theaters for a show. And nothing beats a late-night stroll under the wash of Times Square's millions of twinkling bulbs. It may be 4 a.m., but you'll swear it's the middle of the afternoon. (Thanks to a zoning ordinance, all businesses must display illuminated signs in the area—it's actually against the law not to add that flash.)

Free. Daily.

TKTS DISCOUNT THEATER TICKETS

Broadway at 47th St., New York; www.tkts.com

With the price of Broadway shows closing in at upwards of $100 for decent seats, TKTS is a godsend to less-than-wealthy theater lovers. The more popular TKTS booth at Times Square (just look for lots of people standing in two lines) provides up to 50 percent discounted tickets on Broadway, off-Broadway, and some musical and dance events. Tickets are sold the day of performance for matinees and evening shows. The downtown booth (199 Water St.) sells tickets for evening day of performance and for matinees one day in advance. Generally, you will not be able to get tickets for the hottest shows in town through TKTS, but usually for ones that have been running a while. Lines are long, and you are not guaranteed anything by waiting in line. Have a first, second and third choice in mind. Only cash and travelers checks are accepted.

Free. Daily.

TRINITY CHURCH

Broadway at Wall St., New York, 212-602-0800; www.trinitywallstreet.org

This is the third building to occupy this site; the original was built in 1697. Its famous graveyard, favorite lunchtime spot of workers in the Financial District, contains the graves of Robert Fulton and Alexander Hamilton. The Gothic Revival brownstone church houses a museum. The parish center has a dining room..

Free. Monday-Friday 7 a.m.-6 p.m., Saturday 8 a.m.-4 p.m., Sunday 7 a.m.-4 p.m.

UNION SQUARE GREENMARKET

17th St. E. and Broadway, New York, 212-788-7476; www.cenyc.org

This busy year-round farmers' market is located at Union Square between 14th and 17th Streets and Broadway and Park Avenue. It's a chance to experience a bit of the country in the Big Apple, as farmers and other vendors sell fresh fruits, vegetables, cheeses, homemade pies, herbs, cut flowers and potted plants. Arrive early for the best selection.

Free. Monday, Wednesday, Friday-Saturday 8 a.m.-6 p.m.

UNITED NATIONS

First Avenue at 46th Street, New York, 212-963-8687; www.un.org

The 18-acre headquarters of this peacekeeping organization isn't technically in New York, but situated atop international territory belonging to all member countries. The complex encompasses four buildings, one of which is the Secretariat, an iconic, 39-story structure with green-glass-curtained exterior. Tours of the U.N. are available Monday through Friday and take visitors through various council chambers and the General Assembly Hall. Gifts donated by member countries, such as an ivory carving from China and drums from the Caribbean, are also on display.

Free. Tours: adults $12.50, seniors and students $8, children 5-12 $6.50. Monday-Friday 9:45 a.m.-4:45 p.m. Children under 5 are not permitted on tour.

WALL STREET

Between Broadway and South Street near the East River, Financial District

A flurry of crisp business suits and mobile gadgets, Wall Street is a stretch of pavement that has become synonymous with the U.S. financial industry. Named for the blockade constructed by Dutch colonists to protect themselves from British attacks, today it's known far better as the home of financially and historically relevant sites, including the New York Stock Exchange (NYSE) and Federal Hall. The NYSE, also known as the "Big Board," is the largest exchange in the world based on the value of its securities. As the nation's first capitol, Federal Hall was the sight of George Washington's inauguration, the first congressional meeting and the signing of the Bill of Rights. Today, the area is booming with new potential, as upscale luxury residences and a plethora of retail outlets prosper.

Free. Daily.

WASHINGTON SQUARE PARK

West Fourth Street and Waverly Place, New York

This potter's field-turned-park was once home to the public gallows, but today the hanging around is much more leisurely. Located in the heart of Greenwich Village, this green space is not only a popular haunt for sunbathing students from adjacent New York University, but a haven for chess players and street performers. The park's most famous landmark, Washington Arch, an Arc de Triomphe replica, was built between 1890 and 1892 to replace a wooden arch that had been erected to commemorate the centennial of George Washington's inauguration. In the 1960s, the park was a popular gathering spot for hippies and artists. Today, it's currently a perfect spot for a little New York City people-watching, particularly at the central fountain, though it's been embroiled in controversy as renovation plans for the park call for it to be moved 23 feet east to align with the Arch.

Daily 6 a.m.-1 a.m.

WHITNEY MUSEUM OF AMERICAN ART

945 Madison Ave., New York, 212-570-3600, 800-944-8639; www.whitney.org

In 1931, Gertrude Vanderbilt Whitney founded the Whitney Museum when she purchased a brownstone at 10 West 8th Street and turned it into the Whitney Studio, an exhibition space and social center for young progressive arts. It began with 700 works of contemporary American art, most from Whitney's own collection. Today, at its current location, the museum houses one of the foremost collections of 20th-century American paintings, sculptures, multimedia installations, photographs and drawings from Edward Hopper, John Sloan, Max Weber and more. Well-known for its annual and biennial exhibits that highlight current artists, the museum frequently purchases works from up-and-comers to keep its ever-changing collection fresh.

Admission: adults $15, seniors and students $10, children under 12 free.

Wednesday-Thursday, Saturday-Sunday 11 a.m.-6 p.m., Friday 1-9 p.m.

WOOLWORTH BUILDING

233 Broadway, New York

This Gothic-style skyscraper towering 792 feet above Manhattan's Financial District was built to house the now-defunct five-and-dime's headquarters. Funded completely with cash, the building was completed in 1913, and was the tallest in the world until the 927-feet tall 40 Wall Street came along in 1930. Its interior features a cruciform floor plan with vaulted ceilings, and boasts several humorous gargoyles depicting the building's key players including Mr. Woolworth counting his dimes and architect Cass Gilbert holding a model of the building. Coined the "cathedral of commerce," its opening was celebrated by President Wilson, who pushed a button in the White House to illuminate each floor and the building's façade. Sold by the Woolworth Company in 1998, the building now houses the New York University School of Continuing and Professional Studies' Center for Global Affairs, in addition to other tenants.

Free. Daily.

ZABAR'S

2245 Broadway, New York, 212-787-2000; www.zabars.com

This Upper West Side gourmet grocer is practically a New York icon. As their slogan says, Zabars really is New York. Started as an appetizing counter in 1934 by Louis and Lillian Zabar, the market now stretches nearly the length of an entire city block and sees more than 35,000 loyal customers every week. The grocer is known for both its extensive kitchen-gadget selection as well as its high-quality bagels, smoked fish counter, knishes, olives and cheeses, and there is still always a member of the Zabar family in the store. If you're craving something sweet, Zabar's Café also serves native-to-New York desserts like black-and-white cookies and cheesecake.

Free. Monday-Friday 8 a.m.-7:30 p.m., Saturday 8 a.m.-8 p.m., Sunday 9 a.m.-6 p.m.

SPECIAL EVENTS

BRYANT PARK SUMMER FILM FESTIVAL

42nd St., New York, 212-768-4242; www.bryantpark.org

Park yourself on the lawn at Bryant Park for its weekly film showing on summer evenings. Hundreds come each Monday night to see a movie and hang out once the sun goes down. Check the Web site or local papers to find out what's playing each week. Mid-June-August, Monday.

CENTRAL PARK CONCERTS

72nd St., and Fifth Avenue, New York, 212-860-1370; www.centralparknyc.org

The Great Lawn in Central Park opens itself up to free performances by the New York Philharmonic and the Metropolitan Opera Company each summer. Bring a blanket and a picnic and get there early to ensure a swath of grass. June-August.

FLEET WEEK

Pier 88, New York, 212-245-0072; www.cnrma.navy.mil/fleetweek/

In a scene right out of the Gene Kelly Navy-themed musical, On the Town, Navy and Coast Guard ships gather for a parade up the Hudson River that is a true spectacle of springtime in New York. After the ships dock by the museum, they are open to the public for tours. Expect to find Navy men and women all over the city, looking for a good time. Late May.

GREENWICH VILLAGE HALLOWEEN PARADE

West Fourth Street, New York; www.halloween-nyc.com

Straights, gays, men, women, kids, seniors and everyone in between dress in the wildest of costumes for this annual Halloween tradition in the West Village. Strangers become instant friends and everyone gets into the spirit at what has become the largest Halloween parade in the United States. Late October.

INDEPENDENCE DAY HARBOR FESTIVAL

East River and South Street, Seaport, New York

This is the nation's largest July 4 celebration. Come for fireworks, food stands and live music. Weekend of July 4.

MACY'S THANKSGIVING DAY PARADE

Broadway between 34th and 72nd streets, New York, 212-397-8222;
www.macysparade.com

Amazing floats, cheerful clowns (who are all volunteers and are either Macy's employees or friends and families of Macy's employees), and celebrities are all part of the parade, which starts at 9 a.m. and ends around noon (with Santa's arrival). One of the best viewing spots is on Herald Square in front of Macy's. Thanksgiving day.

NATIONAL PUERTO RICAN DAY PARADE

Fifth Avenue between 45th and 86th streets, New York, 718-401-0404;
www.nationalpuertoricandayparade.org

The National Puerto Rican Day Parade, Inc. was established to bring a national awareness to the Puerto Rican culture and its contribution to the culture and society of the United States. In addition, it promotes the study, improvement and advancement of Puerto Rican culture and the arts by encouraging, promoting, coordinating, developing, managing and participating in various cultural events. Mid-June.

NEW YORK SHAKESPEARE FESTIVAL & SHAKESPEARE IN THE PARK

81st St., and Central Park West, New York, 212-260-2400; www.publictheater.org

The words of Shakespeare ring out at the 2,000-seat outdoor Delacorte Theater in Central Park, near West 81st Street. Free tickets are distributed on the day of the performance at the Public Theater. June-September, Tuesday-Sunday.

NEW YORK CITY MARATHON

New York; www.nycmarathon.org

Which event attracts more than two million spectators nearly 40,000 participants from around the world and 12,000 volunteers? The grueling 26.2-mile New York City Marathon. Whether you're an experienced runner or a couch potato, to stand on the sidelines and to cheer on these amazing athletes during the world's largest marathon is a thrilling and rewarding experience. The event begins on the Staten Island side of the Verrazano-Narrows Bridge, winds through all five boroughs of the city and finishes up by Tavern on the Green restaurant in Central Park. First Sunday in November.

RINGLING BROS. AND BARNUM & BAILEY CIRCUS

Madison Square Garden, Seventh Ave. and 32nd St., New York, 212-465-6741;
www.ringling.com

The Greatest Show on Earth visits the city every spring. Expect the usual circus fare—elephants, trapeze artists, clowns and the like. For a special treat, view the parade of circus people and animals from 12th Avenue and 34th Street to the Garden on the morning before the show opens. March-April.

SAN GENNARO FESTIVAL

Little Italy, Mulberry Street between Canal and Houston Streets, New York;
www.sangennaro.org

More than 75 years old, this giant street festival in Little Italy salutes the patron saint of Naples with a celebratory Mass and a candlelit procession of the Statue of the Saint. More than a million people descend on Little Italy during these 11 days to feast on food from the old country, watch the parades, enjoy the live music and compete for the title of cannoli-eating champion. Mid-September.

ST. PATRICK'S DAY PARADE

Fifth Ave. between 44th and 86th Streets, New York; www.saintpatricksdayparade.com
This is New York's biggest annual parade with approximately 100,000 marchers. Don festive green apparel and join the celebration of Irish heritage. Mid-March.

WESTMINSTER KENNEL CLUB DOG SHOW

Madison Square Garden, 4 Pennsylvania Plaza, New York, 212-213-3165;
www.westminsterkennelclub.org
Nearly 3,000 top dogs and their owners take part in this two-day annual extravaganza leading up to the crowning of Best in Show on the second night of competition. Arrive two hours early each night, at about 6 p.m., and go to the huge backstage area. Here, you will be able to pet the dogs that vied for Best in Breed in competitions held earlier in the day. (Always ask the owner/handler for permission before petting an animal.) The owners and handlers welcome the public since they love showing off their pooches—they may even convince you to buy a future offspring of their show dogs. Best in Group competitions for the seven groups run from 8-11 p.m. each night. You can buy tickets for one or both nights. For the best deal, purchase a general admission, two-day pass. Mid-February.

WINTER AND SUMMER RESTAURANT WEEKS

New York; www.nycvisit.com
Many of the city's finest restaurants offer two- or three-course, fixed-price lunches at bargain prices during two weeks in summer and winter. This is a wildly popular promotion that natives can't wait to experience. Check local newspapers at the beginning of your trip to see which restaurants are participating and make a reservation. February and June.

WHERE TO STAY

★★★6 COLUMBUS

6 Columbus Circle, New York, 212-204-3000; www.sixcolumbus.com
There's an überchic aesthetic and too-cool-for-school vibe at this mod hotel, which replaced a dive that sat here long before it. The lobby's slender leather couch, white shag rug and powder-blue saucer chairs read I Dream of Jeannie, and that '60s feel carries through to the blue-toned Steven Sclaroff-designed rooms, decked out with teak walls, Saarinen-style side chairs and tables, and classic Guy Bourdin prints on the wall. The Euro crowd doesn't seem to mind unloading their Euros for current amenities such as maki from Blue Ribbon Sushi, or shelling out $4,500 a night for the privilege of staying in a two-story loft space with a terrace overlooking Central Park and Columbus Circle.
88 rooms. Restaurant, bar. $351 and up.

★★★60 THOMPSON

60 Thompson St., New York, 212-431-0400, 877-431-0400; www.60thompson.com

Beautiful is the operative term here. Opened in 2001, this boutique hotel's clientele and staff are just as attractive and stylish as the trendy rooms designed by Thomas O'Brien and Aero Studios. Sferra linens cover the dark-wood beds, products by Fresh stock the marble bathrooms and gourmet Dean & DeLuca goods fill the mini-bars. To top it all off, literally, the A60 rooftop lounge—with great downtown views that include water-tower topped lofts and the distant Empire State Building—is open only to members and hotel guests. More exclusive still is the "Thompson Loft"—a two-story penthouse with a marble fireplace and its own private rooftop terrace. Privacy in New York—now that's a beautiful thing.

100 rooms. Restaurant, bar. Fitness center. $351 and up.

★AFFINIA GARDENS

215 E. 64th St., New York, 212-355-1230, 866-246-2203; www.affinia.com

On the outside, Affinia Gardens may not look like anything special; but because it was originally erected as the first all-suite hotel in the 1960s, the roomy suites at this Upper East Side property feel more like home than a hotel. Modern dark-wood furniture and bright-colored sofas and accent pieces lend a cozier feel than the stark-and-sleek options available at so many other high-end hotel options, and some ground-floor suites even have outdoor patios. There's no onsite restaurant, but all rooms have kitchens, and the concierge services include 24-hour takeout food delivery. The hotel has also has a pet program that includes a dog-walking service.

129 rooms. Fitness center. Business center. Pets accepted. $351 and up.

★★★THE ALEX HOTEL

205 E. 45th St. New York, 212-867-5100; www.thealexhotel.com

This 33-story hotel near the Chrysler Building whisks you away from New York's constant bustle to a serene oasis where David Rockwell's minimalist décor proves instantly soothing. Clutter-free guest rooms are awash in a palette of whites, creams and earth tones, while limestone bathrooms have Frette towels and products by Frédéric Fekkai. If you have to stay in the city for more than a quick visit—or just hate to say goodbye—extended-stay suites make your time here comfortable with luxury Poggenpohl-fitted kitchens sporting everything from Sub-Zero refrigerators to Miele dishwashers.

203 rooms. Restaurant, bar. Fitness center. Business center. Pets accepted. $351 and up.

★★ALGONQUIN HOTEL

59 W. 44th St., New York, 212-840-6800; www.algonquinhotel.com

Since 1902 the Algonquin has been popular with theatrical and literary glitterati, most notably members of the legendary Round Table luncheons: The exclusive group of creative types, including Dorothy Parker, Edna Ferber and Harpo Marx, met at the hotel almost daily during the decade following World War II to exchange ideas and barbs (financing for The New Yorker magazine was secured here). Today, it's still loaded with character, from the antique furniture to its most popular current resident, Matilda the cat—the latest in a long line of felines that have called the hotel home since a wayward feline first wandered in and ended up staying in the 1930s. Rooms have recently been remodeled and include comfortable pillow-top beds, duvets and modern amenities like flat-screen TVs. For a special treat, make a reservation for dinner and a cabaret show at the famous Oak Room Supper Club, the hotel's dark-wood paneled restaurant where crooners like Harry Connick, Jr. and Diana Krall got their starts.

174 rooms. Restaurant, bar. Fitness center. Pets accepted. $251-350

★★AMERITANIA HOTEL

230 W. 54th St., New York, 212-247-5000; 800-555-7555;
www.ameritaniahotelnewyork.com

The Art Nouveau Ameritania Hotel's best feature is its proximity to some of Manhattan's most popular sights, including Broadway and Times Square. The large, sleek lobby is bathed in off-white hues and furnished with a mix of contemporary leather chairs and antique sofas. Rooms are chic, with warm tan and brown palettes, checkerboard-pattern carpets and platform beds. You'll also find down comforters, CD players and on-demand movies. Add free coffee in the morning and it's a pretty sweet deal, especially for the location.

219 rooms. $61-150

★★★THE AVALON

16 E. 32nd St., New York, 212-299-7000, 888-442-8256; www.avalonhotelnyc.com

Stately black marble columns and a mosaic floor make an elegant first impression at this Murray Hill boutique hotel. The elegant lobby is warm and inviting, with the look and feel of a mini European palace. Rooms feature desk chairs designed for comfort and functionality, as well as Irish cotton linens and velour bathrobes. Each room also comes with a signature body pillow.

100 rooms. Restaurant, bar. Complimentary breakfast. Fitness center. $151-250

★★★THE BENJAMIN

125 E. 50th St., New York, 212-715-2500, 800-637-8483; www.thebenjamin.com

Set in a classic 1927 building, this hotel has all the high-tech amenities a business traveler could want. It also offers comfortable accommodations in a sophisticated setting with earth tones and contemporary furnishings. A standout amenity is the pillow menu, which offers a choice of 10 different kinds of bed pillows and a guarantee of a refund if you do not wake well rested. The Benjamin's Wellness Spa offers body treatments with a holistic approach. Pets will also be pleased with the Dream Dog Program, offering your four-legged friend a three-choice bed menu, plush dog bathrobe, and more.

209 rooms. Restaurant. Spa. Pets accepted. $351 and up.

★★BENTLEY HOTEL

500 E. 62nd St., New York, 888-969-0069; www.bentleyhotelnewyork.com

It's a bit off the beaten path—just one block from the East River—but this stylishly mod hotel is just a short walk from Upper East Side favorites like Bloomingdale's. Despite the location, the vibe is decidedly downtown, with a sleek brown and polished-steel color scheme that starts in the lobby, which is furnished with dark brown leather sofas and tan club chairs. Shades of brown also color the rooms, which have marble baths, down comforters and

Belgian linens. Many also have striking river views and blackout shades that allow you to sleep past sunrise

196 rooms. Restaurant, bar. $61-150

★★★BOWERY HOTEL

335 Bowery, New York, 212-505-9100; www.theboweryhotel.com

This boutique spot in the Bowery—an area once home to legendary punk bar CBGB and long known for being more gritty than pretty—embodies the area's continuing gentrification. A short walk from Nolita, the East Village, Lower East Side and Soho, the latest venture for hoteliers Eric Goode and Sean MacPherson (Waverly Inn, Maritime Hotel), has a dimly lit lobby with leather- and velvet-upholstered furniture that feels old and cozy, minus any mustiness. The lounge, with its velvet banquettes, dark wood walls and fireplace, draws a cocktail-seeking crowd as do the outdoor patio and small back bar known for its absinthe-based concoctions. Guest suites have wood-slatted floors, marble bathrooms and floor-to-ceiling paned factory windows that overlook the neighboring tenements just to remind you that—despite the HD television, iPod stereo system and docking station, this isn't the Upper West Side. The location may be too rough around the edges for some, but the beautiful lounges, rustic restaurant and free copies of the New York Post will make you feel right at home.

135 rooms. Restaurant, bar. $351 and up.

★★★BRYANT PARK HOTEL

40 W. 40th St., New York, 212-869-0100, 877-640-9300; www.bryantparkhotel.com

For years, this hotel has attracted a who's-who list of designers, media bigwigs and celebs during New York's Fall and Spring Fashion Weeks, thanks to its proximity to the tents erected to host the runway shows across the street. The shows are moving to Lincoln Center this year, but no matter: many of the same fashionistas frequent this boutique property all year round anyway. They enjoy the amenities in the mod rooms (leather chairs, Tibetan rugs and Travertine marble bathrooms) such as high-definition flat-screen televisions, BOSE Wave music systems and Obus Forme sound therapy machines which lull them to sleep with gentle waterfall sounds and wakes them with chirping birds. There's also a loft meeting space that's popular for sample sales, a 70-seat theater-style screening room and "entertainment planner" (really just a clever title for the concierge) at guests' disposal. Japanese restaurant Koi and the large underground Cellar Bar are always packed with the young and fashionable. Book one of the 10 rooms that face the park—these come with terraces to enjoy the lovely views and all the activity that is always going on in Bryant Park.

129 rooms. Restaurant, bar. Fitness center. $251-250

★★★THE CARLTON ON MADISON AVENUE

88 Madison Ave., New York, 212-532-4100; www.carltonhotelny.com

It wasn't long ago that this now-stunning 1904 Beaux Arts building was a run down property that seemed destined for decay. But a $60 million, five-year renovation project headed by architect David Rock-well breathed brand-new life into the hotel. Today, the three-story lobby and lounge areas are bathed in opulent golds and creams, and the sound of the cascading waterfall here serves as a soothing background soundtrack. Rooms are all about what's plush and new, with Frette bedding, free wireless, and iHome systems. Preserving the hotel's original décor was important, too: An ornate 28-foot Tiffany stained-glass dome, discovered during renovations under such thick layers of dirt and tobacco tar that it was thought to be painted black, has been restored. The main downside: no spa or fitness center.

316 rooms. Restaurant, bar. Business center. Pets accepted. $351 and up

★★★★THE CARLYLE, A ROSEWOOD HOTEL
35 E. 76th St., New York, 212-744-1600, 888-767-3966; www.thecarlyle.com

Everyone from heads of state to celebs like Tom Cruise and Katie Holmes favor this classic hotel when they're in New York City, but the attentive and discreet staff is famous for treating all guests like visiting A-listers. Opened in 1930, the classic Art Deco hotel (named for British essayist Thomas Carlyle) is all about understated, old-fashioned elegance. Uniformed elevator operators guide you to floors where rooms and suites are mixed with 60 residential apartments (lucky live-ins get the same perks as hotel guests). The rooms were originally designed by Dorothy Draper and later updated by Mark Hampton, Thierry Despont, Alexandra Champalimaud and other well-known designers. The furnishings range in style from classic British to modern décor, and some of the larger suites include powder rooms, foyers with full wet bars and even grand pianos. Luxurious touches include custom-made Limoges ashtrays, oversized umbrellas at the ready and a significant nod to modern technology with plasma televisions, DVD players and iPod docking stations. Step back in time outside your room by hitting the classic Café Carlyle, where acts include Eartha Kitt and, occasionally, a clarinet-playing Woody Allen.

187 rooms. Restaurants, bar. Fitness center. Spa. Business center. Pets accepted. $351 and up

★★★CHAMBERS

15 W. 56th St., New York, 212-974-5656, 866-204-5656; www.chambershotel.com

From the large front door made from woven walnut wood to the more than 500 pieces of artwork by everyone from John Waters to Do-Ho Suh, the Chambers Hotel feels like a chic downtown gallery that's plopped down into the middle of New York's Midtown retail hub. In addition to the paintings that line the walls of the guest rooms, hallways and other public spaces, the hotel uses warm shades of brown throughout, and the rooms have a loft-like feel with large windows, sleek furniture and mini-bars stocked with Dean and Deluca goods. Massage therapists, babysitters and even personal shoppers from Henri Bendel are a phone call away.

77 rooms. Restaurant, bar. Pets accepted. $351 and up

★★★CITY CLUB HOTEL
55 W. 44th St., New York, 212-921-5500; www.cityclubhotel.com

The City Club Hotel is all about contemporary style and elegance. From the Frette bed linens to the luxury bath products, this intimate boutique hotel spoils its guests with luxurious amenities, not to mention attentive service and stunning appointments. Acclaimed chef Daniel Boulud's DB Bistro Moderne is adjacent to the hotel lobby

65 rooms. Restaurant, bar. $151-250

★★★CROWNE PLAZA HOTEL TIMES SQUARE MANHATTAN

1605 Broadway, New York, 212-977-4000; www.manhattan.crowneplaza.com

With a prominent location on Broadway in the center of Times Square, this contemporary hotel sits steps from the Great White Way's attractions. Guest rooms provide comfortable, high-quality bedding, relaxation CDs, eye masks, earplugs and lavender aromatherapy spray. Guests can even request a quiet-zone floor.
770 rooms. Restaurant, bar. Business center. Fitness center. Pool. $251-250

★★★DOUBLETREE GUEST SUITES TIMES SQUARE-NEW YORK CITY

1568 Broadway, New York, 212-719-1600, 800-222-8733; www.doubletree.com

If you're looking for an all-suite hotel in Times Square, the Doubletree sits in the center of the action. The spacious, two-room suites feature a bedroom and a separate living/dining/work area with a pullout sofa bed, microwave and refrigerator. The Center Stage Cafe in the atrium offers breakfast, lunch and dinner, and the Cabaret Lounge is perfect for an end-of-day cocktail.
460 rooms. Restaurant, bar. Business center. Fitness center. Pets accepted. $351 and up.

★★★DREAM HOTEL NEW YORK

210 W. 55th St., New York, 212-247-2000, 866-437-3266; www.dreamny.com

Vikram Chatwal, the brains behind Time Hotel, turned the former Majestic Hotel into this slumber-themed property in 2004. You'll feel like you've walked into a trippy dream the moment you hit the lobby, where a two-story aquarium and gold Catherine the Great statue are part of the eclectic design mix. The restaurant here is an outpost of the Serafina chain of northern Italian spots known all over town for their specialty pizzas. An Ayurvedic spa was designed by Deepak Chopra to allow guests to massage and meditate their way to peacefulness before turning in for the night in the minimalist rooms, outfitted with feather beds and 300 thread-count Egyptian sheets, and awash in blue lights that create a twilight feel. If a nightcap is more your style, take the elevator up to the Ava Lounge, which offers a seasonal rooftop garden that sits high above the city with views of Times Square and Columbus Circle.
220 rooms. Restaurant, bar. Fitness center. Spa. Pets accepted. $351 and up

★★★DYLAN HOTEL

52 E. 41st St., New York, 212-338-0500, 866-553-9526; www.dylanhotel.com

This 16-story 1903 Beaux Arts structure was once home to the Chemist's Club of New York, which explains the insignia over the stone entryway. The microscopes and test tubes are long gone, but designer Jeffrey Beers experiments with amber lightboxes suspended from the lobby ceiling, and in a nod to its origins, the hotel provides beakers in place of bathroom cups. Rooms are open and airy spaces, with 11-foot ceilings and large windows, and accented with a mix of muted shades, jewel-toned materials and American walnut furniture; bathrooms are outfitted with Carrara marble. If you're feeling experimental, check yourself into the Alchemy Suite, which was once a Gothic chamber created to replicate a medieval alchemist's lab. It still has the original stained-glass windows and vaulted ceilings.
107 rooms. Restaurant, bar. Business center. Fitness center. $351 and up

★★★★★FOUR SEASONS HOTEL NEW YORK

57 E. 57th St., New York, 212-758-5700, 800-545-4000; www.fourseasons.com

Well-heeled travelers kick off their shoes in the 52-story Midtown outpost of this luxe hotel chain, appropriately located steps from shopping-mecca Fifth Avenue. Designed by I.M. Pei, its jaw-dropper is the 33-foot-high backlit onyx ceiling in the lobby (which led Jacqueline Kennedy Onassis to nickname it "The Cathedral.") Sweeping views of Central Park and other parts of the city are part of the allure of the guest rooms, which range in size from 500 to 800 square feet—larger than many New York City apartments—with roomy seating areas (some have furnished terraces, too). Other treats include big marble bathrooms with soaking tubs, and silk drapes that you can control bedside to open or close on those views. Plenty of celebrities have stayed here because they can't get enough of the Four Seasons' signature top-notch service, luxurious spa and fine dining establishments, including L'Atelier de Joël Rubuchon. 368 rooms. Restaurant, bar. Business center. Fitness center. Spa. Pets accepted. $351 and up.

★★★THE GRAMERCY PARK HOTEL

2 Lexington Ave., New York, 212-920-3300; www.gramercyparkhotel.com

Despite being a favorite haunt of the likes of Humphrey Bogart and Babe Ruth, who frequented the bar here, the Gramercy has been known as a low-key (and at times tired) spot since its opening in 1925. When hotelier Ian Schrager gave the place a major overhaul before reopening it in 2006, he managed to make improvements without turning it into yet another cookie-cutter Mid-Century mod property. The lobby now boasts impressive smoked-wood beams, a 10-foot-high fireplace and Moroccan checker-tiled floor. Rooms are decorated in rich reds, royal blues and other jewel tones instead of de rigueur minimalist neutrals, and velvets, leathers and tapestries adorn Julian Schnabel-designed furniture. The Rose Bar is lined with paintings by Andy Warhol, Jean-Michel Basquiat and Schnabel himself. The prettiest perk is something even lifelong New Yorkers never see: keys to the exclusive and elegantly landscaped Gramercy Park, an honor normally reserved for residents of the 39 buildings that surround the oldest private park in the country. 185 rooms. Restaurant, bar. Business center. Fitness center. Spa. Pets accepted. $351 and up.

★★★THE GREENWICH HOTEL

377 Greenwich St., New York, 212-941-8900; www.thegreenwichhotel.com

If individuality is your thing, The Greenwich Hotel should be your auberge of choice. Each of the 88 guest rooms is unique, adorned with global influences such as Parisian antiques, Moroccan tilework, Tibetan rugs and repurposed Japanese lumber. The brainchild of actor/director Robert De Niro (his office is across the street), this boutique property is yet another resplendent addition to the ever-expanding Tribeca 'hood. The 1,700-square-foot Greenwich Suite is a worthy splurge with 30-foot skylit windows, two master bedrooms and a wood-burning stone fireplace. Don't forgo a trip to the sublevel Shibui Spa; it may be your one opportunity to relax under a 250-year-old Japanese wooden farmhouse and lantern-lit swimming pool. For a good gauge of the neighborhood, snag a sidewalk table at Locanda Verde and watch the locals sashay by. 88 rooms. Restaurant, bar. Fitness center. Pool. Spa. Pets accepted. $$$

★HAMPTON INN MANHATTAN CHELSEA

108 W. 24th St., New York, 212-414-1000; www.hamptoninn.com

This easy-on-the-wallet hotel is a good option for those who want to stay downtown but can't afford the exorbitant prices. A 20-story high-rise, the hotel has clean, functional rooms typical of the Hampton brand, and the chain's complimentary "on the house" hot breakfast is served daily in the dining room. No time to sit down and eat? The hotel also offers an "on the run" breakfast bag with a bottle of water on weekdays.

144 rooms. Complimentary breakfast. Business center. Fitness center. $151-250

★★★HILTON CLUB NEW YORK

1335 Avenue of the Americas, New York, 212-586-7000, 800-445-8667; www.hilton.com

This large convention hotel—one of the largest in Manhattan—has a prime Midtown setting. The spacious, contemporary rooms offer work desks, on-demand entertainment systems, marble bathrooms and Internet access. There are several onsite restaurants, bars and shops as well as a fitness center and full-service spa. This is a popular convention hotel, so pay no mind if everyone seems to know each other.

2,058 rooms. Restaurant, bar. Business center. Fitness center. Spa. $251-350

★HOLIDAY INN EXPRESS NEW YORK CITY FIFTH AVENUE

15 W. 45th St., New York, 212-302-9088; www.expressfifth.com

This Holiday Inn is centrally located near Grand Central Terminal, Times Square, Rockefeller Center and other New York City sights. The 22-story hotel was renovated in 2005, and services include a complimentary breakfast and free in-room wireless Internet service.

124 rooms. Complimentary breakfast. Business center. $251-350

★★HOLIDAY INN MANHATTAN-DOWNTOWN SOHO

138 Lafayette St., New York, 212-966-8898, 800-465-4329; www.holiday-inn.com

A friendly, relaxed, and gracious oasis, this Holiday Inn is located in the busy lower section of Soho, on the edge of Canal Street in Chinatown. Business travelers will find the location convenient to Wall Street and the financial district, and leisure travelers will find many attractions, dining options, and shopping nearby.

227 rooms. Restaurant, bar. Business center. Fitness center. $151-250

★★HOLIDAY INN NEW YORK CITY-MIDTOWN-57TH STREET

440 W. 57th St., New York, 212-581-8100; www.holiday-inn.com

This Holiday Inn is situated off busy 9th Avenue in the western section of Upper Midtown Manhattan. Many New York attractions are nearby, including Central Park, Broadway theaters, Carnegie Hall, and plenty of shopping. Guest rooms are quite spacious and decorated with dark woods and relaxing shades of green and burgundy.

597 rooms. Restaurant, bar. Fitness center. Pool. $151-250

★★HOTEL BEACON

2130 Broadway, New York, 212-787-1100, 800-572-4969; www.beaconhotel.com

This Upper West Side hotel was converted from a residential building, and many of its rooms are still leased as long-term apartments. All of the Beacon's spacious rooms are simply furnished and decorated in a floral motif, and one- and two-bedroom suites come with one king or two double beds in each room as well as a pull-out couch, making this a good option for larger families who want to be near neighborhood institutions like the American Museum of Natural History and Lincoln Center. Fully equipped kitchenettes in all the rooms include microwaves and coffeemakers. Otherwise, the hotel restaurant is open 24-hours.

258 rooms. Restaurant. Business center. $151-250

★★★HOTEL ELYSEE

60 E. 54th St., New York, 212-753-1066, 800-535-9733; www.elyseehotel.com

Built in 1926 and named after one of the best French restaurants of that time, the Hotel Elysée combines the charm of an intimate bed and breakfast with the service and style of an upscale boutique hotel. The lobby is elegantly decked out with marble floors and mahogany walls, while the guest rooms are styled in French country décor. Stop by the Club Room for complimentary wine and hors d'oeuvres on weekday evenings and pick up free daily guest passes to the local branch of New York Sports Club at the front desk. Be sure to check out the famous Monkey Bar, littered with statues, pictures and paintings of its name-sake animal. It was once a haunt for celebs like Ava Gardner, Marlon Brando and 15-year hotel resident Tennessee Williams, who lived here until his death in 1983.

103 rooms. Complimentary breakfast. Restaurant, bar. $351 and up.

★★★HOTEL GANSEVOORT

18 Ninth Ave., New York, 212-206-6700, 877-426-7386; www.hotelgansevoort.com

This hotel is just as stylish as its trendsetting neighbors in the Meatpacking District, a neighborhood home to high-end-but-downtown-chic retailers like Scoop and Stella McCartney. Room palettes consist of neutrals with blue-purple splashes. Everything, including headboards, armoires and walls, are awash in leather and fabrics, while 9-foot ceilings add airiness. The hotel is famous for its rooftop destination Plunge, a restaurant, bar and lounge with wraparound views of the city and a 45-foot-long outdoor, heated pool that's surrounded by glass panels and open year-round.

180 rooms. Restaurant, bar. Fitness center. Pool. Spa. Business center. Pets accepted. $351 and up

★★★HOTEL ON RIVINGTON

107 Rivington St., New York, 212-475-2600, 800-915-1537; www.hotelonrivington.com

The super-modern steel-and-glass Hotel On Rivington offers 21 stories of hip and luxurious guest rooms. All have floor-to-ceiling windows for sweeping Manhattan views, and most include balconies. Sensuous details range from velvet sofas and chairs in the living spaces, bathrooms constructed with glitzy Bisazza tiles and glass-enclosed showers with skyline views, to Swedish Tempur-Pedic mattresses and Frette linens. The hotel sits in the heart of the rapidly gentrifying Lower East Side, where there's no shortage of trendy boutiques, hip restaurants and popular local watering holes, including the 1,500-square-foot onsite lounge, 105 Riv.

110 rooms. Complimentary breakfast. Restaurant, bar. Fitness center. Business center. Pets accepted. $351 and up

★★★HÔTEL PLAZA ATHÉNÉE

37 E. 64th St., New York, 212-734-9100, 800-447-8800; www.plaza-athenee.com

The Hôtel Plaza Athénée sits on a strip of prime real estate in Manhattan: a tranquil, tree-lined street just a few blocks from Central Park. The lobby is awash in marble and crystal, but also has a modern feel thanks to wireless Internet access. Rooms have rich cherry furniture and jewel-toned color schemes like maroon and gold, plus nice extras such as Belgian linens and complimentary morning coffee. Some suites boast indoor atriums and outdoor balconies. The nearly 2,449-square-foot Penthouse Duplex suite on the 16th and 17th floors includes two bedrooms, a decorative fireplace, formal dining for 12 and a private terrace running half the hotel's length. If that's your style, you'll probably also love that Barneys New York and the other high-end shops along Fifth Avenue are just steps away.

149 rooms. Restaurant, bar. Fitness center. Business center. Pets accepted. $351 and up

★★HOTEL WALES

1295 Madison Ave., New York, 212-876-6000, 866-925-3746; www.waleshotel.com

This restored 1902 hotel, located on Manhattan's Upper East Side, is the perfect mix of old-world elegance and modern amenity. Reminiscent of a country inn, the cozy décor features original heating pipes and fireplaces, a curved marble lobby staircase, oriental rugs and antique tables. The comfortable guest rooms feature Belgian linens, fresh flowers, Aveda toiletries, and VCRs.

87 rooms. Restaurant. Complimentary breakfast. Fitness center. $251-350

★★★INN AT IRVING PLACE

56 Irving Place, New York, 212-533-4600, 800-685-1447; www.innatirving.com

Step back in time to 19th-century New York at this romantic brownstone hideaway located in a row of 1830s townhouses just south of Gramercy Park. The high-ceilinged guest rooms feature antiques, four-poster beds and couches without sacrificing modern amenities such as remote climate control and Internet access. Enjoy breakfast in bed or take it in the elegant guest parlor. Afternoon tea at Lady Mendl's Tea Salon is a special treat. The staff can arrange special services including an in-room massage or the booking of theater tickets.

12 rooms. No children under 13. Bar. Complimentary breakfast. $351 and up.

★★★INTERCONTINENTAL THE BARCLAY NEW YORK

111 E. 48th St., New York, 212-755-5900, 800-782-8021; www.intercontinental.com

This hotel boasts an opulent lobby with marble floors and fine furnishings. It's a hint of what guests will find in their rooms. An array of convenient hotel services include babysitting service, laundry and dry-cleaning services, a concierge and a 24-hour business center. The clubby Barclay Bar and Grille offers a creative Continental menu.

686 rooms. Restaurant, bar. Business center. Fitness center. $251-350

★★★THE IROQUOIS

49 W. 44th St., New York, 212-840-3080, 800-332-7220; www.iroquoisny.com

The Iroquois underwent a $10 million renovation a few years back that restored this landmark property to its original 1923 elegance. Guest rooms are individually decorated with works of art reflecting New York themes and feature Frette linens and Italian marble baths. Triomphe restaurant features French cuisine, and the Burgundy Room offers a tasty breakfast and cocktails.

114 rooms. Restaurant, bar. $351 and up.

★★★JUMEIRAH ESSEX HOUSE ON CENTRAL PARK

160 Central Park S., New York, 212-247-0300, 888-645-5697;
www.jumeirahessexhouse.com

Opened in 1931, this landmark hotel sits on Central Park and recently underwent a two-year, $90 million refurbishment. Rooms come with custom-designed furniture and other special touches including amber-colored glass sinks, red leather-framed mirrors and wall-to-wall cabinetry for extra storage space. Not everything is a throwback to the mid-20th century, however. Modern touches include touchscreen controls for lighting and music, flat-panel TVs and lighted footpaths to the bathrooms. If you're in need of a little restoration of your own, the in-house spa features a steam bath, sauna and a host of treatments like massages and facials.

515 rooms. Restaurant, bar. Fitness center. Spa. Pets accepted. $351 and up

★★★THE KIMBERLY HOTEL

145 E. 50th St., New York, 212-702-1600, 800-683-0400; www.kimberlyhotel.com

The Kimberly's one- and two-bedroom suites feature living rooms, dining areas and fully equipped separate kitchens. Many have private terraces with city views. A unique perk: Guests may take a complimentary cruise on the hotel's 75-foot yacht on weekends from May through October. For a real treat, book a duplex suite at the Kimberly to enjoy warm woods, deluxe linens and lots of space by New York standards.

193 rooms. Restaurant, bar. Business center. $351 and up.

★★★THE KITANO NEW YORK

66 Park Ave., New York, 212-885-7000, 800-548-2666; www.kitano.com

This Japanese import just south of Grand Central features modern guest rooms with soft tones of beige and tan and soundproof windows that ensure peace and quiet. The rooms also feature duvets, large desks and samplings of green tea. The Nadaman Hakubai restaurant specializes in gourmet Japanese cuisine, and the sun-splashed Garden Cafe features contemporary European and Asian cuisines.

149 rooms. Restaurant, bar. $351 and up.

★★★LE PARKER MERIDIEN

118 W. 57th St., New York, 212-245-5000, 800-543-4300; www.parkermeridien.com

Business-minded types will appreciate the ergonomic touches at this Midtown hotel: built-in 6-foot-long workstations with adjustable Herman Miller Aeron chairs, 32-inch TVs set back in swiveling consoles and roll-away storage compartments for luggage. Junior suites add luxury in the form of two-person, cedar-lined baths and showers. There's a weight room, and both basketball and racquetball courts, but it's the rooftop pool that's a longtime-favorite of locals and tourists alike. Same goes for Norma's, one of three onsite restaurants, which caters to a mix of natives and visitors with popular breakfast items including the "Zillion Dollar Lobster Frittata" and "Artychoked Benedict." The hotel is also famous for it's excellent burger joint.

731 rooms. Restaurant. Fitness center. Pool. Business center. Pets accepted. $351 and up

★★★LIBRARY HOTEL

299 Madison Ave., New York, 212-983-4500, 877-793-7323; www.libraryhotel.com

Bookworms will get a kick out of this concept hotel, located steps from the New York Public and Pierpont Morgan Libraries on what's known as "Library Way." Rooms are identified by one of 10 Dewey Decimal System categories, and 6,000-plus books are shelved throughout the hotel. Whether you're mad for math or hungry for literature, you can choose a room based on more than 60 themes. The rooms are pleasantly unstuffy, thanks to a décor that's heavy on creams, whites and other light colors. Social readers should check out the mahogany-paneled Writers' Den, which has a cozy fireplace and greenhouse.

60 rooms. Complimentary breakfast. Restaurant, bar. $251-350

★★★THE LOMBARDY HOTEL

111 E. 56th St., New York, 212-753-8600, 800-223-5254; www.lombardyhotel.com

An elegant Midtown hotel, the somewhat sleepy Lombardy was built in the 1920s by William Randolph Hearst and features oversized rooms decorated in a classic, old-world style. The marble baths have huge showers and upscale toiletries. Above-and-beyond services include a seamstress and white-glove elevator attendants..

167 rooms. Restaurant, bar. Complimentary breakfast. Business center. Fitness center. No children under 10 years. $251-350

★★★LONDON NYC

151 W. 54th St., New York, 866-690-2029; www.thelondonnyc.com

Anglophiles will love this Midtown luxury hotel which offers the finest elements of British sophistication and understatement. The 500-square-foot London Suites, with bed chamber and separate parlor, were conceptualized by British interior architect David Collins, and are decorated with parquet flooring, custom-woven banquettes and embossed-leather desks, plus tech pleasures like iHome players and Mitel touchscreen phones. If the biggest and best is what you're after, book the 2,500-square-foot penthouse, which is spread out on two floors with 180-degree views that include Central Park and the George Washington Bridge. It also offers a dining room that seats eight and access to the Chef's Table in the hot-and-hyped onsite restaurant Gordon Ramsay at the London. The hotel partners with Quintessentially, a luxury concierge service famous for pulling strings and doing the impossible, like scoring same-night seats to the most popular Broadway shows or chartering a private jet on a moment's notice. If you'd rather stay in, calls across the pond are on the house eight hours a day.

561 rooms. Restaurant, bar. Fitness center. Business center. $351 and up

★★★★THE LOWELL

28 E. 63rd St., New York, 212-838-1400, 800-221-4444; www.lowellhotel.com

Located in a landmark 1920s building on the Upper East Side, the Lowell captures the essence of an elegant country house with a blend of English prints, floral fabrics and Chinese porcelains that surprisingly works. Many suites boast wood-burning fireplaces, a rarity in Manhattan. All rooms are individually decorated, and the Lowell's specialty suites are a unique treat. The Hollywood Suite reflects the 1930s silver-screen era with photos of glamorous ingenues. The English influences extend to the Pembroke Room, where Anglophiles can throw their pinkies up at tea time (breakfast and brunch is also served). But for something uniquely American, check out the clubby Post House, a well-respected New York steakhouse that serves terrific chops.

72 rooms. Restaurant, bar. Fitness center. Business center. Pets accepted. $351 and up

★★★★★MANDARIN ORIENTAL, NEW YORK

80 Columbus Circle, New York, 212-805-8800, 866-801-8880;
www.mandarinoriental.com/newyork

With all that the Mandarin Oriental offers, it's possible you may never want to leave. First, there are the views: The hotel, which occupies the 35th to 54th floors of the Time Warner Center, boasts impressive floor-to-ceiling windows that look out onto Columbus Circle, midtown Manhattan, the Hudson River and Central Park. Then there are the shops and restaurants: They include the buttoned-up shirtmaker Thomas Pink and famed $450-per-person sushi restaurant Masa. Finally, there's the décor: Standard rooms are dressed in black, red, gray or cream colors with Asian cherrywood furniture and fresh orchids, while superior rooms have lavish Spanish marble bathrooms with Italian granite vanities. The best amenity may be the view; each room serves up a panorama of either Central Park or the Hudson River. For the supreme pampering experience reserve the 2,640-square-foot Presidential suite on the 53rd floor, which includes a living and dining area, gourmet kitchen and study, all outfitted with oriental rugs, upholstered silk walls and other Asian artifacts. Dine at the Mandarin's wonderful Asiate restaurant, take a dip in the 75-foot lap pool (rumored to be the largest in Manhattan) or order room service and a movie—and put the high-tech entertainment system that's standard in every room to good use.

248 rooms. Restaurant, bar. Fitness center. Pool. Spa. Business center. Pets accepted. $351 and up

★★MANSFIELD

12 W. 44th St., New York, 212-277-8700, 800-255-5167; www.mansfieldhotel.com

In contrast to the elegant, classic lobby with its original fireplaces, the small rooms at the century-old Mansfield are decidedly modern thanks to recent re-dos. The ebony-stained hardwood floors are complemented by shades of white and tan throughout the spaces. Comfortable beds have pillow-top mattresses and 300-count linens, while bathrooms are stocked with Aveda products. You won't get much in the way of views here, but you'll find comfort in the hotel's M Bar—an intimate lounge with a domed skylight and mahogany bookshelves, as well as the beautifully restored Beaux Arts library, where you can kick back with a book or chess match by the fire. If you can't sleep or just need a quick pick-me-up, there's complimentary cappuccino, espresso, coffee and tea service around the clock in the lobby.

126 rooms. Bar. Fitness center. Business center. Pets accepted. $351 and up

★★★THE MERCER

147 Mercer St., New York, 212-966-6060; www.mercerhotel.com

Housed in a landmark Romanesque revival building, this is a see-and-be-seen hotel that's all about modern luxury. All rooms have sleek Christian Liaigre interiors that artfully mix soothing neutral colors, hardwood floors and rich materials like leather upholstery and 400-count Egyptian-cotton linens. Bathrooms are just as inviting, with oversized marble tubs big enough for two and bath products from Swedish company FACE. Too tired to unpack? No problem—the staff can take care of that. Need a private trainer or an in-room massage? They've got that (and plenty of other personalized services) available, too. If all that weren't enough, Jean-Georges Vongerichten's American-Provençal restaurant, Mercer Kitchen, is onsite.

75 rooms. Restaurant, bar. $351 and up.

★★★THE MICHELANGELO

152 W. 51st St., New York, 212-765-0505, 800-237-0990; www.michelangelohotel.com

If you are an aficionado of all things Italian, book a room at the Michelangelo. Opera music plays in the public spaces, frothy cappuccino and Italian pastries are breakfast standouts and Baci chocolates appear at turndown. The extra-large rooms are decorated in Art Deco, country French or neoclassical style and feature woven fabrics from Italy.

178 rooms. Complimentary breakfast. Restaurant, bar. Fitness center. $351 and up.

★★★MILLENNIUM BROADWAY HOTEL NEW YORK

145 W. 44th St., New York, 212-768-4400, 866-866-8086; www.millenniumhotels.com

Colorful murals that exemplify the 1930s adorn the lobby of this contemporary Midtown hotel, located near Times Square, the Theater District, choice shopping and Grand Central. Spacious guest rooms are tastefully appointed, though somewhat bland, with a satellite TV, minibar, high-speed Internet access, iron and ironing board, hairdryer and views of Manhattan.

750 rooms. Restaurant, bar. Business center. Fitness center. $151-250

★★★MILLENIUM HILTON

55 Church St., New York, 212-693-2001, 800-445-8667; www.hilton.com

This Financial District hotel is a good choice for business travelers who need proximity to Wall Street as well as vacationers who want to be near popular spots like Battery Park, Greenwich Village, Tribeca and Soho. The ho-hum guestrooms in the 55-story skyscraper aren't anything special in terms of décor, but they do have 42-inch flat-screen televisions, high-speed Internet access, personalized voicemail and Hilton's "Serenity Bed" with plush down pillows. Request a room with views of the Statue of Liberty or East River, with its iconic bridges. Fitness facilities are top-notch and include a heated indoor pool.

569 rooms. Restaurant, bar. Business center. Fitness center. Pool. Spa. Pets accepted. $251-350

★★★MILLENNIUM UN PLAZA HOTEL

1 United Nations Plaza, New York, 212-758-1234, 877-866-7529;
www.millennium-hotels.com

Diplomats, business travelers and a few guests from the Rachael Ray show
(the show's official hotel) all find something to like about this Midtown East
hotel located next to the United Nations. Plenty of meeting and banquet space
is available, including a fitness center, pool and even indoor tennis courts.
The rooms are sparsely decorated and have a calm, neutral pallete, allowing
the sweeping views of the U.N. and the rest of the city to take center stage
instead. Unbothered by looming skyscraper neighbors (guest rooms start on
the 28th floor), the hotel has some of the best panoramic views of the city—
making the rooms feel more like private penthouses than part of a hotel. The
only con here: The property is pretty far east, so you'll have to walk several
avenues over to catch the subway at Grand Central Station.

427 rooms. Restaurant, bar. Fitness center. Pool. Spa. Tennis. $251-350

★★★MORGANS

237 Madison Ave., New York, 212-686-0300; www.morganshotel.com

Guest rooms at this Midtown hotel are decorated in soft, muted tones and carry
a modern flair. Asia de Cuba restaurant offers an inventive Asian-Latin menu
courtesy of restaurateur Jeffrey Chodorow. Morgans' Bar is the perfect place for
a late-night elixir. Complimentary breakfast and afternoon tea add to your stay.
113 rooms. Complimentary breakfast. Restaurant, bar. $251-350

★★★THE MUSE

130 W. 46th St., New York, 212-485-2400, 877-692-6873; www.themusehotel.com

Style abounds at this theater district hotel with a triple-arched, limestone-
and-brick façade and lobby that has a 15-foot vaulted ceiling with a mural
that depicts the nine muses. Original artwork celebrating the theater and the
performing arts hangs in each room, decorated in warm colors and cherry
wood furniture. Custom linens and duvet-covered feather beds further en-
liven the spaces. Pets are given special beds and snacks, and the hotel will
arrange sitting services if needed.

200 rooms. Restaurant, bar. Fitness center. Pets accepted. $251-350

★★★NEW YORK MARRIOTT DOWNTOWN

85 West St., New York, 212-385-4900, 800-228-9290; www.marriott.com

This Financial District hotel has great access to Wall Street, and the South
Street Seaport. Guest rooms in the 38-floor building were renovated in spring
2008, and include 32-inch flat-screen TVs, marble bathrooms, beds with
300-thread-count linens and down comforters. There's an indoor pool, too,
but be sure to request the hotel's best perk, if it's available: a room with a
view of New York Harbor and the Statue of Liberty.

497 rooms. Restaurant, bar. Business center. Fitness center. Pool. $351 and up.

★★★NEW YORK MARRIOTT MARQUIS

1535 Broadway, New York, 212-398-1900, 800-843-4898; www.marriott.com

Located in Times Square, this mammoth, family-friendly hotel is a city in
itself—filled with shops, restaurants and theaters, all built around the towering atrium where glass elevators zip up and down at dizzying speeds. The

spacious rooms feature 300-thread count linens, fluffy pillows, down comforters and thick mattresses.

1,950 rooms. Restaurant, bar. Fitness center. $251-350

★★★★THE NEW YORK PALACE

455 Madison Ave., New York, 212-888-7000, 800-804-7035; www.newyorkpalace.com

The moment you step through the Madison Avenue gates of the Villard Mansion and walk down the grand staircase, this hotel's motto, "Old World Elegance—New World Opulence," clicks into place. First built as a luxury apartment building in 1882, the structure was transformed into a hotel in 1980. The spacious and sumptuously appointed rooms throughout the 55-story tower include marble bathrooms, comfortable seating, work desks and large cozy beds. If you're looking to splurge, Triplex Suites are up to 5,000 square feet and boast Art Deco décor and unforgettable views from their 18-foot windows and private rooftop terraces.

93 rooms. Restaurant, bar. Business center. Fitness center. Spa. Pets accepted. $351 and up.

★★★OMNI BERKSHIRE PLACE

21 E. 52nd St., New York, 212-753-5800, 888-444-6664; www.omnihotels.com

Pillow-top mattresses and feather pillows in all the rooms should make it easy to get a good night's sleep amid the never-ending frenzy outside this Midtown luxury hotel. Rooms range in size from a 271-square-foot deluxe—with options for one king-size or two double beds up to the 1,000-square-foot Rodgers & Hammerstein Suite, lavishly appointed with a wraparound terrace, fireplace and spa tub. There's also a sundeck and fitness center on the 17th floor.

396 rooms. Restaurant, bar. Business center. Fitness center. $351 and up.

★★★★★THE PENINSULA NEW YORK

700 Fifth Ave., New York, 212-956-2888, 800-262-9467; www.peninsula.com

Rising 23 stories above some of the best shopping in New York, the Peninsula's Midtown location in the middle of Fifth Avenue is a shopaholic's dream. The Beaux Arts building was completed in 1905 and has luxurious, bright guestrooms with large windows and simple, contemporary furnishings that give nods to the chain's Asian roots with details like lacquered dressers and armoires. Tech-types get their due, too: Bedside controls mean you don't have to move to manage your music, temperature and lighting settings, and flat-screen TVs and speaker phones are within reach of the bathtubs. The hotel's library-like Gotham Lounge serves afternoon tea, which includes a selection of finger sandwiches such as smoked salmon and egg salad. For a spicier cocktail, head to the rooftop lounge Salon de Ning where 1930's Shanghai meets Midtown Manhattan in an exotic blend of pillow-strewn chaises, potent potables and Asian-influenced appetizers. The Peninsula Spa by ESPA continues the Far East theme with rich bamboo floors and orchid arrangements aplenty. Don't forget your swim suit; the glass-enclosed rooftop pool is ideal for an evening dip amidst the city skyline.

239 rooms. Restaurant, bar. Fitness center. Pool. Spa. Business center. $351 and up

★★★THE PLAZA HOTEL

768 Fifth Ave., Upper East Side, 212-546-5499; www.theplaza.com

With a standard for luxury that dates back more than a century, it is no surprise that the renovated Plaza hotel reopened its doors in 2008 to universal pomp and pageantry. After three years and $400 million, The Plaza now bridges Old World enchantment and contemporary technology. Guest rooms are thoughtfully detailed in Beaux Arts-inspired décor with spacious closets, custom Italian Mascioni linens and bathrooms flaunting 24-karat gold-plated Sherle Wagner faucets, handcrafted solid marble vanities, inlaid mosaic tiles and Miller Harris bath products. If that's not enough pampering for you, make your way to the Caudalié Vinotherapie Spa, the first of its kind in the United States, where face and body treatments can—and should—be followed up by a visit to the French Paradox Wine Lounge. Fitness legend Radu Teodorescu (known simply as Radu to his celeb clientele) is the force behind the new 8,300-square-foot fitness center, which includes an Olympic-sized lap pool and basketball court. Stop by the storied Palm Court for sumptuous afternoon tea, or enjoy a cocktail at the Rose Club or Champagne Bar.

282 rooms. Restaurant, bar. Fitness center. Business center. Spa. Pets accepted. $$$$

★★★THE REGENCY HOTEL

540 Park Ave., New York, 212-759-4100, 800-233-2356; www.loewshotels.com

Home of the original power breakfast, where deals are sealed and fortunes made, the Regency consistently ranks as one of New York's top hotels. Combining the appearance of a library and a private club, this hotel provides attentive service that extends beyond the ordinary. Pets are even welcomed in grand style with room service, dog-walking services and listings of pet-friendly establishments. Unwind at Feinstein's, where Grammy-nominated Michael Feinstein entertains nightly or savor a meal at 540 Park or the Library.

353 rooms. Restaurant, bar. Fitness center. Spa. Pets accepted. $351 and up.

★★★RENAISSANCE NEW YORK HOTEL TIMES SQUARE

714 Seventh Ave., New York, 212-765-7676; www.renaissancehotels.com

An extensive makeover by famed designer Jordan Mozer transformed this Marriott-owned hotel from cookie-cutter to au courant. The lobby is modern without being steely, thanks to blue and red leather chairs and funky orb-shaped ceiling fixtures. Rooms have stylish, dark hard-wood furniture and blue and gold accents, plus modern necessities like technology panels where you can plug in all your electronics—iPod, cell phone, laptop—in one place. Bathrooms have robes and LATHER products. The restaurant Two Times Square on the second floor has sweet views of Times Square. (For just-as-cool views of the square, ask for an upper-floor room overlooking Seventh Avenue).

305 rooms. Restaurant, bar. Fitness center. Pets accepted. $251-350

★★★★THE RITZ-CARLTON NEW YORK, BATTERY PARK

2 West St., New York, 212-344-0800, 800-542-8680; www.ritzcarlton.com

Top-notch views of the Statue of Liberty, Ellis Island, New York Harbor and the downtown skyline make the Ritz's quieter downtown, waterfront location on the southwestern tip of Manhattan a great excuse to avoid the chaotic Midtown hotel scene. Harborside rooms are equipped with telescopes, and all the rooms have the typically plush Ritz-style amenities. Bulgari toiletries are in the marble bathrooms, and feather-beds come with 400-thread-count Frette linens, feather duvets and goose-down pillows. If that's not enough to lull you to sleep, a deep-tissue or hot-stone massage at the Prada Beauty Spa should do the trick.

298 rooms. Restaurant, bar. Fitness center. Spa. Business center. Pets accepted. $351 and up

★★★★★THE RITZ-CARLTON NEW YORK, CENTRAL PARK

50 Central Park S., New York, 212-308-9100, 800-542-8680; www.ritzcarlton.com

The Ritz is all about, well, being ritzy. This link in the exclusive hotel chain is no exception, epitomizing New York glamour and sophistication at every turn. Guests barely lift a finger from the time they arrive in the wood-paneled lobby and are escorted to rooms with 400 thread-count French sateen linens, feather duvets and a selection of seven pillow types. Oversized marble bathrooms have deep soaking tubs, Frédéric Fekkai toiletries and a choice of terry-waffle or sateen-cotton bathrobes. Visitors in the park-view rooms get telescopes for bird (or people) watching, and when they tire of that, it's a toss-up between having a jet-lag therapy, facial or other treatment at the second-floor La Prairie spa or taking one of the hotel's on-call Bentleys or limos for a leisurely drive around the park.

259 rooms. Restaurant, bar. Fitness center. Spa. Business center. Pets accepted. $351 and up

★★THE ROGER WILLIAMS

131 Madison Ave., New York, 212-448-7000, 888-448-7788;
www.hotelrogerwilliams.com

The name's a bit lackluster, but we can assure you that there's nothing drab about this recentlly renovated 16-story hotel named for Rhode Island's founder. The modern rooms range from the simple, single-bed superior rooms and Japanese-inspired doubles where furnishings include shoji screens, to garden terrace rooms that have landscaped patios and great city views. All have special touches, whether it's a colorful quilt on the bed or a bright-blue armchair and orange bench in the corner. The unique Help Yourself Breakfast Pantry is a casual, buffet-style service where you can choose from New York specialties like croissants from Balthazar, bagels from H&H or just a complimentary newspaper in the morning. The Mezzanine Lounge is a little more formal, with a menu that changes as the day progresses.

193 rooms. Complimentary breakfast. Restaurant, bar. Fitness center. Business center. $251-350

★★ROOSEVELT HOTEL

45 E. 45th St., New York, 212-661-9600, 888-833-3969; www.theroosevelthotel.com

Named for President Theodore Roosevelt and opened in 1924, this Madison Avenue hotel is situated in the heart of Midtown, where shopping, theater and business converge. The sprawling Colonial American-style building, which is near historic Grand Central Terminal, takes up a full city block and is a tourist stop itself because of its design. Crystal chandeliers and a large clock hang from the soaring ceilings over the large multistory marble lobby; the smaller but equally refined Palm Room has a sky mural on its ceiling. Rooms are simple, and have ergonomic desks, sofas and wireless access. The rooftop lounge, mad46, is a favorite of Times Square office workers who like its 19th floor location with open-air views of Manhattan's skyscrapers.

1,015 rooms. Restaurant, bar. Business center. Fitness center. $251-350

★★★ROYALTON HOTEL

44 W. 44th St., New York, 212-869-4400, 800-697-1791; www.royaltonhotel.com

Many consider the Royalton to be the original boutique hotel. It's the one that set the standard for hipness with its famously spare Philippe Starck design and a fashion-magazine crowd that frequented the lobby bar in the '90s. A recent renovation upped the sophistication level in a quiet, clubby way. The dark lobby, with a mix of icy glass, varnished wood, steel and brass, is softened by a giant fireplace, warm leather-covered walls and furniture upholstered in suede and hide. The large guest rooms have also been updated, and use soft colors like light blues, grays and whites as a backdrop for the built-in banquettes that run from one end of the room to the other. Flowing curtains, down comforters and Philippe Starck-designed bathrooms with five-foot circular tubs and steel sinks continue the cozy-meets-mod aesthetic. Back downstairs, restaurateur John McDonald (Lure Fishbar, Lever House), has overhauled Bar 44 and the intimate 100-seat Brasserie 44 with honey-teak walls, rope arches and white-glass globe lighting.

168 rooms. Restaurant, bar. Business center. Fitness center. Pets accepted. $351 and up.

★THE SALISBURY HOTEL

123 W. 57th St., New York, 212-246-1300; www.nycsalisbury.com

This hotel is conveniently located in the middle of Manhattan and its simple, no-nonsense rooms—available with queen, king or double beds—are quite large by New York City standards (most have kitchenettes and walk-in closets). Business travelers will enjoy the perks of the recently renovated corporate rooms and suites, such as large work areas, dual-line speakerphones and WiFi service. There isn't a restaurant onsite, but room service is available from several nearby ethnic restaurants, and complimentary continental breakfast is served daily in the dining room.

204 rooms. Complimentary breakfast. $251-350

★★★SAN CARLOS HOTEL

150 E. 50th St., New York, 212-755-1800, 800-722-2012; www.sancarloshotel.com

The San Carlos is an elegant, low-key hotel located in the center of Midtown. Rooms are spacious and comfortable with contemporary décor. Amenities such as wet bars, Aveda bath products and flat-screen TVs allow for a luxurious experience while the well-equipped Wi-Fi business center and large desks appeal to the business-minded.

147 rooms. Complimentary breakfast. Restaurant, bar. Business center. Fitness center. $251-350

★★★SHERATON NEW YORK HOTEL AND TOWERS

811 Seventh Ave., New York, 212-581-1000; www.sheraton.com

This large, comfortable hotel is one of Sheraton's flagships. Close to the theater district, the rooms are large by New York standards and all offer ultra-comfortable pillow-top Sheraton Sweet Sleeper Beds. Request a room on the club level for access to complimentary breakfast, hors d'oeuvres and drinks both day and night.

1,748 rooms. Restaurant, bar. Complimentary breakfast. Business center. Fitness center. Spa. $251-350

★★★THE SHERRY NETHERLAND

781 Fifth Ave., New York, 212-355-2800, 877-743-7710; www.sherrynetherland.com

If your style is more classic than contemporary, this landmark 1927 hotel and apartment tower on Fifth Avenue across from Central Park is the address for you. Suites are spacious and decorated with antiques (some even have crystal chandeliers in the bathrooms) and feature full-stocked kitchens and pantries. To keep the property up-to-date, a fitness center and high-speed Internet access have been added.

50 rooms. Fitness center. $351 and up.

★★★THE SHOREHAM HOTEL

33 W. 55th St., New York, 212-247-6700, 800-553-3347; www.shorehamhotel.com

Terrifically situated just off Fifth Avenue, the Shoreham mixes contemporary elegance with smart attention to detail. The rooms are comfortable and spacious with modern furnishings, high-definition television sets, Bose radios, 300-thread count linens and multijet showers. Begin your day with the complimentary coffee and cappuccino service in the spacious, lounge-like lobby and wind down at the spiffy Shoreham Bar with a signature Shoreham Happy Martini and plate of chickpea hummus fries.

177 rooms. Restaurant, bar. Business center. Fitness center. Pets accepted. $251-350

★★★SOFITEL NEW YORK

45 W. 44th St., New York, 212-354-8844; www.sofitel.com

You'll be greeted with a polite "bonjour" at this 30-story French export, a curved, modern limestone-and-glass building in the heart of Midtown. Paris- and New York-influenced Art Deco motifs are mixed throughout the hotel, including in photographs of the two cities in each room. Guest suites are compact and comfortable, with beautiful maple headboards affixed to the walls above the beds and marble baths. Top-floor rooms have private terraces and dazzling city views to boot.

398 rooms. Restaurant, bar. Business center. Fitness center. $351 and up.

★★★SOHO GRAND HOTEL

310 West Broadway, New York, 212-965-3000, 800-965-3000;
www.grandhospitality.com

Still one of just a handful of hotels in Soho, this property was the first to open in the neighborhood in more than a century when it came on the scene in 1996, and it has been a hipster mainstay ever since. The lobby's glass-bottle-paved staircase, cast-iron accents and concrete pillars were designed by William Sofield to mimic the neighborhood's characteristic warehouse lofts. Rooms are downtown-chic, with walls of massive windows, neutral color schemes, leather touches, iPod docks and even a pet goldfish upon request. You can bring along your cat or dog, too—the hotel is owned by pet-products company Hartz Mountain Industries, and offers everything from room service for your pet to on-call veterinarians and even a special pet-limo service. The hotel's Grand Bar & Lounge (a.k.a. "Soho's Living Room") is a good place to start exploring New York nightlife—it has long been popular with both New York's celeb set (Uma Thurman, Kevin Spacey and Heidi Klum) and out-of-towners. The adjoining Yard, open May through September, is a great place to get margaritas and light summer fare under the city sky.

363 rooms. Restaurant, bar. Business center. Fitness center. Pets accepted. $351 and up.

★★★★★THE ST. REGIS NEW YORK

2 E. 55th St., New York, 212-753-4500, 888-625-4988; www.stregis.com/newyork

No New York hotel may be better suited for shoppers than the St. Regis, with its prime location around the corner from Pucci and Japanese department store Takashimaya, and with the famed De Beers boutique right in the lobby. The opulent 1904 Beaux Arts landmark building (restored in a $100 million undertaking in 2006) is an impressive throw-back to old-school New York elegance. The lobby is dripping with gilded cornices and Italian marble, and if that isn't glitzy enough, a large glittering chandelier hangs over the reception desk from the soaring Trompe l'oeil ceiling which resembles a bright-blue sky. A visit to the legendary King Cole Bar—with its famous 1906 Art Nouveau oil mural by Maxfield Parrish—is definitely in order. Ask for a Red Snapper (people call it a Bloody Mary everywhere else, but don't try that here—the bar claims to be its birthplace) and then head to Adour, chef Alain Ducasse's onsite restaurant and wine bar. Guest rooms have a lavish appeal with silk wall coverings and antique furniture. Beds come dressed in soft Egyptian-cotton sheets and feather-down comforters, and the Remède bath amenities are pure indulgence for the skin. If you have any last-minute needs before falling asleep, each floor has its own 24-hour butler.

256 rooms. Restaurant, bar. Business center. Fitness center. Spa. $351 and up.

★★★SURREY HOTEL

20 E. 76th St., New York, 212-288-3700; www.affinia.com

Understated elegance describes this Upper East Side sleeper positioned off Madison Ave. You'll see the old-world charm upon entering the lobby, with its 18th-century English décor, wood-paneled elevators and leather sofas. The studio, one-bedroom and two-bedroom suites have a similar look. World-renowned chef Daniel Boulud's Cafe Boulud serves relaxed-chic French cooking in this refined setting.

132 rooms. Restaurant. Business center. Fitness center. Pets accepted. $351 and up.

★★★TRIBECA GRAND HOTEL

2 Avenue of the Americas, New York, 212-519-6600, 800-965-3000;
www.tribecagrand.com

This edgy-but-elegant hotel is a goldmine for those looking to party like rock stars, or just appear like they do. The soaring triangular atrium off the lobby is where an international roster of DJs spin in the sofa-filled Church Lounge, and the lower level has a 100-seat theater for private movie screenings. Rooms are smallish, but have phones and TVs in the bathrooms, gourmet mini-bars, and, if you request one, a live goldfish to keep you company. Some suites look out over the lounge, which can feel like opening the door into a round-the-clock party, but that's fine by most of the people who stay here. If you're into gadgets, book an "iStudio," tricked out with Apple's latest goods, including G5 computers with film-, photo- and sound-editing software.

201 rooms. Restaurant, bar. Fitness center. Pets accepted. $251-350

★★★★★TRUMP INTERNATIONAL HOTEL & TOWER

1 Central Park W., New York, 212-299-1000, 888-448-7867; www.trumpintl.com

As with most things Trump, this 52-story building at the crossroads of Broadway, Columbus Circle and Central Park is anything but understated. Designed by architects Philip Johnson and Costas Kondylis, only a portion of Trump's black-glass tower—fronted by an unmistakable, massive silver globe sculpture—is taken up by the hotel's 167 rooms. The premises are also home to the lauded French-fusion restaurant Jean Georges and the luxurious 6,000-square-foot Trump spa. Rooms have Trump-style basics: blond wood furnishings, marble bathrooms, European-style kitchens with china, crystal glassware and Christofle serving trays, and amazing park and city views through the floor-to-ceiling windows. Leave it to the Donald to add an extra-special touch by assigning each of the hotel guests their own personal attaché to assist with everything from personalized stationary to a custom-stocked fridge.

167 rooms. Restaurant, bar. Business center. Fitness center. Pool. Spa. Pets accepted. $351 and up.

★★★W NEW YORK-TIMES SQUARE

1567 Broadway, New York, 212-930-7400; www.whotels.com

Located in Times Square, this hotel is just as colorful as its surroundings. The ultra-contemporary lobby, located on the seventh floor, has tile floors and leather benches, and it houses the hip Living Room bar. Guest rooms are minimalist and stylish, with contemporary furnishings in muted grays and dark-wood touches or, in the recently renovated rooms, lavender tones with glass desks and cube-shaped nightstands. It goes without saying that the views from the rooms can't be beat: Watch the action unfold below on Times Square as you relax on your pillow-top bed and goose-down pillow. And though this W doesn't have a Bliss Spa, it does have the homegrown spa's signature products sink-side. Once you're rested and primped, head down to the Blue Fin restaurant and start the night with a cocktail at Whiskey bar before heading out into the square, just outside the lobby doors.

507 rooms. Restaurant, bar. Fitness center. Business center. Pets accepted. $351 and up

★★★W NEW YORK-UNION SQUARE

201 Park Ave. S., New York, 212-253-9119; www.whotels.com

This Union Square outpost of the contemporary hotel chain does a nice job blending an uptown atmosphere with some downtown coolness. Set on the open square with a leafy park in its center, this W (there are four others around Manhattan) located in the 1911 Beaux Arts Guardian Life building has the same clean modern lines and comfortable beds that guests swear by, and twice-daily maid service, as the other locales. There's also an in-hotel lounge and a branch of Todd English's Italian/Mediterranean restaurant Olives, but with the East Village, Tribeca and Soho so close, you're better off heading out on an adventure than staying in.

270 rooms. Restaurant, bar. Fitness center. Pets accepted. $351 and up.

★★★THE WALDORF-ASTORIA

301 Park Ave., New York, 212-355-3000, 800-925-3673; www.waldorfastoria.com

Opened in 1893 by millionaire William Waldorf Astor, this grande dame of New York luxury hotels moved to its present location from a little further south on Fifth Avenue in 1931, and it still retains some of the original hotel's Art Deco interior. The lobby has the decadent feel of a ballroom with its sweeping marble staircases, and glamour seeps from every crevice of the hotel, which sits on a full city block. As you would suspect from such a historic hotel, every room located in the Waldorf Astoria and Waldorf Towers (which has a separate lobby, concierge, long-term leases and roomier suites) is adorned with thick draperies and ornately carved furniture, though some rooms are quite small. The hotel's Bull and Bear Steakhouse & Bar, Inagiku Japanese restaurant, and cocktail terrace overlooking the Park Avenue lobby are always busy. A new Guerlain spa offers complimentary valet parking and relaxing foot baths upon arrival.

1415 rooms. Restaurant, bar. Fitness center. Spa. Business center. Pets accepted. $351 and up

★★★WARWICK HOTEL

65 W. 54th St., New York, 212-247-2700; www.warwickhotelny.com

Originally opened as a residential hotel in 1928, this Midtown Manhattan property has retained its sense of history while remaining current, thanks to its modern amenities and services. The public spaces feature traditional chandeliers, potted flowers, contemporary furnishings and a small library in the lobby while guest rooms have a European-style décor and marble-clad bathrooms. Murals on 54, the onsite Continental cuisine restaurant, is a great choice for dinner, followed by a nightcap at Randolph's Bar, named for the hotel's builder, William Randolph Hearst.

426 rooms. Restaurant, bar. Business center. Fitness center. $251-350

★★★THE WESTIN NEW YORK AT TIMES SQUARE

270 W. 43rd St., New York, 212-201-4679, 866-837-4183; www.westinny.com

This 45-story hotel near Times Square is an oasis in a sea of nonstop action. Regular rooms are kitted out with the hotel's trademarked Heavenly Bed & Bath, and have views of Times Square and the Hudson River. The "Spa-Inspired" guest rooms take relaxation to the next level with aroma air diffusers, a Kinjoy Shiatsu massage chair that can be adjusted to "zero gravity" position and a variety of soothing CDs for your listening pleasure. Book a $2,000-a-night "Renewal suite" and your own personal "host" (in other words, butler) caters to your every wish so you can focus on rejuvenation. There may not be much more you'll need beyond the fresh white roses, orchids and lotus flowers supplied throughout the suite, a bamboo-floored exercise space which includes a spinning cycle and other exercise equipment, and spa bathroom with a Kohler Chromatherapy whirlpool bath, plus cashmere robes and slippers.

863 rooms. Restaurant, bar. Fitness center. Spa. Business center. $251-350

WHERE TO EAT

★★★'21' CLUB

21 W. 52nd St., New York, 212-582-7200; www.21club.com

This classic institution, a former speakeasy with a hidden wine vault, is a place where suited men sip tumblers of Scotch with the guys in the downstairs Bar Room while digging into medium-rare steaks and inflating stories about business and broads. Is this the '50s, or 50-plus years later? That's precisely the beauty of '21' Club, where time seems to have stopped and a who's who of celebrities and power brokers (George Clooney, Bill Gates) eating burgers and Caesar salads provides more noteworthy decoration than the hanging model airplanes downstairs, or the murals and chandeliers in the upstairs dining rooms.

American menu. Lunch (Monday-Friday), dinner. Closed Sunday. $86 and up

★88 PALACE

88 E. Broadway, New York, 212-941-8886

If you are craving dim sum, or a perfect Chinese tea luncheon, consider stopping at 88 Palace, a bustling Chinese restaurant featuring a delicious and authentic selection of dim sum and house-made soups, fish, meats, and rice dishes.

Chinese. Lunch, dinner. $16-35

★★★★ADOUR ALAIN DUCASSE

The St. Regis New York, 2 E. 55th St., New York, 212-710-2277; www.adour-stregis.com

Legendary chef Alain Ducasse's Adour is a dramatic leap from the French master's previous endeavor, Alain Ducasse at the Essex House. Where the Essex House scared away diners with a French elegance rarely seen stateside, Ducasse's Adour is meant to be a subdued yet elegant wine bar. Draped in warm burgundy and gold with a corridor outfitted in leather and walls lined with well-stocked wine coolers and grape vines, the space is a perfectly warm setting for chef Joel Dennis' straightforward but expertly prepared and sophisticated French comfort food. Adour's dishes range from simple and straight-from-the-farm to quietly stunning and intricate. Start off with delicate foie gras or ricotta gnocchi and follow it with an expertly prepared duck breast or the braised wild striped bass. Adour's wine list is among the city's best, and the desserts, created by pastry chef Sandro Micheli, rank accordingly—they include a luxuriously rich dark chocolate sorbet and pear with roasted pecans.

Contemporary French. Dinner. Reservations recommended. Bar. $36-85

★★★AL BUSTAN

827 Third Ave., New York, 212-759-8439; www.albustanny.com

Head to Al Bustan, which means The Orchard, and discover its aromatic and exquisitely fresh Lebanese cooking. Al Bustan is very popular, especially at lunch, as its Midtown location makes it a nice choice for dealmakers. When the sun sets, this restaurant becomes an elegant respite for dinner, offering guests a luxurious dining experience that includes some of the best bread in the city, served with a magnificent array of mezze, not to mention a full menu of authentic Lebanese dishes.

Middle Eastern. Lunch, dinner. Reservations recommended. Bar. $36-85

★★★ALLEN & DELANCEY
115 Allen St., New York, 212-253-5400; www.allenanddelancey.net

amed after the Lower East Side intersection where it's located, this restaurant brings a little more boho chic to the Lower East Side. Thick red-velvet drapes and candles dripping with wax on bookshelves make this seductive gastropub feel like a brothel-like foodie haven. Forget bangers and mash—the kitchen makes normally cringe-worthy animal parts (is that a lamb's neck on your plate?) something to crave. The dining room is so dark you might need a pocket flashlight just to read the menu, so memorize a few signature items just in case, such as the divine porchetta and morcilla with riesling-braised cabbage, hazelnuts and violet mustard, or the poached halibut with Italian olives, artichoke barigoule and roasted tomato. It's hard to resist tossing in a side of the Jerusalem artichokes and bacon for the table.

Contemporary American. Dinner. Reservations recommended. $16-35

★★AMMA
246 E. 51st St., New York, 212-644-8330; www.ammanyc.com

At Amma, an elegant, petite East Side spot serving excellent Indian fare, you'll find tables jammed with eager curry-lovers kvelling over dishes of Goan shrimp, piles of bhel puri, and plates of frizzled okra with tomatoes and onions. This is not your ordinary curry house, though. Amma is stylish and serene, and the service is efficient. The chef, formerly of Tamarind, knows his way around the tandoor oven, and you should by all means order several tandoori dishes like stuffed chicken breasts, crisp and spiced shrimp, or the succulent yogurt-infused lamb chops. Save room for dessert; the rasmalai dumplings are a showstopper.

Indian. Lunch, dinner. Reservations recommended. Jacket required. $36-85

★★AMY RUTH'S
113 W. 116th St., New York, 212-280-8779; www.amyruthsharlem.com

For authentic, homestyle Southern fare, you don't have to head to the Deep South. Chef Carl Redding opened this casual, cozy Harlem restaurant as a tribute to his Alabama grandmother, Amy Ruth, who taught him real Southern cooking. Dishes are named after prominent African Americans, like The Rev. Al Sharpton (fried chicken and waffles), The Ludacris (fried chicken wings), and The C. Virginia Fields (country bread pudding), and pack in crowds of both locals and tourists alike.

Southern. Breakfast, lunch, dinner. $16-35

★★★ANNISA
13 Barrow St., New York, 212-741-6699; www.annisarestaurant.com

At Annisa, a cozy, off-the-beaten-path gem in Greenwich Village, chef/partner Anita Lo and partner Jennifer Scism (who runs the front of the house) bring a bit of Asia and a lot of flavor and savvy style to the contemporary American table. The restaurant's golden glow and elegant, sheer-white curtains draped along the tall walls create a stylish backdrop for the simple, approachable menu. An array of wines by the glass and an able sommelier make pairing wine with dinner a breeze. Due to a recent fire, the restaurant is currently closed; call or check their website for reopening details.

American. Dinner. Reservations recommended. Bar. $36-85

★★★AQUAGRILL

210 Spring St., New York, 212-274-0505; www.aquagrill.com

A perennial favorite for swimmingly fresh seafood (and great dry-aged steak), Aquagrill has a terrific location at the edge of Soho. Take advantage of the stellar outdoor seating in warm months. With its tall French doors flung open to the street, Aquagrill has a European elegance that makes it an irresistible spot to settle in, even if only for a glass of sparkling wine and a dozen (or two) shimmering oysters.

Seafood. Lunch, dinner, brunch. Reservations recommended. Outdoor seating. Bar. $36-85

★★★AQUAVIT

65 E. 55th St., New York, 212-307-7311; www.aquavit.org

The Scandinavian cuisine at Marcus Samuelsson's Midtown eatery is a far cry from the café at IKEA. The super-modern dining room is bright and minimal with angular booths, and the bar has stylish egg-shaped chairs reflecting a sharp Scandinavian aesthetic. The menu emphasizes traditional seafood and game, but with a sophisticated twist (foie gras ganache with quail egg, pickled tomato and mustard; duck atop parsley spätzle, radicchio and root vegetables). The onsite Aquavit Café features a more casual menu of Scandinavian staples including six different kinds of herring, beef Rydberg and, yes, Swedish meatballs. Then there are the dozen-plus housemade aquavits; we recommend both the horseradish and the mango, lime and chili pepper-combo flavors. A great way to try it all: The Sunday smorgasbord ($48 including a Danish Mary) is stocked with herring and hot potatoes, Swedish cheese, gravlax with mustard sauce and, of course, Swedish meatballs.

Scandinavian. Lunch (Monday-Friday), dinner, Sunday brunch. $36-85

★★★ARABELLE

37 E. 64th St., New York, 212-606-4647; www.arabellerestaurant.com

From the dramatic gold dome and brass chandeliers of the main dining area to the exotic atmosphere of the Bar Seine, Arabelle offers a romantic dining experience. The restaurant is situated in the elegant Hotel Plaza Athénée. Several intimate dining alcoves, which serve as extensions of both the Bar Seine and the main dining room, are offered to guests during hours when the main dining is closed. Specialty dishes on the classic American menu include coffee-rubbed New York strip steak and grilled diver sea scallops. There's also a traditional Sunday brunch and afternoon high tea.

American. Lunch (Tuesday-Sunday), dinner (Tuesday-Saturday), Sunday brunch. Reservations recommended. Children's menu. Bar. $36-85

★★ARTISANAL FROMAGERIE & BISTRO

2 Park Ave., New York, 212-725-8585; www.artisanalbistro.com

If you love cheese, then you've found your paradise in this sprawling, dimly lit bistro with buttercream yellow walls and red-checkered floors. Couples nibble on baskets of airy gougères at the bar while cheese-savvy servers hustle pots of gooey fondue to tightly packed wooden tables. It's the quality of the French-style food, from hearty leg of lamb to charred hanger steak, that salvages Artisanal from becoming a kitschy fondue joint and instead makes it a delightful restaurant you will want to return to again and again. Weekend brunch isn't for the cholesterol conscious—the cinnamon sugar dusted beignets are impossible to refuse.

French. Lunch (Monday-Friday), dinner, Saturday-Sunday brunch. $16-35

★★★★ASIATE
80 Columbus Circle, New York, 212-805-8881; www.mandarinoriental.com

French-Asian fare is nothing new—hello, 20th century Vietnam—but it sure is something to write home about if it comes from this restaurant inside the Mandarin Oriental hotel. Asiate offers thoughtful, well-executed East-meets-West fare, like roasted foie gras and glazed eel atop braised daikon in an anise-pineapple broth, and black sea bass with stir-fried Asian vegetables in a ginger-lemongrass consommé. Indeed, everything about this restaurant is noteworthy, from the sweeping views of Central Park, courtesy of the 16-foot-high windows, to the glittering tree-branch sculpture hanging from the ceiling, to the beautiful china on your table and the wine collection, which fills up an entire wall. The chocolate fondant with raspberry granite is the perfect complement to your evening.

Asian, French. Breakfast, lunch (Monday-Friday), dinner, Saturday-Sunday brunch. Reservations recommended. $86 and up.

★★★★AUREOLE
One Bryant Park, 135 West 42nd St., 212-319-1660; www.charliepalmer.com

Owned by Charlie Palmer, Aureole specializes in the kind of stylish yet comfortable fine-dining experience completely devoid of pretension—here, it really is about the food and not a celebrity chef. Aureole now inhabits the famous Bank of America building under the kitchen leadership of executive chef Christopher Lee. Diners receive star treatment from courteous staff doling out hearty dishes such as veal tenderloin and sweetbreads, Australian rack of lamb or crispy black sea bass with French white asparagus. If you crave lighter fare, sit in the bar room where you will see more casual options such as the Aureole grilled burger or the diver sea scallop sandwich. A wine list heavy on European and California labels also includes the restaurant's own sparkling wine, Aureole Cuvée—no doubt a popular choice for the marrying kind of guests that you frequently see here on bended knee, popping the question before dessert.

Contemporary American. Lunch (Monday-Saturday), dinner. Bar. Reservations recommended. $36-85

★★AVRA ESTIATORIO
141 E. 48th St., New York, 212-759-8550; www.avrany.com

At this terrific, airy, and elegant estiatorio, you can eat like they do on the Greek islands, feasting on fresh fish (priced by the pound) simply grilled with lemon, herbs, and olive oil; salads of fresh briny feta and tomato; and loaves of fluffy, warm pita for dipping into assorted garlicky mezze like hummus and tzatziki. Save room for dessert, as the sticky-sweet honey-soaked baklava is not to be missed.

Mediterranean. Lunch (Monday-Friday), dinner, Saturday-Sunday brunch. Reservations recommended. Outdoor seating. Bar. $36-85

★★AZUL BISTRO

152 Stanton St., New York, 646-602-2004; www.azulnyc.com

Located on a sleepy corner of Stanton Street in the now hip 'hood known as the Lower East Side, Azul Bistro is a seductive corner spot with raw wood accents and low lighting. Serving South American fare to the soft rhythms of tango music, Azul makes a nice substitute for a trip to Buenos Aires. While the menu focuses on Argentinean cuisine, you'll also find other Latin American dishes like ceviche and empanadas. Grilled meats are a specialty, like the lamb and the juicy steak dotted with chimichurri sauce (think garlic-pesto). The watermelon sangria should get the night going on the right foot, no matter what you order.

Latin American. Dinner. Reservations recommended. Outdoor seating. $36-85

★★★BABBO

110 Waverly Place, New York, 212-777-0303; www.babbonyc.com

Mario Batali is the rock 'n' roll bad boy of the restaurant world. He's got a notorious temper, a ragtag wardrobe and a cameo in a Bloodsugars' music video to his credit along with all those fabulous restaurants. It's at Babbo where he lets his rebel personality shine; a close friend of R.E.M.'s Michael Stipe, Batali understandably skips Old Blue Eyes and plays whatever he wants over the dining room sound system at this traditional-with-a-twist Italian restaurant. So rock out while tucking into Batali's creative dishes like "mint love letters"—delicate pasta pockets of spicy lamb sausage with just a hint of mint to cool your palette—and melt-in-your-mouth beef cheek ravioli with rich squab liver and black truffles. A $125 "traditional" tasting menu with wine is a song compared to similar menus at other restaurants—and you can bet those places won't likely have that rustic, rock combo all rolled into one.

Italian. Dinner. Reservations recommended. Bar. $36-85

★★★BALTHAZAR

80 Spring St., New York, 212-965-1414; www.balthazarny.com

This warm, noisy French bistro—a hot spot of the '90s and now a reliable standby—is a transporting experience, from the sunshine-yellow walls to the European crowd devouring steak au poivre, duck confit and other "I-must-be-in-Paris" staples. The brunch is among the best in town; the smartest calls are the pillowy brioche French toast and baskets of baked goods—but don't eat that entire croissant or you might not fit between the snugly packed tables when you get up to leave. The late-night menu keeps Balthazar bustling until after midnight seven days a week. No time for a full meal? Stop at the adjacent bakery for one of the city's best baguettes or a crisp, buttery chocolate chip cookie before hitting the Soho shopping circuit.

French. Breakfast, lunch (Monday-Friday), dinner, late-night, Saturday-Sunday brunch. Reservations recommended. Bar. $36-85

★★BAO 111

111 Ave. C, New York, 212-254-7773; www.bao111.com

This sleek little spot on Avenue C gets major snaps for its contemporary brand of Vietnamese fare. Drawing an eclectic crowd, Bao 111 is an alluring space, marked by amber lighting and wood banquettes graced with embroidered pillows. Expect dishes like the signature short ribs skewered with lemongrass, spring rolls with mint and basil, five-spice quail, and crab and shrimp soup with noodles.

Vietnamese. Dinner, late-night. Reservations recommended. Bar. $36-85

★★★BAR BLANC

142 W. 10th St., New York, 212-255-2330; www.barblanc.com

You know what they say about size. Well, lucky for Bar Blanc, which epitomizes the New York maxim, it's all about what you do with what you've got. The compact joint clothed completely in white is refreshingly simple with a casual-chic vibe accompanying a short seasonal menu. Start with the crispy sweetbread salad with sherry-poached cherries, watercress and lemon vinaigrette, and then move to the seared black cod with wilted Arrowleaf spinach, celery root, fennel saffron sauce and salt cod brandade.

Contemporary American. Dinner. Reservations recommended. Bar. $36-85

★★★BAR BOULUD

1900 Broadway, New York, 212-595-0303; www.danielnyc.com/barboulud.html

Conveniently situated across the street from Lincoln Center, Daniel Boulud's most laidback foray into the New York dining scene takes aim at hurried opera- and ballet-goers, offering his world-class cuisine sans frills and fuss. That's not to say, however, that you won't pay a pretty penny for this French pub fare. You stand forewarned on both the early evening crowds and the price of your steak-frites and roasted chicken. But Boulud executes the wine bar concept fittingly. The design pays homage to the winemaking industry with a long vaulted ceiling reminiscent of a wine cellar, a gravel wall conjuring images of vineyard terroir, furnishings made from wine barrel oak. Of course chef Boulud's menu doesn't disappoint. The highlight here, besides the wine, are the over 18 varieties of house-made charcuterie. Best bet is to sip Burgundy wine while sharing some patés and the aioli appetizer, an olive oil-poached cod and Louisiana shrimp garlic dip with quail eggs, veg etables and mussels

French menu. Lunch (Monday-Friday), dinner (Monday-Friday), Saturday-Sunday brunch. Bar. Casual attire. Reservations recommended. Outdoor seating

★★BAR JAMON

125 E. 17th St., New York, 212-253-2773; www.barjamonnyc.com

Mario Batali is turning Spanish on us. After mastering the art of simple Italian fare at Babbo, Lupa, Otto and Esca, he is taking on the Iberian Peninsula with Bar Jamon, an all-tapas restaurant located just above Union Square in the East Village and adjacent to Casa Mono. A menu of Catalan small plates is served up at this ham and wine bar in a convivial setting straight out of Barcelona. A miniature spot with dark wood accents and a marble bar, this crowded watering hole features all sorts of Spanish jamon (pronounced haah-mon), cheeses (manchego, queso de tetilla, valdeon, calabres) and olives. More exciting plates include smoked trout salad with olives and cava-soaked grapes and classics like tortilla Española—all perfectly suited to Spanish wine and sherry.

Spanish. Lunch (Saturday-Sunday), dinner, late-night. Reservations recommended. $15 and under.

★★★BAR MASA

10 Columbus Circle, New York, 212-823-9800; www.masanyc.com

If Masa, chef Masa Takayama's celebrated (and incredibly expensive) Japanese and sushi restaurant, is too hard on your wallet, try going next door to Bar Masa. Both restaurants are located in the Time Warner Center and have some identical items on their menus, but Bar Masa is more affordable and has a casual ambience. The attractive space is narrow, with the bar (topped with an African plank) on one side of the room and long, ultrasuede banquettes and tables on the other. Lunch, dinner and á la carte sushi menus are available, and the restaurant offers a cocktail menu as well as wine and sake lists.

Japanese. Lunch, dinner. Closed Monday. Bar. $36-85

★★★BARBETTA

321 W. 46th St., New York, 212-246-9171; www.barbettarestaurant.com

This classic Italian restaurant opened its doors in 1906 and is still owned by the same family, the Maioglios. Located in a pair of historic early 19th-century townhouses, this restaurant is a classic charmer that's all about elegant, old-world dining. The menu doesn't aim anywhere other than where its heart is—Italy—but don't expect just pasta. The kitchen offers a great selection of seafood, poultry and beef prepared with seasonal ingredients and lively flavors.

Italian. Lunch, dinner. Closed Sunday-Monday. Reservations recommended. Outdoor seating. Bar. $36-85

★★BARBUTO

775 Washington St., New York, 212-924-9700; www.barbutonyc.com

Occupying a trendy space in one of the city's hippest locations, chef and owner Jonathan Waxman, who was seasoned by Alice Waters, developed a successful recipe for a New York City restaurant: a dash of contemporary design combined with a hefty dose of casual yet happening ambience finished with a helping of fabulous food. Funky yet functional garage doors act as the restaurant walls and in warm weather transform Barbuto into an indoor-outdoor dining room, which runs right into the open kitchen. The downside: the modern industrial design doesn't do much to dampen noise. But who needs conversation when you have pan-fried monkfish with farroto and butternut squash purée in need of your attention?

Italian. Lunch, dinner. Reservations recommended. Outdoor seating. Bar. $36-85

★BARNEY GREENGRASS

541 Amsterdam Ave., New York, 212-724-4707; www.barneygreengrass.com

If you like your restaurants with a schmear of character and history, look no further than the 100-year-old Barney Greengrass. Known affectionately as "The Sturgeon King," this appetizing Jewish deli (which moved from its original Harlem location to its current spot in 1929) takes the nickname seriously: Sturgeon and velvety lox top bagels and bialys, and weave through fluffy scrambled eggs with onions for one of the most popular breakfasts on the Upper West Side. Other traditional fare such as herring, sable and whitefish salad have also understandably made this no-frills Formica haven with its surly counter staff a go-to eatery for generations of New Yorkers. Expect a long wait, especially on weekends, when you might bump elbows with the likes of Jerry Seinfeld.

Deli. Breakfast, lunch. Closed Monday. $16-35

★★BECCO
355 W. 46th St., New York, 212-397-7597; www.becconyc.com

Becco, a charming Italian restaurant in Times Square, is a delightful place to relax over a delicious Italian supper before or after the theater, or at lunch for a business meeting. Becco offers great food, gracious service, and a lovely, airy atmosphere. The pre-theater special for which it has become famous, offers authentic homemade pastas in an all-you-can-eat style. You choose three pastas, and they keep dishing them out until you surrender or burst, whichever comes first.

Italian. Lunch, dinner. Reservations recommended. $36-85

★★★BEN BENSON'S STEAKHOUSE
123 W. 52nd St., New York, 212-581-8888; www.benbensons.com

At this popular steakhouse, you'll find yourself elbow to elbow with celebrities, politicians, sports stars and the city's financial elite. As you might expect from a power steak spot, the menu is as big as the egos in the room and includes solid standards like salads, poultry and seafood that are simply and impeccably prepared. The signature selection of USDA dry-aged prime beef is served in nearly a dozen cuts and portion sizes. The huge steaks are matched in size by the burly lobsters. Don't miss the house's signature crispy hash browns.

Steak. Lunch (Monday-Friday), dinner. Reservations recommended. Outdoor seating. Bar. $36-85

★★★BENOIT
60 W. 55th St., New York, 646-943-7373; www.benoitny.com

This former home of La Côte Basque brasserie got a new resident when Alain Ducasse brought the century-old Parisian brasserie Benoit stateside. Attempting to bring the old French favorites to the Big Apple, the menu doesn't deviate from the 50- to -100-year-old recipes for the classics—onion soup gratinée, marinated salmon with warm potato salad and foie gras confit. The paté en croute recipe dates back to 1892. If the new-fangled French that you'll get at Ducasse's higher-end Adour is more your thing, go there or be disappointed.

French. Lunch, dinner. Bar. $36-85

★★BEPPE
45 E. 22nd St., New York, 212-982-8422; www.beppenyc.com

Walk into Chelsea's Beppe, and you may feel yourself leaving the city of New York and entering the lovely land of Italy. At this warm, weathered eatery filled with all the charm of an Italian farmhouse kitchen, you can sample some of chef/owner Cesare Cassella's earthy and divine pasta; a terrific se-

lection of Tuscan-style wood-fired seafood, meat, and game; and a wine list that focuses on gems from Tuscany to Italy's lesser-known regions.
Italian. Lunch, dinner. Closed Sunday. Reservations recommended. Bar. $36-85

★★BEYOGLU
1431 Third Ave., New York, 212-650-0850
There is much to love about this family-run Turkish restaurant on the Upper East Side. From the service, which is warm and friendly, to the dining room, a spacious, stylish, low-lit space, to the easygoing crowd of neighborhood folks, Beyoglu beckons you back as soon as you enter. The real star here is the food, which includes delicious warm pita bread drizzled with olive oil to start and moves on to a terrific variety of appetizers and a heavenly-spiced selection of fragrant rice and assorted kabobs that will leave you clamoring for a ticket to Istanbul ASAP.
Middle Eastern. Lunch, dinner. Reservations recommended. Outdoor seating. Bar. $16-35

★★BICE
7 E. 54th St., New York, 212-688-1999; www.bicenewyork.com
With a convenient location off 5th Avenue in Midtown, Bice (pronounced bee-chee) is easily accessible from Museum Row, Rockefeller Center, and theaters. Subtle lighting, massive urns of fresh flowers, and geometric-shaped ceiling beams add to the warm Mediterranean ambience. An extensive, classic Italian menu is offered, including signature dishes such as tagliolini pasta with lobster, osso buco, and veal and spinach ravioli—the pasta here is homemade. A collection of rare dinner plates created by famed designer Gianni Versace is on display and available to guests for purchase.
Italian. Lunch, dinner. Outdoor seating. Children's menu. Bar. $36-85

★★★BLT MARKET
1430 Sixth Ave., New York, 212-521-6125; www.bltmarket.com
Laurent Tourondel's BLT (Bistro Laurent Tourondel) Market in the Ritz-Carlton hotel is a valentine to all things local and seasonal and another star in Tourondel's constellation of restaurants, which includes BLT Steak and BLT Prime. Diners feast on peak-season ingredients, like spring's pea and ricotta ravioli with spicy sausage, mint and pea shoots. The soft shell crab comes from Maryland, while Jamison Farm provides the lamb, and nearly all of the vegetables come from farms nearby. No matter where it hails from, the food is delicious.
Contemporary American. Breakfast, dinner. Closed Sunday-Monday. Reservations recommended. $36-85

★★★BLUE FIN
1567 Broadway, New York, 212-918-1400; www.brguestrestaurants.com
Located in the W Times Square Hotel, Blue Fin is restaurateur Steve Hanson's (Blue Water Grill, Dos Caminos) elaborate seafood palace. Blue Fin features high-end fish dishes and a stunning array of sushi, sashimi and maki. The bar on the ground floor is always packed with bright young things sipping tall, cool cocktails,.

American, seafood, sushi. Breakfast, lunch (Monday-Friday), dinner, Saturday-Sunday brunch. Outdoor seating. Children's menu. Bar. $36-85

★★★BLUE HILL

75 Washington Place, New York, 212-539-1776; www.bluehillnyc.com

Chef Dan Barber is one of New York's masters of farm-to-table cuisine, using ingredients sustainably grown at the Stone Barns Center for Food and Agriculture, a farm and educational center 30 miles away in the Hudson Valley. (A country-chic dining experience is available at the farm, too.) Much of the produce, from the pickled ramps in the martinis to the shiitake mushrooms in the warm asparagus soup, is grown on the farm. Other ingredients like guinea hen, goat cheese and veal are from local purveyors, and you can taste their freshness. The below-street-level dining room is calm, warm and elegant. Contemporary American. Dinner. $36-85

★★BLUE RIBBON BAKERY

35 Downing St., New York, 212-337-0404; www.blueribbonrestaurants.com

The brothers Bromberg first brought New Yorkers a taste of their creative culinary genius with Blue Ribbon, their hip late-night bistro. They took on the task of baking bread (delicious bread) and decided to offer a menu of salads, small plates, and fresh seasonal entrées. The décor is rustic at this windowed corner spot in the West Village; wood beams, brick walls, and wide-plank floors all add to the casual and relaxed ambience. Whether for lunch, brunch, dinner, or an afternoon pick-me-up, Blue Ribbon Bakery is the perfect spot for a casual and always tasty bite.

American, French. Lunch, dinner, late-night (Friday-Saturday), Saturday-Sunday brunch. Bar. $36-85

★★BLUE RIBBON BRASSERIE

97 Sullivan St., New York, 212-274-0404; www.blueribbonrestaurants.com

Blue Ribbon is everything a good brasserie should be—woody and warm, with a menu that leans heavily on upgraded comfort classics like hanger steak and fried chicken but expertly folds in worldly touches like paella. This candlelit eatery (the crown jewel of the local empire that includes Blue Ribbon Sushi and Blue Ribbon Bakery) excels with its always-fresh raw bar and juicy bomb of a burger. Tip for the chef-obsessed: With a kitchen that serves until 4 a.m., Blue Ribbon has long been a favorite late-night hangout for the toqued set after finishing shifts at nearby restaurants.

International. Lunch, dinner, late-night. Bar. $36-85

★★BLUE SMOKE

116 E. 27th St., New York, 212-447-7733; www.bluesmoke.com

The smell of smoking meat wafts through the entire spacious, airy restaurant, priming your appetite for its stick-to-your-ribs food. Many regional barbecue styles are served here—so expect the likes of saucy Kansas City ribs and dry-rubbed Texas-style fare. While the barbecued ribs and brisket hit the spot, the side dishes are stars in their own right. Gooey macaroni and cheese, smoky baked beans and braised collard greens with bacon will have you licking your plate clean. The burger here is a double-fister, and it can be topped with smoked bacon. The jazz club downstairs and a late-night menu

keep this place jumping past midnight.
American. Lunch, dinner. $16-35

★★BLUE WATER GRILL
31 Union Square W., New York, 212-675-9500; www.brguestrestaurants.com
Overlooking Union Square Park, Blue Water Grill is a buzzing shrine to sea-food, with a raw bar and an extensive menu of fresh fish prepared with global accents and a terrific array of sushi, sashimi and creative maki rolls. The din-ing room is massive with marble columns and floors, and sky-high ceilings. The vibe is spirited and lively. Be warned that conversation may be difficult at peak times.
Seafood. Lunch (Monday-Saturday), dinner, Sunday brunch. Reservations recommended. Outdoor seating. Children's menu. Bar. $36-85

★★BOATHOUSE RESTAURANT
72nd Street and Park Drive N., New York, 212-517-2233;
www.thecentralparkboathouse.com
Central Park is one of the most wonderful places to spend a day in Manhat-tan. It really doesn't matter what the season. The same can be said of the Boathouse Restaurant, an open, airy, and romantic New York icon/restaurant with views of the boaters rowing their way across Central Park pond. Sure, summer is the ideal time to settle in for cocktails on the patio under the cherry blossoms, but this restaurant is equally idyllic in the winter, when snow blankets the park in a soft hush. The menu at the Boathouse is New American, with steak, fish, pasta, and salads sure to please any and all cu-linary desires. Brunch in warmer months is a winner here, but the lines are long, so call ahead.
American. Lunch (Monday-Friday), dinner, Saturday-Sunday brunch. Reser-vations recommended. Outdoor seating. Children's menu. Bar. $36-85

★★★BOND STREET
6 Bond St., New York, 212-777-2500; www.bondstrestaurant.com
High-art sushi and sashimi are the calling cards of Bond Street, a hipster hangout disguised as a modern Japanese restaurant. The whitewashed, airy restaurant has a dark and sexy lower-level bar. Dress to impress here, and expect a wait, even with a reservation; it is all part of the experience.
Japanese. Dinner. Reservations recommended. Bar. $36-85

★★★★BOULEY
163 Duane St., Tribeca, 212-964-2525; www.davidbouley.com
David Bouley recently moved his acclaimed restaurant to a new Tribeca head-quarters and the results are impressive. The dining room's vaulted gold-leafed ceiling is bold, his determination to serve high-end ingredients is fierce, and freebies like a lemon tea cake for ladies to take home for the next morning's breakfast are a godsend. You won't be able to restrain your glee at Bouley's classic-yet-unconventional French fare, like rosemary-crusted rack of lamb in a pool of zucchini-mint purée, and seafood dishes adorned with yuzu and Japanese pickles. The over-the-top mantra doesn't stop at the entrées: The Chocolate Frivolous dessert is an exercise in excess—a plate piled high with

chocolate brûlée, chocolate parfait, chocolate-walnut spice bread, orange-cointreau ganache and a generous scoop of chocolate ice cream. You'll be on a sugar rush all evening.

French. Lunch, dinner. Reservations recommended. $86 and up.

★★★BRASSERIE

100 E. 53rd St., New York, 212-751-4840; www.rapatina.com

As you step inside sleek Brasserie, you may feel all eyes on you, which is probably because they are. The dining room is set down a level, and when you enter, you must walk down a futuristic glass staircase, a dramatic walkway that turns heads. The menu mixes classics and contemporary dishes, from duck cassoulet and frisée aux lardons to onion soup, escargots and goujonettes of sole.

Contemporary. Breakfast (Monday-Friday), lunch (Monday-Friday), dinner, Saturday-Sunday brunch. Reservations recommended. Bar. $36-85

★★★BRASSERIE 8 1/2

9 W. 57th St., New York, 212-829-0812; www.rapatina.com

Located in the sleek, Gordon Bunshaft-designed 9 building on West 57th Street, Brasserie 8 1/2 is the perfect spot for a power lunch, post-work cocktails or a pre-theater meal. A chic, curved staircase is backed by bright, salmon-hued walls and leads down to the long, backlit bar and dramatic, modern art-filled dining room. The kitchen incorporates accents from Asia and the Mediterranean into updated bistro classics.

American, French. Lunch (Monday-Friday), dinner, Sunday brunch. Reservations recommended. Bar. $36-85

★★BRICK LANE CURRY HOUSE

306-308 E. 6th St., New York, 212-979-8787; www.bricklanecurryhouse.com

Brick Lane Curry House is a standout in Curry Row, a stretch of East 6th Street in the East Village that's lined with Indian restaurants. Named for London's Little India dining district, Brick Lane opened to instant raves for its stunning well-spiced Indian cuisine and stylish, hip setting. The décor features walls of paprika and turmeric, and there are wall murals of an Indian beach resort. Some of the dishes, like the seven-ingredient phaal curry, are so fiery that the house will buy you a beer if you can finish.

Indian. Lunch, dinner, late-night. Reservations recommended. Bar. $16-35

★★BRYANT PARK GRILL

25 W. 40th St., New York, 212-840-6500; www.arkrestaurants.com

Located behind the New York Public Library in the leafy tree-lined Bryant Park, the Bryant Park Grill is an airy, vaulted, and stylish spot, with wall-sized windows bringing the park's greenery indoors. An outdoor patio spills out into the park, providing a rare country feel. The simple American menu features salads, steaks, fish, sandwiches and pasta on a straightforward, seasonal menu. The bar is hopping in the summertime, so if mingling with happy hour crowds is your thing, make Bryant Park Grill your destination.

American. Lunch, dinner. Reservations recommended. Outdoor seating. Children's menu. Bar. $16-35*3*

★★★BULL AND BEAR STEAKHOUSE
301 Park Ave., New York, 212-872-4900; www.bullandbearsteakhouse.com

Located in the stately Waldorf-Astoria Hotel, the Bull and Bear Steakhouse is a meat-eater's kingdom. The street-level dining room is elegant in a clubby, macho sort of way, and the steaks, all cut from certified aged Black Angus, are fat, juicy and the way to go, even though the menu does offer a wide variety of other choices, including chicken, lamb, potpie and assorted seafood. Classic steakhouse sides like creamed spinach, garlic mashed potatoes and buttermilk fried onion rings are sinful accompaniments.

American, Steak. Lunch, dinner. Bar. $36-85

★★★CAFÉ BOULUD
20 E. 76th St., New York, 212-772-2600; www.danielnyc.com

The look of the dining room may have changed, thanks to a cosmetic renovation in 2009, but the same exceptional French cuisine continues to flow from the kitchen under the command of chef Gavin Kaysen. Daniel Boulud's more casual eatery, Café Boulud is reminiscent of a buzzing neighborhood brasserie with high ceilings, tightly packed tables and mirrors lining the walls. The menu is divided into categorical themes: tradition, season, garden and world cuisine. It's hard to resist getting traditional with the foie gras au torchon, or dipping into the summer season with Maine peekytoe crab over a carrot purée. For a good smattering of each, opt for the prix fixe lunch. Café Boulud is a popular destination for brunch as well. One look at the viennoiseries basket of pastries and you'll understand why.

French. Lunch, dinner. $36-85

★★CAFÉ DE BRUXELLES
118 Greenwich Ave., New York, 212-206-1830; www.cafebruxellesonline.com

New Yorkers flock to this casual Greenwich Village eatery for out-of-this-world fries (which the Belgians claim to have invented) and steamy mussels. The staff is charming, the menu is packed with fresh, flavorful choices, and the beer selection rivals that of any pub in the city or across the pond, for that matter.

Belgian. Lunch, dinner, Saturday-Sunday brunch. Reservations recommended. Bar. $16-35

★★★CAFÉ DES ARTISTES
1 W. 67th St., New York, 212-877-3500; www.cafenyc.com

Café des Artistes is a timeless New York City classic, boasting incredible floral displays and murals of cavorting nymphs. The restaurant remains an old-guard favorite for its luxurious, sophisticated setting, impeccable service and menu of up-to-the-minute (yet approachable) seasonal French fare. Locals regularly flock to this spot for brunch.

French. Dinner, late-night, brunch. Reservations recommended. Bar. $36-85

★★CAFÉ FIORELLO
1900 Broadway, New York, 212-595-5330; www.cafefiorello.com

If you find yourself taking in a ballet or an opera at Lincoln Center and you don't want to break the bank on dinner because you've just spent your last dime on those tough-to-get tickets, Cafe Fiorello is a great choice for a reasonable, casual and tasty meal. The convivial restaurant has a large outdoor patio for summertime seating and people-watching, while the indoor room is warm and welcoming The menu offers a delicious selection of antipasti, pasta, meat, and fish prepared in the tradition of a Roman osteria, along with classic desserts like a creamy tiramisu.

Northern Italian. Lunch (Monday-Friday), dinner, late-night (Monday-Saturday), Saturday-Sunday brunch. Reservations recommended. Bar. $36-85

★CAFÉ HABANA
17 Prince St., New York, 212-625-2001; www.ecoeatery.com

It's safe to say that if you don't see a crowd of models, musicians and assorted other super-fabulous people strewn out on the sidewalk outside Café Habana, it is closed. Indeed, as soon as this Cuban diner opens, the crowds are there, like metal to a magnet. The space is decked out in vintage chrome, with a food bar and way-cool retro booths, but the draw here is the flawless menu of cheap, straight-up Cuban grub, like rice and beans, terrific hangover-curing egg dishes, fried plantains and molletes.

Cuban, Mexican. Breakfast, lunch, dinner, brunch. $15 and under.

★★CAFÉ LOUP
105 W. 13th St., New York, 212-255-4746; www.cafeloupnyc.com

Café Loup is a neighborhood favorite for simple but stylish French fare. This spacious, airy restaurant has a soothing vibe and is adorned with fresh flowers, lithographs and photographs. If you are in the mood for attitude and a scene, head somewhere else; this is a place where diners come to feel comfortable and simply enjoy a meal.

French. Lunch, dinner. Reservations recommended. Bar. $16-35

★★CAFÉ LUXEMBOURG
200 W. 70th St., New York, 212-873-7411; www.cafeluxembourg.com

This Upper West Side gem has become a favorite of New Yorkers over the years, which explains why it's constantly abuzz with activity. The Art Deco décor with warm, cream-colored walls offers a sophisticated and stylish atmosphere, but it's the consistently good bistro fare that invokes the loyalty. Lunch and dinner menus feature choices like steak au poivre, escargots with garlic butter, and truffle-scented risotto, while duck hash and eggs, Irish oatmeal with brown sugar and cinnamon, and smoked salmon Benedict are standouts on the brunch menu.

American, French. Breakfast (Monday-Friday), lunch (Monday-Friday), dinner, Saturday-Sunday brunch. Reservations recommended. Bar. $36-85

★★CAFÉ SABARSKY
1048 Fifth Ave., New York, 212-288-0665; www.cafesabarsky.com

Located in the Neue Galerie, facing magnificent Central Park on Fifth Avenue, Café Sabarsky offers a taste of Austria in a spectacular New York City setting. With sky-high ceilings, marble pillars, crystal chandeliers, and elegant brocade banquettes, Café Sabarsky feels like a royal chateau in the Austrian Alps. The divine menu, prepared by wonder-chef Kurt Gutenbrunner of Wallse, includes delicious and authentic Viennese pastries and savory Austrian dishes. The wine list is extensive and includes wonderful Austrian red and white varietals.

Continental. Breakfast, lunch, dinner. Closed Tuesday. Reservations recommended. $36-85

★★CAFETERIA

119 Seventh Ave., New York, 212-414-1717; www.cafeteriagroup.com

This 24-hour Chelsea eating house is a late-night hotspot—and at all times during the day—for its easy-to-love American menu in a minimalist whitewashed setting. Cafeteria is a sleek, ramped-up diner with good food, fun cocktails and lots of fabulous attitude that makes it a second home to many-a-model and fashionista.

American. Breakfast, lunch, dinner, late-night, brunch. Outdoor seating. Children's menu. Bar. $16-35

★★★CAPSOUTO FRERES

451 Washington St., New York, 212-966-4900; www.capsoutofreres.com

As its name suggests, Capsouto Freres is owned by the Capsouto brothers who watch over this romantic retreat. Set in a restored 1891 factory in Tribeca, the restaurant has an understated elegance, with original beam floors and exposed brick walls. The eclectic menu features an impressive variety of choices, from calf's liver in sherry vinegar sauce to cassoulet, salmon with green herb sauce and wild Scottish venison. If you are wandering around downtown on a Sunday, the brunch is a great choice, with omelets and excellent French toast at reasonable prices.

French. Lunch (Tuesday-Friday), dinner, Saturday-Sunday brunch. Reservations recommended. Outdoor seating. Bar. $36-85

★★★CARLYLE RESTAURANT

35 E. 76th St., New York, 212-744-1600; www.thecarlyle.com

This lavishly decorated restaurant is housed in the elegant Carlyle Hotel. From the plush velvet walls covered with rare 19th-century prints to the crystal chandeliers and unique floral arrangements, guests will delight in the atmosphere. Meticulous attention is paid to the visual presentation of the gourmet dishes served by a wonderfully attentive staff. Live entertainment includes a pianist and jazz trio.

French. Breakfast, lunch (Monday-Saturday), dinner, Sunday brunch Reservations recommended. Children's menu. Bar. $36-85

★CARMINE'S

2450 Broadway, New York, 212-362-2200; www.carminesnyc.com

If you have an aversion to garlic, do yourself a favor and stay far away from Carmine's, a frenetic, oversized Italian spot in the Upper West Side theater district. Garlic, a prominent ingredient here fills the space. But if you crave hearty portions of zesty, family-style, red-sauced Italian food at reasonable prices, this is your place.

Italian. Lunch, dinner. Reservations recommended. Outdoor seating. Bar. $36-85

★CARNEGIE DELI
854 Seventh Ave., New York, 212-757-2245, 800-334-5606; www.carnegiedeli.com

This is a Jewish deli on steroids—heaps of deliciously fatty pastrami piled between soft slices of rye bread are enough for at least two meals, and mile-high cheesecake wedges could double as door stops. Nothing says American excess like this New York institution, which boasts a personality as large as its portions. Try creatively named sandwiches like Carnegie Haul (pastrami, tongue and salami with relish) or Bacon Whoopee (chicken salad BLT)—and enjoy these hulking sandwiches or a big bowl of matzo ball soup while gazing at the celebrity headshots lining the walls.

Deli. Breakfast, lunch, dinner, late-night. $16-35

★CARRY ON TEA & SYMPATHY
108 Greenwich Ave., New York, 212-989-9735; www.teaandsympathynewyork.com

Anglophiles will love this cozy restaurant in the West Village, where everything from the décor to the food is British through and through. Walls are adorned with the Queen's portrait and royal proclamations, while the menu offers a charming assortment of English fare, such as bangers and mash, and roast beef with Yorkshire pudding.

English. Breakfast, lunch, dinner. $15-35

★★CASA MONO
52 Irving Place, New York, 212-253-2773; www.casamononyc.com

With Casa Mono (which means "monkey house"), a snug little restaurant on the corner of 17th and Irving Place, Mario Batali has stepped from familiar Italian earth onto the culinary and fashion hotbed of Barcelona. Grab a seat at one of the two "eat-at" bars overlooking the open kitchen and watch as the chefs deliver a menu that excites and invigorates in its simplicity. Popular picks include the sepia a la plancha (grilled squid), quail with quince, and oxtail-stuffed piquillo peppers. The decor is understated, and the tables are neat though a bit crowded. But it doesn't matter because this is the sort of place that will make you smile until your face hurts. Claim your sliver of real estate and be patient. You'll soon be rewarded.

Spanish. Lunch, dinner. Reservations recommended. Children's menu. Bar. $15-35

★★CENTOLIRE
1167 Madison Ave., New York, 212-734-7711; www.pinoluongo.com/Centolire.html

Fashionable Upper East Siders use Pino Luongo's Centolire as their elegant dining room and comfy watering hole. The space, soothing and aglow in ultra-flattering light, has a serene vibe with a subtle air of money and power. This is not to say that Centolire is pretentious, because it's not. The service is gracious and the Italian menu of simple, well-articulated flavors is wonderful. However, if you are used to a downtown crowd, you may feel out of place among the aristocratic guests.

Italian. Lunch (Monday-Saturday), dinner, Sunday brunch. Bar. $36-85

★★★'CESCA
164 W. 75th St., New York, 212-787-6300; www.cescanyc.com

Dependably delicious and cozy, the rustic Italian restaurant 'Cesca has been a favorite of Upper West Siders since it opened in 2003. Stenciled white walls, soft lighting and large, circular booths keep the mood relaxed. The open kitchen churns out hits such as parmesan and prosciutto fritters dusted with a surprising kick of cayenne, and orecchiette with crumbled pork sausage and broccoli rabe. A three-course pre-theater menu is available before 6:30 p.m. for crowds catching a show at nearby Lincoln Center. If you need a kickstart before the performance, swing by the long, granite-topped bar for a Tuscan Maple Sidecar with maple syrup and Grand Marnier or a tangy Via Veneto Spritz, bubbling over with Prosecco, Aperol and lemon.

Italian. Dinner, Sunday brunch. $36-85

★★CHAT 'N' CHEW

10 E. 16th St., New York, 212-243-1616; www.chatnchew.ypguides.net

Walk by Chat'n'Chew on a Saturday afternoon and you'll walk straight into a line of twenty-somethings, married couples with strollers, and red-eyed partiers waiting to get inside to feast on one of the best and most reasonably priced brunch menus in the city. Filled with vintage décor and thrift store restaurant finds, this crowded Union Square diner is about quantity (portions are giant) and comfort food. There's roast turkey with gravy, mac 'n' cheese, and hearty breakfast fare like eggs, hash browns, French toast and pancakes. It's not fancy, it's inexpensive, and it's all good.

American. Lunch, dinner, brunch. Outdoor seating. Bar. $15 and under.

★★CHIKALICIOUS

203 E. 10th St., New York, 212-475-0929; www.chikalicious.com

Children are always fantasizing about skipping supper and just having dessert for dinner, and secretly, adults crave the same indulgence. With Chikalicious Dessert Bar, the dream of an all-dessert, all-of-the-time meal has come true. At this quaint and sweetly decorated East Village cake, cupcake, cookie, brownie and muffin depot, you can enjoy haute treats while even watching the pastry chefs in action. Chikalicious opens at 3 p.m., the perfect time for an afternoon snack, or having dessert before (or for) dinner.

Dessert, American. Dinner. Bar. $16-35

★★CHURRASCARIA PLATAFORMA

316 W. 49th St., New York, 212-245-0505; www.churrascariaplataforma.com

Succulent Brazilian barbecue is served in delicious abundance at Churrascaria Plataforma, a loud, high-energy eatery in the theater district. This authentic Riodizio offers main courses of grilled and skewered beef, pork, chicken, sausage, lamb, and fish in all-you-can-eat portions, accompanied by intoxicating caiparinas—tangy, lime-soaked cocktails made from cachaca, a potent alcohol similar to rum.

Brazilian. Lunch, dinner. Reservations recommended. Bar. $36-85

★CITY BAKERY

3 W. 18th St., New York, 212-366-1414; www.thecitybakery.com

Every neighborhood should have a City Bakery, where imaginative salads make veggies exciting, soups are silky and flavorful, and chocoholics rejoice at the creamy, dreamy hot chocolate heady with homemade marshmallows. The caramelized French toast (only available on weekends) and pretzel croissant have legions of fans as well, as do the array of sweet baked treats. Seating in the boisterous, high-ceilinged café is limited, so if you're not the patient type, take your goodies to go and sit in nearby Union Square to munch alfresco. American. Breakfast, lunch, brunch. $15 and under.

★★★CONVIVIO

45 Tudor City Place, New York, 212-599-5045; www.convivionyc.com

If the aging socialites of NYC can get facelifts to increase their appeal, why can't a restaurant? That's exactly what restaurateur Chris Cannon and chef Michael White asked themselves before trading stuffy-and-serious L'Impero for a more casual, food-focused endeavor in the same locale. The result: a bright new star in Tudor City—about as far east as you can be in Manhattan without swimming in the East River—where the pasta sings and the price is palatable. The $59 four-course prix fixe dinner includes winners such as stracciatella (creamy cheese curd, tangy tomato and basil), maccheroni alla carbonara (pillowy pasta laced with pancetta, egg and pecorino) and scotta-dito di agnello (perfectly-grilled lamb chops over escarole in a sizzling salsa verde). Don't be put off by the buttoned-up clientele that frequent the place; as one of the few decent eateries neighboring the United Nations, it gets its share of foreign diplomats on expense accounts.

Southern Italian. Lunch (Monday-Friday), dinner. $36-85

★CORNER BISTRO

331 W. Fourth St., New York, 212-242-9502; www.cornerbistro.ypguides.net

Nothing about this former speakeasy is fancy—the kitchen is the size of a closet, the bar is dark and food comes on either paper or plastic plates—but everything is memorable. The small pub menu is posted on the wall, but skip it and just order the bar's namesake, the legendary Bistro Burger (eight ounces of broiled beef topped with bacon, cheese, onions, lettuce and tomato) and a side of fries. You'll still have money left to plug the jukebox and get a mug or two of $2.50 drafts. But get here early—the line for one of the precious few tables gets long and frustrating, particularly on weekend nights.

American. Lunch, dinner. $15 and under

★★★CORTON

239 West Broadway, New York 212-219-2777; www.cortonnyc.com

White on white is the new black at this trendy Tribeca restaurant. The windowless space epitomizes modern simplicity with lightly stenciled white-washed walls, white linen tablecloths and white Bernardeaud china. Such sophistication is par for the course with old school chef Paul Liebrandt, who works his magic in a state-of-the-art kitchen visible from the dining room through a narrow slit in the wall. The three-course prix fixe menu ($85) may appear fussy at first glance—think foie gras with sour cherries, chioggia beet and marcona almonds, and Montauk cod over razor clam risotto and arugula chantilly—but Liebrandt delivers with exceptionally delicate flavors and farm fresh ingredients. Dessert keeps the culinary bar held high with French treats such as the black cherry clafoutis with sour plum and lemon verbena. At a time when Manhattan foodies are turning their attention toward cheap burger joints and casual no-nonsense menus, Corton proves that exceptional food is always in vogue. Good luck getting a reservation less than a month in advance, but once you're in, you'll be very glad you came.

French. Dinner. Closed Sunday. Reservations recommended. $86 and up

★★★★COUNTRY

90 Madison Ave., New York, 212-889-7100; www.countryinnewyork.com

While swooning over a meal in the opulent dining room is no longer an option—the space is now only for private parties—the downstairs cafe has taken up the helm, offering three square meals a day amidst a sleek atmosphere of leather chesterfields and dark wood moldings. Chef-owner Geoffrey Zakarian, who also runs Country's sister restaurant, Town, is known for his expert execution of dishes that might not necessarily be novel—like bison tenderloin, succulent chicken for two and classic burgers—but nevertheless delight in their perfect marriage of texture and harmonious flavors. It's hard to ignore the four-sided zinc bar anchored in the center of the 28-foot space, and even harder to dismiss seasonal sparkling-wine cocktails such as Sicilian—a blend of white crème de menthe mixed with lime purée, muddled mint leaves, bitters and sparking wine.

American. Breakfast (Monday-Friday), lunch (Monday-Friday), dinner, Saturday-Sunday brunch. $86 and up.

★★★CRAFT

43 E. 19th St., New York, 212-780-0880; www.craftrestaurant.com

Tom Colicchio of *Top Chef*—the sexiest bald head on TV since Kojak—obviously knows food. It shows at his restaurant Craft (part of the Craft chain that includes Craftsteak, Craftbar and 'wichcraft), which emphasizes fresh ingredients and cooking methods as so many other restaurants do, but does so like no other. Diners build their own meals—an exciting or daunting experience, depending on your sense of adventure and food curiosity. First, select a preparation method (roasting, braising, raw), and then the ingredient (halibut, sweetbreads, oysters) for the table. Servers bring plates for everyone in the group to share. The diver scallops and braised short ribs are standouts, while the restaurant's desserts have a deserved cult following—the homemade Boston crème doughnuts with blueberry compote, chocolate malted milk and cheesecake ice cream will not disappoint. The elegantly industrial dining room emulates the menu's work-in-progress theme, with dangling filament light bulbs and exposed brick and iron.

Contemporary American. Dinner. $36-85

★★CRAFTBAR

900 Broadway, New York, 212-461-4300; www.craftrestaurant.com

After the runaway success of Craft, chef/owner Tom Colicchio's magnificent temple to the season's best ingredients, it was only a matter of time before he would open a smaller, more intimate and casual offshoot. Located right next door to its fancier sibling, Craftbar is part wine bar, part Italian trattoria and part American eatery, serving up small plates like signature fried, stuffed sage leaves and crisp fried oysters with preserved lemon, alongside beautiful salads, soups and crusty panini. The veal ricotta meatballs are also the most extraordinary in the country, if not the world.

American, Mediterranean. Lunch, dinner, Saturday-Sunday brunch. Bar. $36-85

★★CRISPO

240 W. 14th St., New York, 212-229-1818; www.crisporestaurant.com

Named after its chef/owner Frank Crispo, this West 14th Street dining room is a staple for fans of rustic, Italian-accented cuisine, like plates of delicious hand-sliced prosciutto di Parma, fresh pastas, grilled chops and seasonal salads. The warm, exposed-brick room gets crowded early on, so plan to reserve a table ahead of time or wait at the bar (not a bad option, although the bar area is tight) for one of the coveted tables to open up.

Italian. Dinner. Reservations recommended. Outdoor seating. Bar. $36-85

★★★CRU

24 Fifth Ave., New York, 212-529-1700; www.cru-nyc.com

The elegantly restrained décor at this Village restaurant oozes wealth in that subtly showy old-money kind of way, and service is warm and proper. The ever-changing menu demands attention with its global influences and creative combinations. East Coast cod packs a Latin punch with chorizo crust and piquillo-blood orange compote, while chilled foie gras over white chocolate and basil elevates the concept of sweet and savory to a new level. An award-winning wine list—it's the size of a phone book and has two volumes, one for whites and one for reds—will make you gasp. Cru boasts an astounding 150,000 bottles from the private collection of its owner, Roy Welland, and sways toward French wines from Burgundy.

Contemporary European. Dinner. Closed Sunday-Monday. $36-85

★★CUB ROOM CAFÉ

131 Sullivan St., New York, 212-677-4100; www.cubroom.com

The Cub Room was one of the first hotspots to open in SoHo, and it has stood the test of time thanks to chef-owner Henry Meer, who keeps the seasonal Mediterranean-accented menu splashy and fresh, offering the perfect brand of upscale fare for the lively bunch that frequents this popular destination. In the chic, living room-style lounge with vintage fabric-covered sofas and a long, serpentine bar, a gregarious and gorgeous crowd sips chilly cocktails, while inside the rustic, country-style dining room boards animate groups, informal lunch dates and happy couples feasting on Meer's solid cooking.

American. Lunch, dinner, late-night, brunch. Children's menu. Bar. $36-85

★★★DA SILVANO

260 Sixth Ave., New York, 212-982-2343; www.dasilvano.com

Da Silvano is a scene and a great one at that. With such a loyal and fabulous following, the food could be mediocre, but the kitchen does not rest on its starry laurels. The kitchen produces wonderful, robust, regional Italian fare and the sliver of a wine bar next door, Da Silvano Cantinetta serves Italian-style tapas paired with a wide selection of wines by the glass. But perhaps the best way to experience Da Silvano is on a warm day, where a seat at the wide, European-style sidewalk cafe offers prime people-watching.

Italian. Lunch, dinner. Reservations recommended. Outdoor seating. Bar. $36-85

★★★★DANIEL

60 E. 65th St., New York, 212-288-0033; www.danielnyc.com

Chef Daniel Boulud is fastidious about details—like the clarity of his veal stock, the flower petals suspended in ice cubes in some of the cocktails and the complimentary basket of warm madeleines at meal's end. But this is what's kept Daniel firmly moored among New York's most elite and elegant restaurants. After a massive redesign in 2008 under the command of famed designer Adam Tihany, the space marries neo-classical sophistication and organic playfulness. Archways and balustrades are bisected by vine-like wrought iron sconces, Limoges chandeliers drape the dining room in warm light and understated leafy table arrangements stand out against otherwise neutral tones. Eating here, you'll happily part with stacks of greenbacks just to dig a fork into his legendary potato-coated sea bass or a dish of succulent veal prepared three ways. The very attentive staff is a highlight, expertly helping well-heeled diners navigate the 1,500-bottle wine list and graciously amending tasting menus to fit your preferences. Choose between three-course prix fixe and six- or eight-course tasting menus, or dine à la carte in the lounge.

French. Dinner. Closed Sunday. Reservations recommened. $86 and up

★★★DAWAT

210 E. 58th St., New York, 212-355-7555; www.restaurant.com/dawat

Serving elegant haute cuisine in a posh, hushed townhouse setting, Dawat is one of the most popular destinations for seekers of upscale, authentic Indian cuisine, including curries, rice dishes, poori, naan and chutneys. The interior is decorated with simple wall groupings of surreal nomadic sculptures, and tables are elegantly set with gleaming copper plates.

Indian. Lunch (Monday-Saturday), dinner. Reservations recommended. Bar. $36-85

★★★DB BISTRO MODERNE

55 W. 44th St., New York, 212-391-2400; www.danielnyc.com

This sexy, ultrastylish Midtown bistro is Daniel Boulud's most casual outpost. His signature DB Burger is an excellent example of creative interpretation. Boulud builds a juicy round of beef and stuffs it with short ribs and sinful amounts of foie gras and truffle. He serves it on a homemade Parmesan brioche bun, with house-stewed tomato confit (instead of ketchup) and a big vat of fries, perfect for sharing.

American, French. Breakfast, Lunch (Monday-Friday), dinner. Reservations recommended. Bar. $86 and up.

★★★★DEL POSTO

85 10th Ave., New York, 212-497-8090; www.delposto.com

If you're looking for checkered tablecloths and the quaint fare of typical red-sauce joints, keep moving. The ambitious, sprawling Del Posto reflects the bold, larger-than-life persona of its famous owner-partner, Mario Batali. At 24,000 square feet, with soaring columns and enough mahogany to give environmentalists palpitations, this high-end Italian restaurant dwarfs its competition in size and style, but still pays attention to tiny details like purse stools for the ladies. Sliced jalapeño peppers in the spaghetti rotti with Dungeness crab will have you reaching for ChapStick to cool your lips. That's the kind

of bold touch one expects from Batali, as is serving whole fish dramatically and expertly portioned tableside by attentive servers. Dinner here is wildly expensive and may leave you wondering how on earth pasta strands made of flour, eggs and water can cost so much ($30 for panzotti, or pasta pockets filled with rabbit). But one taste of dishes like that and the remarkably flaky torta Carotina—sliced and served tableside with cool, creamy gelato—will quickly quell your doubts about whether the meal was worth every penny.
Italian. Lunch (Wednesday-Friday), dinner. $86 and up.

★★DINOSAUR BBQ
646 W. 131st St., New York, 212-694-1777; www.dinosaurbarbque.com
You won't leave hungry at this Harlem barbecue joint. Memphis- and Cuban-style barbecue sandwich platters, two- and three-meat combo plates and slabs of slow pit smoked barbecue pork ribs are served with cornbread as well as your choice of two homemade sides like mac 'n' cheese, Creole potato salad or BBQ fried rice. To wash it all down, choose from 23 draft beers or 26 bottled varieties. And despite Dinosaur's rough and tumble, roadhouse environment (where graffiti in the bathroom is encouraged), dining here is a pleasure with its friendly and accommodating staff.
American, barbecue. Lunch, dinner. Outdoor seating. Bar. $16-35

★★★DISTRICT
130 W. 46th St., New York, 212-485-2999; www.districtnyc.com
Located within the Muse Hotel in Times Square, District is surrounded by Broadway theaters, making it a great spot for pre- and post-theater dining. In keeping with the neighborhood, the restaurant features theatrical décor, including spotlights designed by renowned set designer David Rockwell. Signature dishes on the New American menu include citrus-roasted chicken, grilled Atlantic salmon and diver scallop ceviche.
New American. Breakfast, lunch (Monday-Friday), dinner (Monday-Saturday). Reservations recommended. Bar. $36-85

★★DO HWA
55 Carmine St., New York, 212-414-1224; www.dohwanyc.com
This mom-and-daughter-owned restaurant is always crowded with Village trendsetters. It's one of those perpetually populated restaurants, mostly due to the menu, which features authentic, family-style Korean food at reasonable prices. Sure, there are more elegant, refined places to dine in the city, but Do Hwa's draw is its warm and lively atmosphere that focuses on food and company. If you even want to do your own home-cooking, request a booth with a built-in grill.
Korean. Lunch (Monday-Friday), dinner. Reservations recommended. Bar. $16-35

★★DOS CAMINOS
373 Park Ave. S., New York, 212-294-1000; www.brguestrestaurants.com
With Dos Caminos, Steve Hanson has introduced regional Mexican cuisine to his winning formula of the hip scene, laid-back bar and crowd-pleasing eats. Dos Caminos is loud and always crowded, so don't plan on intimate dining, but certainly plan on colorful, tasty food. The menu reflects the diverse

regions of Mexico, including made-to-order guacamole prepared tableside; warm homemade tacos filled with chile-rubbed shrimp, steak, or pulled pork; and snapper steamed in banana leaves. Wash it all down with potent, icy margaritas.

Mexican. Lunch, dinner, brunch. Reservations recommended. Bar. $36-85

★★★DOVETAIL

103 W. 77th St., New York, 212-362-3800; www.dovetailnyc.com

Neighboring the American Museum of Natural History, Central Park and Lincoln Center, Dovetail is a welcome addition to a tourist heavy, and restaurant slim, locale. Chef John Fraser honors fresh, local ingredients with simple dishes that emphasize flavor over fuss. The pistachio crusted duck with daikon, water greens and sweet and sour plums is succulent and tangy with an even balance of salty and sweet, while the truffle gnocchi alongside Serrano ham and chanterelles is light and airy. Come for the famed Sunday Suppa, an affordable prix fixe menu, or head down to the sherry cellar to watch the magic in the kitchen while you dine. The interior is sleek without being pretentious and modern without being uncomfortable. Brick columns and muslin-covered walls give the space a casual urban vibe, perfect for the Upper West Siders who frequent it.

Contemporary American. Dinner. $36-85

★★★EIGHTY-ONE

45 W. 81st St., New York, 212-873-8181; www.81nyc.com

From elegant, international artisanal ingredients, such as custom-grown lettuces, black truffles from Provence and hand-selected peppercorns, chef Ed Brown offers an array of fine-selected ingredients in each of his dishes: from chestnut and mascarpone ravioli to peekytoe crab salad. Choose a main course such as an organic Scottish salmon with cranberry beans or Cedar River Farm hanger steak. Red velvet hangs as the backdrop and the creative wine cooler that is built into the restaurant's south wall even has four temperature zones to keep all bottles in their ideal climate.

Contemporary American. Dinner, Sunday brunch. Reservations recommended. Bar. $36-85

★ELEPHANT AND CASTLE

68 Greenwich Ave., New York, 212-243-1400; www.elephantandcastle.com

Elephant and Castle feels like a bit of London in the Big Apple. This pub, styled like those found in rainy England, is low-lit and narrow, with dark wood paneling that gives the place a warm vibe that feels welcoming and cozy. The menu is straightforward and includes easy-to-love New York-style fare like Caesar salad, omelets, burgers, and top-notch sandwiches. The beer list is impressive as well. Servers are all trained in the art of latte decoration, a 30-plus-year specialty of the house.

Continental. Breakfast, lunch, dinner, Saturday-Sunday brunch. $16-35

★★★★ELEVEN MADISON PARK

11 Madison Ave., New York, 212-889-0905; www.elevenmadisonpark.com

The large scale of the Art Deco dining room—think high ceilings volumous floral arrangements, hulking light fixtures—contrasts with the modestly-sized food portions. But what does adorn the plate is so thoughtfully conceived, gorgeously executed and alive with flavor that you won't mind. The French-influenced greenmarket cuisine includes such dishes as Muscovy duck glazed with lavender honey, and foie gras terrine with plums, umeboshi and bitter almonds. Here, the trolley really does go ding ding—a mobile martini cart means a cocktail can be prepared at your table. The boozy treats are served with a dish of olives, a small dish of Marcona almonds and a fancy toothpick. Contemporary American. Lunch (Monday-Friday), dinner. Closed Sunday. $86 and up

★★ELMO
156 Seventh Ave., New York, 212-337-8000; www.elmorestaurant.com
Located in the heart of Chelsea, Elmo is a convivial American eatery with a bustling bar serving comfort food that has been tweaked a bit for a fashion-able New York City crowd. There are dishes as retro as Alphabet Soup with fluffy, dill-accented chicken dumplings; a hearty macaroni and cheese; and easy-to-love Hungry Man-type meals featuring meat and potatoes. There's even a Duncan Hines devil's food cake for dessert.
American. Lunch (Monday-Friday), dinner, Saturday-Sunday brunch. Outdoor seating. Bar. $16-35

★★ESSEX RESTAURANT
120 Essex St., New York, 212-533-9616; www.essexnyc.com
Located on the Lower East Side, one of Manhattan's hippest 'hoods, Essex is a warm, inviting, minimalist space marked by skylights, whitewashed brick and sleek black tables. This is a perfect place for cocktails or a dinner date. The menu is as eclectic as the neighborhood, with dishes that pay tribute to the diverse local population—like a potato cake napoleon (a haute version of the knish); the Essex Cubano sandwich; a scallop and mango ceviche; and kasha varnishkes. Late-night, the place turns into a loud and lively DJ party, the perfect prelude to the brunch with all-you-can-drink Bloody Marys, mimosas or screwdrivers.
International. Dinner, late-night, Saturday-Sunday brunch. Closed Monday. Reservations recommended. Bar. $16-35

★★★ESTIATORIO MILOS
125 W. 55th St., New York, 212-245-7400; www.milos.ca
Milos, as it's called for short, is a luxurious, cavernous, whitewashed eatery decorated with umbrella-topped tables and seafood market-style fish displays. Showcasing simple, rustic Greek cooking, this restaurant serves seafood priced by the pound and prepared either perfectly grilled over charcoal or in the Greek style called spetsiota filleted and baked with tomatoes, onions, herbs and olive oil.
Greek, Mediterranean, seafood. Lunch (Monday-Friday), dinner. Reservations recommended. Outdoor seating. Bar. $36-85

★★FANELLI'S CAFÉ
94 Prince St., New York, 212-226-9412
This classic Soho eatery dressed in dark wood, with a long, tavern-style bar up front, has been around since 1872. It remains one of the neighborhood's

best hideaways for honest and hearty American meals like macaroni and cheese, big bowls of hot chili, thick burgers, and classic steaks. Some things are better left unchanged; Fanelli's is one of them.

American. Lunch, dinner, late-night. Children's menu. Bar. $16-35

★★★FELIDIA

243 E. 58th St., New York, 212-758-1479; www.felidia-nyc.com

Celebrated chef and TV personality Lidia Bastianich is the unofficial matriarch of Italian-American cuisine. Her restaurant, Felidia (she and son Joe are partners in Becco), is warm and elegant and draws an elite New York crowd. Diners are expected to eat as they do in Italy, so you'll start with a plate of antipasti or a bowl of zuppe, move on to a fragrant bowl of fresh pasta and then to a grilled whole fish, and finally dessert. The Italian wine list is extra special, so be sure to pair your meal with a few glasses.

Italian. Lunch (Monday-Friday), dinner. Reservations recommended. Bar. $36-85

★★★FIREBIRD

365 W. 46th St., New York, 212-586-0244; www.firebirdrestaurant.com

Set in a lavish double townhouse in Hell's Kitchen, this restaurant and cabaret is furnished like a majestic Russian palace, with ornate antique furniture, intricate china and etched glass, old-world oil paintings and 19th-century photographs. The extravagance extends to the food, with Russian classics like blinis with sour cream and caviar, zakuska (the Russian equivalent of tapas), borscht made with pork and dill and sturgeon baked in puff pastry.

Eastern European. Lunch, dinner. Closed Monday. Reservations recommended. Outdoor seating. Bar. $36-85

★★★THE FOUR SEASONS RESTAURANT

99 E. 52nd St., New York, 212-754-9494; www.fourseasonsrestaurant.com

A sports jacket isn't the only thing you need when dining here. An expense account comes in handy as well, with a menu that charges $45 for Maryland crab cakes and $65 for a rack of lamb with mint jus. Chances are you can find an equally good meal for less elsewhere in Manhattan, but you'll be hard pressed to find a better dining room in which to enjoy it. Both the Grill Room and Pool Room are considered prized destinations among New York's dining elite. The Grill Room hosted JFK's 45th birthday party and boasts walnut-paneled walls and soaring two-story windows. It doesn't get more New York than the Four Seasons Resturant. On the opposite end of the restaurant, the Pool Room is anchored by Mies van der Rohe's legendary white marble pool and surrounded by trees that change with the seasons. Widely spaced tables and exemplary service make either room a good choice for a private affair.

Contemporary American. Lunch, dinner. $86 and up

★FRANK

88 Second Ave., New York, 212-420-0202; www.frankrestaurant.com

Do you love simple, rustic Italian food? If so, you will fall in love with Frank in an instant, for the same reason that throngs of East Villagers are already swooning over this cramped, thrift-store-furnished spot for southern Italian cuisine. You'll find great food, cheap prices and a happening crowd that doesn't mind waiting over an hour to get inside to sit elbow to elbow. Italian. Breakfast, lunch, dinner, brunch, late-night. Reservations recommended. Outdoor seating. Bar. No credit cards accepted. $16-35

★★★GABRIEL'S

11 W. 60th St., New York, 212-956-4600; www.gabrielsbarandrest.com

Gabriel's is the creation of owner Gabriel Aiello, a charming host who knows how to make guests feel at home in this elegant Lincoln Center spot for sumptuous Tuscan fare. (Think gorgonzola tortellini with a shiitake mushroom tomato sauce, lasagne Bolognese and a daily house-made risotto.) The restaurant is elegantly dressed with contemporary art cloaking the warm saffron-toned walls. While Gabriel's may look like a see-and-be-seen hot spot, the restaurant is refreshingly warm and welcoming. Northern Italian. Lunch (Monday-Friday), dinner. Closed Sunday. Reservations recommended. Bar. $36-85

★★★GALLAGHER'S

228 W. 52nd St., New York, 212-245-5336; www.gallaghersnysteakhouse.com

This Times Square steakhouse is a New York City landmark and former speakeasy, and remains decorated as it was the day it opened in November 1927, with worn planked floors, red-checked tablecloths and dark wood-paneled walls covered in old photographs. Specializing in dry-aged beef, the kitchen stays true to simple American fare.

American, steak. Lunch, dinner. Reservations recommended. Bar. $36-85

★★GASCOGNE

158 Eighth Ave., New York, 212-675-6564; www.gascognenyc.com

At this charming Chelsea neighborhood restaurant, the robust regional cuisine of Gascogne fills the air. Paying tribute to southwestern France, the kitchen offers heavenly plates of fill-in-the-blank confit; Armagnac-soaked prunes and foie gras terrine, cassoulet, and monkfish casserole; and a lovely list of wines to match. This is a spot for romance, as the dining room is intimate and candlelit, and the garden out back makes you feel like you are miles from the city.

French. Lunch (Tuesday-Sunday), dinner, Saturday-Sunday brunch. Reservations recommended. Outdoor seating. Bar. $36-85

★★★GEISHA

33 E. 61st St., New York, 212-813-1113; www.geisharestaurant.com

Set in a modern townhouse on the Upper East Side, Geisha is seafood whiz kid Eric Ripert's inspired translation of Japanese cuisine. While he is still manning the stoves at Le Bernardin, here at Geisha, his love affair with seafood is in the open. Dishes include coconut-marinated fluke with coconut ponzu and bowls of tiger shrimp dumplings with toasted pumpkin in a green curry broth. There are also chic platters of sushi, sashimi and signature rolls prepared by a pair of seriously skilled sushi masters.

Japanese. Lunch (Monday-Friday), dinner. Closed Sunday. Reservations recommended. Outdoor seating. Bar. $36-85

★★GHENET ETHIOPIAN RESTAURANT
284 Mulberry St., New York, 212-343-1888; www.ghenet.com

Featuring the fragrant dishes of Ethiopia, Ghenet is a charming spot in Nolita to explore a new and delicious cuisine. The menu reads like a descriptive textbook, with great explanations of all of the menu items, many of which are savory rice dishes and lamb or beef stews to be mopped up with Frisbee-size rounds of homemade flatbread. Owned by a husband-and-wife team, this family-run establishment is all about hospitality, and you will feel like family when you leave.

Middle Eastern. Lunch (Tuesday-Sunday), dinner. Bar. $16-35

★★GIGINO TRATTORIA
323 Greenwich St., New York, 212-431-1112; www.gigino-trattoria.com

Gigino Trattoria has been a local favorite for Italian fare since 1983. Owned by Phil Suarez and Bob Giraldi (partners in Patria and Jean-Georges), this Tribeca gem offers casual, comfortable, family-oriented dining and the delicious, home-style cooking of an authentic Italian trattoria. Generous bowls of pasta, brick-oven pizzas, seasonal produce, game, fish and meats round out the appealing menu.

Italian. Lunch, dinner. Outdoor seating. Children's menu. Bar. $36-85

★★★★GILT
455 Madison Ave., New York, 212-891-8100; www.giltnewyork.com

Located in the Villard Mansion within the New York Palace Hotel, Gilt has been rejuvenated with new chef Justin Bogle and a constantly changing menu that spotlights seasonal flavors (lamb tartare with rhubarb, buckwheat and sorrel, and tandoori-spiced black cod with roasted eggplant, mustard greens and toasted coconut) in three-, five- and seven-course tasting menus. An impressive wine list features 1,400 bottles, including 50 selections under $50. Tippling not your thing? Gilt has assembled an extensive list of nearly 40 teas (like the rare, aged High Mountain oolong tea from Taiwan) chosen with seasonality in mind. The wood-paneled, library-esque 52-seat dining room in this historic mansion is straight out of a Brontë novel, while the contrasting slick bar with futuristic décor suggests a modern club setting, perfect if you're looking for a more casual à la carte dining option. Or slip outside to the Palace Gate, a new seasonal seating area that serves up bar menu favorites amidst the melee of Midtown.

Contemporary American. Dinner (Tuesday-Saturday). Bar (open seven days). Reservations recommended. $86 and up

★★★★GORDON RAMSAY AT THE LONDON
151 W. 54th St., New York, 212-468-8888; www.thelondonnyc.com/gordon_ramsay

The somewhat hushed, polished dining room decorated in a muted palette contrasts starkly with the salty, fiery chef and namesake of this celebrated 45-seat Manhattan restaurant in the London NYC hotel. You won't see TV cameras or hear Gordon Ramsay dropping "F" bombs at a skittish staff like he does on the reality TV shows Hell's Kitchen and Kitchen Nightmares. But you might utter an expletive in amazement at the innovative and expertly prepared cuisine here, including caramelized duck breast, roasted foie gras and ginger poached lobster. A three-tiered "Bon Bon trolley" weighed

down with confections—think peanut brittle, salted caramels and handmade chocolates—provides a playful and sweet finale.
Contemporary European. Dinner. Closed Sunday-Monday. Reservations recommended. $86 and up

★★★★GOTHAM BAR & GRILL
12 E. 12th St., New York, 212-620-4020; www.gothambarandgrill.com
Gotham Bar and Grill opened in 1984 and proves that, just like bangs and skinny jeans, some holdovers from the '80s just get trendier with age. Acclaimed chef Alfred Portale is a perfectionist who pioneered architecturally-inspired food presentation. His edible compositions—the roasted Maine lobster is presented with lobster claws wrapped around the tail which sit atop spaghetti squash along with potato purée and toasted brussels sprout halves—are the stuff of true epicurean delight. Bright and airy with stylish, silk-draped lighting and not a hint of vanity, this landmark feels like a comfortable pair of jeans, albeit with a high-end designer label.
Contemporary American. Lunch (Monday-Friday), dinner. $36-85

★★★★GRAMERCY TAVERN
42 E. 20th St., New York, 212-477-0777; www.gramercytavern.com
Charming Gramercy Tavern is self-assured without being flashy and comfortable without being dull, making it a favorite upscale dining choice for everyone from expense-account suits to serious foodies wondering if the Chioggia beets came from the farmers market down the street (they probably did). Chef Michael Anthony has filled the big toque left behind by Tom Colicchio, and he has infused the classic menu with creative flourishes—from the hazelnut yogurt sauce and red cabbage complementing the halibut to the apple chutney on the foie gras custard—that keep you on your toes just when you think you've got the place pegged. Try a specialty such as the shrimp salad with grapefruit or rack of pork and braised belly, and for dessert, warm chocolate bread pudding. The long bar is a perfect perch from which to enjoy the à la carte menu, plates of cheese and wines by the glass.
Contemporary American. Lunch (Monday-Friday), dinner. Reservations recommended. $86 and up

★GREAT N.Y. NOODLETOWN
28 Bowery, New York, 212-349-0923
It would be impossible to pass Great N.Y. Noodletown off as your own private discovery. Anointed years ago by rave reviews, this bright corner spot continues to draw crowds all day and late into the night. This is not the place for complicated dishes. Treat Great N.Y. Noodletown like a Chinese version of your local coffee shop: avoid preparations that have more than two ingredients and you'll be more than satisfied. The roast meats are top-notch, particularly the crisp-skinned baby pig. Greens are basic and fresh, and the perfectly cooked noodles, naturally, are a must-order.
Chinese. Breakfast, lunch, dinner, late-night. Bar. No credit cards accepted. $15 and under.

★★★HAKUBAI
66 Park Ave., New York, 212-885-7111; www.kitano.com

Located in the Kitano hotel, Hakubai offers authentic Japanese fare in a tranquil space. The menu features a myriad of traditionally prepared seafood dishes like chopped salted squid, vinegar-marinated jellyfish and fried, grilled or simmered flounder. For a special treat, call ahead and reserve a private room for the multi-course chef's choice menu. To savor a simpler meal, choose from the restaurant's selection of sushi, sashimi and maki rolls, as well as udon and soba noodle dishes.

Japanese. Lunch, dinner. Reservations recommended. $36-85

★★★THE HARRISON
355 Greenwich St., New York, 212-274-9310; www.theharrison.com

Since chef Amanda Freitag took the reins in January 2008, she has infused new life into The Harrison, whose sister restaurant, Chelsea's The Red Cat, also has that Mediterranean-American thing down pat. Freitag's menu is both familiar and imaginative—traditional offerings like lamb chops get punched up with anchovy and rosemary, and the seasonal salmon will clear your sinuses thanks to the horseradish crust and red mustard greens. Fries cooked in duck fat are both indulgent and addictive. The candlelit tables are a little too close for comfort, but the reliable food more than makes up for the tight surroundings. Sidewalk seating out front is ideal for enjoying a warm evening and fabulous people-watching in eternally trendy Tribeca.

Contemporary American. Dinner. $36-85

★★★HARRY CIPRIANI
781 Fifth Ave., New York, 212-753-5566; www.cipriani.com

If you are searching for a place to see and be seen by New York's most moneyed crowds, Harry's is your spot. Located across the street from Central Park, this posh Midtown West restaurant features Italian cuisine and clipped service at an astronomical price point.

American, Italian. Lunch, dinner. Reservations recommended. Bar. $36-85

★★★HEARTH
403 E. 12th St., New York, 646-602-1300; www.restauranthearth.com

White walls, recessed lighting and red ceilings add to the warm setting at Hearth. Guests can dine in the main area, fronting the street, the four-seat bar/chef's table, facing the kitchen or the intimate, cozy back room, which is ideal for groups ordering the five-course tasting menu. Specialties include ricotta tortellini with spring vegetables; roasted monkfish; and braised veal breast with sweetbreads, onions and morels. For dessert, try the carrot cake with candied pecans and cinnamon raisin ice cream.

American. Dinner. Reservations recommended. Bar. $36-85

★HEARTLAND BREWERY
35 Union Square West, New York, 212-645-3400; www.heartlandbrewery.com

Stained woods, exposed-brick walls and a substantial mahogany bar add to the early Americana décor at the high-spirited Heartland Brewery. Large steel beer vats set behind glass walls in this large space at the rear of the restaurant complete the setting. Located in Union Square off Chelsea and the

Village, the restaurant serves its own microbrew from the central Heartland Brewery in Brooklyn (there are six Heartland restaurants in all).
American. Lunch, dinner. Outdoor seating. Children's menu. Bar. $16-35

★★HOME RESTAURANT
20 Cornelia St., New York, 212-243-9579; www.homerestaurantnyc.com
Like many New York City apartments, Home Restaurant is tiny. The understated wood dining room is small. The tables are small (some generously-sized diners think too small). Even the menu is small with only a handful of dishes offered. But what Home lacks in size, it makes up in flavor. Every dish is made from local farm-fresh, sustainable products. Even the wines come from regional vineyards in the Hudson Valley, Finger Lakes and North Fork of Long Island. The mac and cheese, with or without chorizo, is gooey and delightful, while the coriander-crusted double cut pork chop caters to a more sophisticated appetite. Don't leave Home without trying the butterscotch pudding. There's an adorable outdoor garden too, if you can find an open table.
Contemporary American. Lunch, dinner. $16-35

★★★I TRULLI
122 E. 27th St., New York, 212-481-7372; www.itrulli.com
This Gramercy restaurant envelops you with warmth, whether in the winter with its hearth-style, wood-burning fireplace or in the summer when the lovely outdoor courtyard garden opens up for under-the-stars dining. This is a true neighborhood refuge, with charming service that features the rustic Italian cuisine of the Apulia region. Favorites include ricotta-stuffed cannelloni, orecchiette with veal ragu and fantastic calzones made by hand and baked to a golden brown in the wood-burning oven.
Italian. Lunch (Monday-Friday), dinner. Reservations recommended. Outdoor seating. Bar. $36-85

★★IL BUCO
47 Bond St., New York, 212-533-1932; www.ilbuco.com
While the Mediterranean food here is some of the most honest and well executed of its kind in the city, Il Buco is all about atmosphere. This East Village escape is low-lit and relaxed, filled with antiques (many for sale) and sturdy farmhouse tables that give the restaurant the soft, inviting charm of a rural Spanish farmhouse. Romance is always an attraction, but visiting with friends is just as lovely. You'll have a great meal and feel right at home.
Italian, Mediterranean. Lunch (Tuesday-Saturday), dinner. Bar. $36-85

★★IL CORTILE
125 Mulberry St., New York, 212-226-6060; www.ilcortile.com
Il Cortile has been a pillar of Italian cuisine in Little Italy since 1975. This lower Manhattan neighborhood trattoria, located amid the bustling streets of Little Italy and Chinatown, offers heaps of authentic Italian fare—antipasti, pasta, fish, poultry, and beef, prepared with love and a nod to old country tradition. The restaurant has a sunny indoor garden room that will make you feel like you are dining somewhere on the Mediterranean. There are classical Roman sculptures and archways throughout the property.
Italian. Lunch, dinner, late-night. Outdoor seating. $36-85

★★★IL MULINO

86 W. Third St., New York, 212-673-3783; www.ilmulinonewyork.com

West Village's Il Mulino is the kind of Italian spot where the service is excellent and the rich, heavy food is read from long lists of specials and served in portions impossible to finish (the herb-crusted lamb chops are massive). Tableside theatrics include hand-tossed Caesar salads and whole fish filleting that give guests even more of a show. Il Mulino is a boy's club with lots of loud, brash eaters who don't mind the wince-worthy tabs.

Italian. Lunch (Monday-Friday), dinner. Closed Sunday. Reservations recommended. Bar. $86 and up.

★★INO

21 Bedford St., New York, 212-989-5769; www.cafeino.com

Ten years ago, the concept of Italian-style grilled sandwiches was ground-breaking (and inspired copies everywhere). Today, this panini pioneer is still as good as ever. The tiny (25-seat) restaurant has everything you could ask for: wonderful wines and cheese, hot and crispy panini in combinations such as Italian sausage with butternut squash mustard, rucola and fontina, and wonderfully satisfying breakfast options, including an Italian BLT (pancetta, tomato, arugula and lemon mayo) and a truffled egg toast that you'll crave afterward. Best of all, Ino serves until 2 a.m., making it the perfect spot for a casual breakfast, lunch or a late-night snack.

Italian. Lunch, dinner, late-night. $16-35.

★★★INSIEME

777 Seventh Ave., New York, The Michelangelo Hotel, 212-582-1310;
www.restaurantinsieme.com

From the owners of the downtown darling Hearth comes Insieme and its as different from its sister restaurant as Times Square is from the East Village. This separate take on Italian cuisine was, however, inspired by unity, bringing "together," as the name says, traditional and contemporary Italian cuisine on one menu. For example the insalata di misticanza of lettuce, vegetables, three-year-old parmesan and balsamic vinegar is countered by an octopus carpaccio with soffritto crudo, fennel, sweet potato and red wine vinaigrette; the clam linguine by mushroom risotto; and the lamb accented by squash, tomato confit, green olive and mint.

Italian. Breakfast, lunch (Monday-Friday), dinner (Monday-Saturday), Saturday-Sunday brunch. Reservations recommended. Bar. $36-85

★JACKSON HOLE

1611 Second Ave., New York, 212-737-8788; www.jacksonholeburgers.com

If you crave a thick, juicy burger and don't mind a loud crowd and a fast-paced—sometimes even frenetic—setting, then Jackson Hole is the place for you. This is a top spot to feast on burgers offered in various sizes and weights with an almost infinite variety of toppings.

American, Mexican. Breakfast, lunch, dinner, late-night, Saturday-Sunday brunch. Outdoor seating. Bar. $16-35

★★★★★JEAN GEORGES
1 Central Park West, New York, 212-299-3900; www.jean-georges.com

So this is what fabulous looks and tastes like. The minimalist dining room is Grade-A sexy—it resembles an extra-large egg, thanks to the curved white seating, soft round lighting, pale white walls and sheer drapes. The soaring ceiling and windows and the dainty Spiegelau stemware contribute to the delicate, airy feeling, but that's as far as your attention will veer from the real star of the show: Jean-Georges Vongerichten's ethereal Asian-influenced French cuisine (roasted sweetbreads with pickled white asparagus and coriander; young garlic soup with frog's legs). Vongerichten is a master at layering flavor, making each bite a hit parade of taste—striking you first with smoky squab, chasing it with poignantly sweet summer peas, then following with a refreshing hint of peppermint. Savor his flawless technique in a three-course meal ($98) or a seven-course procession of signature dishes ($148). For a more casual rendezvous with Jean Georges' tantalizing cuisine, settle for a table at the outdoor Terrace or neighboring Nougatine.

French. Lunch (Monday-Friday), dinner. Closed Sunday. Reservations recommended. $86 and up

★★★JEWEL BAKO
239 E. Fifth St., New York, 212-979-1012

This shoebox-sized true "jewel" of a place in East Village serves delicately mastered sushi and sashimi, as well as more traditional Japanese meals. Jewel Bako is owned by a husband-wife team who place a premium on gracious hospitality. The dining areas are calming and elegant, with diffused light peeking through the wooden ceiling slats. The restaurant's small size and popular following make reservations a must.

Japanese, sushi. Dinner. Closed Sunday. Reservations recommended. $36-85

★JING FONG
20 Elizabeth St., New York, 212-964-5256

If the New York Stock Exchange trading floor were a restaurant, Jing Fong would be it. This Hong Kong-style dim sum banquet hall is never without frenzy. Gesturing diners vie for the attention of jacketed waiters wheeling carts heaped high with plates of steamed pork buns, sticky rice with pork in lotus leaf and other traditional dim sum goodies. Get your game face on: The competition can get stiff between diners battling over that last basket of dumplings.

Chinese. Lunch, dinner. $16-35

★JOHN'S PIZZERIA
278 Bleecker St., New York, 212-243-1680; www.johnsbrickovenpizza.com

For many pizza aficionados, when it comes to John's Pizzeria, there simply is no other. This decades-old standard, located on a congested block of Bleecker Street in Greenwich Village, is almost a dive in terms of décor, but it doesn't matter; the pizza—gorgeous, piping hot, bubbling mozzarella-topped pies—is divine.

Italian. Lunch, dinner. No credit cards accepted. $16-35

★★★JOJO

160 E. 64th St., New York, 212-223-5656; www.jean-georges.com

Dining at Jojo's is more akin to a meal at a friend's apartment than a restaurant—as long as that friend has a palatial Upper East Side townhouse, a knack for cooking flawless French cuisine and goes by the name Jean-Georges. The interior can waver on prissy and overdone, but one bite of the ricotta ravioli with spring vegetables, and you'll hardly care. The poached lobster is unique with a tangy lemon risotto and caramelized fennel, while the duck is perfectly cooked in sweet and sour shallots. Desserts are extraordinary. Raspberry crisp, gooey chocolate cake, poached peaches, warm madeleines. Take your pick; they're all rich and satisfying.

French. Lunch, dinner. $36-85

★★★★KAI

822 Madison Ave., New York, 212-988-7277; www.itoen.com/kai/

To reach this serene Japanese restaurant, you must first pass through the tea shop Ito En downstairs, which makes Kai seem like a hidden gem of some sort—and actually, it is. The atmosphere is hushed and the décor sleek and minimalist, right down to the single flower on each table. Kai specializes in kaiseki, a Japanese multicourse seasonal tasting menu, for $85, while a prix fixe omakase (chef's choice) menu is $150-$200 per person, while the Kagoshima Wagyu steak is $16 per ounce with a five-ounce minimum. If the kaiseki has you parched, opt for hot or cold sake or one of more than a dozen teas on hand—you are above a tea shop after all.

Japanese. Lunch, dinner. Closed Sunday-Monday. $86 and up

★KELLEY & PING

127 Greene St., New York, 212-228-1212; www.eatrice.com

This trendy pan-Asian eatery has been full of slinky Soho hipsters since opening day. The menu of fiery fare served at this cafeteria-style teashop, noodle bar, and Asian grocery reflects many regions of Asia, including China, Vietnam, Korea and Thailand. For those who can't make a decision about what to eat, the menu offers combination platters that include spring rolls, chicken satay, dumplings and duck pancakes.

Pacific-Rim, Pan-Asian. Lunch, dinner. Reservations recommended. Children's menu. $16-35

★★★KURUMA ZUSHI

7 E. 47th St., New York, 212-317-2802

Kuruma Zushi is an understated, small Japanese spot located on the second floor of a less-than-impressive Midtown building, with only a tiny sign to alert you to its presence. Incredibly fresh fish is served with freshly grated wasabi and bright, fiery shavings of ginger. Many consider this the pinnacle of sushi, unfortunately it also comes with a high price tag.

Japanese. Lunch, dinner. Closed Sunday. Reservations recommended. $86 and up.

★★★★L'ATELIER DE JOËL ROBUCHON

57 E. 57th St., New York, 212-758-5700; www.fourseasons.com/newyork

This is lauded chef Joël Robuchon's fourth outpost of L'Atelier worldwide, and he further establishes his talented flair for flavor with an ambitious small-plate French menu by way of Asia. "L'Atelier," which means "workshop" in French, offers a dizzying array of small-tasting portions on the regular menu, making your choices—from frog's legs croquettes to crispy langoustines—a bit overwhelming. But that's like saying a lottery jackpot is too big. The restaurant offers a mixture of table and counter seating similar to that of a sushi restaurant; if you're more inclined to keep tabs on the open kitchen rather than your dining companion, opt for a spot at the v-shaped bar.

French. Dinner. Reservations recommended. Bar. $86 and up.

★★L'EXPRESS
249 Park Ave. South, New York, 212-254-5858; www.lexpressnyc.com

Open 24 hours a day for omelets, frisée au lardons, steak frites and other traditional bistro fare, L'Express of Gramercy is a perfect choice for an off-hour snack, a late-night meal or a quiet breakfast of eggs, coffee and a newspaper. At prime lunch and dinner hours, this replica of a French brasserie can get a bit jammed, but if you don't mind the hustle and bustle, you'll have yourself a nice Parisian-style meal.

French. Breakfast, lunch, dinner, late-night, brunch. Bar. $16-35

★★★★LA GRENOUILLE
3 E. 52nd St., New York, 212-752-1495; www.la-grenouille.com

Decked out with more flowers than a royal wedding, this lovely and luxurious French restaurant is the kind of place where you'll want to dress up and carry a French phrase book so you can converse with the waiter. La Grenouille—which means "frog" in French, though this is actually a prince of a place—is where the most glittery and powerful personalities (Truman Capote in years past, Martha Stewart today) have dined since 1962, enjoying the polished service that is the pinnacle of attentiveness. Just as the cashmere twin set and diamond studs worn by the socialite at the next table will never go out of style, neither will the French classics on the menu here, from frog's legs to Dover sole. Notoriously pricey, La Grenouille has added an affordable $49 theater menu (before 6:30 p.m. and after 9 p.m.), making it—at last!—a upscale dining option even for those on a budget.

French. Lunch (Tuesday-Friday), dinner. Closed Sunday. Jacket required. Bar. $86 and up

★★LA PALAPA
77 St. Marks Place, New York, 212-777-2537; www.lapalapa.com

La Palapa is a lively Iberian hot spot in West Village that seems tailor made for large, loud groups of friends who are on a budget. While the room could seem claustrophobic to some, with gaggles of couples and hordes of singles sitting at candlelit tables, somehow it seems cozy. The specialty is paella, offered in five different varieties.

Mexican. Lunch, dinner, Saturday-Sunday brunch. Reservations recommended. Outdoor seating. Bar. $16-35

★★LAFAYETTE GRILL & BAR
54 Franklin St., New York, 212-732-5600; www.lafgrill.com

Located in lower Manhattan, Lafayette Grill & Bar offers a relaxed ambience for high-powered business lunches, special-occasion dinners or simply rubbing elbows with the locals. The room features high brick walls, sooty woods and a worn dance floor where, live music, dance lessons and performances in tango, flamenco, salsa, and belly dancing provide entertainment several times a week.

Mediterranean. Lunch, dinner. Reservations recommended. Bar. $16-35

★★★★★LE BERNARDIN
155 W. 51st St., New York, 212-554-1515; www.le-bernardin.com

It's hard to keep food in your mouth when your jaw keeps dropping in awe. And awestruck you'll be at chef Eric Ripert's skilled transformation of everything that swims into his pristine dishes. A sure thing since it opened in 1986, Le Bernardin has really hit its stride under perfectionist Ripert. Since he succeeded chef Gilbert Le Coze in 1995, Ripert has continued Le Bernardin's tradition of serving luxurious French seafood with a modern and international flavor (yuzu in the fluke marinade, and salmon served with a jalapeño emulsion). Ripert has divided the menu into playfully named sections: "Almost Raw" (oysters, kampachi), "Barely Touched" (poached white tuna, warm lobster carpaccio) and "Lightly Cooked" (pan-roasted monkfish, poached halibut). A handful of meat dishes available upon request—like seared Kobe beef and pan-roasted squab—will make carnivores sit up and take notice, too. With its butterscotch leather chairs and beige fabric-covered walls, Le Bernardin feels a bit like a corporate dining room, but enormous sprays of seasonal, twiggy flowers soften the décor. The prix fixe dinner menu is $109; the tasting menu with wine is $220.

French. Lunch (Monday-Friday), dinner. Closed Sunday. Reservations recommended. $86 and up

★★★★LE CIRQUE
151 E. 58th St., Midtown, 212-644-0202; www.lecirque.com

in 2006 when it moved from its old digs at the New York Palace Hotel to the Bloomberg Tower in Midtown. Toss in a new chef, Craig Hopson, and a revitalized menu and you've got a winning combination. Plump foie gras ravioli is a standout appetizer, while lamb served with flaky eggplant in filo, goat cheese and a red pepper purée seals the deal for the entrées. Le Cirque's impresario-owner, Sirio Maccioni, presides over his creation each night, looking over a more subdued dining room compared to the outlandish previous space—there's no longer a baroque-carnival feel, but more of an Upper East Side party atmosphere, albeit encased in a gold tent. The new futuristic glass and steel space is more suited to Midtown's business crowd and the sometimes-cold Le Cirque service. But a towering napoleon dessert can make up for any missteps you may encounter from your waiter.

Contemporary French, Italian. Lunch (Monday-Friday), dinner. Closed Sunday. Reservations recommended. Jacket required. $36-85

★★LE COLONIAL
149 E. 57th St., New York, 212-752-0808; www.lecolonialnyc.com

Serving sophisticated French-Vietnamese fare, Le Colonial is a Midtown favorite. The room feels like colonial Saigon come to life, with tall bamboo, spinning ceiling fans, lazy palms and diffused lighting. The menu offers the vibrant spiced chile-tinged signature dishes of the region and includes such treats as glossy spring rolls filled with shrimp, pork, and mushrooms; tender ginger-marinated duck with a tamarind dipping sauce; and grilled loin of pork paired with a lively mango and jicama salad.

Vietnamese, French. Lunch (Monday-Friday), dinner. Reservations recommended. Bar. $36-85

★★★LE PERIGORD

405 E. 52nd St., New York, 212-755-6244; www.leperigord.com

Midtown's Le Perigord is one of New York's old-time favorites for sophisticated French dining. The menu of classic dishes includes the restaurant's signature game selection (in season) and is geared for diners who define gratification in terms of impeccable service, haute nouvelle French cuisine and a quiet, sophisticated dining room.

French. Lunch (Monday-Friday), dinner. Reservations recommended. Jacket required. Bar. $86 and up.

★★★LE REFUGE

166 E. 82nd St., New York, 212-861-4505; www.lerefugenyc.com

Located within walking distance of the Metropolitan Museum of Art and the lush greenery of Central Park, Le Refuge is a classically charming French restaurant offering a small slice of Paris on New York's Upper East Side. A sophisticated crowd gathers at Le Refuge for its Parisian elegance and its impressive wine list that pairs up perfectly with the selection of simple, bistro-style fare, such as farm-raised duck with fresh fruit and filet mignon with peppercorn sauce.

Continental, French. Dinner. Reservations recommended. Outdoor seating. Children's menu. Bar. $36-85

★★LE SOUK

47 Ave. B, New York, 212-777-5454; www.lesoukny.com

The fragrant and seductive foods of Morocco and Egypt are served with warm hospitality at this East Village hideaway. Amber lighting and hookah pipes lend an opium den quality to the dining room that doubles as a stage for belly dancers. The menu includes Moroccan specialties like chicken cooked in a tagine; moulekaya—a rich and savory Egyptian stew; and toasty pita bread with assorted mezze (think Middle Eastern tapas like stuffed grape leaves, hummus, baba ghanoush and the like). A tray of desserts arrives in show-and-tell style, and the selection includes everything from chocolate mousse cake to baklava.

Middle Eastern. Dinner. Outdoor seating. Bar. $16-35

★★LES HALLES

411 Park Ave. S, New York, 212-679-4111; www.leshalles.net

Chef Anthony Bourdain (author of behind-the-scenes memoir *Kitchen Confidential*) brought Les Halles into the culinary limelight a few years back. Despite all the hype, this brasserie remains a genuine star for amazing cuts of steak and terrific takes on pork, chicken, moules and, of course, heaps of frites. The front serves as a French-style butcher shop (modeled after the French marketplace, Les Halles), while the crowded bistro-style dining room feels like it belongs in some natty arrondissement in Paris.

French. Breakfast, lunch, dinner, Saturday-Sunday brunch. Bar. $36-85

★★LES HALLES DOWNTOWN
15 John St., New York, 212-285-8585; www.leshalles.net

This classic French brasserie is located in lower Manhattan and is within easy walking distance of Wall Street, the Stock Exchange and Battery Park. The rich interior features brass foot rails, globe lighting, dark mahogany walls, leather banquettes and framed posters. The menu boasts staple fare such as steak-frites and burgers.

French, steak. Lunch, dinner, Saturday-Sunday brunch. Children's menu. Bar. $16-35

★LOMBARDI'S
32 Spring St., New York, 212-941-7994; www.firstpizza.com

Arguably the best pizza in the city is served at Lombardi's, a timeworn institution in Little Italy. Straight from the coal-fired oven, these pies are served sizzling hot and smoky from the coal's char, with thin, crispy crusts and fresh toppings. The service can be lazy but is always friendly, and the tables are tight, but it adds to the amicable ambience. This is not Mobil Four-Star dining, but Four-Star eating, and when you crave pizza and a bottle of red, nothing is better.

Pizza. Lunch, dinner. Outdoor seating. No credit cards accepted. $15 and under.

★★LONDEL'S SUPPER CLUB
2620 Frederick Douglas Blvd., New York, 212-234-6114; www.londelsrestaurant.com

This Harlem supper club delights diners with fast, friendly service and home-style American fare that pops with Cajun and Southern flavors. Entrées like honey barbecued baby back ribs, Southern fried chicken and pan-seared salmon with coriander butter will make you feel as if a Southern grandmother is in the kitchen, and the Sunday Gospel Brunch will inspire you.

Southern. Lunch, dinner, Saturday-Sunday brunch. Closed Monday. Reservations recommended. Bar. $16-35

★★LUCKY STRIKE
59 Grand St., New York, 212-941-0772; www.luckystrikeny.com

Lucky Strike was one of the first downtown hot spots from Keith McNally, the king of the distressed Parisian chic brasserie. Filled with smoky mirrors, wine-stacked walls and a dressed-down vintage French vibe, Soho's Lucky Strike is still a super-cool spot to slink down into a sexy banquette and feast on perfect bistro standards like steak frites, frisée and goat cheese salad, steamed mussels and juicy roast chicken.

American, French. Lunch, dinner, late-night, brunch. Bar. $16-35

★★LUPA OSTERIA ROMANA
170 Thompson St., New York, 212-982-5089; www.luparestaurant.com

There are several sure things about Lupa, celebrity chef Mario Batali's wonderfully rustic, Roman osteria: the line for a table will wind its way down Thompson Street. The heavenly spaghettini with spicy cauliflower ragout will leave you wondering how you ever hated cauliflower. The antipasti board—a massive butcher block piled high with house-made cured meats and sausages—will leave you unable to eat these heavenly pork products anywhere else. For all these reasons and more (like wine, atmosphere, service, and style), Lupa is, hands-down, one of the most beloved spots for earthy and satisfying Roman fare. It's worth the wait.

Italian. Lunch, dinner. Outdoor seating. Bar. $16-35

★★LUSARDI'S

1494 Second Ave., New York, 212-249-2020; www.lusardis.com

This well-established neighborhood staple is a favorite among Upper East Siders craving reliable Italian fare in a modest, unpretentious setting. The menu sticks to the plates that Italian restaurants do best—antipasti, fresh composed salads, hearty bowls of pasta, olive oil-grilled fish and tender slow-cooked meats braised in red wine. This is a lovely restaurant with a gracious staff and a wonderful wine list to complement the cuisine.

Italian. Lunch, dinner. Reservations recommended. Bar. $36-85

★★★MALONEY & PORCELLI

37 E. 50th St., New York, 212-750-2233; www.maloneyandporcelli.com

Named for the restaurant owner's attorneys, Maloney & Porcelli prepares simple, well-executed cuisine served in a classic, clubby environment. The New American menu offers straightforward choices like a raw bar, thin-crust pizza and filet mignon. The wine list contains some real gems as well, making Maloney & Porcelli a favorite for Midtown dining.

American, steak. Lunch (Monday-Friday), dinner. Reservations recommended. Outdoor seating. Bar. $36-85

★★★★★MASA

10 Columbus Circle, New York, 212-823-9800; www.masanyc.com

When you surrender this much cash (at least $450 a head—or more, depending upon availability of ingredients—before drinks and tip) and power (the chef decides what you'll eat), the food better be flawless. Luckily, chef Masa Takayama's creations are, and when you put yourself entirely in his expert hands, he'll regale you with an array of five to six appetizers, 20 to 25 different types of fresh seafood and a dessert course. The chef is infatuated with high-end, luxury ingredients such as truffles (white truffle tempura; black truffles on oysters), caviar (a generous scoop of which tops tuna belly), Ohmi beef and foie gras. Seafood is flown in daily from Japan. There are just 26 seats; ask if you can sit at the sushi counter, composed of a single slab of Japanese cypress Hinoki wood, so you can watch Takayama and his team of chefs at work.

Japanese. Lunch (Tuesday-Friday), dinner. Closed Sunday. Reservations recommended. $86 and up

★★★MATSURI

369 W. 16th St., New York, 212-242-4300; www.themaritimehotel.com

Located in the Meatpacking District's Maritime Hotel, Matsuri is an Asian wonderland. From the bamboo and paper-lanterned movie set décor to the shimmering sushi, sashimi and expertly plated haute Japanese stylings, this restaurant is an ode to the exotic senses of the Far East, attracting glamorous crowds seeking high-style fare and flair.

Japanese. Dinner. Reservations recommended. Bar. $36-85

★★MAX

51 Ave. B, New York, 212-539-0111; www.max-ny.com

Delicious and cheap are two words commonly used to describe Max, a no-frills joint for terrific red sauce, pasta, lasagna and all sorts of dishes whose names end in "parmagiana." Other words to throw into the mix include crowded, loud and no reservations, all of which means that you'd better be prepared to wait and to shout to be heard. But that's part of Max's charm, and the food makes it worthwhile.

Italian. Dinner. Outdoor seating. Bar. No credit cards accepted. $16-35

★★★MAYA

1191 First Ave., New York, 212-585-1818; www.modernmexican.com/mayany

A native of Mexico City, Maya's talented chef/owner Richard Sandoval knows authentic Mexican cuisine. His popular Upper East Side restaurant is perpetually packed with neighborhood locals who love the hacienda-style room—wood-paneled walls accented with native art and terracotta tiled floors—and such dishes as cordero en mole verde; a lamb shank braised in a chocolate sauce with pan-roasted potatoes; and chayote squash with baby carrots. The house mariscada—a mammoth bowl bobbing with sea scallops, shrimp, mussels and clams, served with black rice and a coriander seed-red pepper emulsion—is superb.

Mexican. Dinner. Reservations recommended. Bar. $36-85

★★MELBA'S

300 W. 114th St., New York, 212-864-7777; www.melbasrestaurant.com

A small, chic space with granite tables, chandeliers and sophisticated black and white décor provides a delightful environment for the equally delightful cuisine at Melba's. A menu of updated soul food classics and contemporary American choices delights the palate and keeps Harlem's locals coming back for more. Macaroni with pepper jack, cheddar and mozzarella cheeses; wine-braised beef short ribs with cheddar grits; and BBQ turkey meatloaf are just a few of the entree choices that bring a hint of elegance to your dinner, while desserts like homemade vanilla ice cream and grandma's sweet potato pie will make you feel like a kid again.

American. Dinner, Sunday brunch. Closed Monday. Reservations recommended. Bar. $16-35

★★★MERCER KITCHEN

99 Prince St., New York, 212-966-5454; www.jean-georges.com

This sleek, sexy room inside Soho's Mercer Hotel is the brainchild of star chef Jean-Georges Vongerichten. Here, he practices his talent for comfort food, albeit the most luxe, delectable, gourmet kind of home cooking you'll ever taste. The menu includes several kinds of pizzas topped with ingredients like black truffle and fontina cheese, and every entrée may be accompanied by sides like unctuous macaroni or corn pudding.

American, Continental. Breakfast, lunch, dinner, late-night, Saturday-Sunday brunch. Reservations recommended. Bar. $36-85

★★ THE MERMAID INN
96 Second Ave., New York, 212-674-5870; www.themermaidnyc.com

This seafood eatery boasts a well-stocked raw bar and is decked out with framed maritime maps and fish prints, plus dishes of goldfish pretzels on the bar. A double-cut pork chop (East Village location) and a grilled hanger steak (Upper West Side location) infiltrate the otherwise exclusively seafood menu, and the short-but-well-chosen wine list complements the ocean fare. A lobster sandwich bears chunks of celery and comes heaped on a buttery brioche roll with a side of Old Bay-seasoned fries, and complimentary chocolate pudding served in a demitasse cup rounds out the night. The dark wooden tables are placed liberally throughout the dining room, back garden and front patio, so it never gets too noisy.

American, seafood. Dinner. Reservations recommended. Outdoor seating. Bar. $16-35

★★MESA GRILL
102 Fifth Ave., New York, 212-807-7400; www.mesagrill.com

Food Network fans know chef Bobby Flay as the red-haired chef who is a master of the grill. Today, he's practially an empire, with multiple restaurants under his helm, cookbooks and numerous television appearances. But Mesa Grill, which opened in 1991, was his first restaurant, and above all else, Flay is the king of all things spicy. Dishes like the shrimp and roasted garlic corn tamales, New Mexican spice-rubbed pork tenderloin with crushed pecan butter, and sixteen-spice duck breast with carrot-habanero sauce and a chorizo-goat cheese tamale with thyme, prove that his food keeps getting better and better. The service can be clunky, but your focus will be on the food.

Southwestern. Lunch (Monday-Friday), dinner, brunch (Saturday-Sunday). $35-85

★★MI COCINA
57 Jane St., New York, 212-627-8273; www.micocinany.com

Authentic regional Mexican cuisine is featured at Mi Cocina, a cozy, colorful and lively West Village favorite for outstanding Latin dishes. The menu offers easy-to-love dishes like crisp, savory quesadillas and soft tacos fashioned from fresh corn and filled specialties such as ancho-rubbed pulled pork. There are vibrant regional specialties as well like the rich, chocolate moles of Oaxaca and the lime- and chile-marinated fish from the seaside region of Veracruz. Margaritas are wonderfully tart with lots of fresh lime juice and, of course, quite a bit of tequila. This restaurant is all about good food and fun.

Mexican. Lunch (Monday-Friday), Dinner. Reservations recommended. Outdoor seating. Children's menu. $16-35

★MICKEY MANTLE'S
42 Central Park S., New York, 212-688-7777; www.mickeymantles.com

Located on Central Park South, Mickey Mantle's is an easy and smart choice when you want to catch a game and have a good meal without the roar of a crowded sports bar. This elegant dining room is a good option if you're wandering around Central Park and get hungry for straightforward, tasty American fare. Burgers, steaks, seafood and pastas are on the menu, and guests will love the celebrity wine list. In season, the Yankees are always on the 30 flat-screen TVs here. You'll also find a nice collection of rare baseball memorabilia (some available for sale) and sports-themed art on the walls.

American. Lunch, dinner. Reservations recommended. Outdoor seating. Children's menu. Bar. $16-35

★★★★THE MODERN

9 W. 53rd St., Midtown, 212-333-1220; www.themodernnyc.com

The Modern, an elegant sun-lit Midtown addition to restaurateur Danny Meyer's dense portfolio (which includes Blue Smoke, Gramercy Tavern and Union Square Café) is really two restaurants in one—the sophisticated Dining Room and a less-formal Bar Room. Split up into two rooms separated by frosted glass, both restaurants reside in The Museum of Modern Art, one of the most elegant buildings in New York. In fact, most seats afford great views of the MoMA sculpture garden next door, so don't be surprised to catch glimpses of a Miró or a Picasso as you dine. Still, chef Gabriel Kreuther—who took home the James Beard Award for Best Chef: New York City in 2009—tries his darndest to take your attention from the masterpieces outside to those on your plate with his bold, flavorful food, and he succeeds. The romantic, 85-seat Dining Room offers more elegant dishes like chorizo-crusted codfish with white cocoa bean purée and harissa oil; roasted lobster with chanterelles, heart of palm and chamomile blossom nage; and a Pennsylvania duck breast with a black trumpet marmalade, fleischschneke and banyuls jus. In the less-formal Bar Room, you can find an earthy menu emphasizing small plates with big tastes, such as a pasta dish elevated by chewy, salty escargots and fragrant wild mushrooms. A not-to-miss dessert is the pistachio dark-chocolate dome with pistachio ice cream and amaretto gelée. It's essentially edible art.

French, Contemporary American. Lunch (Monday-Friday), dinner. Closed Sunday. $36-85

★★★MOLYVOS

871 Seventh Ave., New York, 212-582-7500; www.molyvos.com

Located near Carnegie Hall and City Center, Molyvos is a great choice before or after a dance or concert, with a wonderful menu of modern Greek specialties such as assorted mezze served with warm pita, grilled whole fish, stunning takes on lamb and an impressive international wine list. The restaurant feels like it fell from the shores of Mykonos, thanks to its blue-and-white tiles and sturdy wooden tables.

Greek. Lunch, dinner. Reservations recommended. Bar. $36-85

★★MOMOFUKU SSÄM BAR

207 Second Ave. (at 13th St.), New York, 212-254-3500; www.momofuku.com

Star chef David Chang dabbles in pork the way great artists work in clay or watercolor. His steamed pork belly buns (also available at nearby Momofuku Noodle Bar), regional country ham selections and crispy pig's head torchon make Chang New York's reigning prince of pork. The jewel in his crown is bo ssäm—a hefty roasted Boston pork butt that takes six to eight hours to prepare. (Ordering this dish in advance for a party of at least six is the only way to get a reservation.) It's served with Chang's interpretation of traditional accoutrements: kimchi, oysters, Korean rice and bibb lettuce. Communal tables keep the mood here light and fun, and the hipster staff is blissfully helpful. If you're craving more of a challenge, try getting a table at sister property and restaurant-of-the-moment Ko; the ultra-strict reservation policy may be frustrating, but if you get in, it doesn't take long to see what all the fuss is about.

Asian. Lunch, dinner. $16-35

★★★MR. K'S
570 Lexington Ave., New York, 212-583-1668; www.mrks.com

Forget any thoughts you may have had about Chinese food because Midtown's Mr. K's breaks all the rules, bringing New Yorkers wonderful, upscale, exotic dishes from various regions of China and serving them in an ultra elegant, posh setting filled with fresh flowers, plush banquettes and, most notably, waiters who know the meaning of service.

Chinese. Lunch, dinner. Reservations recommended. Bar. $36-85

★★NAM
110 Reade St., New York, 212-267-1777; www.namnyc.com

The fresh, spicy flavors of Vietnam are on the menu at Nam, a chic, breezy, bamboo-accented restaurant in Tribeca. Giving a city-slicker kick to this Asian cuisine, Nam offers Vietnamese classics like noodle dishes, soups, spring rolls, green papaya salads and simply magnificent seafood dishes. The crispy whole red snapper is slathered in chile and lime and served with steamed jasmine rice, while the steamed sea bass is a fleshy, sweet dish, accompanied by stewed tomatoes.

Vietnamese. Lunch (Monday-Friday), dinner. Bar. $16-35

★★★NOBU
105 Hudson St., New York, 212-219-0500; www.myriadrestaurantgroup.com

Chef Nobuyuki Matsuhisa solidified his darling status here when he opened this, the first of his New York City eateries, in 1994. The sleek restaurant backed by Robert De Niro broke traditional sushi rules with its pioneering Japanese-South American style, serving concoctions like scallops drizzled with hot pepper sauce and slivers of velvety yellowtail studded with rounds of jalapeño. Nobu's miso-marinated black cod has inspired countless imitations, but it's gotten easier to try the real deal now that there are 17 Nobu restaurants around the world, from Miami to Milan. If you can't get a table at Nobu here in New York, try its sister spot Nobu Next Door (212-334-4445) one door down, where the menu is almost exactly the same but the no-reservations policy (except for dinner parties of five or more) makes it a good last-minute option.

Japanese. Lunch (Monday-Friday), dinner. $36-85

★★★OCEANA
1221 Avenue of the Americas, New York, 212-759-5941; www.oceanarestaurant.com

Highly regarded Oceana serves practically every fish in the sea, from halibut to tuna, dorado to turbot. Scallops, lobster and glistening oysters are also on the menu. The service is warm and efficient, and the cream-colored, nautical-themed room (portholes dot the walls) is peaceful and comfortable, making Oceana a perennial favorite for Midtown power lunchers and pre-theater diners. The wine list is impressive, with a good number of seafood-friendly options at a variety of price points.

Seafood. Lunch (Monday-Friday), dinner. Closed Sunday. Reservations recommended. Outdoor seating. Jacket required. Bar. $86 and up.

★★THE ODEON

145 W. Broadway, New York, 212-233-0507; www.theodeonrestaurant.com

Hot spots come and go but the crowds eventually come home to Odeon, the original hipster restaurant in Tribeca (which used to serve the likes of Andy Warhol back in the day). Odeon is refreshingly simple and straighforward, offering well-executed bistro classics such as a rich and crispy croque monsieur, a thick and juicy hamburger with cheese and bacon, and a nice omelet with fries. Order one of the potent martinis and you pretty much have a meal that is guaranteed to hit the spot.

Contemporary American. Lunch, dinner, late night. $16-35

★★★OLIVES

201 Park Ave. S., New York, 212-353-8345; www.toddenglish.com

Celebrity chef Todd English's eclectic restaurant in the W Union Square Hotel has an open kitchen, an open-hearth fireplace and deep, oval banquettes. The menu stars English's standard, but well-presented, Mediterranean formula: boldly flavored dishes that are impeccably prepared and artfully presented. His signature tart filled with olives, goat cheese and sweet caramelized onions is a winner, but the menu also offers lamb, fish, homemade pastas and pizzas from the wood oven.

Mediterranean menu. Breakfast, lunch, dinner, late-night, brunch. Reservations recommended. Bar. $36-85

★★★ONE IF BY LAND, TWO IF BY SEA

17 Barrow St., New York, 212-255-8649; www.oneifbyland.com

This classic French restaurant, set in a restored, turn-of-the-century carriage house in Greenwich Village that was once owned by Aaron Burr, is one of New York's most romantic eateries (and the setting for many marriage proposals). Dark and elegant, the hushed, candlelit, two-story dining room is richly appointed with antique sconces, oriental carpets and blazing fireplaces. The menu here is straight-ahead French, with seasonal accompaniments and modern flourishes that add design to the plate.

American, French. Dinner, Sunday brunch. Bar. $36-85

★★OSTERIA AL DOGE

142 W. 44th St., New York, 212-944-3643; www.osteria-doge.com

Times Square's Osteria al Doge is a warm restaurant that feels like a seaside town near Venice. The room is warmly decorated with blue, green and yellow accents; hardwood floors; a large wood bar; and a balcony overlooking the main dining area. This restaurant is a solid standby for Venetian-inspired seafood dishes like whole branzino with cherry tomatoes, olives and potatoes; a bouillabaisse-style seafood stew; and house-made trenette pasta with crabmeat.

Italian. Lunch (Monday-Friday), dinner. Reservations recommended. Bar. $36-85

★★★OSTERIA DEL CIRCO
120 W. 55th St., New York, 212-265-3636; www.osteriadelcirco.com

Owned by Sirio Maccioni of Le Cirque fame, Osteria del Circo in Midtown carries on his signature brand of homespun hospitality in a more casual, yet no less spirited, atmosphere. The rustic menu of Italian fare includes delicious homemade pastas as well as thin Tuscan-style pizzas, classic antipasti and signature main courses such as salt-baked Mediterranean sea bass and brick-pressed chicken. Entrées are available in both large and small portions, and meals can be eaten in either the dining room, ablaze with banquettes in dazzling colors, in the lounge or on the street-side patio.

Italian. Lunch (Monday-Friday), dinner. Reservations recommended. Outdoor seating. Bar. $36-85

★★OTTO ENOTECA PIZZERIA
1 Fifth Ave., New York, 212-995-9559; www.ottopizzeria.com

Mario Batali's bustling pizza joint near Washington Square Park is one of the few spots in the city where a large group can dine really well and not break the bank. Thin pizzas (like the memorable pane frattau, made with tomato and pecorino romano and topped with a velvety sunny side up egg) are crisped on a griddle, while $9 pastas (spaghetti alla carbonara, rigatoni with escarole and Italian sausage) are hearty and satisfying. It's the housemade gelato that's out of this world, especially the fruity and unexpected olive-oil flavor. The staff is highly knowledgeable about wine—no small feat, as there are more than 700 Italian bottles on the menu.

Italian. Lunch, dinner. $15 and under

★OUR PLACE
1444 Third Ave., New York, 212-288-4888; www.ourplaceuptown.com

Our Place could be mistaken for just another neighborhood Chinese joint, but once you try their sophisticated cuisine, you'll agree it's a notch or two above. The dining room and staff are so pleasant and professional it's worth dining in, but if you must stay at home it's by far the highest-quality Chinese delivery on the Upper East Side.

Chinese. Lunch, dinner, Saturday-Sunday brunch. Reservations recommended. $16-35

★★OYSTER BAR
Grand Central Terminal, Lower Level, New York, 212-490-6650; www.oysterbarny.com

Chaos has never been more fun than at the Oyster Bar. Packed to the gills at lunch and dinner daily, this Grand Central Station icon is a famous cocktail spot and one of the best places to gorge on all sorts of seafood. The room makes you feel as though you have gone back in time, with vaulted subway-tiled ceilings and waiters who have been working here for ages. As for the grub, there are more than two dozen varieties of oysters to choose from, as well as all sorts of chowders and fish entrées. If it swims or just sits in water, it's on the menu, which changes daily based on market availability.

Seafood. Lunch, dinner. Closed Sunday. Bar. $16-35

★★★PARK AVENUE WINTER, SPRING, SUMMER, AUTUMN

100 E. 63rd St., New York, 212-644-1900; www.parkavenyc.com

Park Avenue Café reinvented itself in 2007 into another restaurant—actually, into four other restaurants. The venue is now Park Avenue Winter, Spring, Summer or Autumn, depending on the season, and the focus, of course, is on seasonal ingredients. In winter, for example, nosh on expertly done organic salmon with parsnip puree or grilled veal chops, and a few weeks later, sample dishes like roasted leg of lamb or peekytoe crabcake from the spring menu. The seasons motif goes beyond the rotating menu, too: Every three months or so, the restaurant's entire décor shifts to reflect the mood of what's just outside. Now that's fresh.

American. Lunch, dinner, brunch. Reservations recommended. Bar. $36-85

★★★PATROON

160 E. 46th St., New York, 212-883-7373; www.patroonrestaurant.com

Owner Ken Aretsky's popular, clubby Patroon is a chic steakhouse, but the terrific kitchen turns out wonderful seafood and poultry dishes, too. Steak Diana (named for Aretsky's wife) is prepared tableside with brown butter, shallots and wine. A rooftop deck makes summertime fun with great grilled fare and chilled cocktails.

American. Lunch, dinner. Closed Saturday-Sunday. Reservations recommended. Outdoor seating. Bar. $36-85

★PATSY'S PIZZERIA

509 Third Ave., New York, 212-689-7500; www.patsyspizzeriany.com

Folks in New York take their pizza seriously, and with a pizza joint on what seems like every corner, the competition is fierce. But Patsy's remains a favorite among pie connoisseurs, consistently serving wonderful pizza with thin, crisp but chewy crusts, with an array of toppings for every appetite. Patsy's original location in Harlem is an easy, casual place, with gingham tablecloths, wood floors, and a welcoming, seasoned waitstaff.

Italian, pizza. Lunch, dinner. Bar. No credit cards accepted. $16-35

★★★PAYARD PATISSERIE & BISTRO

1032 Lexington Ave., New York, 212-717-5252; www.payard.com

Payard is the perfect pit stop for lunch if you're shopping on Madison Avenue or headed to the theater. The main attraction is the sublime confections (tarts, cakes, macaroons, oh my), which are some of the best you'll find this side of the Seine. While the sweets delight, don't discount the savory entrées like braised veal cheeks with rosemary polenta. Payard serves one of the best cups of coffee in the city—strong and balanced in that very French fashion—best enjoyed leisurely, with a cookie and a magazine at one of the cozy bistro tables beneath oversized, whimsical glass light fixtures that look like floating balloons.

French. Lunch, dinner. Closed Sunday. Bar. $36-85

★★PEARL OYSTER BAR

18 Cornelia St., New York, 212-691-8211; www.pearloysterbar.com

This New England clamshack by way of the West Village has many outstanding seafood options, from briny raw oysters and clam chowder with smoky bacon to whole-grilled fish and bouillabaisse. Really, there's only one item you need to think about: the lobster roll. The one here will bring you to your knees. A toasted, buttery hot dog bun cradles chunks of sweet lobster and shares the plate with a nest of shoestring fries. It's a perfect mix of sweet, salty, crunchy and creamy. The secret's long been out on the food here, so expect a wait despite a long-overdue expansion a few years back.

American, seafood. Lunch (Monday-Friday), dinner. Closed Sunday. $16-35

★★★★★PER SE

10 Columbus Circle, New York, 212-823-9335; www.perseny.com

Per Se bears the same blue front doors as French Laundry (its country cousin in Napa Valley) and has similar high-end flourishes like nine varieties of salt, plus chef Thomas Keller's legendary "oysters and pearls" dish of Island Creek oysters, creamy tapioca and caviar. But the 64-seat Per Se in the Time Warner Center, with its neutral brown palette and silver accents, feels more cosmopolitan and overtly ambitious in ways the pastoral French Laundry is not. Yet at its heart, Per Se offers the fine-dining indulgences fans worship Keller for (artisanal butter; a fierce focus on fresh ingredients), and it'll still take you five hours to stuff yourself silly on foie gras and truffles as a cavalcade of servers fawn over you. (The daily-changing nine-course tasting menu—vegetarian option available—is $275, and a $175 five-course lunch menu is available Friday through Sunday.) So what if the East Coast setting is a bit more buttoned-up? You won't miss the original a bit.

Contemporary American. Lunch (Friday-Sunday), dinner. Jacket required. Reservations recommended. $86 and up

★★★PERIYALI

35 W. 20th St., New York, 212-463-7890; www.periyali.com

Offering authentic Greek fare in a soothing Mediterranean-accented setting, elegant, recently revamped Periyali serves octopus marinated in red wine, sautéed sweetbreads with white beans, grilled whole fish, and mezze such as taramosalata (caviar mousse), melitzanosalata (grilled-eggplant mousse) and spanakopita (spinach and cheese pie).

Greek. Lunch (Monday-Friday), dinner. Reservations recommended. Bar. $36-85

★★★PETROSSIAN

182 W. 58th St., New York, 212-245-2214; www.petrossian.com

Caviar, caviar and caviar are the reasons for visiting this elegant, art deco-style eatery inspired with ornate mirrors and marble sculptures. In addition to the great salty roe, you'll find an ultra-luxurious brand of Franco-Russian cuisine that includes classics such as borscht, assorted Russian tapas including smoked salmon (served with cold shots of vodka—ask for Zyr, one of the best from Russia), and other glamorous plates, including foie gras prepared several ways and, of course, beef Stroganoff.

Continental, French. Lunch (Monday-Saturday), dinner, Saturday-Sunday brunch. Reservations recommended. Bar. $36-85

★★★★PICHOLINE

35 W. 64th St., New York, 212-724-8585; www.picholinenyc.com

Chef Terrance Brennan's French-Mediterranean cuisine continues to impress at Picholine, which opened in 1993 and seems to get more distinguished with age. The refined menu lacks the fussiness of some French restaurants—you won't find overly rich sauces and heavy, buttery entrées here—but it doesn't skimp on elegance. The fare is simple, seasonally driven and clean in construction: Hearty rabbit comes with fresh tagliatelle and wild snails, while wild striped bass is served with corn chorizo and chanterelle escabéche. Pull up to the bar and try the cheese flights, which are organized by country of origin, and make a good pre- or post-theater treat. The service is poised in the windowless lavender dining room, which gets its sparkle from an enormous chandelier overhead.

French. Dinner. Closed Sunday-Monday. Reservations recommended. $86 and up

★PIE BY THE POUND

124 Fourth Ave., New York, 212-475-4977; www.piebythepound.com

At Pie by the Pound, a slick little pizza joint in the East Village, pizza by the slice is taboo. Ditto for pizza by the pie. The pizzas at Pie are long and rectangular, with scissors used to slice off just the amount you want. You can have your very own pizza party by selecting a variety of pizzas topped with fresh and tasty ingredients like crispy potato, tallegio, and walnuts or pillowy mozzarella, tomato, and basil. Once you make your selections, your slices are weighed, and you pay by the pound, not by the slice.

Pizza. Lunch, dinner. Children's menu. $15 and under.

★PIG HEAVEN

1540 Second Ave., New York, 212-744-4887; www.pigheaven.biz

The name may be intimidating, but they're not guilty of false advertising. The spare ribs, roast pork and suckling pig are some of the best found outside Chinatown (the roast duck is fantastic, too). And with the delightful and contemporary décor, Pig Heaven is just as much for dining out as for dining in.

Chinese. Lunch, dinner, late-night. Outdoor seating. Bar. $16-35

★★PING'S

22 Mott St., New York, 212-602-9988

Be sure to pack your sense of culinary adventure when you go to Ping's, a Chinatown favorite for dim sum and gorgeous live seafood cooked up to order. The room is usually filled to capacity with Chinese families and lawyers on break from nearby courthouses, but do not be deterred by the crowds. The steamed pork buns alone make Ping's worth the wait.

Chinese, seafood. Lunch, dinner, brunch. $16-35

★★PIPA

38 E. 19th St., New York, 212-677-2233

Pipa, a lively and sultry restaurant and tapas bar in the Flatiron District, serves up some of the most delicious modern Spanish food in the city in a setting of a designer's dream. The eclectic décor of the candlelit dining room, which features antiques, exposed brick walls and crystal chandeliers should come as no surprise, as the restaurant occupies the ground floor of ABC Carpet & Home, one of the city's swankiest furniture and accessories stores, making it a perfect shopping pit stop.

Spanish. Lunch, dinner. Reservations recommended. Bar. $36-85

★★★POST HOUSE
28 E. 63rd St., New York, 212-935-2888; www.theposthouse.com

The Post House elevates the typical steakhouse with polished parquet floors, wainscoting and leather armchair seating. The menu includes wonderful salads, signature appetizers such as cornmeal-fried oysters and a shimmering raw bar as well as such entrées as grilled chicken, rack of lamb, prime rib, filet mignon and the signature stolen Cajun rib steak.

Steak. Lunch, dinner, Saturday-Sunday brunch. Reservations recommended. Bar. $36-85

★★PRAVDA
281 Lafayette St., New York, 212-226-4944; www.pravdany.com

Vodka is the main theme at Pravda, a sexy, subterranean bar and lounge in Soho. As for the menu, it pretty much matches what might be served at a Russian vodka bar: caviar, blinis, assorted smoked fish, and black bread—perfect nibbles for late-night revelers of the less-hungry, supermodel or European expatriate type. Pravda's interior, like its caviar, is dark and luxuriously decadent.

Eastern European. Dinner, late-night. Reservations recommended. Bar. $16-35

★★PRUNE
54 E. First St., New York, 212-677-6221; www.prunerestaurant.com

A place that serves 10 different kinds of Bloody Marys (like the Caesar, served with Boodles gin, clam juice and a pickled egg) obviously knows a thing or two about brunch. That's why you'll wait north of 90 minutes on weekend mornings for a seat in the snug-though-charming dining room. If you tough it out, your prize is delicious fare like roasted marrow bones with sea salt and parsley salad or grilled mackerel atop pickled beets and saffron aioli. Don't skimp on the vegetable sides, which include artichokes bathed in tarragon butter and escarole with Merquez sausage. Lunch and dinner offerings are equally innovative and consistently sensational, and service is pleasantly cheery.

Contemporary American. Lunch (Monday-Friday), dinner, Saturday-Sunday brunch. $16-35

★★RAOUL'S
180 Prince St., New York, 212-966-3518; www.raouls.com

Cramped quarters and a rushed waitstaff are part of the charm of this downtown bistro mainstay. Opened in the 1970s by the Alsatian Raoul brothers, the restaurant has grown from a struggling neighborhood eatery to a bustling Manhattan hotspot for scene-seeking locals and tourists in the know. Tightly packed tables provide a bustling atmosphere, especially in the main dining room. (For a quieter dining experience, request a table in the covered garden behind the kitchen or in the upstairs loftspace—don't mind the clairvoyant.) Signature dishes include the artichoke vinaigrette soaked in Raoul's famous

dressing and extra peppery steak au poivre with French fries. Portions are generous, but it's worth leaving a bit on your plate in order to save room for the profiteroles.
French. Lunch, dinner. $16-35

★★THE RED CAT
227 10th Ave., New York, 212-242-1122; www.theredcat.com
Folksy but also art-house cool, the Red Cat is the kind of unpretentious restaurant that leaves you wondering why there simply aren't more places like it. With its art-adorned barn walls, warm red banquettes and hanging iron lanterns, this neighborhood Mediterranean-American charmer is frequented by horn-rimmed-glasses-wearing professionals who sit solo at the bar, tearing into the thick double-cut pork chop and sipping a glass of peppery pinot noir. The vegetables are so fresh and thoughtfully prepared—rapini comes sautéed in garlic and chili flakes—that you'll wonder whether there really is a farm out back from which the chef is plucking his ingredients.
Contemporary American. Lunch (Tuesday-Saturday), dinner. $16-35

★★REDEYE GRILL
890 Seventh Ave., New York, 212-541-9000; www.redeyegrill.com
You can't miss the bright red entrance to Redeye Grill, which sits just 50 feet from Carnegie Hall in Midtown. Its name comes from the dreaded overnight flight linking the West and East coasts, and that link is exactly what inspires its seafood-heavy menu as well as its design. The soaring dining room features Mission-style furnishings and is anchored by a sushi and smoked fish bar, flanked by bronze shrimp sculptures.
American, seafood. Lunch, dinner, late-night, brunch. Outdoor seating. Bar. $36-85

★★★REMI
145 W. 53rd St., New York, 212-581-4242; www.remi-ny.com

The cuisine of Venice is the focus of the menu at Remi, an airy, lofty restaurant in Midtown decorated with ornate Venetian blown-glass lights, hand-painted murals of the Italian city's romantic canals and teak flooring. Remi has long been a favorite for local business people who want to dish over lunch but also makes a terrific choice for drinks, dinner or a visit before or after the theater. The kitchen's specialty is handmade pastas, but the menu also features contemporary Mediterranean takes on fish, beef, poultry and game. A "cicchetti" menu of Venetian tapas is also available at the bar.
Italian. Lunch, dinner. Reservations recommended. Outdoor seating. Bar. $36-85

★REPUBLIC
37 Union Square West, New York, 212-627-7172; www.thinknoodles.com
Located on Union Square West, Republic is perpetually packed with trendy locals who seek out the restaurant's signature Asian noodle dishes. The interior is bright and attractive with high ceilings, orange bar stools, blond wood benches and pasta-inspired black-and-white photography. Be ready to sit on communal picnic tables and shout above the din, but the troubles of pitch and the less-than-comfy seating vanish when the steaming bowls arrive, brimming with Thai, Japanese, and other East Asian varieties of noodles. For an

entertaining dining experience, sit at the bar that faces the open kitchen. Pacific-Rim, Asian. Lunch, dinner. Outdoor seating. Children's menu. Bar. $16-35

★★★RIINGO

205 E. 45th St., New York, 212-867-4200; www.riingo.com

Marcus Samuelsson, the heartthrob, boy-wonder chef behind the very popular contemporary Scandinavian spot Aquavit, is the man behind Riingo, his Asian outpost in Midtown's Alex Hotel. Japanese for "apple," Riingo is a sleek and sexy bi-level space featuring dark ebony woodwork, bamboo floors and luxurious banquettes that offer a sublime setting for supping on Samuelsson's inventive brand of Japanese-American fare.

American, Japanese, sushi. Breakfast, lunch, dinner, brunch. Reservations recommended. Outdoor seating. Bar. $36-85

★★ROCK CENTER CAFÉ

20 W. 50th St., New York, 212-332-7620; www.rockcentercafeny.com

Located in Rockefeller Center, this contemporary American/Italian restaurant is an ideal place to relax under blue summer skies with cool cocktails; or to grab a seat and watch the ice skaters slip, slide and crash all winter long under the twinkling Christmas tree. The Rock Center Café is one of those places that never fails to satisfy with a broad menu of terrific salads, sandwiches, burgers and generously sized seasonal entrées.

American, Italian. Breakfast, lunch, dinner, brunch. Reservations recommended. Outdoor seating. Children's menu. Bar. $36-85

★★★ROSA MEXICANO

61 Columbus Ave., New York, 212-977-7700; www.rosamexicano.com

One of the first restaurants to introduce New Yorkers to authentic Mexican cuisine, Rosa Mexicano was founded by chef Josefina Howard in the early 1980s. It remains an essential stop for anyone who craves strong, chilly margaritas and knockout bowls of guacamole mixed tableside to your desired level of heat (mild to scorching). The menu is a tribute to the regional home-cooking of Mexico—steamy pork tamales; chicken in a rich, savory blanket of mole; terracotta cazuelas brimming with shrimp, tomatoes, garlic and chiles; and a longtime entrée signature, budin Azteca, a wonderful tortilla casserole with layers of shredded chicken and cheese.

Mexican. Lunch (Monday-Friday), dinner (Saturday-Tuesday), Saturday-Sunday brunch. Reservations recommended. Outdoor seating. Bar. $16-35

★★★RUTH'S CHRIS STEAK HOUSE

148 W. 51st St., New York, 212-245-9600; www.ruthschris.com

At this steakhouse chain near Times Square, aged prime Midwestern beef is broiled to your liking and served on a heated plate, sizzling in butter, a staple ingredient used generously in most entrées. Sides like creamed spinach and fresh asparagus with hollandaise are perfect companions to any dish.

Steak. Lunch (Friday), dinner. Reservations recommended. Bar. $36-85

★★★SAKAGURA

211 E. 43rd St., New York, 212-953-7253; www.sakagura.com

At this subterranean hideaway in Midtown, you'll find one of the most extensive sake collections in the city, as well as a talented knife-wielding team of sushi chefs chopping up delicious sashimi. (There is no sushi here, though, as it is forbidden to serve rice with sake.) Sakagura is tough to find; you enter through the lobby of an office building and follow a small gold sign that points you toward this buried basement space. The hunt is worth it.

Japanese. Lunch (Monday-Friday), dinner. Reservations recommended. $36-85

★★★SAN PIETRO

18 E. 54th St., New York, 212-753-9015; www.sanpietro.net

Located on a busy Midtown street, glitzy San Pietro is owned and run by the three Bruno brothers, who grew up on a family farm along the Amalfi Coast in the southern Italian region of Campagna. They pay homage to their homeland by serving traditional dishes—antipasti, pasta, poultry, fish, veal and beef—accented with seasonal ingredients. The wine list contains a knockout selection of southern Italian wines to complete the experience.

Southern Italian. Lunch, dinner. Closed Sunday. Reservations recommended. Bar. $36-85

★★SARABETH'S

423 Amsterdam Ave., New York, 212-496-6280; www.sarabethswest.com

During the nearly inevitable hour-long wait for a table on Sunday mornings, you may wonder if pancakes and eggs are worth it. The answer? Absolutely. This brunch mainstay is favored by a J.Crew-clad, preppy set seeking otherworldly ricotta lemon pancakes and three-egg omelets in a faux-country setting. If you can't bear the wait, pick up a selection of scones, muffins and a jar of jewel-toned homemade jam (we like strawberry peach, mixed berry or plum cherry) from the bakery counter. Lunch and dinner offerings like chicken pot pie are just what you'd expect—hearty and homey.

American. Breakfast, lunch, dinner. Whitney Museum location: lunch only (closed Monday). Lord & Taylor location: lunch only. $16-35

★★SARDI'S

234 W. 44th St., New York, 212-221-8440; www.sardis.com

This icon in the theater district, established in 1921, is one of those old-time favorites that essentially stays the same year after year. For some places, though, no change is a good thing. Sardi's still serves as a cafeteria of sorts for many theater celebrities (diners can check out the signed celebrity photos which cover the walls), and still offers hearty Continental signatures like stuffed cannelloni (veal, beef, or sausage), serviceable antipasti (this is not the restaurant's strong suit), and solid simple dishes like rotisserie-roasted chicken and grilled filet mignon. Yes, the brilliant baked Alaska is still on the menu, and it's still a monster—a tasty one at that.

Continental. Lunch, dinner. Closed Monday. Reservations recommended. Bar. $36-85

★★SAVORE

200 Spring St., New York, 212-431-1212; www.savoreny.com

Located on a lovely block in Soho, Savore is a quiet little gem that offers Tuscan dining in a relaxed and authentic countryside setting. At Savore, you'll feel like you are dining in Europe. Meals are not rushed, service is leisurely, and the food is simple and delicious—the menu features earthy pastas, grilled whole fish, braised meats and fresh salads. An extensive wine list offers numerous interesting bottles as well as nearly 40 selections by the glass. All you crave after dinner is a ticket to Italy.

Italian. Lunch, dinner, Saturday-Sunday brunch. Reservations recommended. Outdoor seating. Bar. $36-85

★★★SAVOY

70 Prince St., New York, 212-219-8570; www.savoynyc.com

Located on two floors of a Soho townhouse, Savoy embodies the art of organic, seasonal cuisine. In fact, chef Peter Hoffman can be seen loading up his bike with the freshest finds from the Union Square farmers market early in the morning to prepare the day's menu. The beauty of Savoy is that produce is allowed to shine on its own with little adornment. Asparagus might be simply grilled and topped with sea salt and shaved Parmesan, and entrées typically have no more than five main ingredients. Savoy can be this side of precious (check out the honey from Hoffman's rooftop hives), but the freshness and high quality of the food can't be beat. The fireplace makes this charming setting a must in winter, while heavy wooden beams overhead and warm walls surrounding the small dining room give Savoy a country-in-the-city feel.

American, Mediterranean. Lunch (Monday-Saturday), dinner. Reservations recommended. Bar. $36-85

★★SCHILLER'S LIQUOR BAR

131 Rivington St., New York, 212-260-4555; www.schillersny.com

A Lower East Side hipster haunt from Keith McNally, the king of the distressed vintage Parisian brasserie, Schiller's Liquor Bar is bursting at its authentic subway-tiled seams with the most up-to-the-minute stars and scene-seekers. Though, unlike competing scenes, the diversely inspired grub here is consistently tasteful and affordable.

French, English, Southern. Breakfast, lunch, dinner, Saturday-Sunday brunch. Reservations recommended. Bar. $16-35

★★★SEA GRILL

19 W. 49th St., New York, 212-332-7610; www.rapatina.com/seagrill

The Sea Grill is home to some of the most delicious seafood in the city, paired with an enchanting setting. This lavish, ocean-blue restaurant houses a slick bar and offers prime wintertime views of ice skaters twirling on the rink under the twinkling Christmas tree at Rockefeller Plaza. Summertime brings alfresco dining and lots of icy cocktails to pair up with the fantastic contemporary seafood menu. Crab cakes are its signature, and other dishes—salmon, cod, halibut and skate—are just as special, as the kitchen infuses dishes with techniques and flavors from Asia and the world at large.

Seafood, Japanese sushi. Lunch (Monday-Friday), dinner. Closed Sunday. Reservations recommended. Outdoor seating. Bar. $36-85

★★SERAFINA FABULOUS PIZZA

1022 Madison Ave., New York, 212-734-2676; www.serafinarestaurant.com

At this mini-chain of velvet-roped pizza joints, you can start the evening off with a simple meal of tasty Italian fare like wood-fired pizzas, salads, antipasti, pasta, seafood and meat; and then stay and hang out in the bar to sip cool cocktails and listen to the DJs tunes. Serafina is casual but hip, with a generally young and gorgeous European crowd that comes in more for the see-and-be-scene vibe than the terrific pizza.

Italian. Lunch, dinner. $36-85

★SERENDIPITY 3

225 E. 60th St., New York, 212-838-3531; www.serendipity3.com

Don't let the crush of people ogling knickknacks for sale dampen your desire to indulge in a signature frozen hot chocolate or three-scoop "drugstore" sundae at this Upper East Side sweet shop. There are few places in New York as playful as Serendipity, where both kids and kids-at-heart can unabashedly worship at the altar of sweets. Serendipity feels like an Alice in Wonderland tea party come to life, complete with multicolored Tiffany lamps (some of them real), a tiny space and larger-than-you-can-imagine sticky treats. "Serious" food is available, too, from burgers and hot dogs to meatloaf and pasta.

American, dessert. Lunch, dinner. $16-35

★SETTEPANI BAKERY & CAFÉ

196 Lenox Ave., New York, 917-492-4806; www.settepani.com

In addition to scrumptious pastries and artisan breads, this family-run bakery in Harlem—whose name means "seven breads"—offers a delectable menu of paninis, pastas, quiches and salads. Everything at Settepani is freshly made on the premises and, like the flagship store in Brooklyn, they offer a wide range of specialty coffees and teas.

American, bakery. Breakfast, lunch, dinner, brunch. Outdoor seating. Children's menu. $15 and under.

★★★SHUN LEE PALACE

155 E. 55th St., New York, 212-371-8844; www.shunleepalace.com

A favorite choice for Chinese-food-loving New Yorkers who want something a little more refined than some of the places in Chinatown, Shun Lee specializes in Hunan, Cantonese and Szechuan classics. Its following is not unfounded: The food here is flavorful and light, with many authentic, time-intensive dishes you won't find at neighborhood Chinese spots. The Beggar's Chicken, for example, is a vegetable-, pork- and seafood-stuffed chicken wrapped in lotus leaves and packed in clay soil before baking for several hours. Vegetarians who wrestle with the carnivore-crave—particularly the Peking duck variety—will find salvation in the Veggie Duck Pie, a tofu take on the famous delicacy, pancake, hoisin sauce and all. Shun Lee's sister restaurant, Shun Lee on the Upper West Side (43 W. 65th St., 212-595-8895), serves similar food and is a popular choice with the Lincoln Center crowd.

Chinese. Lunch, dinner. $16-35

★★★SMITH & WOLLENSKY

797 Third Avenue, New York, 212-753-1530; www.smithandwollensky.com

The original steakhouse for which the national chain was modeled, this 390-seat, wood-paneled dining room in Midtown is renowned for sirloin steaks and filet mignon but also offers lamb and veal chops. Sides are huge and straightforward, with the likes of creamed spinach and hash browns. Good wines and personable service complete the experience.

Steak. Lunch, dinner. Reservations recommended. Outdoor seating. Bar. $36-85

★★SOBA-YA

229 E. Ninth St., New York, 212-533-6966; www.sobaya-nyc.com

Tucked away on a side street in Lower East Village, Soba-Ya is a tiny, serene space that is the neighborhood's perennial favorite for Japanese noodle dishes. Noodles come both hot and cold, plus you can watch the soba and udon noodles being cut and hung to dry like wears in an old laundry house. Although the noodles make the best impression, the rest of the menu deserves attention as well, like tempura vegetables with spicy curry sauce and an excellent assortment of sakes, organized on the menu for pairing. Bamboo, rice paper and paper lanterns add to the traditional décor.

Japanese. Lunch, dinner. $16-35

★★★SOUTH GATE

Jumeirah Essex House, 154 Central Park South, New York, 212-484-5120;
www.jumeirahessexhouse.com

Alain Ducasse moved out and Eleven Madison Park's Kerry Heffernan moved in—after the place got a no-holds-barred facelift that transformed the space into a gleaming, imposing, high-ceilinged dining room focused on floor-to-ceiling windows looking out on the park. The menu hosts satisfactory seafood and experimental plates like seared foie gras with tarragon and muscat and pear wafers. The crowd is what you'd expect at a high-end Midtown hotel restaurant—local expense-account opportunists and their jet-setting guests.

Contemporary American. Lunch, dinner, Sunday brunch. Reservations recommended. Bar. $36-85

★★★SPARKS STEAK HOUSE

210 E. 46th St., New York, 212-687-4855; www.sparkssteakhouse.com

A Manhattan mainstay since 1966, Sparks delivers the boys club style and brisk service often associated with old-school steak joints. Give or take the décor, this midtown behemoth delivers on flavor. The menu encompasses all the steakhouse standards: shrimp cocktail, creamed spinach, hash brown potatoes, and a surprisingly small array of beef cuts. (Don't come craving a ribeye.) But what is on the meat menu is excellent. The New York sirloin is the signature dish, slightly charred and salty on the outside, but still rare. No need for steak sauce, which is a good thing since the waitstaff doesn't take kindly to the request. The wine list is hefty and offers a nice range of vintages and prices.

Steak. Lunch, dinner. $36-85

★★SPICE MARKET

403 W. 13th St., New York, 212-675-2322; www.jean-georges.com

Spice Market, the first project from dynamic chef duo Jean-Georges Vongerichten and Gray Kunz, is like something out of the Kasbah—an authentic Moroccan escape with deep color-stained wood panels; authentic Indian furniture; and sari-wrapped waitresses. As for the fare, there's magic on the plate. Out of the 60-foot-long open kitchen (complete with its own sultry food bar) parades fragrant, exotically spiced, family-style dishes inspired by Morocco and the Far East—satays and summer rolls, dosa and pho; and fragrant pulled-oxtail hot pots with coriander chutney and kumquats. With stunning banquettes and an attractive clientele aglow with amber candle-light, Spice Market is easily a contender for New York's sultriest scene.

Pacific-Rim, Pan-Asian. Lunch, dinner, late-night. Reservations recommended. Outdoor seating. Bar. $36-85

★STAGE DELI

834 Seventh Ave., New York, 212-245-7850; www.stagedeli.com

Stage Deli in Midtown is one of New York's most favored between-the-bread restaurants, offering lovely sandwiches crafted from rye bread, pastrami, tongue, brisket, mustard, mayo, and half-sour pickles, as well as comforting standards like chicken noodle soup. This is a hectic and bustling deli, with cafeteria-style tables.

Deli. Breakfast, lunch, dinner, late-night. Children's menu. $16-35

★★STEAK FRITES

9 East 16th St., New York, 212-675-4700; www.steakfritesnyc.com

Located down the block from the Union Square Greenmarket, Steak Frites is the perfect rest stop after shopping for the season's best produce. Open for Saturday and Sunday brunch, it is popular on weekends, when locals grab outdoor tables and people-watch. At night, the restaurant is lively and has a rich European flair, decorated with vintage posters and long leather banquettes. This is a fun restaurant in which to hang out and just have drinks, but it's also an ideal spot to hunker down for a dinner of the signature steak frites with a bold red wine.

French. Lunch, dinner, brunch. Outdoor seating. Bar. $16-35

★★★STRIP HOUSE

13 E. 12th St., New York, 212-328-0000; www.striphouse.com

From the neon sign out front to the loungy interior with burgundy banquettes, red velvet walls and pictures of semi-nude burlesque girls on the walls, this is a far cry from Steak 'n' Shake, or even Peter Lugers. Many a business deal is made over plump shrimp cocktail and thick bone-in strip steak or dry aged ribeye. Don't skimp on the sides; the truffled creamed spinach tops the list, but the mashed potatoes are a close second. It's no surprise at this machismo palace that the portions are huge, and the theme carries through to dessert where a single slice of chocolate cake is enough to feed a family of five.

Steak. Lunch, dinner. $36-85

★★SUEÑOS

311 W. 17th St., New York, 212-243-1333; www.suenosnyc.com

Walk by Chelsea's Sueños and you will most likely spy a crowd of people gathered on the sidewalk, looking through a large front window, drooling. The porthole gives sidewalk voyeurs a view of the kitchen, where Mexican-cuisine diva Sue Torres executes orders of her addictive modern regional Mexican cuisine. There are fat, steamy empanadas filled with fava beans and drunken goat cheese; heavenly pork tamales steamed in banana leaves and plated in a fiery lather of ancho beurre blanc; and tortilla-crusted Chilean sea bass with a chile rajas tamale. The restaurant is lively and hip, decorated in bright colors and filled with the sweet smell of handmade fresh corn tortillas.

Mexican. Dinner. Closed Monday. Reservations recommended. Bar. $36-85

★★★★SUGIYAMA

251 W. 55th St., New York, 212-956-0670; www.sugiyama-nyc.com

This may be the closest you'll get to Japan without hopping on a plane. The minimalist Sugiyama (tiny bamboo lanterns offer minimal sparkle to an otherwise spartan, booth-filled space) offers innovative and interesting takes on traditional Japanese food that you won't find elsewhere in the city. It specializes in kaiseki, three-, five- or eight-course seasonal tasting menus that emphasize harmony in flavor, texture, color and shape. The menu typically progresses from cold dishes (mixed greens with Japanese mushrooms) to hot (beef tenderloin grilled on a hot stone), producing a taste bud-pleasing medley of flavors and sensations. A chef's choice kaiseki menu (called omakase) is also available.

Japanese. Dinner. Closed Sunday-Monday. $36-85

★★★SUMILE

154 W. 13th St., New York, 212-989-7699; www.sumile.com

Sumile, a windowless and soothing Zen space in the West Village, feels like a movie set with star-quality guests to match. The menu is a celebration of Japanese ingredients and contrasting textures, temperatures and flavors. Innovative plates include striped bass in a nori sauce or roasted miso cod. This is not a place for timid eaters.

Japanese. Lunch (Monday-Friday), dinner. Reservations recommended. Outdoor seating. Bar. $36-85

★★SURYA

302 Bleecker St., New York, 212-807-7770; www.suryany.com

Surya is a sleek, low-lit restaurant and boîte in the West Village that offers the most stylish setting in the city for contemporary Indian cuisine. The lounge is a chic place to stop in for a cocktail, like the house "tajmapolitan" (a cosmopolitan with cinnamon). After that drink, you might want to move into the sultry dining room for dinner (beef-free), featuring a wonderful list of inspired vegetable dishes like birianyi—basmati rice perfumed with sweet spices and served with raita—and urulakilangu katrika koze, spiced potatoes and eggplant served with paratha (griddle-fried bread). In warm weather, you can dine outside in the restaurant's lovely leafy garden.

Indian. Lunch, dinner. Outdoor seating. Bar. $16-35

★★★SUSHI OF GARI

402 E. 78th St., New York, 212-517-5340; www.sushiofgari.com

Sushi of Gari is one of those spots frequented by New Yorkers in the know. This Upper East Side restaurant is always packed to capacity with sushi-loving trendsetters, and at times, it's hard to hear yourself order, let alone have a conversation. If you're sticking to the basics, try the kanpachi (Japanese yellowtail) and the toro (fatty tuna).

Japanese, sushi. Dinner. Closed Monday. Reservations recommended. $36-85

★★★SYLVIA'S

328 Lenox Ave., New York, 212-996-0660; www.sylviassoulfood.com

Critics may say that Sylvia's has lost some of its soul since it spawned cookbooks and a line of food products including canned black-eyed peas and jarred "Sassy Sauce." But this legendary Harlem soul-food eatery—which Sylvia Woods opened with her husband Herbert in 1962 in a luncheonette where she had formerly waitressed—is still a go-to spot for everything fried, smothered and sauced in the Southern comfort tradition. All of the usual faves are here: catfish, chicken livers, ribs, waffles and fried chicken, grits, collard greens, coconut cake, banana pudding—we could go on. President Barack Obama has been seen dropping in for fried chicken, as has former President Bill Clinton. Don't miss the Sunday gospel brunch; you'll leave with a spring in your step and your belly full.

American, Southern. Breakfast, lunch (Monday-Saturday), dinner, Sunday brunch. $16-35

★★★TABLA

11 Madison Ave., New York, 212-889-0667; www.tablany.com

Much like the mixed cuisine that it serves, Tabla is two restaurants in one. The main dining room occupies a sophisticated balcony-level space with crisp white tablecloths, warm candlelight and golden mosaics on the walls, and serves new American cuisine accented by Indian spices and flavors. Downstairs, the Bread Bar includes an outdoor patio and caters to a more casual crowd with home-style Indian cuisine. No matter where you choose to dine, views of Madison Square Park and the Flatiron building are yours for the taking. The menu changes daily, but standouts include the Tabla crab cakes, blended with papadum and served alongside avocado salad and tamarind chutney, slow-cooked wild striped bass, and the roasted skate with coconut and steamed south Indian rice noodles. For a quick bite, nothing beats the pulled lamb and mustard-mashed potato naanini sandwich (be sure to grab an extra napkin or two).

Contemporary Indian. Lunch, dinner. $36-85

★★★TAMARIND

41-43 E. 22nd St., New York, 212-674-7400; www.tamarinde22.com

The fragrant cuisine of India is served at Tamarind, an elegant restaurant in the Flatiron District with a lively bar and a serene and beautiful dining room. The attraction here is a menu of dishes showcasing perfect flavors—spicy, sweet, sour and hot play together wonderfully on the plate. The kitchen serves stunning samosas, naan, poori, chutneys and traditional curries, alongside more contemporary dishes.

Indian menu. Lunch, dinner. Bar. Jacket required. Reservations recommended. $36-85

★★TAVERN ON THE GREEN

Central Park at W. 67th St., New York, 212-873-3200; www.tavernonthegreen.com

Tavern is a bit like the Hummer of restaurants—showy, too expensive and a so-called remodeled classic that's really just a clunky novelty beneath its shiny veneer. No amount of murals, over-the-top topiaries or twinkling lights can disguise what can often be an uneven dining experience amid mobs of tourists. That said, there will always be hordes of visitors revving up their credit cards to enjoy pricey classics such as lobster bisque and prime rib just for the privilege of eating in beautiful Central Park near the urban-yet-bucolic Sheep Meadow. Afternoon tea service is a nice alternative to the pomp and pageantry of dinner, and the warm scones with sweet jam and Devonshire cream make an ideal four o'clock snack. At press time, the future of the restaurant was uncertain. So call ahead before heading out.

American. Lunch (Monday-Friday), dinner, Saturday-Sunday brunch. Reservations recommended. $36-85

★★★TERRACE IN THE SKY

400 W. 119th St., New York, 212-666-9490; www.terraceinthesky.com

Set high in the sky on the top floor of a pre-war Columbia University-area building, this restaurant offers panoramic views of the city and a rich selection of eclectic fare to match. The haute menu of seared sweetbreads, foie gras torchon, smoked salmon, lobster and caviar make dining a luxe event. Terrace in the Sky is an ideal romantic excursion with its elegant linen-topped tables, soft candlelit ambience and views that are truly beyond compare.

French, Mediterranean. Lunch (Friday), dinner (Tuesday-Saturday), Sunday brunch. Closed Monday. Reservations recommended. Outdoor seating. $36-85

★★★THOR

107 Rivington St., New York, 212-475-2600, 800-915-1537; www.hotelonrivington.com

Though its name conjures images of the Norse god of thunder, Thor (an acronym for its location inside the Hotel on Rivington) is a subdued and stylish spot for contemporary takes on American comfort food classics. A sampling from the large selection of small plates could make a meal in itself, from the red beet terrine with horseradish and fresh goat cheese to the crispy cod sticks with malt vinegar foam and tartar sauce. Entrées include butter poached whole lobster with creamed cauliflower and truffles. Late-night the restaurant offers abbreviated versions of the dinner menu.

American. Breakfast, lunch, dinner, late-night, Saturday-Sunday brunch. Reservations recommended. Bar. $36-85

★★★TOCQUEVILLE

1 E. 15th St., New York, 212-647-1515; www.tocquevillerestaurant.com

Owned by husband Marco Moreira (chef) and wife Jo-Ann Makovitzky (front-of-house manager), Tocqueville will calm you the moment you walk through the tall, blond doors into the small, elegant room warmed with butter-yellow walls. Chef Moreira offers impeccably prepared, inventive New

American fare crafted with care from seasonal ingredients handpicked from local farmers and the nearby Greenmarket. American, French. Lunch, dinner. Closed Sunday. Bar. $36-85

★★★TRATTORIA DELL'ARTE
900 Seventh Ave., New York, 212-245-9800; www.trattoriadellarte.com

Trattoria dell'Arte is the perfect choice if Carnegie Hall or a performance at City Center is on your list. This lively and popular restaurant offers easy, approachable Italian cuisine in a comfortable, neighborly setting. The scene here is festive, so expect it to be loud with diners enjoying the generous plates of homemade pastas, selections from the colorful antipasti bar, seafood and meats, all prepared in simple Mediterranean style.

Italian. Lunch, dinner, Sunday brunch. Reservations recommended. Bar. $36-85

★★★TRIBECA GRILL
375 Greenwich St., New York, 212-941-3900; www.tribecagrill.com

This New York icon from Drew Nieporent (Nobu, Montrachet) and partner Robert De Niro is a shining example of how a restaurant should be run. First, hospitality—the service is warm, attentive and knowledgeable without pretension. Second, atmosphere—the Grill is a comfortable, urban dining room with exposed brick walls, oil paintings by Robert De Niro, Sr., and a magnificent cherry wood. Third, food—the kitchen features an approachable, seasonal American menu with dishes from the simple to the ornate. Finally, wine—Tribeca Grill offers an impressive wine program. It's as easy as that.

American. Lunch, dinner, Sunday brunch. Reservations recommended. Outdoor seating. Children's menu. Bar. $36-85

★★TURKISH KITCHEN
386 Third Ave., New York, 212-679-1810; www.turkishkitchen.com

Be prepared to enjoy your food at this bustling Gramercy outpost for authentic Turkish fare. The restaurant specializes in the well-spiced cuisine of of Turkey, with dishes of tender lamb, beef and chicken, as well as soft, warm bread for dipping in assorted mezze. The deep red-stained walls, the low blue ceiling and the Arabic décor warm the room. Service, which is friendly and knowledgeable, can be slow.

Mediterranean, Turkish. Lunch, dinner, Sunday brunch. Reservations recommended. $36-85

★★★UNCLE JACK'S STEAKHOUSE
440 Ninth Ave., New York, 212-244-0005; www.unclejacks.com

This classic steakhouse (which has a new Midtown location as well as a Queens outpost) sticks to well-prepared cuts of beef, from Kobe to USDA prime cuts like the porterhouse or T-bone. Traditional sides such as creamed spinach or garlic mashed potatoes complete every meal, as does the extensive wine selection, which is peppered with bottles from just about every corner of the world.

Steak. Lunch, dinner. $36-85

★★★UNION SQUARE CAFÉ
21 E. 16th St., New York, 212-243-4020; www.unionsquarecafe.com

One of New York's most revered restaurants, Union Square Café set a new standard for seasonal greenmarket cuisine when it opened nearly 25 years ago, and it continues to be a go-to spot for everyone from tourists to trendoids. The menu hasn't changed much since the start, but why mess with a good thing? Plus, the dishes feel timeless rather than dated due to the ever-changing seasonal touches on the menu, like sugar snap pea salad tagliatini and pan-roasted chicken atop asparagus bread pudding. The restaurant's creamy walls and warm wood floors and chairs are so comfortable that you might feel like you're eating at an old friend's house. And in many ways, you are.

Contemporary American. Lunch, dinner. Reservations recommended. $36-85

★★★VERITAS
43 E. 20th St., New York, 212-353-3700; www.veritas-nyc.com

Wine, wine and more wine. With a list more than 192,000 bottles deep, thanks mainly to the Park B. Smith wine collection becoming available, wine is the keystone of any meal at Veritas. And what better accompaniment to award-winning wine than gourmet French fare? Black truffles, foie gras and frogs legs all play a part in chef Gregory Pugin's sophisticated menu. The Wagyu filet with béarnaise croquets and shishito peppers in a bordelaise sauce is perhaps the most memorable dish on the menu. Sidestep the sweets for the ever-changing assortment of cheeses. The interior is neutral and modern, leaving the focus entirely on the food and wine. After all, in vino veritas.

French. Lunch, dinner. $36-85.

★★VICTOR'S CAFÉ
236 W. 52nd St., New York, 212-586-7714; www.victorscafe.com

Long before the mojito became as popular as the cosmopolitan, these minty rum drinks from Cuba were the cocktail of choice at Victor's, a popular theater district restaurant that feels like an elegant throwback to Havana, decorated with tall palm trees and filled with the rhythmic sounds of Cuban jazz. Aside from the terrific cocktails, Victor's is a festive place to feast on top-notch contemporary Cuban cuisine, like roasted marinated pork with rice and beans, picadillo, fried plantains and tostones.

Cuban. Lunch, dinner. Reservations recommended. Bar. $36-85

★VIRGIL'S REAL BARBECUE
152 W. 44th St., New York, 212-921-9494; www.virgilsbbq.com

While everyone has an opinion about barbecue, most will agree that Virgil's is a top choice. Manners are thrown to the wind at Virgil's, a sprawling hog pit located in the hear of Times Square where ribs, juicy chicken, tomato-based pulled pork, Memphis pit beans and spicy collard greens are gobbled up pig-style. The noise can be deafening, but there really isn't time to talk once the food arrives. The warm, fluffy buttermilk biscuits usually quiet hungry guests quite quickly. The warm décor, which features firewood ovens, raw wood floors, an extended bar, dark wood accents and rolls of paper towels on each table, is a perfect complement to the down-home cuisine.

American. Lunch, dinner. Children's menu. Bar. $36-85

★★★VONG

200 E. 54th St., New York, 212-486-9592; www.jean-georges.com

At Vong, Jean-Georges Vongerichten, the sensational Alsatian-born chef, creates French riffs on fiery Thai classics, incorporating spices and flavors of the East with a New York sensibility. The Midtown restaurant feels like a wistful night in the Orient: it's furnished with rouge-paneled booths covered with silk pillows in brilliant ruby tones; the walls are painted crimson red and accented with gold leaf; and mirrored table-tops reflect the radiance.

Thai, French. Lunch (Monday-Friday), dinner. Reservations recommended. Outdoor seating. Bar. $36-85

★★★WALLSE

344 W. 11th St., New York, 212-352-2300; www.wallserestaurant.com

Enter this charming restaurant and you are instantly transported to Vienna via 11th Street in the West Village. Decorated with contemporary art and filled with antique furnishings, charcoals banquettes and a long, romantic stretch of rich mahogany bar (where the cocktails are crisp), chef Kurt Gutenbrunner's eatery is a personal and delicious ode to the hearty yet delicate cuisine of his native Austria. The thin, golden-crusted Wiener schnitzel should not be missed. A terrific selection of Austrian wines complements the meal, and a sweet slice of strudel is the perfect finish.

Continental. Dinner, brunch. Reservations recommended. Bar. $36-85

★★★WATER CLUB

East 30th Street and East River, New York, 212-683-3333; www.thewaterclub.com

Special occasions were made for the Water Club, a lovely restaurant with romantic views of the East River. While poultry and beef are on the menu, the nautical Water Club is known for its seafood. In addition to a gigantic raw bar, you'll find an impressive selection of lobster, scallops, cod, tuna, salmon and other fresh, ever-changing selections. On a sunny day, settle in on the deck with a fiery Bloody Mary in hand and watch the ships sail by.

American, seafood. Lunch, dinner, Sunday brunch. Reservations recommended. Outdoor seating. Bar. $86 and up.

★★★WD-50

50 Clinton St., New York, 212-477-2900; www.wd-50.com

Dining at WD-50 is part feast and part science experiment, thanks to heralded chef Wylie Dufresne's cutting-edge techniques. Here, even mayonnaise goes from plain-Jane to wow as Dufresne fries it and serves it in a neat row of white pellets alongside calf's tongue. The restaurant also serves squab with carob and cream soda, a combination that you likely won't find anywhere else. Even the carb-averse can dive into a plate of noodles, which are actually made of ground shrimp. The food here intrigues, but more important, it's delicious. Pack your sense of adventure and be prepared to spend—the 12-course tasting menu costs $215 with wine pairings.

Contemporary American. Dinner. Closed Monday-Tuesday. Reservations recommended. $36-85

★★★WOO LAE OAK

148 Mercer St., New York, 212-925-8200; www.woolaeoakSoho.com

This sleek, cavernous multiplex-style space in Soho offers some of the best Korean barbecue in the city. Guests grill marinated meats and seafood to a savory char on granite, smokeless grill tables. Melt-in-your-mouth creamy black cod simmered in a sweet-hot, garlicky soy sauce is a one of the restaurant's most famous plates, but it's hard to find a bad choice on the menu. Korean. Lunch, dinner. Reservations recommended. Bar. $36-85

★★ZARELA

953 Second Ave., New York, 212-644-6740; www.zarela.com

This colorful and spirited Mexican eatery in Midtown is renowned for its killer margaritas and delicious regional Mexican fare. Loud and lively, the bar is always packed with a rowdy after-work crowd that lingers well into the evening. Upstairs, in the more intimate yet still boisterous dining room, you'll feast on some of chef/owner Zarela Martinez's vibrant dishes, from rich enchiladas to luxuriously savory moles.
Mexican. Lunch (Monday-Friday), dinner. Reservations recommended. Bar. $16-35

★★★ZOE

90 Prince St., New York, 212-966-6722; www.zoerest.com

Thalia and Stephen Loffredo opened Zoe in the heart of Soho more than 15 years ago, and they have managed to maintain its chic yet comfortable American bistro vibe and inspired cooking. The focal point of the restaurant is the open kitchen with its imported Italian wood-burning oven, which, along with original tile work and pastel walls, creates a simple, rural atmosphere. The menu offers creative, sophisticated American standards painted with global accents, seasonal flourishes and an extensive, heavily American wine list. There is also a terrific cocktail list and a tempting menu of bar snacks. Contemporary American. Lunch, dinner, Saturday-Sunday brunch. Reservations recommended. Children's menu. Bar. $36-85

SPAS

★★★★THE SPA AT FOUR SEASONS HOTEL NEW YORK

57 E. 57th St., New York, 212-758-5700; www.fourseasons.com

This subterranean spa reflects the Four Seasons' signature style with an unobtrusive-yet-attentive staff and a penchant for luxurious details. The quiet space located beneath the hotel lobby provides services inspired by international practices, but eschews New Age notions. You can schedule acupressure combined with back-walking ($230) here, but you'll have to go elsewhere if you want your chakras balanced. The Four Seasons New York Signature Therapeutic Massage ($295), draws from four complementary traditions (shiatsu, Thai stretching, Swedish massage and reflexology) to ensure you're de-stressed and as loose-limbed as possible. Or go native with the Big Apple Antioxidant Body Treatment ($275), which uses two apple-based preparations—an apple/brown sugar scrub with Vichy shower followed by an apple body butter massage—and capitalizes on the natural enzymes in the fruit to leave your skin with a dewy glow.

★★★★★THE PENINSULA SPA BY ESPA

700 Fifth Ave., New York, 212-903-3910, 800-262-9467; www.peninsulaspa.com

When a superlative spa refuses to rest on its laurels by constantly adding improvements, you should plan on becoming a regular. This much-loved spa at the Peninsula has undergone a complete renovation in conjunction with spa consultants ESPA. It's part of a collaboration that began in 2006 with a super swanky re-do of the spa chain's flagship Hong Kong property. The sparkling new addition here is the only ESPA spa in the city, and the only place to try signature treatments like the Yin Uplifter ($465), designed to rid you of chills with a stone massage and application of clay mixed with cinnamon, licorice and ginger before you're placed in a linen wrap. Meanwhile, the Yang Soother ($465) addresses overheated or sensitive skin with a body treatment that mixes chrysanthemum, black lychee and marine mud or algae that leaves skin as smooth as silk. (Both treatments last for two hours.) The commanding space on the 21st and 22nd floors of the hotel, with skyline views, 12 treatment rooms, one couples' suite and private lounges is as relaxing as it gets. Locker rooms offer aromatherapy showers plus steam, sauna and thermal suites.

★★★★★THE SPA AT MANDARIN ORIENTAL, NEW YORK

80 Columbus Circle, New York, 212-805-8880; www.mandarinoriental.com/newyork

Sweeping views of Central Park and the Hudson River from floor-to-ceiling windows aren't the only thing that'll put this 35th-floor hotel spa at the top of your list of favorites. First, book a 90-minute block of time, then consult with the top-notch staff to determine the best treatments to fill it. Asian-influenced services range from relaxing (the signature Thai Yoga Massage combines kneading with gentle yoga poses and assisted stretching; $315-$325) to rejuvenating (Ama Releasing Abhyanga loosens congestion and promises to free your body of toxins with a combination of exfoliation, cleansing and massage; $450-$470). While you're alleviating tension, take advantage of complimentary amenities, including an Oriental Tea Lounge, vitality pool and amethyst-crystal steam chamber, all awash in soothing beiges and golds.

QUEENS (NEW YORK)
WHAT TO SEE
AMERICAN MUSEUM OF THE MOVING IMAGE

35th Avenue at 36th Street, Astoria, 718-784-4520; www.movingimage.us

On the site of historic Astoria Studios, where many classic early movies were filmed, this museum is devoted to the art and history of film, television and video and their effects on American culture. Exhibits are constantly changing but often include costumes, publicity materials and production designs. There are also two theaters with film and video series and screenings on weekends.

Admission: adults, seniors, students and children 8-18 $7, children under 8 free. Tuesday-Friday 10 a.m.-3 p.m.

ASTORIA

At the northwest end of Queens, 718-286-2667; www.nycvisit.com

This Hellenic community, just 15 minutes from Midtown Manhattan, offers the best Greek food this side of Athens. Astoria has an estimated Greek population of 70,000—one of the largest communities outside of Greece—which means that the area is alive with music, culture, saganaki and baklava. Food markets, gift shops, bakeries, restaurants and intimate cafes await. Finish an excursion by relaxing on a sunny day with a cup of Greek coffee in nearby Astoria Park and take in a great view of upper Manhattan. If you want to combine this experience with other area attractions, the American Museum of the Moving Image and the historic Kaufman Astoria Motion Picture Studios are also located in Astoria.

CLEARVIEW PARK GOLF COURSE

202-12 Willets Point Blvd., Flushing, 718-229-2570; www.clearview.americangolf.com
Clearview is recognized as one of the best courses for beginners in the New York area, so it's no surprise that it fills up quickly on weekends. You should also expect your round to take a little longer than normal, but the prices reasonable. The rough is deep, but if you can keep your shots straight, you can avoid it. A par-70 course, Clearview plays just over 6,200 yards from the back tees but that belies the challenge of the narrow fairways.
Admission: prices vary. Daily.

FLUSHING MEADOWS-CORONA PARK

Flushing and Metropolitan Avenues, Flushing, 718-217-6034; www.nycgovparks.org
Originally a marsh, this 1,255-acre area became the site of two World's Fairs (one in 1939 and a second in 1964). It is now the home of the United States Tennis Association National Tennis Center, where the U.S. Open is held annually. The park is also the site of some of the largest cultural and ethnic festivals in the city. Facilities include an indoor ice rink, carousel, 87-acre Meadow Lake and playground for children.
Free. Daily.

ISAMU NOGUCHI GARDEN MUSEUM

32-37 Vernon Blvd, Long Island City, 718-204-7088; www.noguchi.org
Sculpture fans will want to visit the Isamu Noguchi Museum, just a short trip from Manhattan. Housed in the sculptor's former studio, complete with an outdoor sculpture garden, the museum is filled with Noguchi stone, metal and woodwork.
Admission: adults $10, seniors and students $5, children under 12 free. Wednesday-Friday 10 a.m.-5 p.m., Saturday-Sunday 11 a.m.-6 p.m.

P.S. 1 CONTEMPORARY ART CENTER

22-25 Jackson Ave., Long Island City, 718-784-2084; www.ps1.org/warmup
Housed in a newly renovated, four-story building that was once a public school, this premier center for arts on the cutting edge specializes in the avant-garde, conceptual and experimental. The venue also features the Warm Up Music Series, which attracts the hippest of DJs and crowds to its Saturday afternoon through evening outdoor "Warm Up" parties in its courtyard. All ages are welcome.
Admission: adults $5, seniors and students $2. Thursday-Monday, noon-6 p.m. Warm Up Series: $10, Saturday 2-9 p.m.

QUEENS BOTANICAL GARDEN

43-50 Main St., Flushing, 718-886-3800; www.queensbotanical.org

Plants and amenities showcased at this diverse garden include large roses, herbs, woodland and bird gardens and an arboretum. The garden hosts art exhibits in the gallery building, including a fascinating photographic exposé by Ed and Joyce Morrill. .

Free. April-October, Tuesday-Sunday 8 a.m.-6 p.m.; November-March, Tuesday-Sunday 8 a.m.-4:30 p.m.

THE QUEENS MUSEUM OF ART

New York Building, 25th Avenue and 76th Street, Flushing, 718-592-9700;
www.queensmuseum.org

Interdisciplinary fine arts presentations and major traveling exhibitions are displayed here. The permanent collection includes a 9,000-square-foot panorama of New York City, the world's largest three-dimensional architectural model, and an informative exhibit on New York's World's Fairs.

Admission: adults $5, seniors and children 5-18 $2.50, children under 5 free. Wednesday-Friday 10 a.m.-5 p.m., Saturday-Sunday noon-5 p.m.

UNION STREET

Union and Main streets, Flushing

This section of Flushing, located one long block past Main Street, is home to a large, culturally-rich Korean community. Tiny shops feature American and Korean clothing and wedding gowns from both cultures. Gift shops sell miniature collectibles, and food markets offer exotic foods and spices. Korean restaurants serve traditional barbecue dishes and other items; many eateries are open 24 hours a day.

SPECIAL EVENTS
AQUEDUCT

11000 Rockaway Blvd., South Ozone Park, 718-641-4700

Take a short ride on the subway to Queens for an afternoon of thoroughbred races, held from late October through early May. Races take place Wednesday through Sunday and begin at 1 p.m.

Free. Gates open at 11 a.m.

BELMONT PARK

2150 Hempstead Turnpike, Elmont, 516-488-6000; www.nyra.com

This 430-acre racetrack is the home of the third jewel in horse racing's Triple Crown, the Belmont Stakes. This major spectacle is held in June and attracts gamblers, horse lovers and spectators from all walks of life. It's one of the oldest annual sporting events in the nation, so make your plans in advance and reserve seats early.

Admission: adults $2, children under 12 free. Hours vary.

U.S. OPEN TENNIS

Flushing Meadows-Corona Park, USTA National Tennis Center, Flushing,
718-760-6200; www.usopen.org

Tennis fans swarm to the U.S. Open tennis tournament each September. You can see your favorite players, the stars of tomorrow and a host of celebrities in the audience at this upper-tier sporting event. Tickets go on sale in late May or by the beginning of June, and those matches held closer to the finals sell out first. Buying a ticket to the Arthur Ashe Stadium, the main court, gives you admission to all the other courts on the grounds.

Admission: prices vary. Late August-early September.

WHERE TO STAY
★★★CROWNE PLAZA HOTEL NEW YORK-LAGUARDIA AIRPORT
104-04 Ditmars Blvd., East Elmhurst, 718-457-6300, 800-227-6963;
www.crowneplaza.com

The Crowne Plaza LaGuardia boasts a location and accommodations that are perfectly suited for both business and leisure travelers. Rooms feature TVs, stereos and refrigerators. A state-of-the-art fitness center with cardio and weight equipment, an indoor pool, sauna and sundeck provide you with ways to unwind while a business center with printing, fax, copying and secretarial services takes the stress out of working. LaGuardia airport is located across the street, and JFK is only eight miles away. Other nearby attractions include Citi Field and the National Tennis Center.

353 rooms. Restaurant, bar. Complimentary breakfast. Business center. Fitness center. Pool. $151-250

★★HOLIDAY INN
144-02 135th Ave., Jamaica, 718-659-0200, 800-972-3160; www.holiday-inn.com

If you have an early flight, this hotel, located only a half-mile from JFK Airport and minutes from LaGuardia Airport, is the perfect pick. Business travelers will enjoy the 24-hour business center and tourists can use the free shuttle service to get to the subway. Rooms offer basic décor, but include amenities such as refrigerators and work desks.

360 rooms. Restaurant, bar. Business center. Fitness center. Pets accepted. Pool. $151-250

WHERE TO EAT
★★CAVO
42-18 31st Ave., Astoria, 718-721-1001; www.cavoastoria.com

A beautiful and pleasant escape, Cavo is a sprawling Mediterranean restaurant with a stone patio and a wonderful, lush garden that will leave you wanting to set up and never leave. The menu features all the wonders of the Mediterranean, from assorted savory pastas; to whole fish with lemon and herbs; rack of lamb; and assorted mezze.

Mediterranean. Dinner, late-night. Reservations recommended. Outdoor seating. Bar. $16-35

★★CHRISTOS HASAPO-TAVERNA
41-08 23rd Ave., Astoria, 718-726-5195; www.christossteakhouse.com

Christos Hasapo is a restaurant with dual personalities, and both are approachable. By day, locals crowd into this butcher shop to purchase their day's beef. But at night, the shop turns into a Greek steakhouse, serving Astoria's finest selection of meat, prepared simply and to perfection every time.

Greek. Dinner. Outdoor seating. Bar. $36-85

★ELIAS CORNER

24-02 31st St., Astoria, 718-932-1510

Elias Corner, a cult favorite, is a bit garish, decked out in turquoise and far from subtle in the décor department. But the color scheme does not seem to deter the herds of folks who come here to feast on the restaurant's standout Greek fare. Typically, that includes fish, lamb, and, of course, a selection of mezze with warm, puffy pita.

Greek menu. Dinner. Casual attire. Outdoor seating. No credit cards accepted. $16-35

★★IL TOSCANO

42-05 235th St., Douglaston, 718-631-0300; www.iltoscanony.com

Don't let the tuxedo-clad waitstaff intimidate you; this is a casual, neighborhood restaurant with a menu of dependable Italian classics and a nice wine selection. The homemade lasagna bolognese is rich and delicious. There is a special Sunday Family dinner menu if you choose to tote the kids.

Italian. Dinner. Closed Monday. Reservations recommended. Bar. $16-35

★JACKSON DINER

37-47 74th St., Jackson Heights, 718-672-1232; www.jacksondiner.com

Bright, open, and airy, the Jackson Diner has been a Queens favorite for years, serving authentic Indian cuisine in a bright and casual setting. The enormous buffet lunch is a steal, and the à la carte dinner menu is a terrific taste of the kitchen's talents: yogurt-marinated lamb chops, assorted dosas and tasty appetizers to share among the table, like coconut-flecked chicken, fried fish and flaky samosas.

Indian. Lunch, dinner. $15 and under.

★KABAB CAFÉ

25-12 Steinway St., Astoria, 718-728-9858

Kabab Café may not look like much from the outside, but on the inside, it's a different story. Creamy, zesty, and ridiculously good, the appetizers here are truly remarkable, reaching beyond the ordinary trio to more exotic treats like eggah (an Egyptian omelet) and foul (a white bean salad with puréed tomatoes, lemon juice, spices and olive oil).

Middle Eastern. Lunch, dinner. Closed Monday. No credit cards accepted. $15 and under.

★KUM GANG SAN

138-28 Northern Blvd., Flushing, 718-461-0909; www.kumgangsan.net

Kum Gang San, a Korean barbecue, sushi and seafood stalwart, never closes. You can choose to spend part of the day hanging out by the indoor waterfall while having a lunch of blistering barbecue, crisped scallion and seafood pancakes, or hit the sushi bar for plates of panchan—Korean-style tapas-like crab claw with hot pepper and soy-marinated short ribs. In the wee hours, you might join the late-night revelers and watch the fresh fish coming in from the seafood markets.

Korean. Lunch, dinner, late-night. $16-35

★★MANDUCATIS

1327 Jackson Ave., Long Island City, 718-729-4602; www.manducatis.com

Owned by Vicenzo Cerbone, Manducatis is a family-run operation serving the home-style dishes of Italy's best mamas. The terracotta room has an earthy, countryside appeal, as does the menu. Expect delicate homemade pastas topped with soft pillows of milky mozzarella. The kitchen also turns out lovely fish and meat dishes and has an extensive wine list that includes many rare wines from small Italian producers.

Italian. Lunch (Monday-Friday), dinner. Bar. $16-35

★★MOMBAR

2522 Steinway St., Astoria, 718-726-2356

Mombar is a warm, family-owned Egyptian restaurant with stunning authentic décor and intimate banquettes. Owner El Sayed is there all the time, to cook, to chat and to guide you through a meal you will never forget. While his menu changes daily, you can't go wrong with the mezze plate or any of his clay pot stews: Moulekaya, an aromatic stew made from Egyptian greens with braised rabbit or chicken; or the fragrant, soft lamb pulled from a tagine filled with a messy stew of raisins, almonds and olives.

Middle Eastern. Dinner. Closed Monday. Children's menu. $16-35

★★★PICCOLA VENEZIA

42-01 28th Ave., Astoria, 718-721-8470; www.piccola-venezia.com

Piccola Venezia, an old-world trattoria offering authentic northern Italian fare, features delicious homemade pastas and a menu of salads, antipasti, seafood, meat and game prepared with imported ingredients and a nod to the wonderful culinary traditions of northern Italy. The prix fixe menus are an inexpensive way to sample the fare.

Italian. Lunch (Monday-Friday), dinner. $36-85

★★PING'S SEAFOOD

83-02 Queens Blvd., Elmhurst, 718-396-1238

As you might expect, this Chinese restaurant specializes in fish, but not just any fish. Bring along a sense of culinary adventure if you decide to dine here, as the restaurant features tanks filled with all sorts of wild sea creatures for you to experiment. The restaurant also offers dim sum, including steamed pork buns and shrimp dumplings.

Chinese. Breakfast, lunch, dinner. $16-35

★★RESTAURANT 718

35-01 Ditmars Blvd., Astoria, 718-204-5553

Restaurant 718 marks the official arrival of a French bistro to the big fat Greek scene of Astoria. This sweet, cozy Parisian bistro offers standards like duck terrine and steak frites, but also features Spanish-accented plates like grilled tuna with chorizo and soy-cherry sauce; roasted duck with Serrano ham; and, in a respectful nod to the neighborhood, tzatziki with endive.

French. Lunch, dinner, late-night, Saturday-Sunday brunch. Reservations recommended. Bar $16-35

★S'AGAPO TAVERNA
34-21 34th Ave., Astoria, 718-626-0303
At this neighborhood taverna, a taste of the Greek Isles is served up with charm every night of the week. The restaurant specializes in swimmingly fresh grilled seafood as well as classic mezze, such as tangy, garlicky tzatziki. The only potential downside to S'Agapo is that the place can get cramped at times, as tables are very cozy.
Greek. Lunch, dinner. $16-35

★SRIPRAPHAI
64-13 39th Ave., Woodside, 718-899-9599; www.sripraphairestaurant.com
The only downside to this restaurant is that you may have to wait in a line that stretches out the door to get a table. The menu is filled with authentic Thai dishes like noodle bowls, green papaya salad, chile-rubbed pork and fire-breathing dishes of green curry that will set your mouth ablaze with spice.
Thai. Lunch, dinner. Closed Wednesday. Outdoor seating. No credit cards accepted. $15 and under.

★★TOURNESOL
50-12 Vernon Blvd., Long Island City, 718-472-4355; www.tournesolnyc.com
Tournesol is a sunny French bistro just across the river from Manhattan in Long Island City that could have been transported from Paris. Dancing with typical Parisian attributes—romantic music, a sidewalk café, bistro tables, floor-to-ceiling French doors and tin ceilings—this cheery favorite offers up friendly service and a rustic menu of standards like rabbit stew, braised beef cheeks, frisée au lardons and country pâté.
French. Lunch (Tuesday-Sunday), dinner, Saturday-Sunday brunch. Reservations recommended. Outdoor seating. Bar $16-35

★★★UNCLE JACK'S STEAKHOUSE
39-40 Bell Blvd., Bayside, 718-229-1100; www.unclejacks.com
This once-speakeasy now-steakhouse (which has two Manhattan locations) comforts with well-prepared beef cuts, from Kobe to USDA prime cuts like the porterhouse or T-bone. The sides are mostly traditional, like creamed spinach and garlic potatoes.
Steak. Lunch (Monday-Friday), dinner. $36-85

STATEN ISLAND (NEW YORK)
WHAT TO SEE
CONFERENCE HOUSE
7455 Hylan Blvd., Staten Island, 718-984-6046; www.conferencehouse.org
Built in the mid-1680s by an English sea captain, this was the site of an unsuccessful meeting on September 11, 1776, between British Admiral Lord Howe, Benjamin Franklin, John Adams and Edward Rutledge to discuss terms of peace to end the Revolutionary War. The meeting helped create the phrase the "United States of America."
Admission: adults $3, seniors and children $2. April-mid-December, Friday-Sunday 1-4 p.m.

THE GREENBELT/HIGH ROCK

200 Nevada Ave., Egbertville, 718-667-2165

Who ever said Staten Island was a landfill never visited the Greenbelt. This 85-acre nature preserve harbored within a 2,500-acre park makes visitors feel far removed from the bustle of New York City.

Free. Daily.

HISTORIC RICHMOND TOWN

441 Clarke Ave., Staten Island, 718-351-1611; www.historicrichmondtown.org

This outdoor museum complex depicts three centuries of the history and culture of Staten Island and the surrounding region. Daily life and work of a rural community is shown in trade demonstrations and tours of shops and buildings. Among the restoration's 27 historic structures are the Historic Museum; and Voorlezer's House, the oldest surviving elementary school in the United States dating back to 1695.

Admission: adults $5, seniors $4, children 5-17 $3.50, children under 5 free. September-June, Wednesday-Sunday 1-5 p.m.; July-August, Wednesday-Friday 11 a.m.-5 p.m., Saturday-Sunday 1-5 p.m.

JACQUES MARCHAIS MUSEUM OF TIBETAN ART

338 Lighthouse Ave., Staten Island, 718-987-3500; www.tibetanmuseum.com

Perched on a steep hill with views of the Atlantic Ocean, this museum houses the collection of Jacqueline Norman Klauber, who became fascinated with Tibet as a child. Highlights of the exhibits include a series of bright-colored masks and a large collection of golden thangkas or religious images, plus terraced sculpture gardens and a koi pond.

Admission: adults $5, seniors and students $3, children under 6 free. Wednesday-Sunday 1-5 p.m.

SNUG HARBOR CULTURAL CENTER

1000 Richmond Terrace, Staten Island, 718-448-2500; www.snug-harbor.org

Founded in 1833 as a seamen's retirement home, Snug Harbor is now a performing and visual arts center with 28 historic buildings featuring Greek Revival and Victorian architecture.

Dailysunrise-sunset.

STATEN ISLAND ZOO

614 Broadway, Staten Island, 718-442-3100; www.statenislandzoo.org

Maintained by the Staten Island Zoological Society, the zoo boasts a large collection of native and exotic reptiles, varied species of rattlesnakes, amphibians, marine reef fishes, mammals and birds. Kids will enjoy the miniature farm.

Admission: adults $8, seniors $6, children 3-14 $5, children under 3 free. Daily 10 a.m.-4:45 p.m.

NEWBURGH

See also Fishkill, New Paltz, Poughkeepsie, West Point

This manufacturing city was General George Washington's headquarters from 1782 until 1783. Newburgh was also the site where he announced the end of the Revolutionary War and officially disbanded the army. The town is only 12 miles north of the West Point Military Academy and boasts a quaint historic district.

WHAT TO SEE
NEW WINDSOR CANTONMENT STATE HISTORIC SITE
374 Temple Hill Road, Vails Gate, 845-561-1765; http://www.nysparks.state.ny.us/sites/
The Cantonment was the last winter encampment of the Continental Army, occupied from 1782 to 1783. Today, the site features demonstrations of 18th-century military life including muskets and artillery, woodworking, black-smithing and camp life activities.
Free. Monday, Wednesday-Saturday 10 a.m.-5 p.m., Sunday 1-5 p.m. Closed Tuesday.

STORM KING ART CENTER
Old Pleasant Hill Road, Mountainville, 845-534-3115; www.stormking.org
This 500-acre sculpture park contains a museum with a permanent collection of 20th-century sculpture. Be sure to see Richard Serra's commissioned work, Schunnemunk.
Admission: adults $10, seniors and students $9, children 5-17 $7, children under 5 free. April-October, Wednesday-Sunday 10 a.m.-5:30 p.m.; June-August also Saturday 10 a.m.-8 p.m. Closed November-March.

WASHINGTON'S HEADQUARTERS STATE HISTORIC SITE
84 Liberty St., Newburgh, 845-562-1195; http://www.nysparks.state.ny.us/sites/
The Jonathan Hasbrouck house was General George Washington's headquarters for nearly a year and a half at the close of the Revolutionary War, and the first official publically owned historic site in the United States, opening its doors in 1850. The onsite museum has permanent and changing exhibits, an audiovisual program, tours and special events reflecting the war.
Mid-April-October, Monday-Saturday 10 a.m.-5 p.m., Sunday 1-5 p.m. Closed Tuesday.

WHERE TO STAY
★HOWARD JOHNSON INN
95 Route 17K, Newburgh, 845-564-4000, 800-446-4656; www.hojo.com
The rooms at this chain hotel are surprisingly large, though somewhat basic. The real draw of the property is the location, putting you within minutes of West Point Military Academy, Woodbury Commons and the Washington Headquarters sites.
74 rooms. Restaurant, bar. Complimentary breakfast. Pool. Tennis. $61-150

★★QUALITY INN
90 Route 17K, Newburgh, 845-564-9020; www.qualityinn.com
Within two miles of the airport, this property is in the heart of the Hudson Valley and directly off the highway. Guest rooms are standard but comfortable, and if you can't sleep, complimentary coffee is always on hand in the lobby.
120 rooms. Bar. Complimentary breakfast. Business center. Fitness center. Pool. Pets accepted. $61-150

WHERE TO EAT

★★BEEBS

30 Plank Road, Newburgh, 845-568-6102; www.beebsbistro.net

Originally built as a tavern for passing travelers in the mid 19th century, this charming little restaurant serves up dependable American staples such as shepherd's pie and filet mignon. Scotch drinkers will be awed by the impressive selection offered.

American. Lunch, dinner, brunch. Reservations recommended. Bar. $16-35

★CAFÉ PITTI

40 Front St., Newburgh, 845-565-1444

For a low-priced option near the Newburgh's waterfront, this is the place. Enjoy casual Italian fare like pizza, pasta and warm sandwiches.

Italian. Lunch, dinner. Reservations recommended. Outdoor seating. Bar. $15 and under.

★★COSIMO'S ON UNION

1217 Route 300 Union Ave., Newburgh, 845-567-1556; www.cosimosunion.com

Popular with locals, this neighborhood eatery specializes in traditional Italian favorites like fried calamari and chicken Valvostana. Most of the desserts are made in house and worth the calories.

Italian. Lunch, dinner. Outdoor seating. Children's menu. Bar. $16-35

★★IL CENA'COLO

228 S. Plank Road, Newburgh, 845-564-4494

The daily specials are the way to go at this Italian restaurant. Signatures include osso bucco, and pasta with buffalo mozzarella and sun-dried tomatoes. The waitstaff is professional and friendly.

Italian. Lunch (Monday-Friday), dinner. Closed Tuesday. Reservations recommended. Bar. $36-85

NIAGARA FALLS

See also Buffalo, Lockport

Higher falls exist, but Niagara is an impressive and must-see natural wonder. On the border with Canada, the American Falls are 184 feet high, the Canadian Horseshoe, 176 feet. The two are separated by Goat Island. For several hours in the evening, the beauty of the falls continues in a display of colored lights playing over the water.

Originally, after the glacial period, the falls were seven miles downstream at the Niagara escarpment. Rocks have crashed from top to bottom, causing the falls to retreat at a rate averaging about one foot per year. With a flow of more than 200,000 cubic feet of water per second, Niagara has a power potential of about four million horsepower. Electrical production is controlled by agreements between the United States and Canada so that each receives a full share while the beauty of the cataracts is preserved. Kitschy souvenir shops and amusement parks surround the area.

WHAT TO SEE
AQUARIUM OF NIAGARA
701 Whirlpool St., Niagara Falls, 716-285-3575, 800-500-4609;
www.aquariumofniagara.org

See more than 1,500 aquatic animals from around the world here, including sharks, otters, piranha, endangered Peruvian penguins and exotic fish. There is a free outdoor sea lion pool with shows every 90 minutes and shark feedings on alternate days.

Admission: adult $9.50, senior $7.50, children 4-12 $6, children under 3 free. Daily 9 a.m.-5 p.m.

ARTPARK
450 S. Fourth St., Lewiston, 716-754-4375, 800-659-7275; www.artpark.net

This 150-acre state park and summer theater is devoted to the visual and performing arts. Events at the 2,300-seat theater with lawn seating include musicals, classical concerts by the Buffalo Philharmonic Orchestra, dance programs, jazz and pop music concerts. During the summer, free Tuesday night concerts draw large crowds.

Prices and showtimes vary.

CASTELLANI ART MUSEUM
Niagara University, 5795 Lewiston Road, Niagara Falls, 716-286-8200;
www.niagara.edu/cam

The more than 3,700 artworks at this museum range from the Hudson River School to contemporary sculpture. It boasts a first-rate Folk Arts Program, including exhibits, artist demonstrations and performances. The collection of mid-20th century pieces by artists such as DeKooning, Rauschenberg and Bearden is of particular interest.

Free. Tuesday-Saturday 11 a.m.-5 p.m., Sunday 1-5 p.m.

CAVE OF THE WINDS
2153 Juron Drive, Niagara Falls, 716-278-1770; www.niagarafallslive.com

Elevators from Goat Island take you 175 feet deep into the Niagara Gorge. From the elevator, walk over a series of wooden walkways to Hurricane Bridge, where you'll feel the spray at the base of the American Falls. Waterproof garments (including shoes) are supplied.

Admission: adults $10, children 6-12 $7, children under 6 free. May-October, daily 9 a.m.-7:30 p.m.

DEVIL'S HOLE STATE PARK
Robert Moses Parkway N., Niagara Falls, 716-284-4691; www.nysparks.state.ny.us

Enjoy views of the lower Whirlpool rapids and Power Authority generating plant, with a walkway leading along the Niagara River. There is also fishing, nature trails and picnicking. In the winter, Devil's Hole is a prime spot for snowshoeing and cross-country skiing.

Free. Daily.

GOAT ISLAND

Niagara Falls, 716-278-1762; www.niagarafallslive.com

Goat Island separates the Canadian Horseshoe and American Falls. Drives and walks in a 70-acre park offer the closest possible views of the falls and upper rapids. Smaller Luna Island and Three Sister Islands can be reached by a footbridge.

Free. Daily.

MAID OF THE MIST BOAT TOUR

Prospect Point Niagara Falls, 716-284-4233; www.maidofthemist.com

Maid of the Mist debarks from the base of the Observation Tower at Prospect Point and takes passengers on a 30-minute boat tour near the base of the American and Horseshoe Falls. Waterproof gear is supplied, but you should expect to get wet anyway.

Admission: adults $13.50, children 6-12 $8.30, children under 6 free. June-September, daily 10 a.m.-8 p.m.

NIAGARA FALLS STATE PARK

Robert Moses Parkway, Niagara Falls, 716-278-1770; www.nysparks.state.ny.us

This park, the oldest state park in the nation, provides many views of Niagara Falls and the rapids above and below the cataract from Prospect and Terrapin points, Luna Island and other locations. It was designed by Frederick Law Olmsted, who also laid out New York's Central Park. The 282-foot Prospect Park Observation Tower offers peerless views of each of the falls.

Free. Daily.

NIAGARA GORGE DISCOVERY CENTER

Robert Moses Parkway, Niagara Falls

This educational center showcases geological formation and the history of the falls. There is a great 180-degree multi-screen theater and audiovisual presentation as well as a rock garden and gorge overlook.

Admission: $5. June-October, daily.

NIAGARA POWER PROJECT VISITOR CENTER

5777 Lewiston Road, Lewiston, 866-697-2386; www.nypa.gov/vc/niagara.htm

All that water goes to good use at the Niagara plant, one of the largest hydroelectric power outposts in the world. Tour the glass-enclosed observation building and be sure to step onto the outdoor balcony for spectacular views of the Niagara River Gorge. For those interested in seeing how the whole system works, there is a nice hands-on exhibit with a functioning hydropower turbine model.

Daily9 a.m.-5 p.m.

NIAGARA SCENIC TROLLEY

139 Niagara St., Niagara Falls, 716-278-1796; www.niagarafallsstatepark.com

This three-hour, eco-friendly guided train ride travels from Prospect Point to Goat Island and back. It has seven stopovers, including the Cave of the Winds, the Maid of the Mist, Terrapin Point and Three Sister Islands. Ride all day for one price.

NIAGARA FALLS STATE PARK

Niagara Falls is almost an American tourist cliché. But it's still one of the most spectacular natural sites in the country, and Niagara Falls State Park (established in 1885 as Niagara Reservation State Park)—the oldest state park in the United States—offers wonderful opportunities to stroll the area. In warmer months, tickets can also be purchased for a ride on the Viewmobile, which tours the entire park, so that if you get tired at any point, you can hop on for a ride.

Whether you're up for a walk or just want to cruise along, start at the Visitor Center to obtain maps of the park, watch a wide-screen film about the falls and purchase a Niagara Master Pass. The Pass allows savings on all the major attractions in the park, including the Observation Tower, the geological museum, a guided walking tour, the boat tour and more. From the Visitor Center, walk toward the river to the Observation Tower (closed in winter). The Tower rises some 200 feet above the base of the gorge and presents terrific views of all three falls—Horseshoe, American and Bridal Veil. The glass elevator ride is fun, too. The elevator goes down to the dock from which the Maid of the Mist boat tour departs. This narrated 30-minute boat ride, in operation since 1846, goes to the base of American Falls and into the ring of Horseshoe Falls.

From the Tower, turn right and follow the pedestrian walkway to the edge of American Falls. Follow the walkway upriver and cross the Goat Island Pedestrian Bridge. On Goat Island are picnic grounds, a restaurant, a gift shop and snack bars. Follow the path to the Bridal Veil Falls overlook. Here, too, is the Cave of the Winds attraction, a boardwalk that leads right into the Bridal Veil Falls. Continue around the downriver point of the island to Terrapin Point. This overlook sits just a few yards from the top of Horseshoe Falls and reveals the full power of the rushing water. From there, walk up the side of the island and follow the pedestrian bridge onto Three Sisters Island. This trio of small islands yields an excellent view of the river's upper rapids.

Admission: adults $2, children 6-12 $1, children under 6 free. April-October, daily.

OLD FORT NIAGARA STATE HISTORIC SITE

Robert Moses Parkway, Youngstown, 716-745-7611; www.oldfortniagara.org
This restored fort, which dates back to 1679 and has been held by France, Great Britain and the United States, played an important role in the French and Indian War and in the War of 1812. The buildings on the site are the oldest in the Great Lakes region and include the "French Castle," constructed by the French in 1726. Living history programs and reenactments occur frequently.
Admission: adults $10, children 6-12 $6, children under 6 free. September-June, daily 9 a.m.-5 p.m.; July-August, daily 9 a.m.-7 p.m.

WHIRLPOOL STATE PARK

Robert Moses Parkway and Niagara Rapids Blvd., Niagara Falls, 716-284-4691;
www.nysparks.state.ny.us
Take in splendid views of the famous Niagara River Gorge whirlpool and rapids. Ongiara Trail brings you down into the gorge for great fishing opportunities.
Free. Daily.

WINTERGARDEN

Rainbow Blvd., Niagara Falls, 716-285-8007

This seven-story indoor tropical park has more than 7,000 trees, shrubs and flowers, a glass elevators and elevated walkways. It's adjacent to the falls and Convention Center, and popular for wedding ceremonies in one of the onsite chapels. Daily 9 a.m.-9 p.m.

WHERE TO STAY

★★BEST WESTERN SUMMIT INN

9500 Niagara Falls Blvd., Niagara Falls, 716-297-5050, 800-404-8217;www.bestwestern.com

You won't miss any of the comforts of home at the Best Western Summit Inn, only seven miles from the falls. Rooms feature all the amenities you'd expect from a chain hotel: satellite television, alarm clocks, hair dryers, coffee and tea makers, ironing boards and high-speed Internet access. And just like mom, they don't want your busy day to start on an empty stomach; a complimentary continental breakfast is included in your stay.

88 rooms. Complimentary breakfast. Fitness center. Pool. Pets accepted. $61-150

★COMFORT INN, THE POINTE

1 Prospect Pointe, Niagara Falls, 716-284-6835, 800-284-6835; www.choicehotels.com

This hotel is literally at the point of the American side of the falls, and you can hear the roar of the rushing water as you approach the entrance. Like any Comfort Inn, this outlet in the chain doesn't offer a lot of amenities, but its terrific location and no-frills price make it worth consideration if you're in town to see one of America's most amazing natural wonders.

118 rooms. Complimentary breakfast. Fitness center. $61-150

★★★CROWNE PLAZA NIAGARA FALLS

300 Third St., Niagara Falls, 716-285-3361, 888-444-0401; www.ichotelsgroup.com

This recently renovated property is a refreshing change from the more touristy hotels that pervade Niagara Falls. Rooms are cheerfully decorated with duvet-topped beds. The new, well-equipped fitness center is open 24 hours while the Old Falls Sports Bar & Grille is a prime spot for a burger or a brew while catching a sports game.

391 rooms. Restaurant, bar. Fitness center. Pool. Casino. $251-350

★★HOLIDAY INN GRAND ISLAND

100 Whitehaven Road, Grand Island, 716-773-1111; www.holidayinn.com

This hotel is located 12 miles from Niagara Falls and 10 miles from Buffalo. It offers an indoor/outdoor pool, children's pool, game room, tennis court and more. A golf course and marina are adjacent to the hotel.

263 rooms. Restaurant, bar. Business center. Fitness center. Pool. $61-150

★★★THE RED COACH INN

2 Buffalo Ave., Niagara Falls, 716-282-1459, 866-719-2070; www.redcoach.com

Modeled after the Old Bell Inn in England, the Red Coach Inn has welcomed guests since 1923. Situated just 1,500 feet from the falls and near many other attractions, the English Tudor house has antique furniture, floral curtains and linens, whirlpool tubs and amazing views in its guest accommodations. Most suites have kitchens and fireplaces. Continental breakfast is included and champagne, fruit and cheese await you upon arrival.

19 rooms. Restaurant, bar. Complimentary breakfast. $151-250

WHERE TO EAT
★COMO RESTAURANT
2220 Pine Ave., Niagara Falls, 716-285-9341; www.comorestaurant.com

This little gem of a restaurant is located in Niagara Falls' Little Italy. Family-owned and -operated since 1927, the Como Restaurant is popular with locals who come for traditional and tasty Italian fare. If you're eating on the run, the onsite deli offers a selection of pasta dinners and luncheon plates as well as soups, sandwiches and pizzas.

Italian. Lunch, dinner. Reservations recommended. Children's menu. Bar. $16-35

★HONEY'S NIAGARA FALLS
2002 Military Road, Niagara Falls, 716-297-7900; www.honeysniagara.com

With its red and yellow-striped awning, Honey's is hard to miss. Located at the Prime Outlet Mall of Niagara Falls, this restaurant is great for a post-shopping meal with the family.

American. Lunch, dinner, late-night. Outdoor seating. Children's menu. Bar. $15 and under.

★★THE RED COACH INN
2 Buffalo Ave., Niagara Falls, 716-282-1459; www.redcoachinn.com

Exposed beams, upholstered banquettes and chairs, and dark wood create a cozy, old-world atmosphere at The Red Coach Inn restaurant. Signature dishes include juicy Black Angus filet mignon and Australian lobster tail. In warm weather, opt to sit on the patio.

Continental. Lunch, dinner. Reservations recommended. Outdoor seating. Children's menu. $16-35

ONEIDA

See also Cazenovia, Hamilton, Herkimer, Rome, Skaneateles, Syracuse, Utica

Perhaps the best-known of the 19th-century American "Utopias" was established at Oneida in 1848 by John Humphrey Noyes, leader of the "Perfectionists." The group held all property in common, practiced complex marriage and undertook other social experiments. Faced with hostile attacks by the local population, the community was dissolved in 1880. In 1881, the Oneida Community became a stock corporation, and the silverware factory it built remains a major industry, making Community Plate and William A. Rogers silver.

WHAT TO SEE
MADISON COUNTY HISTORICAL SOCIETY, COTTAGE LAWN MUSEUM
435 Main St., Oneida, 315-363-4136; www.mchs1900.org

An 1849 Gothic Revival cottage designed by Alexander Jackson Davis includes Victorian period rooms; historical and traditional craft archives; a stagecoach from 1862; and an adjacent agricultural museum. The barn also houses exhibits in summer.

Admission: $5. Monday-Friday, 10 a.m.-4 p.m.

THE MANSION HOUSE

170 Kenwood Ave., Oneida, 315-361-3671; www.oneidacommunity.org

A communal home built in the 1860s for the utopian Oneida Community; the Mansion House is a National Historic Landmark and has been continually inhabited since its completion. The property includes a museum, restaurant, manicured gardens, overnight facilities and residential apartments (some occupied by descendants of original community members).

Admission: $5. Daily.

VERONA BEACH STATE PARK

Route 13 and Oneida Lake, Oneida, 315-762-4463, 800-456-2267; www.nysparks.com

Located on the shores of Lake Oneida, this park offers a swimming beach and bathhouse, as well as shaded spots for picnicking and camping. Come winter, cross-country skiing and ice fishing are both popular activities. Hunting is allowed with a permit.

Free. Daily.

WHERE TO STAY
★SUPER 8

215 Genesee St., Oneida, 315-363-5168; www.super8.com

For those looking to test their luck at the Turning Stone Casino, but don't want to pay the price to stay at the resort, this is a good option. Only three miles down the road, this no-nonsense hotel offers clean rooms and a complimentary breakfast. Most rooms also include refrigerators for added convenience.

39 rooms. Complimentary breakfast. Business center. $61-150

★★TURNING STONE CASINO RESORT

5218 Patrick Road, Verona, 315-361-7711, 800-771-7711; www.turning-stone.com

As one of the largest hotels in Central New York State, this sprawling complex provides five different lodging options ranging from bed-and-breakfast-like comfort at The Inn to modern luxury in The Lodge. The onsite casino, spa, golf course and multiple dining options offer plenty of opportunity to kick back and enjoy the surroundings.

281 rooms. Restaurant, bar. Fitness center. Spa. Casino. Golf. $151-250

ONEONTA

See also Cooperstown, Stamford

Oneonta lies deep in the hills at the western edge of the Catskills, and it was here in 1883 that the Brotherhood of Railroad Trainmen had its beginnings. A branch of the State University College of New York is located here.

WHAT TO SEE
HANFORD MILLS MUSEUM
County Routes 10 and 12, East Meredith, 607-278-5744, 800-295-4992;
www.hanfordmills.org
Originating as a mill built in 1840, this museums examines the evolution of technology and power generation. The original water-powered sawmill, gristmill and woodworking complex are all onsite and demonstrations of antique machinery occur regularly.
Admission: adults $8.50, seniors $5, children under 13 free. Mid-May-mid-October, Tuesday-Sunday 10 a.m.-5 p.m.

HARTWICK COLLEGE
5200 South Park Ave., Hamburg, 607-431-4200; www.hartwick.edu
This rural college boasts an archived collection of works by Willard Yager, Judge William Cooper and John Christopher Hartwick. The Hall of Science displays fresh and saltwater shells and the Yager Museum contains more than 10,000 American Indian artifacts as well as the Van Ess Collection of Renaissance and Baroque Art.
Free. Daily.

NATIONAL SOCCER HALL OF FAME
Wright National Soccer Campus, 18 Stadium Circle, Oneonta, 607-432-3351;
www.soccerhall.org
Whether you refer to it as soccer or football, you'll be at home amongst the sports paraphernalia at this hall of fame. Displays and exhibits on "the beautiful game" range from youth, amateur and collegiate to professional soccer. On display are trophies, mementos, historical items and uniforms. Real soccer addicts will enjoy the video theater where soccer films dating from 1930s are played.
Admission: adults $12.50, seniors $8.50, students $9.50, children 6-12 $7.50, children under 6 free. April-June, daily 10 a.m.-5 p.m.; July-August, daily 9 a.m.-6 p.m.; September-March, Wednesday-Sunday 10 a.m.-5 p.m.

WHERE TO STAY
★★★CATHEDRAL FARMS COUNTRY INN
4158 Highway 23, Oneonta, 607-432-7483, 800-327-6790
This country inn—a servants' house built in the 1930s—is located 20 minutes from Cooperstown and the Baseball Hall of Fame. The property offers rooms and suites, an outdoor heated pool and Jacuzzi and an onsite restaurant.
19 rooms. Restaurant. Pool. $151-250

★★HOLIDAY INN
5206 State Highway 23, Oneonta, 607-433-2250; www.hioneonta.com
Conveniently located near SUNY at Oneonta and Cooperstown Baseball Hall of Fame, this chain hotel provides upscale rooms with microwaves and refrigerators, workdesks and complimentary wireless Internet.
120 rooms. Restaurant, bar. Fitness center. Pool. Pets accepted. $61-150

WHERE TO EAT

★CHRISTOPHER'S

Route 23, Southside Oneonta, 607-432-2444; www.christopherslodging.com

For a casual meal, Christopher's is a good pick. Portions are enormous and the rustic lodge-like ambiance is complete with stuffed moose heads and fieldstone fireplaces.

American. Lunch, dinner. Children's menu. Bar. $16-35

★★FARMHOUSE

5649 State Highway 7, Oneonta, 607-432-7374; www.farmhouserestaurant.com

Recently under new management, this restored farmhouse from the 1780s offers a quaint country atmosphere to enjoy simple American fare. The Maryland blue crab cakes are a local favorite as is the chicken parmesan.

American, seafood. Lunch (Monday-Friday), dinner. Closed Tuesday. Children's menu. Bar. $16-35

OSWEGO

See also Elmira, Finger Lakes

Oswego's location on Lake Ontario, at the mouth of the Oswego River, made it an important trading post and a strategic fort as early as 1722. Today, as a seaway port and northern terminus of the State Barge Canal, Oswego carries on its industrial and shipping tradition. The town has the largest U.S. port of entry on Lake Ontario.

WHAT TO SEE

FORT ONTARIO STATE HISTORIC SITE

1 E. Fourth St., Oswego, 315-343-4711; www.nysparks.state.ny.us/sites/

The original fort was built by the British in 1755, taken by the French, and eventually used as a U.S. Army installation from 1840 to 1946. This strategic fort commanded the route from the Hudson and Mohawk valleys to the Great Lakes and was later used as an emergency refugee camp for Holocaust victims in the 1940s.

May-October, Tuesday-Sunday 10 a.m.-4:30 p.m.

H. LEE WHITE MARINE MUSEUM

W. First Street Pier, Oswego, 315-342-0480; www.hleewhitemarinemuseum.com

Though it doesn't look like much from the outside, this museum features 12 rooms of artifacts relating to 300 years of Oswego Harbor and Lake Ontario history. The prize of the collection is the US Army LT-5 tugboat, that survived the Normandy Invasion.

Admission: adults $5, children 5-12 $3, children under 5 free. September-June, daily 1-5 p.m.; July-August, daily 10 a.m.-5 p.m.

SELKIRK SHORES STATE PARK

7101 State Route 3, Pulaski, 315-298-5737, 800-456-2267; www.nysparks.state.ny.us

Popular with locals for the beautiful sunsets, this state park is perched on a bluff above Lake Ontario and offers swimming, fishing and boating areas. Free. Daily.

WHERE TO STAY
★BEST WESTERN CAPTAIN'S QUARTERS
26 E. First St., Oswego, 315-342-4040; www.bestwestern.com
Convenient for parents visiting their kids at SUNY Oswego, this chain includes amenities like complimentary breakfast, an indoor swimming pool, hot tub, sauna and steam room, and fitness center. Many guest rooms have lake-views and free high-speed Internet.
93 rooms. Complimentary breakfast. Fitness center. Pool. $61-150

OYSTER BAY
See also Huntington, Long Island
On the North Shore of Long Island, this town gets its name from the oysters that have made Long Island famous with seafood-lovers. History buffs love Oyster Bay, too: President Teddy Roosevelt's summer residence, Sagamore Hill, is here.

WHAT TO SEE
PLANTING FIELDS ARBORETUM AND COE HALL
1395 Planting Fields Road, Oyster Bay, 516-922-9201; www.plantingfields.org
The 409-acre estate of the late William Robertson Coe has immaculately landscaped gardens, including large collections of azaleas and rhododendrons, greenhouses and forested trails. The estate mansion also houses a museum.
Admission: adults $6.50, seniors and students $5, children 7-12 $2, children under 7 free. Daily 9 a.m.-5 p.m.

RAYNHAM HALL MUSEUM
20 W. Main St., Oyster Bay, 516-922-6808; www.raynhamhallmuseum.org
This historic colonial house museum with a Victorian wing was the home of Samuel Townsend, a prosperous merchant, and the headquarters for the Queen's Rangers during the Revolutionary War. There is a traditional Victorian garden onsite.
Admission: adults $5, seniors and students $3, children under 6 free. September-June, Tuesday-Sunday 1-5 p.m.; July-August, Tuesday-Sunday noon-5 p.m.

SAGAMORE HILL NATIONAL HISTORIC SITE
20 Sagamore Hill Road, Oyster Bay, 516-922-4788; www.nps.gov/sahi
The former home of President Theodore Roosevelt, this 23-room mansion has been painstakingly preserved and shows off many animal trophies that Roosevelt caught during his legendary hunting trips. The house also features exotic gifts that Roosevelt received from his overseas travels, as well as original furnishings and paintings. Nearby is the Theodore Roosevelt Sanctuary, which cares for injured birds and offers nature walks. The whole experience is a must for history buffs and fans of this amorous president.
Admission: adults $5, children under 16 free. Wednesday-Sunday 10 a.m.-5 p.m.

THEODORE ROOSEVELT SANCTUARY & AUDUBON CENTER

134 Cove Road, Oyster Bay, 516-922-3200; www.ny.audubon.org

Owned by the National Audubon Society, the memorial contains 12 acres of forest and nature trails. The sanctuary serves as a memorial to Theodore Roosevelt's pioneering conservation achievements. Museum contains displays on Roosevelt and the conservation movement, including bird exhibits. Adjacent in Young's Cemetery is Theodore Roosevelt's grave.

Free. Monday-Friday 9 a.m.-5 p.m., Saturday-Sunday noon-5 p.m.

SPECIAL EVENT
FRIENDS OF THE ARTS LONG ISLAND SUMMER FESTIVAL

Planting Fields Arboretum, 1395 Planting Fields Road, Oyster Bay, 516-922-0061;
www.fotapresents.org/summerfest.asp

For the ultimate evening in great music and relaxation, venture out to this beautiful 409-acre Gold Coast estate. The annual festival specializes in blues, jazz and easy listening concerts and has offered up such artists as Michael Feinstein, David Sanborn, David Benoit and Natalie Cole. Try lawn seats: This way you can bring a picnic with your favorite wines and cheeses. Arrive at least 1 ½ hours before the concert starts to scope out your spot on the lawn. One negative: the concerts go on rain or shine.

Admission: prices vary. June-September.

WHERE TO STAY
★EAST NORWICH INN

6321 Northern Blvd., East Norwich, 516-922-1500, 800-334-4798;
www.eastnorwichinn.com

This suburban hotel could use a facelift, but the rooms are spacious and clean and the business center makes it a good choice for those traveling for work. 65 rooms. Complimentary breakfast. Business center. Fitness center. Pool. $61-150

WHERE TO EAT
★★★MILL RIVER INN

160 Mill River Road, Oyster Bay, 516-922-7768; www.millriverinn.com

The menu at this creative American restaurant changes weekly. Sample such favorites as Australian rack of lamb with a fig and almond couscous or the pan-seared diver scallops with toasted pine nuts.

American. Dinner. Reservations recommended. Bar. $36-85

PALMYRA

See also Rochester

In 1820, in the frontier town of Palmyra, 15-year-old Joseph Smith had a vision that led to the founding of a new religious group—the Church of Jesus Christ of Latter-Day Saints, better known as the Mormon Church. Members of the LDS church believe the Angel Moroni led Smith to Palmyra's Hill Cumorah, where he unearthed golden tablets he translated into the *Book of Mormon.*

WHAT TO SEE
ALLING COVERLET MUSEUM
122 William St., Palmyra, 315-597-6737; www.historicpalmyrany.com

Housed in an old newspaper printing office, this small museum boasts the largest collection of American Jacquard and hand-woven coverlets in the country. There is also a quilt room with looms and antique weaving tools.
Admission: adults $2, seniors $1.50, children 13-18 $1, children under 13 free. June-September, daily 1-4 p.m.

BOOK OF MORMON HISTORIC PUBLICATION SITE
217 E. Main St., Palmyra, 315-597-5982; www.hillcumorah.org

Between June 1829 and March 1830, the first edition of 5,000 copies of the Book of Mormon was printed here at a cost of $3,000. Today the site contains the original printing press, and demonstrates how printing and bindery was done in the 19th century.
Free. Daily.

HILL CUMORAH
603 State Route 21, Palmyra, 315-597-5851; www.hillcumorah.org

This is the site where the golden plates from which Joseph Smith translated the Book of Mormon were delivered to him. A monument to the Angel Moroni now stands at the crest of the hill. The visitor center has religious exhibits and films.
Free. Daily.

JOSEPH SMITH HOME
29 Stafford Road, Palmyra, 315-597-4383; www.hillcumorah.org

Mormon leader Joseph Smith lived in this house as a young man and had his first vision nearby in the Sacred Grove. The interior is filled with early 19th century décor.
Free. Daily.

PALMYRA HISTORICAL MUSEUM
132 Market St., Palmyra, 315-597-6981; www.historicpalmyrany.com

Displays feature 19th-century items including furniture, toys and household items, as well as exhibits examining the influence that Palmyra had on American history over the past two centuries. The restored museum is a former hotel and tavern.
Admission: adults $2, seniors $1.50, children 12-18 $1, children under 12 free. May-September, Tuesday-Saturday 11 a.m.-4 p.m.; October-April, Tuesday-Thursday 10 a.m.-5 p.m.

SPECIAL EVENT
THE HILL CUMORAH PAGEANT
603 State Route 21, Palmyra, 315-597-5851; www.hillcumorah.org

More than 600 cast members re-enact scenes from the Book of Mormon at Hill Cumorah to an exuberant crowd of thousands. The Sacred Grove is open for self-guided tours year-round. There is seating for 9,000 provided, but get there early. Mid-July.

WHERE TO STAY
★★QUALITY INN
125 N. Main St., Newark, 315-331-9500; www.qualityinn.com
This no-frills chain hotel has basic clean rooms and large windows. There is also a microwave and refrigerator in each room.
107 rooms. Restaurant, bar. Fitness center. Pool. Pets accepted. $61-150

PITTSFORD
See also Rochester
This darling town about eight miles from Rochester has a downtown district that is the definition of quaint. Shops, cafes and restaurants line the sidewalks. Stop for a pleasant afternoon in rural New York.

WHERE TO STAY
★★BROOKWOOD INN
800 Pittsford-Victor Road, Pittsford, 585-248-9000, 800-396-1194;
www.thebrookwoodinn.com
Located in historic Bushnell's Basin, this sweeping property sits on the canal and is only minutes from downtown Rochester. The two-story Grande Lobby is modern and comfortable, and the rooms continue the updated theme with mahogany furnishings, rich fabrics and flat-screen TVs.
108 rooms. Restaurant, bar. Business center. Fitness center. Pool. $61-150

WHERE TO EAT
★★★RICHARDSON'S CANAL HOUSE
1474 Marsh Road, Pittsford, 585-248-5000; www.richardsonscanalhouse.net
This is the oldest working tavern on the Erie Canal and is on the National Register of Historic Buildings. The bright-yellow structure, dating back to the early 1800s, houses a New American dining room and a pub for more casual fare. Start your meal with the house-smoked apple sausage with grainy mustard and black lentils before moving on to the perfectly prepared steak frites or grilled Block Island swordfish.
American. Lunch (Tuesday-Friday), dinner. Closed Sunday. Outdoor seating. Bar. $36-85

★VILLAGE COAL TOWER
9 Schoen Place, Pittsford, 585-381-7866; www.villagecoaltower.com
Originally used to store coal for boats traveling through the Erie Canal, this historic building has become a favorite for those looking for friendly service and good food.
American. Breakfast, lunch, dinner. Outdoor seating. Children's menu. $15 and under.

PLATTSBURGH
See also Ausable Chasm
The Cumberland Bay area of Lake Champlain has been a military base since colonial days. Plattsburgh, at the mouth of the Saranac River, has a dramatic history in the struggle for U.S. independence. The British won the Battle of Lake Champlain off these shores in 1776. Here, in 1814, Commodore

Thomas Macdonough defeated a British fleet from Canada by an arrangement of anchors and winches that enabled him to swivel his vessels completely around, thus giving the enemy both broadsides. While this was going on, U.S. General Alexander Macomb executed the Redcoats on shore with the help of school-boys and the local militia. Today, Plattsburgh accommodates both industry and resort trade.

WHAT TO SEE
ALICE T. MINER COLONIAL COLLECTION
9618 Main St., Chazy, 518-846-7336; www.minermuseum.org
Housed in a 19th century colonial home, this museum has a collection of household furnishings including a 17th century table, oil lamps and antique quilts. Explore the Lincoln room which keeps books and letters relating to past presidents and others.
Free. April, by appointment; May-December, Tuesday-Saturday 10 a.m.-4 p.m.

KENT-DELORD HOUSE MUSEUM
17 Cumberland Ave., Plattsburgh, 518-561-1035; www.kentdelordhouse.org
This historic 1797 house served as British officers' quarters during the Battle of Plattsburgh in the War of 1812. Inside, there is a collection of period furnishings and an apothecary.
Admission: adults $5, students $3, children under 12 $2. Tuesday-Friday, 9 a.m.-3:15 p.m.

WHERE TO STAY
★★BEST WESTERN THE INN AT SMITHFIELD
446 Route 3, Plattsburgh, 518-561-7750, 800-243-4656; www.bestwestern.com
Situated near Lake Champlain, this property offers well-appointed rooms and friendly service. Indulge in complimentary, freshly baked cookies upon your arrival.
120 rooms. Complimentary breakfast. Fitness center. Pool. Pets accepted. $61-150

★★HOLIDAY INN
412 Route 3, Plattsburgh, 518-561-5000; www.holiday-inn.com
New beds and pillows have been added to each guest room making the rooms here a tad more comfortable than your average chain hotel. The Adirondack Mountains and Lake Champlain are nearby, providing a myriad of recreational activities.
102 rooms. Restaurant, bar. Business center. Fitness center. Pool. $61-150

WHERE TO EAT
★★★ANTHONY'S
538 Route 3, Plattsburgh, 518-561-6420; www.anthonysrestaurantandbistro.com
An elegant, candlelit setting and unobtrusive, crisp service round out the dining experience at Anthony's where the menu includes such continental fare as grilled lamb sausage with an apple-mango chutney and broiled sea scallops with an herb butter.
American. Lunch, dinner. Children's menu. Bar. $16-35

PORT JEFFERSON

See also Smithtown, Stony Brook

On a harbor that leads to the Long Island Sound, Port Jefferson is all about its waterfront and offshore activities. You can swim, boat, fish, sail—you get the idea. Port Jeff (as locals refer to it) also has art galleries, restaurants and cafes, and shops worth a peek.

WHAT TO SEE
THOMPSON HOUSE

93 N. Country Road, East Setauket, 631-941-9715

Historian Benjamin F. Thompson was born in this early 18th century saltbox house, which is now authentically furnished to depict 18th-century life on rural Long Island. There is also a well-maintained herb garden onsite.
June-mid-October, Saturday-Sunday 1-4 p.m.

WHERE TO STAY
★★DANFORD'S ON THE SOUND

25 E. Broadway, Port Jefferson, 631-928-5200, 800-332-6367; www.danfords.com

Rooms at this waterfront hotel are updated and bright, with warm nautical tones and views of either Long Island Sound or historic Port Jefferson. Modern amenities include flat-screen TVs and iPod home docks. Some rooms have balconies.
86 rooms. Restaurant, bar. Fitness center. Spa. $251-350

★★★THE INN AND SPA AT EAST WIND

5720 Route 25A, Wading River, 631-929-3500; www.eastwindlongisland.com

This Long Island resort is set on 25 acres of landscaped grounds. Rooms and suites are traditionally decorated but feature modern amenities like free wireless Internet access and CD players. The new Spa at East Wind is a sprawling, soothing space with plenty of treatment rooms for hot stone massages, body wraps and facials. The onsite Desmond's restaurant is the perfect spot for romantic dinner.
50 rooms. Restaurant, bar. Business center. Fitness center. Pool. Spa. $251-350

WHERE TO EAT
★★★DESMOND'S

5720 Route 25A, Wading River, 631-846-2335; www.eastwindlongisland.com

This classic restaurant located inside the Inn at East Wind serves everything from sea scallops wrapped in bacon to porterhouse steak with truffle bordelaise. Tables are topped with white linens and the service is precise and professional. The pub offers more casual fare for lunch and dinner, with favorites such as a roasted turkey club and chopped salad with gorgonzola and raspberry vinaigrette.
American. Lunch, dinner, Sunday brunch. $16-35

★★WAVE

25 E. Broadway, Port Jefferson, 631-928-5200; www.danfords.com

Whether you choose to dine inside or alfresco, you'll enjoy fantastic panoramic waterfront views. The décor carries a nautical theme, but remains far from overdone. Seafood is, of course, the way to go here, with dishes such as sesame-crusted Ahi tuna and Alaskan king crab legs.

Seafood. Breakfast, lunch, dinner, Sunday brunch. Bar. $16-35

POUGHKEEPSIE

See also Fishkill, Hyde Park, Newburgh, New Paltz, Rhinebeck

Many people know this Hudson River town as the site of Vassar College, founded in 1861 by a brewer named Matthew Vassar. The Smith Brothers also helped put Poughkeepsie (p'KIP-see) on the map with their cough drops, once made here. For a brief time during the Revolutionary War, this town was the state capital. It was here in 1788 that New York ratified the Constitution.

WHAT TO SEE
BARDAVON OPERA HOUSE
35 Market St., Poughkeepsie, 845-473-5288; www.bardavon.org

This 1869 building is the oldest operating theater in the state and one of the top performance houses in the Hudson Valley. It presents various dance, theatrical and musical performances, as well as Hudson Valley Philharmonic concerts. Check the Web site for performance schedules.

Prices and showtimes vary.

JAMES BAIRD STATE PARK
14 Maintenance Lane, Pleasant Valley, 845-452-1489; www.nysparks.state.ny.us

This 590-acre park has a championship 18-hole golf course and driving range, tennis, hiking trails, cross-country skiing, playground and nature center. If you get hungry, there is a restaurant overlooking the golf course and numerous picnic areas.

Dailysunrise-sunset.

LOCUST GROVE
2683 South Road, Poughkeepsie, 845-454-4500; www.lgny.org

Former house of Samuel F. B. Morse, inventor of the telegraph, it was remodeled into a Tuscan villa in 1847. Many of his possessions still remain onsite, including telegraph equipment and various paintings by Morse. The house also has alternating exhibits of dolls, fans, costumes, books and souvenirs acquired by the Young family (owners following Morse); paintings, art objects and American furnishings. There is also a wildlife sanctuary and park (180 acres) with hiking trails and picnic area.

Admission: adults $10, children 6-18 $6. March-December, daily 10 a.m.-5 p.m.

MID-HUDSON CHILDREN'S MUSEUM
75 N. Water St., Poughkeepsie, 845-471-0589; www.mhcm.org

This interactive children's museum features more than 50 exhibits including a gravity roll, Da Vinci inventions, virtual reality and climb-through-the-heart exhibit. The Hudson Valley is also examined through the Hudson River mural and Diving Bell exhibit.

Admission: adults and children 2-18 $6.50, children under 1 free. Tuesday-Friday 9:30 a.m.-5 p.m., Saturday-Sunday 11 a.m.-5 p.m.

VASSAR COLLEGE

124 Raymond Ave., Poughkeepsie, 845-437-7000; www.vassar.edu

Vassar was started as a women's college in 1865, but has since gone co-ed. The 1,000-acre campus was the first to have an art gallery onsite, the Frances Lehman Loeb Art Center and continues to boast an impressive and diverse collection of works. Be sure to stroll by the chapel to see the intact Tiffany windows.

Free. Daily.

WHERE TO STAY

★★COURTYARD BY MARRIOTT

2641 South Road/Route 9, Poughkeepsie, 845-485-6336; www.marriott.com

Only a few miles from the Vassar campus, this hotel is ideal for visiting parents and business travelers. The rooms are spacious and have desks and high-speed Internet.

149 rooms. Restaurant, bar. Fitness center. Pool. $61-150

★HOLIDAY INN EXPRESS

2750 South Road, Poughkeepsie, 845-473-1151; www.holiday-inn.com

Recently renovated, this chain property has comfortable rooms and a 24-hour business center. Relax by the outdoor pool in summer.

121 rooms. Complimentary breakfast. Business center. Fitness center. Pool. $61-150

★★★OLD DROVERS INN

196 E. Duncan Hill Road, Dover Plains, 845-832-9311; www.olddroversinn.com

This historic inn was built in 1750 and is arguably the oldest continuously operated inn in the United States. Each room is decorated with fine antiques. The service is top-notch, too, and the setting is sublime. Their restaurant, The Tap Room, is a must-visit.

7 rooms. Restaurant. Complimentary breakfast. $151-250

★★★POUGHKEEPSIE GRAND HOTEL

40 Civic Center Plaza, Poughkeepsie, 845-485-5300, 800-216-1034;
www.pokgrand.com

Located adjacent to the Civic Center in the heart of the Hudson Valley, this hotel boasts plenty of meeting space and caters to a business traveler crowd and wedding parties.

195 rooms. Restaurant, bar. Complimentary breakfast. Fitness center. $61-150

★★★TROUTBECK INN

515 Leedsville Road, Amenia, 845-373-9681, 800-978-7688; www.troutbeck.com

This English country-style inn and conference center sits on 600 acres near the Berkshire foothills and features rooms beautifully appointed with over-stuffed furnishings and elegant fabrics. Try for a room with a fireplace and whirlpool bath in the wonderful Garden House, which overlooks the formal walled English garden.

42 rooms. Restaurant, bar. Complimentary breakfast. Fitness center. Pool. Spa. Tennis. $151-250

WHERE TO EAT

★★AROMA OSTERIA

114 Old Post Road, Wappingers, 845-298-6790; www.aromaosteriarestaurant.com

You can't miss this Tuscan farmhouse-inspired canary yellow building. Classic Italian cuisine is served with aplomb and on warm days, the outdoor patio is great spot to sit and while away the afternoon with a cappuccino. You can't go wrong with any of the pasta dishes.

Italian. Lunch (Tuesday-Saturday), dinner. Closed Monday. Reservations recommended. Outdoor seating. Bar. $16-35

★★BEECH TREE GRILL

1 Collegeview Ave., Poughkeepsie, 845-471-7279; www.beechtreegrill.com

This casual eatery continues to draw locals because of its friendly service and reasonably priced fare. The beer selection is extensive and many say the juicy Angus burgers are second to none in the Hudson Valley.

American. Lunch (Tuesday-Saturday), dinner, Sunday brunch. Reservations recommended. Bar. $16-35

★★★CHRISTOS

155 Wilbur Blvd., Poughkeepsie, 845-471-3400; www.christoscatering.com

Internationally influenced American cuisine is served in this elegant, wood-paneled dining room lit by sparkling chandeliers where smooth service from tuxedo-clad waiters and a golf course view combine for a relaxing ambience. The wine list includes excellent selections for all price ranges.

American. Lunch, dinner. Closed Sunday-Monday. Reservations recommended. Bar. $16-35

★★COSIMO'S TRATTORIA & BAR

120 Delafield St., Poughkeepsie, 845-485-7172; www.cosimospoughkeepsie.com

While the restaurant is large with five separate dining rooms, the atmosphere is cozy and intimate with a wood-fired brick oven and rustic Tuscan décor accenting the space. Regulars swear by the chicken penne. No matter what your entrée, don't leave without tasting the house-filled cannoli with chocolate chips.

American, Italian. Lunch, dinner. Reservations recommended. Outdoor seating. Children's menu. Bar. $16-35

★COYOTE GRILL

2629 South Road, Poughkeepsie, 845-471-0600; www.coyotegrillny.com

Come for the drinks, but stay for the food at this hip downtown Poughkeepsie restaurant. The drink menu is overwhelming, but if you stick to one of their mojitos, you're in for an accomplished treat. The Texas bleu crab cakes are a nice starter and the seafood paella doesn't disappoint.

American, Mexican. Lunch, dinner, Sunday brunch. Reservations recommended. Children's menu. Bar. $16-35

★★LE PAVILLON

230 Salt Point Turnpike, Poughkeepsie, 845-473-2525; www.lepavillonrestaurant.com

Head back in time as you step into this 200-year-old farmhouse with classic French accents and aromas. Escargot is a popular choice as is the coq au vin.

Request a table on the patio if the weather allows.

French. Dinner. Closed Sunday-Monday. Reservations recommended. Outdoor seating. Bar. $16-35

RHINEBECK

See also Hyde Park, Kingston, Poughkeepsie

Rhinebeck was once known as "violet town" because it claimed to produce more hothouse violets than any other town in the United States. Today the town is better known for its charming boutiques and restaurants as well as beautifully restored historic homes.

WHAT TO SEE

HUDSON RIVER NATIONAL ESTUARINE RESEARCH RESERVE

Highway 9G, Annandale, 845-889-4745; www.dec.ny.gov

The Hudson River is an estuary, running from Manhattan to Troy, N.Y. More than 5,000 acres of this estuarine land have been reserved for the study of its life and ecosystems. The Reserve includes Piermont Marsh and Iona Island in Rockland County, Tivoli Bays in Dutchess County and Stockport Flats in Columbia County. The reserve's headquarters has lectures, workshops, special exhibits and public field programs.

Free. Daily.

MONTGOMERY PLACE

55 Montgomery place, Annandale, 845-758-5461; www.hudsonriverheritage.org

This 1805 mansion estate along the Hudson River was remodeled in the mid-1800s in the Classical-revival style. The grounds contain a coach house; visitor center; greenhouse with rose, herb, perennial and woodland gardens; a museum; and a garden shop. Bring your walking shoes, as there are numerous scenic trails with views of the cataracts that meet the Hudson.

Admission: adults $5, children 5-17 $3, children under 5 free. May-October, Saturday-Sunday 10 a.m.-5 p.m.

OLD RHINEBECK AERODROME

42 Stone Church Road, Rhinebeck, 845-752-3500; www.oldrhinebeck.org

A self-proclaimed "living" museum of aviation boasts one of the largest collections of antique airplanes and engines. Automobiles, motorcycles and paraphernalia from the Lindbergh era are also on display. Planes from World War I and earlier are flown in air shows on weekends. Biplane air rides are also available.

Admission: adults $10-20, seniors and children 13-17 $8-15, children 6-12 $3-5, children under 5 free. Mid-May-October, daily 10 a.m.-5 p.m.

WHERE TO STAY

★★★BEEKMAN ARMS

6387 Mill St., Rhinebeck, 845-876-7077, 800-361-6517;
www.beekmandelamaterinn.com

This historic inn (America's oldest continually run inn) is the perfect weekend escape. Guest rooms vary in size greatly, so be sure to request a larger room when booking, but all have country décor and include private baths,

TVs and a complimentary decanter of sherry. Savor fine cuisine onsite or visit many local attractions including the Roosevelt and Vanderbilt estates, the Culinary Institute of America and the Rhinebeck Aerodrome's World War I Air Show. Many of the rooms feature fireplaces.
23 rooms. Restaurant, bar. $151-250

WHERE TO EAT
★★CALICO RESTAURANT AND PATISSERIE
6384 Mills St., Rhinebeck, 845-876-2749; www.calicorhinebeck.com
This cozy neighborhood bistro serves delicious American fare with a French twist. But regardless of whether you choose to nosh on pork tenderloin or vegetable napoleon, save room for dessert; the pastry chef works wonders with the likes of brown butter tarts, Milanese macaroons and truffle cakes. American, French. Lunch, dinner, Sunday brunch. Closed Monday-Tuesday. Reservations recommended. Bar. $36-85

★★GIGI TRATTORIA
6422 Montgomery St., Rhinebeck, 845-876-1007; www.gigihudsonvalley.com
With rich tangerine tones and loft-like detailing, this Hudson Valley restaurant presents an inventive menu of pastas, seafood and cheeses. For a quick bite, try one of the signature flatbreads (we recommend the rustica with farm fennel sausage, broccoli rabe and red chili flakes). The wine list is also reasonable and varied.
Italian, Mediterranean. Lunch, dinner. Reservations recommended. Outdoor seating. Bar. $16-35

RIVERHEAD
See also Greenport, Southold
Suffolk County's thousands of acres of rich farmland, first cultivated in 1690, have made it one of the leading agricultural counties in the United States. Potatoes, corn and cauliflower are abundant here. Riverhead also sees its fair share of vineyards (though many prefer to head further out for wine tasting). Once in serious decline, Riverhead is perking up thanks to entrepreneurs who have made the most of its prime location between Long Island's North and South Forks.

WHAT TO SEE
ATLANTIS MARINE WORLD
431 E. Main St., Riverhead, 631-208-9200; www.atlantismarineworld.com
A themed aquatic park meant to recall the lost Greek isle, Marine World also houses the Riverhead Foundation for Marine Research and Preservation, where you can witness marine animals being nursed back to health. The sand-shark lagoon is another worthwhile stop.
Admission: adults $21, seniors and children 3-17 $18, children under 3 free. Daily 10 a.m.-5 p.m.

BRIERMERE FARMS
4414 Sound Ave., Riverhead, 631-722-3931; www.briermere.com
Forget about calories when you walk up to this small roadside farm stand

and bakery. The many varieties of homemade fruit and cream pies are worth every delectable bite. From traditional flavors like cherry and peach to more exotic tastes such as blackberry apple and blueberry cream, the pies are so stocked with fresh fruit that they are actually heavy to carry. Also indulge in Briermere's home-baked breads, muffins and cookies. For healthier interests, they also sell fresh fruits and vegetables. Go early in the day for the best selection and be ready to wait in line on just about any day of the summer.
Free. Monday-Thursday, 9 a.m.-5 p.m., Friday-Sunday 9 a.m.-5:30 p.m.

BROOKHAVEN NATIONAL LABORATORY

2 Center St., Upton, 631-344-8000; www.bnl.gov
The Exhibit Center Science Museum is housed in the world's first nuclear reactor built to carry out research on the peaceful aspects of nuclear science. Participatory exhibits, audiovisual presentations and historic collections are inside.
Free. Mid-July-August, Sunday.

MARTHA CLARA VINEYARDS

6025 Sound Ave., Riverhead, 631-298-0075; www.marthaclaravineyards.com
Martha Clara Vineyards is no stranger to success. Owned by Robert Entenmann, of Entenmann baking fame, the winery has grown from an 18-acre hobby to more than 100 acres of award-winning vines. Aim to visit on a weekend to enjoy a horse-drawn carriage tour around the property, including where the grapes are grown.
Free. Monday-Friday 11 a.m.-5 p.m., Saturday 11 a.m.-7 p.m., Sunday 11 a.m.-6 p.m.

PALMER VINEYARDS

108 Sound Ave., Riverhead, 631-722-9463; www.palmervineyards.com
Opened in 1986, this 55-acre winery is one of the most acclaimed on the North Fork, with an interesting, eclectic variety of wines. Palmer Vineyards offers everything from cabernet franc to chardonnay to special reserve wines that have a unique, robust flavor. Pack a picnic, enjoy a tasting and tour, and buy a bottle to enjoy with lunch.
Free. June-October, daily 11 a.m.-6 p.m.; November-May, daily 11 a.m.-5 p.m.

PINDAR VINEYARDS

37645 Main Road, Peconic, 631-734-6200; www.pindar.net
Even though Long Island's wine country does not have the reputation of Napa Valley, this well-known winery and its smaller counterparts are making a name for themselves. On 550 lush acres, Pindar is the North Fork's largest winery and one of the most established. Founded in 1979, it offers free tastings of their 16 varieties of wine.
Daily 11 a.m.-6 p.m.

SUFFOLK COUNTY HISTORICAL SOCIETY

300 W. Main St., Riverhead, 631-727-2881; www.suffolkcountyhistoricalsociety.org
Dating back to 1886, this museum chronicles Suffolk County's colorful history and rich traditions in farming, whaling and American Indian culture. Displays

include furniture, tools, antique bicycles and carriages and a library containing newspapers, books and photographs relating to Suffolk and its people.
Free. Tuesday-Saturday 12:30-4:30 p.m.

TANGER OUTLET CENTER
1770 W. Main St., Riverhead, 631-369-2732; www.tangeroutlet.com
This outdoor outlet mall is a great place to pick up almost any kind of merchandise—clothes, china, jewelry—at below retail prices. The mall has nearly 200 stores, most of them name brands such as Banana Republic and Williams-Sonoma.
Free. Monday-Saturday 9 a.m.-9 p.m., Sunday 10 a.m.-8 p.m.

VINTAGE TOURS
Peconic, 631-765-4689; www.vintagetour1.com
Vintage Tours will pick you up at your hotel in a comfortable 15-passenger van and take you to at least three wineries in a five- to six-hour jaunt. Also included are behind-the-scene winery tours, a gourmet picnic lunch suited to your tastes and stops at the North Fork's wonderful farm stands for the best in fresh vegetables and fruit.
Admission: adults $70, Monday-Friday; $80, Saturday-Sunday.

WHERE TO STAY
★★BEST WESTERN EAST END
1830 Route 25, Riverhead, 631-369-2200, 800-528-1234;
www.bestwesterneastend.com
Don't worry if you forgot to pack a toothbrush; this chain hotel is located just down the road from the Tanger outlet shops. Rooms are spacious, although somewhat outdated, and some include patios or balconies. Located at the split of the North and South Forks, this makes a good home base for exploring all of eastern Long Island.
100 rooms. Restaurant, bar. Complimentary breakfast. Business center. Fitness center. Pool. Pets accepted. $151-250

ROCHESTER
See also Finger Lakes, Palmyra, Pittsford
Rochester is a high-tech industrial and cultural center and the third-largest city in the state. Its educational institutions include the University of Rochester with its Eastman School of Music and Rochester Institute of Technology with its National Technical Institute for the Deaf. The Vacuum Oil Company, a predecessor of Mobil Oil Corporation, was founded here in 1866. The city also has a symphony orchestra and professional theatre.
Rochester has had its share of famous citizens, too: Susan B. Anthony, champion of women's rights; Frederick Douglass, black abolitionist and statesman; George Eastman, inventor of flexible film and founder of Kodak; Hiram Sibley, founder of Western Union; and musicians Mitch Miller, Cab Calloway and Chuck Mangione.

WHAT TO SEE
GENESEE COUNTRY VILLAGE & MUSEUM
1410 Flint Hill Road, Mumford, 585-538-6822; www.gcv.org

This 19th-century working village has 68 restored and furnished buildings, where locals in period costumes teach you about what life in this part of the country was like more than 150 years ago. The village also boasts an art gallery, "base ball" (it was spelled as two words in the 19th century) park, nature center and heirloom gardens.

Admission: adults $15, seniors and students $12, children 4-16 $9, children under 4 free. Mid-May-mid-October, Tuesday-Friday 10 a.m.-4 p.m., Saturday-Sunday 10 a.m.-5 p.m.

GEORGE EASTMAN HOUSE
900 East Ave., Rochester, 585-271-3361; www.eastmanhouse.org

Kodak founder George Eastman's 50-room mansion and gardens contain restored rooms with their original 1920s furnishings and décor. Adjacent to the house is the archive building; eight exhibit spaces display an extensive collection of 19th- and 20th-century photography representing major photographers of the past 150 years, as well as a chronological display of the evolution of photography.

Admission: adults $10, seniors $8, students $6, children 5-12 $4, children under 5 free. Tuesday-Wednesday, Friday-Saturday 10 a.m.-5 p.m., Thursday 10 a.m.-8 p.m., Sunday 1-5 p.m.

HAMLIN BEACH STATE PARK
1 Camp Road, Hamlin, 585-964-2462; www.nysparks.state.ny.us/parks

This park is most famous for it's soft sandy beach and boat launches, but there is also an excellent environmental education center with self-guided nature tours.

Daily6 a.m.-10 p.m.

HIGH FALLS IN THE BROWN'S RACE HISTORIC DISTRICT
60 Brown's Race, Rochester, 585-325-2030; www.ci.rochester.ny.us

This is the area between Inner Loop and Platt and State streets, along the Genesee River Gorge. One of Rochester's earliest industrial districts has been renovated to preserve the area where flour mills and manufacturers once operated and Eastman Kodak and Gleason Works originated. Today, the district still houses businesses in renovated historic buildings such as the Eastman Technologies Building. Center at High Falls, on Brown's Race Street, is an interpretive museum with hands-on interactive exhibits on the history of the area, as well as information on other attractions to visit in Rochester. Brown's Race Market has been transformed from a maintenance facility of the Rochester Gas and Electric Corporation into three levels of attractions including a nightclub, jazz club and restaurant. A laser light show can be viewed at dusk from the pedestrian bridge that crosses the Genesee River.

Free. Daily.

MEMORIAL ART GALLERY (UNIVERSITY OF ROCHESTER)

500 University Ave., Rochester, 585-276-8900; www.mag.rochester.edu

The permanent collection has more than 12,000 pieces of art spanning 50 centuries and includes masterworks by Monet, Matisse and Homer. In addition to its well-balanced permanent stock, the Gallery offers a year-round schedule of temporary exhibitions, lectures, concerts, tours and family activities.

Admission: adults $10, students, seniors and military $6, children 6-18 $4, children under 6 free. Wednesday, Friday-Sunday 11 a.m.-5 p.m., Thursday 11 a.m.-9 p.m.

ROCHESTER HISTORICAL SOCIETY

485 East Ave., Rochester, 585-271-2705; www.rochesterhistory.org

The Rochester Historical Society, the brainchild of anthropologist Louis Henry Morgan, was established in 1860 only to languish as the Civil War loomed over Rochester and the nation. In 1887, Mrs. Caroline Perkins, philanthropist and wife of businessman Gilman H. Perkins, revived the Society and led it to local prominence. For decades the Society has collected and preserved what today amounts to over 200,000 objects and documents. The headquarters for the society is "Woodside," a Greek Revival mansion dating back to 1839, which contains a collection of portraits and memorabilia, costumes, a reference library and a manuscript collection.

Free. Monday-Friday 9 a.m.-3 p.m.

ROCHESTER INSTITUTE OF TECHNOLOGY

1 Lomb Memorial Drive, Rochester, 585-475-2411; www.rit.edu

It's not just about techies here. This prestigious university covers everything from photography to computer science, criminal justice to bioinformatics. The National Technical Institute for the Deaf is also located here. When visiting, be sure to stop by the Bevier Gallery or grab your skates and head to the Frank Ritter Memorial Ice Arena.

Free. Daily.

ROCHESTER MUSEUM & SCIENCE CENTER

657 East Ave., Rochester, 585-271-4320; www.rmsc.org

Kids will love this hands-on museum where science and nature come to life. Local history is explored through exhibits such as Flight to Freedom: Rochester's Underground Railroad and Rochester's 1873 time capsule. The onsite Strasenburgh Planetarium hosts astronomy and laser-light shows.

Admission: adults $10, seniors and students $9, children 3-18 $8, children under 3 free. Monday-Saturday 9 a.m.-5 p.m., Sunday 11 a.m.-5 p.m.

SENECA PARK ZOO

2222 St. Paul St., Rochester, 585-336-7200; www.senecaparkzoo.org

Animals from all over the world reside at this zoo, including African elephants, penguins, orangutans and polar bears. Aviary fans might enjoy the free-flight bird room (just watch for dive-bombs). The Rocky Coasts features underwater viewing of polar bears and seals.

Admission: adults $7-9, seniors $6-8, children 3-11 $4-6, children under 3 free. January-March, daily 10 a.m.-4 p.m.; April-October, daily 10 a.m.-5 p.m.; November-December, daily 10 a.m.-4 p.m.

STRONG MUSEUM
1 Manhattan Square, Rochester, 585-263-2700; www.strongmuseum.org
As the second largest children's museum in the U.S., the Strong Museum features a myriad of exhibits, 25,000 toys, dolls, miniatures and more. There is also an interactive 3-D exhibit based on the Children's Television Workshop program Sesame Street. The glass atrium features a street scene with an operating 1956 diner and 1918 carousel.
Admission: adults $10, seniors $9, children 2-15 $8, children under 2 free. Monday-Thursday 10 a.m.-5 p.m., Friday-Saturday 10 a.m.-8 p.m., Sunday noon-5 p.m.

SUSAN B. ANTHONY HOUSE
17 Madison St., Rochester, 585-235-6124; www.susanbanthonyhouse.org
Susan B. Anthony lived here for 40 years and was arrested at her house in 1872 for voting illegally in the presidential election. The Victorian brick building contains mementos of the women's suffrage movement and antique furnishings.
Admission: adults $6, seniors $5, students and children under 13 $3. Tuesday-Sunday 11 a.m.-5 p.m.

SPECIAL EVENT
LILAC FESTIVAL
Highland Park, Rochester, 585-256-4960; www.lilacfestival.com
Put on your purple garb. This 10-day festival features more than 500 varieties of lilacs (as long as they bloom in time) and an immense assortment of other floral varieties. There are guided garden tours, arts and craft booths and a parade. Live entertainment lights up the city by nightfall.
Free. Mid-May.

WHERE TO STAY
★★CLARION HOTEL
120 E. Main St., Rochester, 585-546-6400, 877-424-6423;
www.clarionriversidehotel.com
This large chain hotel is situated on the banks of the Genesee River in downtown Rochester and is directly connected to the Rochester Riverside Convention Center. Guest rooms are newly remodeled to include data ports and upgraded bathrooms.
465 rooms. Restaurant, bar. Fitness center. Pool. Pets accepted. $61-150

★COMFORT INN
1501 Ridge Road West, Rochester, 585-621-5700, www.comfortinn.com
Business travelers will enjoy the close proximity to the airport, as well as the complimentary newspaper service and free wireless Internet access. Rooms are standard, but spacious and some include whirlpool tubs.
82 rooms. Complimentary breakfast. Fitness center. Pets accepted. $61-150

★★★CROWNE PLAZA

70 State St., Rochester, 585-546-3450, 866-826-2831; www.rcpny.com

This Crowne Plaza offers a convenient location in the center of downtown Rochester. Airport shuttle service, a concierge, same-day laundry service and a business center with an array of offerings provide convenience, while a well-equipped fitness facility and an outdoor heated pool offer onsite recreation.

362 rooms. Restaurant, bar. Business center. Fitness center. Pool. Pets accepted.

$61-150

★★HOLIDAY INN HOTEL & SUITES MARKETPLACE

800 Jefferson Road, Rochester, 585-475-9190, 888-465-4329; www.hirochesterairport.com

From the free airport shuttle service to the free DVD rentals, there are numerous perks at this chain property. Rooms have been updated and include refrigerators and microwaves, and work stations for business travelers.

120 rooms. Restaurant, bar. Complimentary breakfast. Business center. Fitness center. Pool. $61-150

★★★HYATT REGENCY ROCHESTER

125 E. Main St., Rochester, 585-546-1234, 800-492-8804; www.hyatt.com

A skywalk connects the hotel to the convention center, which is located near shopping, entertainment, wineries and the airport. You will find well-appointed rooms and a health club, extraordinary meeting space and a friendly staff.

338 rooms. Restaurant, bar. Business center. Fitness center. Pool. $151-250

★★★STRATHALLAN HOTEL

550 East Ave., Rochester, 585-461-5010, 800-678-7284; www.strathallan.com

This European-style hotel offers warm and spacious studios and one-bedroom suites. Located in a stately residential neighborhood, the property is convenient to area attractions such as the Rochester Museum & Science Center and the George Eastman House. The award-winning restaurant offers dishes such as sweet potato-crusted Hawaiian snapper in a country club setting, and the bar is a quiet place to relax.

156 rooms. Restaurant, bar. Business center. Fitness center. $151-250

WHERE TO EAT

★DINOSAUR BAR-B-QUE

99 Court St., Rochester, 585-325-7090; www.dinosaurbarbque.com

It's all about meat at this casual smoke shack. Housed in a turn-of-the-century railroad station adjacent to the Genesee River, this local favorite offers chicken, beef and pork in Cuban, cajun, jerk and just about any other style of barbecue that you can imagine. Live blues is performed Monday through Saturday nights.

Barbecue. Lunch, dinner. Bar. $36-85

★★★THE GRILL AT STRATHALLAN

550 East Ave., Rochester, 585-461-5010; www.strathallan.com

This sophisticated yet casual Mediterranean dining room serves fresh, cre-

ative and elegantly prepared food paired with selections from an extensive wine cellar. Seafood dishes, such as sesame-crusted tuna with bok choy, is a great choice. There are also a number of tasty vegetarian options.
American. Breakfast, lunch (Monday-Friday), dinner. Closed Sunday. Jacket required. $36-85

★★★MARIO'S ITALIAN STEAKHOUSE
2740 Monroe Ave., Rochester, 585-271-1111; www.mariosviaabruzzi.com
This charming villa is built and decorated in authentic central Italian style. Mario's unique Italian cuisine includes signatures like steak Diane, and pork loin and fig chutney. The Sunday brunch has won many accolades.
Italian. Dinner, Sunday brunch. Outdoor seating. Children's menu. Bar. $16-35

★★★ROONEYS
90 Henrietta St., Rochester, 585-442-0444; www.rooneysrestaurant.com
This atmospheric downtown spot, with intimate mood lighting and white silk tablecloths, is housed in an 1860 tavern; and the original bar is still in use. Many of the meat dishes are wood-grilled; and there's often venison, though the menu changes daily.
Continental. Dinner. Bar. $16-35

ROME
See also Oneida, Utica
Originally the site of Fort Stanwix, where, during the Revolutionary War, tradition says the Stars and Stripes were first flown in battle. The author of the "Pledge of Allegiance," Francis Bellamy, is buried in Rome. Griffiss Air Force Base is located here as well.

WHAT TO SEE

DELTA LAKE STATE PARK
8797 Highway 46, Rome, 315-337-4670; www.nysparks.state.ny.us/parks
Anglers flock to this park for the surplus of trout, walleye and bass in the region. Because the park is situated on a peninsula that juts into the Delta Reservoir, there is also a protected beach for swimming. Hiking trails provide spectacular views from the upper bluffs.
Free. Daily.

ERIE CANAL VILLAGE
5789 New London Rd., Rome, 315-337-3999, 888-374-3226; www.eriecanalvillage.net
Take trips on a restored section of the Erie Canal aboard a mule-drawn 1840 canal packet boat, The Chief Engineer. Buildings that remain from the 1840s canal village include a church, blacksmith shop, train station, museums, schoolhouse, Victorian home and stable.
Admission: adults $10, seniors $7, children $5, children under 5 free. June-August, Wednesday-Saturday 10 a.m.-5 p.m., Sunday noon-5 p.m.

FORT RICKEY CHILDREN'S DISCOVERY ZOO

5135 Rome-New London Road, Rome, 315-336-1930; www.fortrickey.com

Focusing specifically on hands-on animal interaction, this rural zoo is located in a restored 18th-century British fort. Programs put children in direct contact with such rare animals as African pygmy goats, red-tailed boa constrictors and hedgehogs.

Admission: adults $9.50, seniors $8, children 2-15 $6.50, children under 2 free. Mid-May-mid-June, September daily 10 a.m.-4 p.m.; Mid-June-August, daily 10 a.m.-5 p.m.

FORT STANWIX NATIONAL MONUMENT

112 E. Park St., Rome, 315-338-7730; www.nps.gov/fost

Visit this reconstructed fortress built in 1758. It was also here that the Iroquois signed a treaty opening territory east of the Ohio River to colonial expansion. Known as "the fort that never surrendered," Fort Stanwix was besieged by the British in 1777, but under Col. Peter Gansevoort, troops repelled the attack. Today, the site includes costumed guides, a film covering the history of the fort and a museum.

Free. April-December, daily 9 a.m.-5 p.m.

WHERE TO STAY
★★THE BEECHES INN

7900 Turin Road, Rome, 315-336-1775, 800-765-7251; www.thebeeches.com

Situated on 52 acres, this intimate family-owned inn has sizeable rooms decorated with country furnishings. The staff is friendly, and offers personalized service that includes complimentary bottled water and fresh fruit with each evening turndown service.

70 rooms. Restaurant. Business center. Pool. $61-150

★★QUALITY INN

200 S. James St., Rome, 315-336-4300; www.qualityinnrome.com

This is your standard chain hotel with convenient highway access, clean rooms and a seasonal outdoor pool. There is a 24-hour Denny's restaurant onsite.

103 rooms. Restaurant. Business center. Fitness center. Pool. Pets accepted. $61-150

WHERE TO EAT
★★THE BEECHES

7900 Turin Road, Rome, 315-336-1700; www.thebeeches.com

With heavy English décor and hearty dishes, this getaway is more reminiscent of a London pub than an inn in New York. Signature dishes include rack of lamb with mint jelly and Normandy pork, sautéed with apples and shallots in Applejack Brandy.

Lunch (Tuesday-Friday), dinner, Sunday brunch. Closed Monday. Children's menu. Bar. $16-35

★★SAVOY
255 E. Dominick St., Rome, 315-339-3166; www.romesavoy.com
Pasta is the focus at this intimate Italian restaurant, replete with live piano music and antique photographs. Go with one of the family recipe dishes like Aunt Fannie's fettuccine or Doug's homemade ravioli.
Italian. Lunch (Monday-Friday), dinner. Children's menu. Bar. $16-35

ROSLYN

See also Westbury

More than 100 historic sites dot this village in Nassau County in Long Island. Once called Hempstead Harbor, Roslyn adapted its new name in 1844 to avoid being confused with all the other "Hempsteads" in the region. Roslyn is just east of the Town of North Hempstead. You can understand the bemusement.

WHAT TO SEE
NASSAU COUNTY MUSEUM OF ART

1 Museum Drive, Roslyn, 516-484-9337; www.nassaumuseum.com
This museum is housed in a mansion that was once owned by poet William Cullen Bryant and later lived in by steel tycoon Henry Clay Frick. Temporary exhibits have covered a wide range of topics, from Napoleon, the Civil War and American Revolution, to the surrealist art of Dali. The museum's permanent collection showcases works of many 19th- and 20th-century American and European artists.
Admission: adults $10, seniors $8, children $4. Tuesday-Sunday 11 a.m.-4:45 p.m.

WHERE TO EAT
★★★BRYANT & COOPER STEAK HOUSE

Two Middleneck Rd., Roslyn, 516-627-7270; www.bryantandcooper.com
Have a drink at the bar or feast in the dark wood and marble-accented dining room at this classic steakhouse. The filet mignon is particularly good.
Steak. Lunch, dinner. Bar. $36-85

★★★GEORGE WASHINGTON MANOR

1305 Old Northern Blvd., Roslyn, 516-621-1200; www.georgewashingtonmanor.com
This historic building was once the home of Roslyn founder Hendrick Onderdonk, host to President George Washington during his 1790 Long Island visit. American continental cuisine is served in a colonial room complete with six fireplaces, original wood beams and antique furnishings.
American. Lunch, dinner, Sunday brunch. Bar. $16-35

RYE

See also White Plains

Rye is a quiet village on a harbor that opens into Long Island Sound. John Jay, the nation's first Supreme Court chief justice, lived and is now buried in Rye.

WHERE TO EAT
★★★LA PANETIERE
530 Milton Road, Rye, 914-967-8140; www.lapanetiere.com
Set in a charming 19th-century house in lower Westchester County, La Pane-tiere serves stunning, contemporary French fare. The kitchen focuses on lo-cal, seasonal ingredients, searching out nearby farmers for fish, poultry and produce. The dining room has an original wood-beamed ceiling that gives it rustic warmth that is balanced with elegant tapestries and beautiful 19th-century furnishings.
French menu. Lunch (Tuesday-Friday), dinner. Bar. $36-85

SACKETS HARBOR
See also Thousand Islands, Watertown
This is a lakeside resort area for the eastern Lake Ontario region. Two major battles of the War of 1812 occurred here. In the first barrage, the British war-ships invading the harbor were damaged and withdrew. A landing force was repulsed in the second battle.

WHAT TO SEE
SACKETS HARBOR BATTLEFIELD STATE HISTORIC SITE
505 W. Washington St., Sackets Harbor, 315-646-3634;www.nysparks.state.ny.us/sites/
This site witnessed two battles between the British and the Americans during the War of 1812. Today, the location maintains a Federal-style Union Hotel, which dates back to 1818; a Commandant's House; a former US Navy Yard and a visitor center.
Admission: adults $3, seniors, students, military $2, children under 13 free. Mid-May-early September, Wednesday-Saturday 10 a.m.-5 p.m., Sunday 1-5 p.m.; Mid-September-mid-October, Friday-Saturday 10 a.m.-5 p.m., Sunday 1-5 p.m.

WESTCOTT BEACH STATE PARK
12224 Route 3, Sackets Harbor, 315-938-5083; www.nysparks.state.ny.us
Located along sheltered Henderson Bay, this park offers fantastic swimming and boating options. Black bass fishing is also popular. Campsites provide water views.
Free. May-mid-October, daily.

WHERE TO STAY
★ONTARIO PLACE HOTEL
103 General Smith Drive, Sackets Harbor, 315-646-8000, 800-564-1812;
www.ontarioplacehotel.com
A nice option for families, this small hotel provides mini-suite rooms that can sleep up to five and include refrigerators, microwaves and whirlpools. The décor could use an update, but the price can't be beat.
38 rooms. Complimentary breakfast. Pets accepted. $61-150

SAG HARBOR
See also Amagansett, East Hampton, Shelter Island, Southampton
This great whaling town of the 19th century provided prototypes from which

James Fenimore Cooper created characters for his sea stories. Sheltered in a cove of Gardiner's Bay, the economy of Sag Harbor is still fueled by the sea, attracting wealthy New Yorkers who come to retreat and relax in this chic summertime community by the beach.

WHAT TO SEE
CUSTOM HOUSE
Main and Garden streets, Sag Harbor, 631-692-4664; www.splia.org
This building served as a custom house and post office during the late 18th and early 19th centuries. Antique furnishings and historic documents are on exhibit in the converted museum.
Admission: adults $3, seniors and children $2. June-mid-October, Saturday-Sunday 1-5 p.m.

ELIZABETH A. MORTON NATIONAL WILDLIFE REFUGE
784 Noyac Road, Sag Harbor, 631-286-0485; www.fws.gov/refuges
At one time, Native American tribes inhabited this 187-acre plot of land. Today, a variety of birds—some endangered—call it home at different times of the year. Bring your binoculars; you're likely to see osprey, terns and water birds.
Dailysunrise-sunset.

SAG HARBOR WHALING AND HISTORICAL MUSEUM
200 Main St., Sag Harbor, 631-725-0770; www.sagharborwhalingmuseum.org
Listed on the National Register of Historic Places, this museum, housed in a mansion, celebrates Sag Harbor's long history of whaling. It features items such as the tools used to harpoon whales, a replica of a whaleboat, whale teeth and bones and other materials associated with whaling.
Admission: adults $5, seniors and students $3, children under 12 free. Mid-May-October, daily 10 a.m.-5 p.m., Sunday 1-5 p.m.

WHERE TO EAT
★★★AMERICAN HOTEL
49 Main St., Sag Harbor, 631-725-3535; www.theamericanhotel.com
Located in the atmospheric American Hotel is an elegant and romantic restaurant filled with Empire and Victorian antiques and furnishings. The menu offers American and French classics, and an excellent wine list. Seafood is a good choice here, from the Atlantic lobster to the pan-seared divers scallops.
American, French. Lunch, dinner. Reservations recommended. Outdoor seating. Bar. $36-85

★★ESTIA'S LITTLE KITCHEN
1615 Sag Harbor, Sag Harbor, 631-725-1045;
www.eatshampton.com/LittleKitchen.htm
This local roadside hangout takes the "little" in its name seriously. Space is limited and the décor isn't much, but the kitchen serves up fresh inventive American dishes, and service is friendly and low-key.
American. Breakfast, lunch, dinner. Reservations recommended. Closed Tuesday. $16-35

★★IL CAPUCCINO
30 Madison St., Sag Harbor, 631-725-2747; www.ilcapuccino.com
You may reek of garlic upon leaving this cute Italian restaurant, but it'll be worth it. The menu is filled with straightforward dishes like lasagna and homemade ravioli that are consistently delicious. The wine list has winners as well.
Italian. Dinner. Children's menu. Bar. $16-35

★★SPINNAKER'S
63 Main St., Sag Harbor, 631-725-9353
Located in the heart of downtown Sag Harbor, this local spot provides fresh seafood and burgers without the hefty Hamptons prices. The lobster salad is a must.
American, International. Lunch, dinner, Sunday brunch. Reservations recommended. Children's menu. Bar. $16-35

SARANAC LAKE
See also Lake Placid, Tupper Lake, Wilmington
Surrounded by Adirondack Park, the village of Saranac Lake was first settled in 1819 when Jacob Moody, who had been injured in a sawmill accident, retired to the wilderness, built a log cabin at what is now Pine and River streets and raised a family of mountain guides. The qualities that attracted Moody and made the town a famous health resort in the 19th century continue to lure visitors who come for the fresh, mountain air and a relaxing environment.

WHAT TO SEE
ROBERT LOUIS STEVENSON MEMORIAL COTTAGE
11 Stevenson Lane, Saranac Lake, 518-891-1462;
www.adirondacks.com/robertlstevenson.html
This modest farmhouse is where Robert Louis Stevenson lived while undergoing treatment for what is believed to have been tuberculosis from 1887 to 1888. Today, the building contains a collection of photographs, letters and memorabilia from Stevenson's life.
Admission: $5. July-mid-September, Tuesday-Sunday 9:30 a.m.-noon, 1-4:30 p.m.

SIX NATIONS INDIAN MUSEUM
Adirondack Park, Buck Pond Road, Onchiota, 518-891-2299
Indoor and outdoor exhibits portray the life of Native Americans, with a council ground, types of fires, and ancient and modern articles. There are also frequent lectures on the culture and history of the Iroquois Confederacy.
Admission: adults $2, children $1. July-August, daily 10 a.m.-6 p.m.

SPECIAL EVENTS
ADIRONDACK CANOE CLASSIC
Adirondack Marina, Saranac Lake, 518-891-2744, 800-347-1992;
www.saranaclake.com
Also known as the 90-miler, this three-day, 90 mile race from Old Forge to Saranac Lake is held every fall and embarked upon by roughly 250 canoes, kayaks and guide-boats. The course follows the historic "Highway of the Adirondacks." Early September.

WINTER CARNIVAL

30 Main St., Saranac Lake, 518-891-1990; www.saranaclakewintercarnival.com

Claiming to be the oldest winter carnival in the country, this 10-day festival includes an illuminated ice palace, skating, skiing and snowmobile races and a snowshoe-softball game. There is also a parade and fireworks. Early February.

WHERE TO STAY
★★★★★THE POINT

Highway 30, Saranac Lake, 518-891-5674, 800-255-3530; www.thepointresort.com

Exceptionally well-heeled travelers seeking a glamorous stay in the wilderness head straight for the Point. This former great camp of William Avery Rockefeller revives the spirit of the early 19th-century Adirondacks, when the wealthy came to rusticate in this sylvan paradise. No signs direct visitors to this intimate camp, and a decidedly residential ambience is maintained. The resort has a splendid location on a 10-acre peninsula on Upper Saranac Lake. Rooms feature Adirondack twig furnishings, stone fireplaces, elegant bathrooms and luxe antiques. From snowshoeing and cross-country skiing to water sports, trail hikes and croquet, you'll find a variety of outdoor activities. All guest requests are well catered to. Will you be in the mood for champagne and truffle popcorn at 4 a.m.? At your service. Gourmet dining figures largely in the experience and with a nod to the patrician past, guests don black-tie attire twice weekly at the communal dining table in the resort's great room.

11 rooms. Restaurant, bar. Spa. No children allowed. Beach. Tennis. $351 and up.

★★THE HOTEL SARANAC

100 Main St., Saranac Lake, 518-891-2200, 800-937-0211; www.hotelsaranac.com

This historic red brick hotel is located in the heart of downtown Saranac Lake. There is a country-like feeling to the décor, and basic guest rooms feature bedspreads similar to hand-sewn quilts. Many of the rooms also offer a lovely city view. The hotel is the tallest building in downtown, and a large sign with the hotel's name sits on top so it never hard to find.

86 rooms. Restaurant, bar. Business center. $61-150

★★SARANAC INN GOLF & COUNTRY CLUB

125 County Route 46, Saranac Lake, 518-891-1402; www.saranacinn.com

For basic and no frills accommodations, Saranac Inn Golf & Country Club offers a comfortable stay. Situated off Highway 30, it is approximately 30 minutes from Lake Placid and close to the shores of Upper Saranac Lake. The property sits on more than 350 acres of rolling hills and a sea of trees. Golfers can enjoy a game of golf on the beautiful 18-hole golf course.

10 rooms. Restaurant, bar. Golf. Mid-October-April. $61-150

SARATOGA SPRINGS

See also Glens Falls, Johnstown, Schenectady

Saratoga Springs is a resort city that is rural yet decidedly cosmopolitan. Much of the town's Victorian architecture has been restored. The city boasts the natural springs, geysers and mineral baths that first made the town famous, as well as internationally recognized harness and thoroughbred racing and polo, respected museums and the Saratoga Performing Arts Center.

WHAT TO SEE
HISTORIC CONGRESS PARK
Canfield Casino and Union Ave., Saratoga Springs, 518-584-6920
Both the Museum of the Historical Society and the Walworth Memorial Museum are housed in the historical 1870 Canfield Casino. The museums trace the history of the city's growth. Exhibits change frequently, but often include gambling paraphernalia, antique photographs and negatives and period furnishings.
Admission: adults $5, seniors and students $4, children under 12 free. June-August, Monday-Saturday 10 a.m.-4 p.m., Sunday 1-4 p.m.; September-May, Wednesday-Saturday 10 a.m.-4 p.m., Sunday 1-4 p.m.

NATIONAL BOTTLE MUSEUM
76 Milton Ave., Ballston Spa, 518-885-7589; www.nationalbottlemuseum.org
Glass in all shapes and for all purposes, including antique bottles, jars and dinnerware are on display. There is even a miniature model of a glass furnace, as it would have appeared in the 1800s. Classes in flameworking and lampworking are offered weekly. June-September, daily 10 a.m.-4 p.m.; October-May, Monday-Friday 10 a.m.-4 p.m.

NATIONAL MUSEUM OF DANCE
99 S. Broadway, Saratoga Springs, 518-584-2225; www.dancemuseum.org
Dedicated to American professional dance, the museum boasts an impressive collection of photographs, costumes, artifacts and videos immortalizing the art of dance. The only permanent exhibit here is the Hall of Fame, which has honored such greats as Fred Astaire, George Balanchine and Martha Graham. Kids will enjoy the Discovery Room, where a stage and wearable costumes allow children to put on their own dance performances.
Admission: adults $6.50, seniors and students $5, children 3-12 $3, children under 3 free. Mid-March-December, Tuesday-Sunday 10 a.m.-4 p.m.

NATIONAL MUSEUM OF RACING AND HALL OF FAME
191 Union Ave., Saratoga Springs, 518-584-0400, 800-562-5394;
www.racingmuseum.org
This museum is appropriately situated across from historic Saratoga Race Course, the oldest operating thoroughbred race-track in the country. Exhibitions on the history and mechanics of thoroughbred racing include the stories of racing champs Man o' War, Secretariat, Seattle Slew and Affirmed. The building also contains exhibits on Saratoga's gambling heyday. There are training track tours in summer.
Admission: adults $7, seniors and students $5, children under 6 free. November-December, Tuesday-Saturday 10 a.m.-4 p.m., Sunday noon-4 p.m.; January-March, Wednesday-Saturday 10 a.m.-4 p.m., Sunday noon-4 p.m.; April-October, Monday-Saturday 10 a.m.-4 p.m., Sunday noon-4 p.m.

SARATOGA PERFORMING ARTS CENTER

108 Avenue of The Pines, Saratoga Springs, 518.587.3330; www.spac.org

The SPAC is one of the premier performing arts venues in the region, drawing diverse art and theater acts from near and far. There is a majestic amphitheater with seats for 5,000 under cover and a sprawling lawn beyond, as well as the Little Theatre, a 500-seat indoor showcase for chamber music. Bring a picnic and make an afternoon of it.

Prices and showtimes vary.

SARATOGA SPA STATE PARK

19 Roosevelt Drive, Saratoga Springs, 518-584-2535; www.saratogaspastatepark.org

This 2,200-acre park is home to the performing arts center, mineral bath houses, Saratoga Automobile Museum and the Saratoga Spa Golf Course, among other recreational outlets. Trails snake throughout the natural preserve, and wide-open meadows become prime snowshoeing and cross-country skiing spots in winter.

Free. Daily.

YADDO GARDENS

Union Ave., Saratoga Springs, 518-584-0746; www.yaddo.org

An artists' retreat since 1926, this Victorian Gothic mansion's famous residents have included Flannery O'Connor, Leonard Bernstein and John Cheever. The mansion is closed to the general public, but landscaped gardens are open year round. Daily

8 a.m.-sunset.

WHERE TO STAY

★★GIDEON PUTNAM RESORT AND SPA

24 Gideon Putnam Road, Saratoga Springs, 518-584-3000; www.gideonputnam.com

Built in 1930 and located in Saratoga Spa State Park, this Georgian Revival structure greets guests with beautifully landscaped grounds and an expansive, marble-tiled lobby. In addition to bike rentals, cross-country skiing, tennis, golf, swimming and ice skating, guests can indulge in numerous relaxing treatments and the rejuvenating mineral springs at the adjacent Roosevelt Baths and Spa.

120 rooms. Restaurant, bar. Business center. Fitness center. Spa. $251-350

★GRAND UNION MOTEL

120 S. Broadway, Saratoga Springs, 518-584-9000; www.grandunionmotel.com

Guests looking for a nice place to stay without the frills and huge dollar signs will find the Grand Union Motel to be a good choice. It's conveniently located near the downtown shopping district of Saratoga Springs, Saratoga Spa State Park and the Saratoga Springs Race Track. The Crystal Spa is also on premise. Guest rooms are small and bland, but clean with access from the exterior.

64 rooms. Pool. Spa. Pets accepted. $61-150

★★HOLIDAY INN

232 Broadway, Saratoga Springs, 518-584-4550; www.spa-hi.com

This nicely landscaped Holiday Inn sits on the corner of Broadway and Circular streets, within a few blocks of downtown Saratoga Springs. Light colors are used inside the public areas, creating a bright setting. Each guest room features two phones, a coffee maker, refrigerator and microwave.

168 rooms. Restaurant, bar. Business center. Fitness center. Pool. Pets accepted. $151-250

★★THE INN AT SARATOGA

231 Broadway, Saratoga Springs, 518-583-1890, 800-274-3573;
www.theinnatsaratoga.com

The Inn at Saratoga is a 150-year-old Victorian home with a large covered porch and a lot of character. It is the oldest operating hotel in Saratoga Springs and located only a short stroll from downtown. Guest rooms are bright and airy with plush bedding and upscale furnishings. The onsite restaurant serves exceptional American fare.

42 rooms. Restaurant, bar. Complimentary breakfast. $61-150

★★THE SARATOGA HILTON

534 Broadway, Saratoga Springs, 518-584-4000, 888-866-3591;
www.thesaratogahotel.com

There is a sleek, contemporary feeling when entering the expansive public space of this high-rise building. Huge fresh flowers and leather furniture with sleek lines decorate the lobby. Guest rooms are spacious and updated with soothing color tones and luxury bedding. Located adjacent—and almost connecting to—the City Center, the hotel is on the edge of the charming downtown shopping district, so it is accessible to all the town has to offer. Take in horse races, music, museums, performing arts, nature walks, mineral baths and more.

242 rooms. Restaurant, bar. Business center. Fitness center. Pool. $151-250

WHERE TO EAT
★★★CHEZ PIERRE

979 Route 9, Gansevoort, 518-793-3350, 800-672-0666;
www.chezpierrerestaurant.com

Joe and Pierrette Baldwin's romantic French restaurant serves inspired cooking—like the classic steak au poivre flambé and veal Oscar, a veal cutlet topped with crabmeat, asparagus and hollandaise sauce—in a setting accented with murals painted by local artists and framed pictures of the owners' homeland. If you're in the mood for seafood, opt for the lobster Newburg or filet of sole Marguery with white wine and a mussels and shrimp cream sauce.

French. Dinner. Closed Monday. Reservations recommended. Bar. $36-85

★OLDE BRYAN INN

123 Maple Ave., Saratoga Springs, 518-587-2990; www.oldebryaninn.com

Built in 1832, this restaurant was originally a log cabin and still retains the original wood floors and brick walls, making for a rustic and unique setting. Booths and tables are available, and the lounge has many personalized pewter mugs hanging above the bar for frequent visitors. The menu offers something for everyone and includes options such as sandwiches, salads, seafood and steak.

American. Lunch, dinner. Outdoor seating. Children's menu. Bar. $16-35

★★PRIMO'S RESTAURANT

231 Broadway, Saratoga Springs, 518-583-1890, 800-274-3573; www.theinnatsaratoga.com

The atmosphere is casual and welcoming at this small yet charming restaurant located within the Inn at Saratoga. There are 15 tables and a covered porch outside with a few additional tables for dining. The romantic Victorian décor includes ornate chandeliers, vintage light fixtures, arched doorways and chairs upholstered in a floral pattern. Many pictures of historic Saratoga Springs adorn the walls and a gas fireplace makes the room cozy in winter.

American. Dinner. Reservations recommended. Outdoor seating. Bar. $16-35

SAUGERTIES

See also Hudson, Kingston, Woodstock

At the confluence of Esopus Creek and the Hudson River, Saugerties was a port of call for riverboats. The town was famous for building racing sloops and for the production of fine paper, leather and canvas. Today, pristine Victorian homes line the main streets and boutiques and restaurants have cropped up downtown.

WHAT TO SEE

OPUS 40 & QUARRYMAN'S MUSEUM

50 Fite Road, Saugerties, 845-246-3400; www.opus40.org

An environmental sculpture rises out of this abandoned bluestone quarry. More than six acres of fitted bluestone were constructed over 37 years by sculptor Harvey Fite. Today it is the site of Sunset Concert series and other programs. There is also a Quarryman's Museum on the property which houses a collection of 19th century tools used in the quarries.

Admission: adults $10, seniors and students $7, children 6-18 $3, children under 6 free. June-mid-October, Friday-Sunday 11:30 a.m.-5 p.m.

WHERE TO STAY

★COMFORT INN

2790 Route 32 N., Saugerties, 845-246-1565, 877-424-6423; www.choicehotels.com

This chain hotel is located in a residential neighborhood, but provides easy access to Interstate 87. Guest rooms come standard with wireless Internet, refrigerators and cable TV. Free coffee is available in the lobby.

65 rooms. Complimentary breakfast. Pets accepted. $61-150

WHERE TO EAT

★★CAFE TAMAYO

89 Partition St., Saugerties, 845-246-9371; www.cafetamayo.com

This friendly, bistro-style establishment features French- and Italian-influenced American fare made with local farm-fresh ingredients, including goat cheese, herbs, and various game. The confit of duck with wild rice and red onion marmalade is a specialty.

American. Dinner. Closed Monday-Wednesday. Reservations recommended. Bar. $36-85

★★NEW WORLD HOME COOKING
1411 Route 212, Saugerties, 845-246-0900; www.ricorlando.com

There's plenty of action at this bright eatery where an open kitchen and eclectic menu keep diners coming back again and again. The cajun shrimp are a local favorite, as are the pan-seared string beans.

American, International. Lunch (Saturday-Sunday), dinner. Outdoor seating. Children's menu. $16-35

★★RED ONION
1654 Route 212 at Glasco Turnpike, Saugerties, 845-679-1223;
www.redonionrestaurant.com

Many locals come for the cocktails and stay for the dependable food, ranging from traditional pub fare like fish and chips to all-American steak tartar. The cone of perfectly-crisped French fries is a good addition to any meal.

American, International. Dinner, Sunday brunch. Closed Wednesday. Reservations recommended. Outdoor seating. Bar $16-35

SCHENECTADY
See also Albany, Howes Cave, Johnstown, Saratoga Springs, Troy

Schenectady is one of the oldest cities in the nation, settled by Dutch traders in the mid-17th century. The city offers a unique blend of the old and the new, from row houses of the pre-Revolutionary War stockade era to the bustle of the modern downtown. In the early 1900s, General Electric Co. had its headquarters here. Today, the city is influenced by eclectic arts and diverse cultures thanks to the multiple ethnic communities that have settled here.

WHAT TO SEE

THE HISTORIC STOCKADE AREA
32 Washington Ave., Schenectady, 518-374-0263; www.historicstockade.com

This district is filled with privately owned houses, many dating to colonial times and marked with historic plaques. The Schenectady County Historical Society offers guided tours of their buildings, and also maintains a historical museum with a collection of Sexton and Ames paintings, a 19th-century dollhouse, and a genealogical library.

Free. Daily.

PROCTOR'S THEATRE
432 State St., Schenectady, 518-346-6204; www.proctors.org

This former vaudeville palace and movie house functions as a regional performing arts center hosting touring Broadway shows, dance, opera and plays. The space can seat up to 2,700 and houses a 1931 Wurlitzer theater organ. Prices and showtimes vary.

THE SCHENECTADY MUSEUM AND PLANETARIUM AND SCHENECTADY HERITAGE AREA

15 Nott Terrace Heights, Schenectady, 518-382-7890; www.schenectadymuseum.org

As an early headquarters for General Electric Co., Schenectady has a long history with the appliance giant, and many relics to show for it including a collection of early 20th century appliances and TVs. The museum also has exhibits and programs on art, history, science and technology, and a planetarium.

Admission: adults $6.50, seniors $5.25, children 4-12 $4, children under 4 free. Tuesday-Saturday 10 a.m.-5 p.m.

UNION COLLEGE

807 Union St., Schenectady, 518-388-6000; www.union.edu

This is the country's first campus planned by an architect, and has original buildings dating back to 1812. One of the most prestigious buildings on campus is Nott Memorial, the only 16-sided building in the Northern Hemisphere. Be sure to visit Jackson Garden that comprises eight acres of landscaped and informal plantings.

Free. Daily.

WHERE TO STAY

★★★GLEN SANDERS MANSION INN

1 Glen Ave., Scotia, 518-688-2138; www.glensandersmansion.com

The inn is a 1995 addition to the Glen Sanders Mansion restaurant, which is housed in the original historic residence. Rooms feature comfortable, elegant furnishings and make for the perfect weekend retreat. Complimentary fresh fruit, cookies and coffee are served throughout the day.

22 rooms. Restaurant. Complimentary breakfast. $61-150

★★HOLIDAY INN

100 Nott Terrace, Schenectady, 518-393-4141; www.hischenectady.com

Conveniently located within walking distance of Union College and Proctor's Theatre, this chain property is nicer than most with spacious rooms, a 24-hour fitness center and indoor pool. Request a room that does not overlook the indoor pool to avoid potential noisiness.

184 rooms. Restaurant, bar. Complimentary breakfast. Fitness center. Pool. $61-150

SHANDAKEN

See also Hunter, Kingston, Woodstock

This Catskill Mountain town carries the Iroquois name meaning "rapid waters." Shandaken is a town in the Catskills with easy access to New York City—a rare combo. It is home of the highest peak in the Catskills, Slide Mountain and is also the home of Esopus Creek, one of the finest wild trout fisheries in the East. Skiing, hiking and hunting are popular in this area of mountains and streams.

WHAT TO SEE
BELLEAYRE MOUNTAIN

Route 28, Shandaken, 845-254-5600, 800-942-6904; www.belleayre.com

Cherished wilderness since the 1880s, this ski mountain boasts steep inclines, varied terrain and a comfortable mountainside resort. There are 41 runs and a half-pipe, as well as cross-country trails.

Admission: prices vary. November-mid-April, daily.

WHERE TO STAY
★★★THE COPPERHOOD INN & SPA

70-39 Route 28, Shandaken, 845-688-2460; www.copperhood.com

This European-style oasis with elegant, inviting rooms and helpful staff overlooks the rushing waters of the Esopus Creek. Guests can take advantage of an extensive range of spa services and recreational activities or simply lounge and enjoy nature. The inn's menu includes such dishes as free-range chicken with sun-dried tomatoes and tarragon purée.

15 rooms. Restaurant, bar. Fitness center. Pool. Spa. Tennis. $251-350

SHELTER ISLAND

See also East Hampton, Greenport, Sag Harbor

Quakers, persecuted by the Puritans in New England, settled Shelter Island in Gardiner's Bay off the east end of Long Island. The island is reached by car and pedestrian ferry from Greenport, on the North Fork of Long Island, or from North Haven (Sag Harbor), in the south. There is a monument to the Quakers and a graveyard with 17th-century stones. Two museums recount the area's history: the 18th-century Havens House and the 19th-century Manhanset Chapel. Also here is the 2,200-acre Nature Conservancy's Mashomack Preserve, with miles of trails for hiking and educational programs. The island offers swimming, boating, miles of sandy shoreline, biking, hiking, tennis and golfing.

WHERE TO STAY
★★PRIDWIN BEACH HOTEL AND COTTAGES

81 Shore Road, Shelter Island, 631-749-0476, 800-273-2497; www.pridwin.com

It doesn't get much more intimate than the Pridwin. Situated along Cresent Beach, the property offers swimming, boating and kayaking as well as hiking, biking and tennis. Guest rooms are quaint and cozy with floral bedspreads and a country décor. Request a room with a water view or one of the private cottages that includes a fireplace.

40 rooms. Restaurant, bar. Complimentary breakfast. Pool. Beach. Tennis. Closed November-April. $151-250

WHERE TO EAT
★★★CHEQUIT INN

23 Grand Ave., Shelter Island, 631-749-0018; www.shelterislandinns.com

This casual Victorian inn was originally built around a maple tree that, now enormous, still shades the terrace that overlooks Dering Harbor. Try the home-style Atlantic cod fish and chips with fresh tartar sauce, a proprietary specialty. Continental. Lunch, dinner. Reservations recommended. Outdoor seating. Children's menu. Bar. $16-35

★★★RAM'S HEAD INN

108 Ram Island Drive, Shelter Island, 631-749-0811; www.shelterislandinns.com

At this inn tucked away at a far corner of Shelter Island, meals include fare like roast loin rack of lamb with garlic pommes Anna and wild salmon with wilted spinach and morels.

Continental. Dinner, brunch. Closed November-April. Reservations recommended. Outdoor seating. Children's menu. Bar. $36-85

SKANEATELES

See also Auburn, Finger Lakes, Oneida, Seneca Falls, Syracuse

Skaneateles (skany-AT-les) was once a stop on the Underground Railroad. Today, pristinely maintained Victorian homes and upscale boutiques continue to draw vacationers (like former President Bill Clinton in 1999) to this quiet resort town at the north end of Skaneateles Lake.

WHAT TO SEE
MID-LAKES NAVIGATION BOAT TRIPS

11 Jordan St., Skaneateles, 315-685-8500, 800-545-4318; www.midlakesnav.com

Choose between a 32-mile cruise along shoreline of Skaneateles Lake.

Admission: prices vary. July-August, Monday-Saturday.

SPECIAL EVENT
POLO MATCHES

Skaneateles Polo Club Grounds, 813 Andrews Road, 315-685-7373

Adjust your fancy brim and don your Sunday best. Make an afternoon at the Skaneateles Polo Club. This "gentleman's sport" is no longer that; it is an exciting pastime for the entire family.

Admission: prices vary. July-August, Sunday.

WHERE TO STAY
★THE BIRD'S NEST

1601 E. Genesee St., Skaneateles, 315-685-5641

Family owned for more than 30 years, this hotel-motel has a decidedly seventies feel, which carries into the guest rooms as well. The property includes a fishing pond and a few short hiking paths.

30 rooms. Complimentary breakfast. Pool. Pets accepted. $61-150

★★★★MIRBEAU INN & SPA

851 W. Genesee St., Skaneateles, 315-685-5006, 877-647-2328; www.mirbeau.com

This 12-acre Finger Lakes country estate, filled with ponds, gardens and woodlands, seems to have leapt off the canvases of Claude Monet. Delightful Provençal fabrics and French country furnishings make the rooms cozy and comfortable while fireplaces and soaking tubs add romance. The friendly staff is available when you need them and unobtrusive when you don't. With winsome views of the lily pond and footbridge and the fresh-from-the-garden taste of the dishes, the restaurant truly transports diners. The European-style spa is both modern and charming.

34 rooms. Restaurant, bar. Fitness center. Spa. $251-350

★★★SHERWOOD INN

26 W. Genesee St., Skaneateles, 315-685-3405, 800-374-3796;
www.thesherwoodinn.com

Beautifully furnished with an aura of refinement, this 1807 inn, a former stagecoach stop, has fantastic views of Clift Park and Skaneateles Lake. Guest rooms are tastefully decorated with wood furniture and antique pieces. Some rooms even boast canopy beds and fireplaces. Stop in at the inn's tavern to enjoy a pint on the original bar dating back to 1807. 25 rooms. Restaurant, bar. Complimentary breakfast. Business center. $151-250

WHERE TO EAT
★★★★GIVERNY

851 W. Genesee St., Skaneateles, 315-685-1927, 877-647-2328; www.mirbeau.com

Named after painter Claude Monet's French country home, this elegant dining room, under the confident direction of executive chef John Russ, delivers the best of Provençal cooking in a cozy, romantic setting. Try the four- or five-course tasting menu or dine à la carte on dishes such as butter-braised Maine lobster with squash risotto or sautéed foie gras with caramelized pear. The wine list includes selections from around the world, and around the corner, with local Finger Lakes wineries highlighted.

American, French. Breakfast, lunch, dinner. Reservations recommended. Outdoor seating. Bar. $36-85

SPA
★★★★SPA MIRBEAU

851 W. Genesee St., Skaneateles, 315-685-1927, 877-647-2328; www.mirbeau.com

Fourteen thousand square feet of tranquility await at the Spa Mirbeau, whose beautiful natural surroundings serve as the inspiration for everything from the herbal-infused steam rooms to body wraps and facials. After some pre-treatment relaxation in the resting area—complete with heated foot pools— you're ready to head to one of 18 treatment rooms. More than just a massage, the Monet's Favorite Fragrance massage blends essential oils of herbs and flowers from the Finger Lakes region to create an aromatherapy treatment that stimulates the senses. The expansive fitness center offers everything from meditation to Pilates.

SMITHTOWN

See also Huntington, Port Jefferson, Stony Brook

Smithtown includes six unincorporated hamlets and three incorporated villages and is situated near several state parks on eastern Long Island. Legend has it that the town's settler, Richard Smith, was told by Native Americans that he would be granted the rights to the amount of land that he could traverse in one day on a bull. The land he covered that day in 1665 is said to be the approximate location of Smithtown today.

WHERE TO STAY
★★★MARRIOTT ISLANDIA LONG ISLAND

3635 Express Drive, Islandia, 631-232-3000, 800-228-9290; www.marriott.com

This convenient hotel is located just off the Long Island Expressway near Islip McArthur Airport. Guests will find a wide range of comforts including cable TV, coffee and tea makers and luxurious bedding with down comforters and pillows, and plush cotton linens. Bistro Five-Eight, the hotel's elegant restaurant, offers American fare.

278 rooms. Restaurant, bar. Business center. Fitness center. Pool. $61-150

★★★SHERATON LONG ISLAND HOTEL
110 Motor Parkway, Hauppauge, 631-231-1100, 800-325-3535;
www.sheraton.com/longisland
Comfortable guest rooms, contemporary-styled public spaces and amenities like an indoor pool and fitness center attract both business and leisure travelers to this comfortable hotel. After visiting nearby beaches, relax at the Piano Bar for a cool cocktail.

209 rooms. Restaurant, bar. Business center. Fitness center. Pool. $151-250

SOUTHAMPTON
See also Bridgehampton, East Hampton, Riverhead, Sag Harbor
Southampton is the most formal of the fabled Hamptons, attracting the high society who summer here in their vast mansions overlooking Lake Agawam and the Atlantic dunes. The village center boasts terrific shopping in the form of Saks Fifth Avenue, Ralph Lauren and more. And the town's Parrish Art Museum is a terrific spot to browse the ever-changing collections.

WHAT TO SEE
CONSCIENCE POINT NATIONAL WILDLIFE REFUGE
North Sea Road, Southampton, 631-286-0485; www.fws.gov
With 60 acres, this refuge is known for its maritime grasslands. A host of birds and fowl call this area home in the colder months, and a different variety migrate here in the warmer season. The refuge opened in 1971 and over the years has played host to many guests, both feathered and not.
Admission: prices vary. Hours vary.

OLD HALSEY HOUSE
249 S. Main St., Southampton, 631-283-2494
This 1648 structure is the oldest English frame house in the state. It acted as the headquarters for English general William Erskine during the American Revolution. Today, the house is a museum exhibiting furniture from the 17th and 18th centuries.
Admission: $3. Mid-July-mid-September, Tuesday-Sunday 11 a.m.-5 p.m.

PARRISH ART MUSEUM
25 Jobs Lane, Southampton, 631-283-2118; www.parrishart.org
One of the top museums on eastern Long Island, the Parrish is most well known for its collection of 19th- and 20th-century American paintings and prints by local artists. There is also a sizeable display of Japanese woodblock prints. The museum was built in 1898 as a repository for Samuel Longstreth Parrish's Italian Renaissance art collection. The museum often hosts lectures, workshops and children's programs.
Admission: adults $7, seniors and students $5, children under 18 free. June-mid-September, Monday-Saturday 11 a.m.-5 p.m., Sunday 1-5 p.m.;

Mid-September-May, Monday, Thursday-Saturday 11 a.m.-5 p.m., Sunday 1-5 p.m.

SHINNECOCK INDIAN OUTPOST

Old Montauk Highway, Southampton, 631-283-8047; www.shinnecocktradingpost.com

This funky shop sells Native American crafts, clothes and glassware. There's also an onsite moccasin store that proclaims itself the home of America's original shoe. If you're hungry, the deli is a good bet for a quick morning coffee and a bagel. June-August, daily 6:30 a.m.-7 p.m.; September-May, daily 6:30 a.m.-6 p.m.

SOUTHAMPTON HISTORICAL MUSEUM

17 Meeting House Lane, Southampton, 631-283-2494;
www.southamptonhistoricalmuseum.org

This mansion, built in 1843, depicts Southampton's colorful history. It has original furnishings, photos and quilts, as well as Montauk and Shinnecock Indian artifacts on display. The museum's grounds include a one-room schoolhouse, drugstore, paint shop, blacksmith shop and carpentry store. Admission: adults $4, children under 17 free. Tuesday-Saturday 11 a.m.-5 p.m., Sunday 1-5 p.m.

WHERE TO STAY
★★SOUTHAMPTON INN

91 Hill St., Southampton, 631-283-6500, 800-732-6500; www.southamptoninn.com

Situated on five acres of rolling lawns, this Tudor-style inn offers rooms with classic country furnishings, new Tempur-Pedic mattresses and toiletries by Gilchrist and Soames. The activity options are endless with biking, kayaking, fishing, tennis and a pool only a few steps away.

90 rooms. Restaurant, bar. Business center. Pool. Pets accepted. Tennis. $151-250

WHERE TO EAT
★★COAST GRILL

1109 Noyack Road, Southampton, 631-283-2277;
www.therestaurantsweb.com/thecoastgrill.html

This cute local eatery overlooks Wooley Pond and draws quite a crowd during peak season. The kitschy décor includes pink walls and hanging painted fish. The food is always good and the portions are generous. The signature clam chowder is a must.

American, seafood. Dinner. Closed Wednesday. Bar. $16-35

★GOLDEN PEAR

99 Main St., Southampton, 631-283-8900; www.goldenpearcafe.com

If you're looking for the local spot to scarf down a bowl of chili or laze over a hot cup of coffee, the Golden Pear is it. Choose a spot at the counter to get in on any Hampton gossip. The restaurant is small so don't be surprised if you have to wait for a table during summer.

American. Breakfast, lunch. $16-35

★★JOHN DUCK JR.

15 Prospect St., Southampton, 631-283-0311

Located in a converted farmhouse, this restaurant has been a family affair for more than a century. The country ambiance is in full swing throughout the five separate dining rooms including a glassed-in porch. Sunday brunch here is a treat.

American, German. Lunch, dinner, Sunday brunch. Closed Monday. Children's menu. Bar. $16-35

★★LE CHEF

75 Jobs Lane, Southampton, 631-283-8581; www.lechefbistro.com

Le Chef brings a touch of France to the east end of Long Island. The baby rack of lamb with mint and pan-roasted potatoes is particularly good, as is the nut-crusted local flounder. Save room for dessert; the signature French vanilla crepes are (not surprisingly) delicious.

French. Lunch, dinner, brunch. Bar. $16-35

★★LOBSTER INN

162 Inlet Road, Southampton, 631-283-1525

Locals come more for the fresh-off-the-boat seafood than the rustic interior. Nevertheless, it's hard to find a fresher lobster in town. In summer, the outdoor tables are a nice spot to while away the afternoon.

American, seafood. Lunch, dinner. Outdoor seating. Children's menu. Bar. $16-35

★★MIRKO'S

Water Mill Square, Water Mill, 631-726-4444; www.mirkos.com

Professionally run by a husband-and-wife team, this small American bistro is off the beaten path, and all the more charming because of it (especially during the summer months when Main Street can feel more like Manhattan). Dine alfresco if a table is available.

American. Dinner. Reservations recommended. Outdoor seating. Bar. $36-85

SOUTHOLD

See also Greenport, Riverhead

This community on Long Island is close to more than a dozen vineyards and countless museums and cultural activities. It is located on Long Island Sound, just across from Connecticut.

WHAT TO SEE
GREENPORT POTTERY

64725 Main Road, Southold, 631-477-1687; www.greenportpottery.com

For a great selection of homemade pottery, this is the place to go on the North Fork. The owner creates beautiful lamps, vases, mugs, dishes, decorative plates and other items in his shop. You can custom order items, and he will ship just about anywhere. In addition to the fine craftsmanship, the pottery is extremely reasonably priced—just a fraction of what comparable shops in the tonier Hamptons would charge.

Free. Wednesday-Monday 10 a.m.-5 p.m.

HORTON POINT LIGHTHOUSE AND NAUTICAL MUSEUM

Lighthouse Park, 54325 Main Road, Southold, 631-765-5500

Built in 1847, this lighthouse resembles a church and includes a lighthouse keeper's residence. The onsite museum showcases maps, sea bounty, paintings and more.

Admission: $2. June-mid-October, Saturday-Sunday 11:30 a.m.-4 p.m.

THE OLD HOUSE

Cases Lane and Route 25, Cutchogue, 631-734-7122;
www.cutchoguenewsuffolkhistory.org

This 1649 house is an example of early English architecture and contains well-preserved furnishings from the 17th and 18th centuries. While you're here, stop by the Wickham Farmhouse and the Old Schoolhouse Museum for more antique displays.

Free. July-August, Saturday-Monday 1-4 p.m.

SOUTHOLD INDIAN MUSEUM

1080 Bayview Road, Southold, 631-765-5577; www.southoldindianmuseum.org

This museum celebrates Long Island's Native American history and features displays of artifacts such as weapons, tools and pottery, as well as other items used by the Long Island Algonquins.

Admission: $1. July-August, Saturday-Sunday 1:30-4:30 p.m.; September-June, Sunday 1:30-4:30 p.m.

WHERE TO EAT

★★SEAFOOD BARGE

62980 Main Road, Southold, 631-765-3010; www.seafoodbarge.com

Don't let the unassuming exterior food you. The restaurant has beautiful waterfront views thanks to its location on the Port of Egypt marina. Enjoy traditional seafood favorites like New England clam chowder alongside more imaginative dishes such as pan-seared Ahi tuna with peas, asparagus and cipollini onions.

Seafood. Lunch, dinner. Bar. $16-35

SPRING VALLEY

See also Tarrytown

This quaint village is about 22 miles due north of New York City and only five miles from the New Jersey border. It is a nice retreat from the bustle of Manhattan, especially in warm months.

WHAT TO SEE

HISTORICAL SOCIETY OF ROCKLAND COUNTY

20 Zukor Road, New City, 845-634-9629; www.rocklandhistory.org/home.php

This museum of county history is located in the Jacob Blauvelt House, a circa 1832 Dutch farmhouse and barn. The collection showcases relics from the various culture that have inhabited Rockland County, from the Native Americans through the 20th century.

Free. Tuesday-Sunday 1-5 p.m.

WHERE TO STAY

★FAIRFIELD INN SPRING VALLEY NANUET

100 Spring Valley Marketplace, Spring Valley, 845-426-2000, 800-228-2800;
www.marriott.com

This standard hotel chain is a good option for those looking for an affordable room in the vicinity of New York City. Guest rooms are basic, but spacious and all have large windows. Complimentary breakfast and an outdoor pool are added bonuses.

104 rooms. Complimentary breakfast. Fitness center. Pool. $61-150

★★HOLIDAY INN

3 Executive Blvd., Suffern, 845-357-4800; www.holiday-inn.com

Appealing to both business and leisure travelers, this hotel offers wireless Internet access, in-room work stations and convenient access to the highway. It's a good place for kids too with free meals at the onsite restaurant and an indoor pool.

228 rooms. Restaurant, bar. Business center. Fitness center. Pool. $61-150

★★★HILTON PEARL RIVER

500 Veterans Memorial Drive, Pearl River, 845-735-9001; www.hilton.com

Only 20 miles from Manhattan, the Hilton Pearl River boasts a relaxed, country park-like setting on 17 verdant acres overlooking the adjacent links of the Blue Hill golf course. Guest rooms are spacious and feature French country-styled décor along with high-thread-count sheets and toiletries from Crabtree & Evelyn. The hotel's restaurant, La Maisonette, serves contemporary American cooking with a French twist.

150 rooms. Restaurant, bar. Business center. Fitness center. Pool. Pets accepted. $151-250

STAMFORD

See also Howes Cave, Oneonta

Stamford, located along the west branch of the Delaware River, has a large historic district dating from the Victorian era including numerous former inns. The nearby hamlet of Hobart is chock full of antique bookstores. And close-at-hand Andes bustles with terrific galleries, shops and restaurants.

WHAT TO SEE

LANSING MANOR

Highways 30 and 23, North Blenheim, 607-588-6061, 800-724-0309

This 19th-century manor house depicts life of an Anglo-Dutch household in the mid-1800s. There are period furnishings and antiques throughout the house. The tours, offered on the half hour, are worth waiting for.

Free. June-mid-October, Wednesday-Monday 10 a.m.-5 p.m.

MINE KILL STATE PARK

161 Mine Kill State Park, North Blenheim, 518-827-6111; www.nysparks.state.ny.us

This state park is known for its reservoir fishing, where you're likely to catch bass, trout or walleye. Picnicking, hiking and swimming are other popular past times.

Free. Daily sunrise-sunset.

ZADOCK PRATT MUSEUM

1828 Homestead, Prattsville, 518-299-3395; www.prattmuseum.com

Period furnishings and memorabilia pack this former summer residence of industrial magnate Zadock Pratt. There is also an educational center with rotating exhibits exploring the history of the region.

Free. June-August, Thursday-Sunday 1-4 p.m.

STONY BROOK

See also Port Jefferson, Smithtown

Originally part of the Three Village area first settled by Boston colonists in the 17th-century, Stony Brook became an important center for the shipbuilding industry on Long Island Sound in the 1800s.

WHAT TO SEE
THE MUSEUMS AT STONY BROOK

1200 N. Country Road, Stony Brook, 631-751-0066; www.longislandmuseum.org

This complex comprises three museums. The Melville Carriage House exhibits 90 buggies from a collection of horse-drawn carriages; the Art Museum features changing exhibits of American art; and the Blackwell History Museum has rotating exhibits on many historical themes, as well as displays of period rooms and antique decoys.

Admission: adults $9, seniors $7, children 6-17 $4, children under 6 free. Thursday-Saturday 10 a.m.-5 p.m., Sunday noon-5 p.m.

STALLER CENTER FOR THE ARTS

Nicholas Road and Route 347, Stony Brook, 631-632-7235; www.staller.sunysb.edu

On the SUNY campus, this venue houses a 1,049-seat main theater, three experimental theaters, an art gallery, a 400-seat recital hall and an electronic music studio. The Summer International Theater Festival is also hosted here. Prices and showtimes vary.

WHERE TO STAY
★★★THREE VILLAGE INN

150 Main St., Stony Brook, 631-751-0555, 888-384-4438; www.threevillageinn.com

This harborside inn has elegant rooms overlooking the water and a quaint small town vibe. Enjoy village shopping and museums, or simply relax with a stroll on the beach. Stony Brook University is nearby. 26 rooms. Restaurant, bar. $151-250

WHERE TO EAT
★★★MIRABELLE

150 Main St., Stony Brook, 631-584-5999; www.restaurantmirabelle.com

With a seasoned French chef and former food writer as proprietors, this restaurant rivals many in the city. In its new location at the historic Three Village Inn, Mirabelle heralds refurbished dining rooms and a continued classic appeal. Menu items are a twist on classical French fare, accented with the freshest herbs; and the wine list highlights local vintners. Standout dishes on the menu include the shredded braised rabbit leg with kimchee and the seared organic salmon with a ragout of flageolet beans and pearl onions.

French. Lunch (Tuesday-Friday), dinner, Sunday brunch. Closed Monday. Reservations recommended. $85 and up

SYRACUSE

See also Auburn, Camillus, Cazenovia, Finger Lakes, Oneida, Skaneateles

Syracuse began as a trading post at the mouth of Onondaga Creek. Salt was produced from wells here from 1796 to 1900. Industry began in 1793, when Thomas Ward began making wooden plows. Shortly after 1800, a blast furnace was built that produced iron utensils, and during the War of 1812, cast ammunition for the Army. When the Erie Canal reached town in the late 1820s, Syracuse's industrial future was assured. Today the city has many large and varied industries.

WHAT TO SEE

BEAVER LAKE NATURE CENTER

8477 E. Mud Lake Road, Baldwinsville, 315-638-2519

This 600-acre nature preserve with 10 miles of trails and boardwalks also has a 200-acre lake that serves as a rest stop for migrating ducks and geese and a visitor center. In the winter, the preserve is popular with cross-country skiers and snowshoers. Other programs include maple sugaring and guided canoe tours.

Daily7:30 a.m.-sunset.

ERIE CANAL MUSEUM

318 Erie Blvd. E., Syracuse, 315-471-0593; www.eriecanalmuseum.org

Indoor and outdoor exhibits detail the construction and operation of the Erie Canal, including a 65-foot reconstructed canal boat from which exhibits are seen. A re-created general store and post office are other interesting stops within the museum.

Free. Tuesday-Saturday 10 a.m.-5 p.m., Sunday 10 a.m.-3 p.m.

EVERSON MUSEUM OF ART

401 Harrison St., Syracuse, 315-474-6064; www.everson.org

The first I.M. Pei-designed museum houses a permanent collection of American art and a collection of American ceramics, with changing exhibits. Look for the works of such familiar masters as Jackson Pollock and Andrew Wyeth. It is also the home of the Syracuse China Center for the Study of American Ceramics.

Admission: $5. Tuesday-Friday, Sunday noon-5 p.m., Saturday 10 a.m.-5 p.m.

LANDMARK THEATRE

362 S. Salina St., Syracuse, 315-475-7980; www.landmarktheatre.org

This historic theater was built in 1928 as Loew's State Theatre in the era of vaudeville movie houses. The interior architecture is filled with carvings, chandeliers and ornate gold decorations. Concerts, plays, dance recitals and classic movies are hosted there frequently. Check the Web site for specific dates and showtimes.

Prices and showtimes vary.

ONONDAGA HISTORICAL ASSOCIATION MUSEUM

321 Montgomery St., Syracuse, 315-428-1864; www.cnyhistory.org

Examining the history of Syracuse and the Onondaga County region is the aim here with changing and permanent exhibits ranging from architecture to transportation to cultural diversity. Those with an interest in beer will enjoy the small collection of artifacts depicting the history of brewing beer in Syracuse.

Admission: $7. Wednesday-Friday 10 a.m.-4 p.m., Saturday-Sunday 11 a.m.-4 p.m.

ROSAMOND GIFFORD ZOO AT BURNET PARK

1 Conservation Place, Syracuse, 315-435-8511; www.rosamondgiffordzoo.org

This small zoo traces the origin of life from 600 million years ago, with exhibits on animals' unique adaptations and animal/human interaction. Such exotic animals as the red panda, the white-spotted bamboo shark and the Madagascar hissing cockroach all call Rosamond home.

Admission: adults $6.50, seniors and students $4.50, children 3-15 $4, children under 3 free. Daily 10 a.m.-4:30 p.m.

ST. MARIE AMONG THE IROQUOIS

Syracuse, 315-453-6767; www.onondagacountyparks.com

St. Marie Among the Iroquois is a re-creation of a 17th-century French mission that once occupied a place on the shores of Onondaga Lake. The onsite museum explores the history of the Iroquois and their interaction with the French. Blacksmithing, cooking, carpentry and gardening demonstrations take place as well.

Admission: adults $3, seniors $2.50, children 6-17 $2, children under 6 free. May-mid-October, Tuesday-Friday 9:30 a.m.-2:30 p.m., Saturday-Sunday noon-5 p.m.

SYRACUSE UNIVERSITY

University Ave. at University Place, Syracuse, 315-443-1870; www.syr.edu

Founded in 1870, this private research university is most noted for the Maxwell School of Citizenship and Public Affairs, Newhouse School of Public Communications, College of Engineering and 50,000-seat Carrier Dome where football, basketball and lacrosse all draw students and area locals. Free. Daily.

SPECIAL EVENTS

BALLOON FEST

Jamesville Beach Park, Apulia Road, Jamesville, 315-435-5252; www.syracuseballoonfest.com

Occurring the second weekend in June, this massive festival often includes more than 40 hot-air balloons, as well as live music, food and arts and crafts. Mid-June.

NEW YORK STATE FAIR

State Fairgrounds, 581 State Fair Blvd., Syracuse, 315-487-7711; www.nysfair.org

Over 375 acres of rides, food, entertainment and midway games appear here every summer, and swarms of people come out to enjoy them. Over 12 days in late August to early September, the fairgrounds host everything from butter-sculpture competitions to lumberjack races. Late August.

WHERE TO STAY

★★COURTYARD BY MARRIOTT

6415 Yorktown Circle, East Syracuse, 315-432-0300; www.marriott.com

After a complete renovation of the property, this chain hotel now provides guest rooms with luxury bedding, complimentary Internet access, new furniture and sizeable work stations for business travelers. The hotel is only minutes from Syracuse University.

149 rooms. Restaurant. Business center. $61-150

★★★DOUBLETREE HOTEL SYRACUSE

6301 Highway 298, Syracuse, 315-432-0200; www.doubletree.com

This comfortable hotel caters to the business travelers who visit the corporate park in which it is located and the area's surrounding businesses. Amenities include signature Sweet Dreams beds, MP3 docking stations and Herman Miller work chairs.

250 rooms. Restaurant, bar. Business center. Fitness center. Pool. $61-150

★★EMBASSY SUITES

6646 Old Collamer Road, Syracuse, 315-446-3200, 800-362-2779;
www.embassy-suites.com

For a little extra room with an affordable price tag, this is a good option. All guest rooms include a private bedroom and separate living space with two flat-screen TVs, a refrigerator, microwave and dining table.

215 rooms. Restaurant, bar. Complimentary breakfast. Business center. Fitness center. Pool. $61-150

★★★GENESEE GRANDE HOTEL

1060 E. Genesee St., Syracuse, 315-476-4212, 800-365-4663;
www.geneseegrande.com

Befitting its name, the Genesee Grande is a luxurious hotel in the University Hill section of downtown Syracuse. Rooms have soft, comfortable beds, flat-screen TVs and Brazilian granite baths. Gracious service complements the grand surroundings.

159 rooms. Restaurant, bar. Complimentary breakfast. Fitness center. $61-150

★★HOLIDAY INN

6555 Old Collamer Road S., East Syracuse, 315-437-2761, 800-465-4329
www.holiday-inn.com

Boasting brand new mattresses in every guest room, this chain hotel is conveniently located near Syracuse University and the Carrier Dome, as well as many corporate headquarters. The indoor pool is a nice amenity for kids.

203 rooms. Restaurant, bar. Complimentary breakfast. Fitness center. Pool. $61-150

★★★THE MARX HOTEL AND CONFERENCE CENTER

701 E. Genesee St., Syracuse, 315-479-7000, 877-843-6279; www.marxsyracuse.com

Located in downtown Syracuse, this chic, contemporary hotel has rooms featuring desks with ergonomic seating and high-speed Internet access. There's also a fully equipped fitness center. Those on a working vacation can order room service for breakfast, lunch or dinner and the complimentary van service transports sightseers.

279 rooms. Restaurant, bar. Business center. Fitness center. Spa. Pets accepted. $61-150

★★★SHERATON UNIVERSITY HOTEL AND CONFERENCE CENTER

801 University Ave., Syracuse, 315-475-3000, 800-395-2105;
www.sheratonsyracuse.com

Bordering Syracuse University and the surrounding hospitals, this hotel is within walking distance of downtown civic centers, restaurants, entertainment arenas and other attractions. Service is friendly, and rooms have been updated with plush beds. The 24-hour business center is ideal for business travelers in a last minute scramble.

236 rooms. Restaurant, bar. Business center. Fitness center. Pool. $151-250

WHERE TO EAT
★BROOKLYN PICKLE

2222 Burnet Ave., Syracuse, 315-463-1851

If you want to relive your college days, when enormous slapdash sandwiches constituted a high-end meal, stop for a sub at Brooklyn Pickle. The restaurant is clean and the young staff is friendly. Your best bet is to order the sub for which the restaurant was named.

Deli. Lunch, dinner. Closed Sunday. Outdoor seating. $15 and under.

★★COLEMAN'S

100 S. Lowell Ave., Syracuse, 315-476-1933; www.colemansirishpub.com

March 17th is a daily celebration at this Tipperary Hill restaurant. A tribute to everything Irish in Syracuse, the menu is packed with winning classics like corned beef and cabbage and juicy Reuben sandwiches. Weekend evening diners are treated to live Irish music.

Irish. Lunch, dinner. Outdoor seating. Children's menu. Bar. $15 and under.

★★GLEN LOCH MILL

4626 North St., Jamesville, 315-469-6969; www.glenloch.net

Housed in a mill dating back to 1827, the restaurant has a rustic appeal. The fresh seafood is the main attraction with dishes like coconut-crusted tilapia and deep-fried haddock.

Seafood, steak. Dinner, Sunday brunch. Closed Monday. Outdoor seating. Children's menu. Bar. $16-36

★★★PASCALE

204 W. Fayette St., Syracuse, 315-471-3040; www.pascalerestaurant.com

Centrally located in Armory Square, a revitalized sector of downtown Syracuse, this restaurant features eclectic international food served in a contemporary setting. The menu changes seasonally, but the mixed grill is a top option year-round. The wines-by-the-glass list is extensive and affordable. American. Dinner. Closed Sunday. Outdoor seating. Children's menu. Bar. $16-35

TARRYTOWN

See also Spring Valley, White Plains, Yonkers

The village of Tarrytown and the neighboring villages of Irvington and Sleepy Hollow were settled by the Dutch during the mid-1600s. The name Tarrytown was taken from the Dutch word "tarwe," meaning wheat. On September 23, 1780, the British spy Major John Andre was captured while carrying the detailed plans for West Point given to him by Benedict Arnold. The village and the area were made famous by the writings of Washington Irving, particularly The Legend of Sleepy Hollow, from which this region takes its name.

WHAT TO SEE
KYKUIT, THE ROCKEFELLER ESTATE

Highway 9 N. and N. Broadway, Sleepy Hollow, 914-631-3992; www.hudsonvalley.org

This six-story stone mansion was home to three generations of the Rockefeller family. Sitting atop a hill, the name means "lookout" in Dutch and befittingly affords sweeping views of the Hudson River. Today, the house is amass with antiques and period furnishings. The property also includes extensive gardens featuring an important collection of 20th-century sculpture acquired by Governor Nelson A. Rockefeller, including works by Alexander Calder, Constantin Brancusi and Pablo Picasso. Scheduled tours running 2 1/2 hours depart approximately every 15 minutes from Philipsburg Manor. Children under five are not permitted.

Admission: adults $23, seniors and children 5-18 $21. May-October, Wednesday-Monday 9 a.m.-5 p.m.

LYNDHURST

635 S. Broadway, Tarrytown, 914-631-4481; www.lyndhurst.org

Considered one of the best examples of the Gothic Revival style in the United States, this marble mansion built in 1838 for William Paulding, mayor of New York City, sits on 67 landscaped acres overlooking the Hudson River. The interior includes exquisite stain-glass windows, soaring arched ceilings and intricate period furniture like canopy beds and writing desks.

Admission: adults $12, seniors $11, children 6-16 $5, children under 6 free. Mid-April-October, Tuesday-Sunday 10 a.m.-5 p.m.; November-mid-April, Saturday-Sunday 10 a.m.-4 p.m.

MUSIC HALL THEATER

13 Main St., Tarrytown, 914-631-3390; www.tarrytownmusichall.org

One of the oldest remaining theaters in the county, this 1885 structure now serves as a center for the arts. Big-name performers like Wynton Marsalis and Tony Bennet have performed here, and it also has hosted an impressive share of movie premieres.

Prices and showtimes vary.

OLD DUTCH CHURCH OF SLEEPY HOLLOW

42 N. Broadway, Tarrytown, 914-631-1123; www.olddutchburyingground.org

This 1685 church structure of Dutch origins was built on what was the Manor of Frederick Philipse and is widely considered the oldest church in New York State. The stone and wood structure has been restored and showcases a replica of the original pulpit inside. Sleepy Hollow Cemetery surrounds the church and free tours are given of both sites on Sunday at 2 p.m.

Free. June-August, Monday, Wednesday-Thursday 1-4 p.m., Saturday-Sunday 2-4 p.m.; September-October, Saturday-Sunday 2-4 p.m.

PHILIPSBURG MANOR

381 N. Broadway, Sleepy Hollow, 914-631-3992; www.hudsonvalley.org

Head back in time with a visit to this colonial farm and trading site from the mid-1700s. Tour the 300-year-old manor house and a restored operating gristmill. A highlight is the exhibit on slavery in the colonial north. There is also a wooden millpond bridge across the Pocantico River.

Admission: adults $12, seniors $10, children 5-17 $6, children under 5 free. April-October, Wednesday-Monday 10 a.m.-6 p.m.; November-December, Saturday-Sunday 10 a.m.-4 p.m.

SLEEPY HOLLOW CEMETERY

540 N. Broadway, Sleepy Hollow, 914-631-0081; www.sleepyhollowcemetery.org

Surrounding the Old Dutch Church, the burial grounds contain graves of Washington Irving, Andrew Carnegie and William Rockefeller among others. Legend has it that Washington Irving used this cemetery to gain inspiration for character names for his novel.

Monday-Friday 8 a.m.-4:30 p.m., Saturday-Sunday 8:30 a.m.-4:30 p.m.

SUNNYSIDE

W. Sunnyside Lane, Tarrytown, 914-631-8200; www.hudsonvalley.org

Washington Irving's Hudson River estate contains much of his furnishings, personal property and library. A guide in traditional period dress will lead you through the 1830s residence, explaining Irving's eclectic architectural decisions in designing Sunnyside and its grounds.

Admission: adults $12, seniors $10, children 5-17 $6, children under 5 free. April-October, Wednesday-Monday 11 a.m.-6 p.m.; November-December, Saturday-Sunday 10 a.m.-4 p.m.

VAN CORTLANDT MANOR

500 S. Riverside Ave., Croton on Hudson, 914-631-8200; www.hudsonvalley.org

Explore this post-Revolutionary War estate of the prominent Van Cortlandt family. A highlight is the 18th-century tavern onsite. Frequent demonstrations of open-hearth cooking, brickmaking and weaving are held in the nearby tenant house.

Admission: adults $12, seniors $10, children 5-17 $6, children under 5 free. June-August, Thursday-Sunday 11 a.m.-6 p.m.; November-December, Saturday-Sunday 10 a.m.-4 p.m.

WHERE TO STAY
★★★CASTLE ON THE HUDSON
400 Benedict Ave., Tarrytown, 914-631-1980, 800-616-4487;
www.castleattarrytown.com

Built between 1897 and 1910, this hotel has panoramic views of the Hudson River and the historic Hudson Valley. The rooms and suites are romantically furnished with four-poster or canopied beds. The grounds are meticulously maintained and feature tennis courts and a pool. Equus restaurant is a destination in its own right, and its three rooms suit a variety of moods. The Tapestry and Oak rooms resemble a European castle with stone fireplaces and beamed ceilings while the conservatory style of the Garden Room has scenic river views.

31 rooms. Restaurant, bar. Fitness center. Pool. Spa. Tennis. $251-350

★★COURTYARD BY MARRIOTT
475 White Plains Road, Tarrytown, 914-631-1122, 800-589-8720; www.courtyard.com

The best thing about this chain hotel is the easy access it provides to many of the surrounding tourist attractions like Kykuit and the Sunnyside Estate. Rooms are clean and basic, but include high-speed Internet and ergonomically designed work spaces.

139 rooms. Restaurant, bar. Business center. Fitness center. Pool. $151-250

★★★DOUBLETREE HOTEL TARRYTOWN
455 S. Broadway, Tarrytown, 914-631-5700; www.doubletree.com

This hotel features comfortable rooms with complimentary wireless Internet access and flat-screen TVs. The public area is impressive with Adirondack-styled beamed ceilings and detailed stonework. The newly renovated fitness center is an added perk.

247 rooms. Restaurant, bar. Business center. Fitness center. Pool. Tennis. $251-350

★★★TARRYTOWN HOUSE ESTATE AND CONFERENCE CENTER
49 E. Sunnyside Lane, Tarrytown, 914-591-8200, 800-553-8118;
www.tarrytownhouseestate.com

Located only 24 miles from Manhattan, this lovely estate was built in the late 1800s and has views overlooking the Hudson River Valley. The comfortable rooms mix country touches with a modern sensibility. Dine in the hotel's Sleepy Hollow Pub with its billiards table, fireplace and numerous wines-by-the-glass.

212 rooms. Restaurant. Complimentary breakfast. Business center. Fitness center. Pool. Tennis. $151-250

WHERE TO EAT
★★★★BLUE HILL AT STONE BARNS
630 Bedford Road, Pocantico Hills, 914-366-9600; www.bluehillstonebarns.com

An extension of Blue Hill restaurant in Manhattan set in the Pocantico Hills, Blue Hill at Stone Barns is not only a restaurant but also a working farm and educational center dedicated to sustainable food production. The dining room is a former dairy bar that has been converted into a lofty, modern space with vaulted ceilings, dark wood accents and earthy tones. Diners can choose three-, four- or five-course meals from a variety of dishes such as pancetta wrapped trout or lamb with local rapini, chickpeas and chorizo. Desserts are freshly made and hard to resist, like the chocolate torte with salted peanuts, caramel, and coffee ice cream.

American. Dinner, Sunday lunch. Closed Monday-Tuesday. Reservations recommended. Bar. $85 and up.

★★CARAVELA

53 N. Broadway, Tarrytown, 914-631-1863; www.caravelarestaurant.com

The paella is the thing to order at this intimate Brazilian restaurant with a friendly staff and local appeal. It's also a smart idea to bring friends along since servings of this aromatic dish, packed with everything from sausage to chicken to clams, is generous.

Brazilian, Portuguese. Lunch, dinner. Reservations recommended. Outdoor seating. Bar. $16-35

★★★EQUUS

400 Benedict Ave., Tarrytown, 914-631-3646; www.castleattarrytown.com

Choose from three charming dining rooms at this restaurant within the Castle on the Hudson. The menu includes standouts such as bacon-wrapped chicken roulade with sweet corn pudding and pistachio-crusted tuna with grape tomatoes and arugula.

French, American. Breakfast, lunch, dinner, brunch. Jacket required. Bar. $36-85

★★SANTA FE

5 Main St., Tarrytown, 914-332-4452; www.santaferestaurant.com

A favorite with locals, this bright Southwestern spot offers good food, a friendly waitstaff and more than 30 premium tequilas from which to choose. Be sure to specify if you aren't a fan of hot and spicy.

Mexican, Southwestern. Lunch, dinner. Bar. $16-35

THOUSAND ISLANDS

See also Alexandria Bay, Clayton, Ogdensburg, Sackets Harbor

This group of more than 1,800 islands on the eastern U.S.-Canadian border, at the head of the St. Lawrence River, extends 52 miles downstream from the end of Lake Ontario. Slightly more than half of the islands are in Canada. Some of them are five miles wide and extend more than 20 miles in length. These rocky slivers of land are noted for their scenery and numerous parks, including St. Lawrence Islands National Park. The Thousand Islands Bridge and Highway (seven miles long) between New York and Ontario mainlands crosses several of the isles and channels. Many of the Islands were settled during the early 1900s by American millionaires, whose opulent summer residences and private clubs made the area renowned throughout the world. The Seaway Trail, a 454-mile national scenic byway, runs through the Thousand Islands region along the southeastern shore of Lake Ontario and beside the St. Lawrence area.

Uncluttered villages, boat tours, museums, walks, water sports and abundant freshwater fishing make the Thousand Islands a popular vacation center.

TICONDEROGA

See also Crown Point, Lake George

An Iroquois word meaning "land of many waters," this resort area lies on the ancient portage route between Lake George and Lake Champlain. For almost 200 years, it was the site of various battles involving American Indians, French, British, Canadians, Yankees and New Yorkers.

WHAT TO SEE
FORT TICONDEROGA

Route 74, Ticonderoga, 518-585-2821; www.fort-ticonderoga.org

This fort was built in 1755 by the Quebecois, who called it Carillon, and was successfully defended by the Marquis de Montcalm against a more numerous British force in 1758. It was captured by the British in 1759, and by Ethan Allen and the Green Mountain Boys in 1775 (known as the first victory of the Revolutionary War). The stone fort was restored in 1909. The largest collection of cannons in North America is assembled on the grounds, and the museum houses weapons, paintings and articles about the daily lives of the soldiers garrisoned here during the Seven Year and Revolutionary wars. There are costumed guides that give tours and fire cannons daily.

Admission: adults $15, seniors $13.50, children 7-12 $7, children under 7 free. Mid-May-mid-October, daily 9:30 a.m.-5 p.m.

HANCOCK HOUSE

6 Moses Circle, Ticonderoga, 518-585-7868; www.thehancockhouse.org

The home of the Ticonderoga Historical Society is a replica of the house built for John Hancock on Beacon Street in Boston. It is maintained as a museum and research library. The rooms display various period furnishings as well as exhibits presenting social and civil history from the 1700s through the present.

Free. Wednesday-Sunday 10 a.m.-4 p.m.

HERITAGE MUSEUM

Montcalm Street and Tower Avenue, Ticonderoga, 518-585-2696;
www.ticonderogaheritagemuseum.org

Learn about the early days of Ticonderoga's civilian and industrial history at this old paper company-cum-museum. There is an appealing children's workshop onsite.

Free. June, September-mid-October Saturday-Sunday 10 a.m.-4 p.m.; July-August, daily 10 a.m.-4 p.m.

WHERE TO STAY
★CIRCLE COURT

6 Montcalm St., Ticonderoga, 518-585-7660; www.circlecourtmotel.com

This "tourist home" was first established in 1918 in response to the growing automobile travel trend. Today, the small motel offers standard rooms (with tired and outdated furnishings) and a friendly staff. Lake George is only a short distance away.

16 rooms. Pets accepted. $61-150

WHERE TO EAT
★CARILLON RESTAURANT
872 Route 9N, Ticonderoga, 518-585-7657; www.carillonrestaurant.com

Carillon may not look like much from the outside, but inside, the staff is friendly and the food is hearty and good. Surf and turf is the way to go, unless you're a sucker for baby back ribs, which are particularly tasty here.
American. Dinner. Closed Wednesday. $15 and under.

TUPPER LAKE
(See also Lake Placid, Saranac Lake)

In the heart of the Adirondack resort country and surrounded by lakes, rivers and mountains, Tupper Lake offers hunting, fishing, boating, mountain climbing, skiing, camping, snowmobiling, golf, tennis and mountain biking amid magnificent scenery. Head to the Junction section of town to explore the buildings of Tupper Lake's early days, including the Grand Union Hotel.

WHAT TO SEE
HISTORIC BETH JOSEPH SYNAGOGUE
Miller and Lake St., Tupper Lake, 518-359-7229; www.northcountryfolklore.org

This restored version of the area's first synagogue is itself based on the Eastern European synagogues familiar to early Jewish settlers. The gallery features Adirondack art and artists, and the complex often hosts concerts.
Free. July-August, daily 11 a.m.-3 p.m.

SPECIAL EVENT
WOODSMEN'S DAYS
14 Second St., Tupper Lake, 518-359-9444; www.woodsmendays.com

Logging demonstrations, chainsaw carving and axe throwing are some of the events that dominate this annual outdoor event held at Tupper Lake Municipal Park. Second weekend in July.

WHERE TO STAY
★SHAHEEN'S
314 Park St., Tupper Lake, 518-359-3384, 800-474-2445; www.shaheensmotel.com

Nature surrounds at Shaheen's where rooms boast peaceful forest views. The rooms could use a makeover, but they are clean and the staff is eager to please.
31 rooms. Complimentary breakfast. Pool. $61-150

UTICA
See also Herkimer, Oneida, Rome

Near the western end of the Mohawk Trail, Utica has been a manufacturing and trading center since its early days. By 1793 there was stagecoach service from Albany. The opening of the Erie Canal brought new business. The first Woolworth "five and dime" opened here in 1879.

WHAT TO SEE
CHILDREN'S MUSEUM
311 Main St., Utica, 315-724-6128; www.museum4kids.net

One of the nation's oldest children's museums includes hands-on exhibits teaching history, natural history and science. Highlights include an Iroquois exhibit with a section of Long House, a well-stocked dress-up area, and outdoor railroad display.

Admission: adults $9, seniors $8, children 2-17 $7, children under 2 free. Monday-Tuesday, Thursday-Friday 9:30 a.m.- 3 p.m., Saturday 9:45 a.m.-3:15 p.m.

F.X. MATT BREWING COMPANY
830 Varick St., Utica, 315-642-2480; www.saranac.com

Started by a German-born immigrant in 1885, this is one of only a few regional breweries left in the country. A visit includes a plant tour, trolley ride, a visit to the 1888 Tavern and free beer or root beer samples (for those under 21).

Admission: adults $5, children under 12 free. June-August, Monday-Saturday 1-4 p.m., Sunday 1-3 p.m.; September-May, Friday-Saturday, 1 p.m., 3 p.m.

MUNSON-WILLIAMS-PROCTOR ARTS INSTITUTE
310 Genesee St., Utica, 315-797-0000; www.mwpai.org

This institute comprises a museum, performing arts center and well-regarded art school. The Museum of Art boasts a sizeable collection of 18th-, 19th- and 20th-century American and European paintings and sculpture displayed throughout 20 galleries. Adjacent to the main building is Fountain Elms, a Victorian house museum, with five mid-19th-century rooms and various changing exhibits. It's worth visiting the art school galleries to observe up-and-coming talent.

Free. Tuesday-Saturday 10 a.m.-5 p.m., Sunday 1-5 p.m.

UTICA ZOO
99 Steele Hill Road, Utica, 315-738-0472; www.uticazoo.org

More than 250 exotic and domestic animals roam this 80-acre zoo including Siberian tigers, red pandas and Burmese pythons. There is also a small Children's zoo.

Admission: adults $6.75, seniors $5.75, children 4-12 $4.25, children under 4 free. Daily 10 a.m.-5 p.m.

WHERE TO STAY
★BEST WESTERN GATEWAY ADIRONDACK INN
175 N. Genesee St., Utica, 315-732-4121; www.bestwestern.com

All of the amenities you'd expect from a Best Western hotel are here from in-room wireless Internet access for business travelers to a game room for the kids. The guest rooms could use a facelift, but they are spacious and clean. The hotel is only minutes from many local universities and the Stanley Theater.

89 rooms. Complimentary breakfast. Business center. Fitness center. Pets accepted. $61-150

★★HOLIDAY INN

1777 Burrstone Road, New Hartford, 315-797-2131; www.holiday-inn.com

Conveniently situated near some of Central New York's top tourist destinations including the Baseball Hall of Fame, Colgate University and the Munson Williams Proctor Institute, this chain hotel offers guest rooms and suites with basic décor. Added amenities include a business center and outdoor pool.

100 rooms. Restaurant, bar. Business center. Fitness center. Pool. Pets accepted. $61-150

★★RADISSON HOTEL-UTICA CENTRE

200 Genesee St., Utica, 315-797-8010; www.radisson.com

This upscale chain hotel is a pleasant surprise. The lobby and public areas are bright and tastefully decorated. The soothing décor carries into the guest rooms where large picture windows and contemporary furnishings provide an updated atmosphere. Additional perks include a large fitness facility, indoor pool and hot tub.

158 rooms. Restaurant, bar. Business center. Fitness center. Pool. $61-150

WHERE TO EAT
★★★HORNED DORSET

Highway 8, Leonardsville, 315-855-7898

Apple orchards and farmland create a bucolic backdrop for the first-class New American cooking and impeccable European service found at this historic inn with its charming, expansive dining rooms. There are rooms in the inn should you wish to stay longer and savor the rural setting.

French. Dinner. $36-85

WARRENSBURG

See also Bolton Landing, Lake George, Lake Luzerne

Near Lake George, Warrensburg is an old-time village in the heart of a year-round tourist area and is populated with campgrounds, dude ranches and antiques shops. Activities include canoeing, fishing, golf, swimming, tubing, skiing, horseback riding and biking, among others. The fall foliage here is especially beautiful.

WHAT TO SEE
WARRENSBURG MUSEUM OF LOCAL HISTORY

47 Main St., Warrensburg, 518-623-2928

Exhibits detail the history of Warrensburg from the time it became a town to present day. Artifacts on display include photographs, industry tools and everyday household items.

Free. Hours vary.

SPECIAL EVENT
WORLD'S LARGEST GARAGE SALE AND FOLIAGE FESTIVAL

Warrensburg, 518-623-2161; www.warrensburggaragesale.com

Self-proclaimed as the largest garage sale in the world, this annual fall event draws dealers, collectors and curious consumers from across the country. Food vendors and crafts dealers also arrive in great numbers. Everything from vintage treasures to old junk can be found at this massive sale. Free. First weekend in October.

WHERE TO STAY
★★★FRIENDS LAKE INN
963 Friends Lake Road, Chestertown, 518-494-4751; www.friendslake.com

A stay at this restored 19th-century inn offers cross-country skiing, a private beach and canoeing on Friends Lake. Many of the Adirondack-styled rooms feature soaring ceilings, river rock-enclosed fireplaces and whirlpool tubs. The inn's New American menu features dishes such as braised Chilean sea bass with a tomato fennel broth and ancho-rubbed lamb chops with a minted pea purée. 17 rooms. Restaurant, bar. Pool. $251-350

WHERE TO EAT
★★FRIENDS LAKE INN
963 Friends Lake Road, Chestertown, 518-494-4751; www.friendslake.com

With its original tin ceiling and rustic wood beams, this restaurant exudes country charm. Yet the food is anything but simple. Standout dishes include Hudson Valley duck breast in a mandarin thyme reduction atop orzo and spinach, and caramelized sea scallops with ginger polenta cake and roasted red peppers.

American, seafood. Lunch, dinner. Reservations recommended. Outdoor seating. Children's menu. Bar. $36-85

★★★MERRILL MAGEE HOUSE
3 Hudson St., Warrensburg, 518-623-2449; www.merrillmageehouse.com

Situated in the heart of the Adirondack Mountains, the Merrill Magee offers comfortable, relaxed accommodations—and delicious dining. The inn's dinner menu includes New York strip steak with mushroom and tomato ragu and shrimp Florentine, and jumbo shrimp sautéed with bacon, garlic and spinach. Continental. Dinner, Sunday lunch. Closed Tuesday-Wednesday. Reservations recommended. Outdoor seating. Bar. $16-35

WATERLOO
See also Geneva, Seneca Falls

The Church of Jesus Christ of Latter-Day Saints (Mormon) was founded by Joseph Smith and five other men in a small log cabin here on April 6, 1830. The site is commemorated at the Peter Whitmer Farm.

WHAT TO SEE
MCCLINTOCK HOUSE
14 E. Williams St., Waterloo, 315-568-2991

Prominent players in the first Women's Rights Convention and the Underground Railroad, Thomas and Mary Ann McClintock were progressive Quakers activists in the Waterloo community in the mid-1800s. Today, the house that they resided in from 1836 to 1856 is open to the public, with tours available on weekends. Many of their personal affects still remain in the house.

Free. June-August, Thursday-Sunday 1-4 p.m.

PETER WHITMER FARM

1451 Aunkst Road, Waterloo, 315-539-2552

Visit the site where the Church of Jesus Christ of Latter-Day Saints was organized with six members in 1830. This tiny log building housed Joseph Smith while he translated the Book of Mormon, and also marks the spot that Joseph performed some of his first priesthood ordinances.

Free. Daily.

TERWILLIGER MUSEUM

31 E. Williams St., Waterloo, 315-539-0533; www.waterloony.com/library.html

This historical museum houses collections dating from 1875 and includes Native American displays and authentic full-size vehicles. There is a replica of a general store that provides a glimpse of life as it was in the 1920s. The recently restored Fatzinger Hall on the Library's second floor seats 140, and hosts Spring and Fall programs featuring dance, theater productions, music and public lectures. Five rooms are furnished to depict a specific era.

Admission: adults $3. Tuesday-Friday 1-4 p.m.

WATERLOO MEMORIAL DAY MUSEUM

35 E. Main St., Waterloo, 315-539-9611; www.waterloony.com/MdayMus.html

Mementos of the Civil War, World War I, World War II, the Korean conflict, Vietnam and the first Memorial Day are on exhibit in this 20-room mansion furnished to depict the 1860-1870 period. Mid-April-mid-May, September-mid-December Tuesday-Saturday 10 a.m.-5 p.m.; Mid-May-August, Tuesday-Sunday 10 a.m.-5 p.m.

WHERE TO STAY
★★HOLIDAY INN

2468 Mound Road, Waterloo, 315-539-5011; www.hiwaterloo.com

This chain hotel is conveniently located near Seneca Lake, Watkins Glen International Speedway, the Finger Lakes Wine Festival and the Waterloo Premium Outlets. Guest rooms are small, but clean and bright, offering views of either the courtyard or the outdoor pool. The small onsite gym is a nice added amenity.

148 rooms. Restaurant, bar. Fitness center. Pool. Pets accepted. Tennis. $61-150

WATERTOWN

See also Clayton, Sackets Harbor

Watertown lies along the Black River, 11 miles east of Lake Ontario and 22 miles south of the St. Lawrence. Within the city, the river falls more than 100 feet, which makes for great whitewater rafting. During a county fair in 1878, young Frank W. Woolworth originated the idea of the "five-and-dime" store.

WHAT TO SEE
AMERICAN MAPLE MUSEUM

9753 Main St., Croghan, 315-346-1107; www.lcida.org/maplemuseum.html

If you've ever been curious how maple syrup goes from the tree to the table, this museum will answer all of your questions. Along with exhibits on the history of maple syrup and sugar production techniques, the former school building has displays of maple syrup production equipment, logging tools and an American Maple Hall of Fame.

Admission: adults $4, children 5-14 $1, children under 5 free. June, Monday, Friday-Saturday 11 a.m.-4 p.m.; July-mid-September, Monday-Saturday 11 a.m.-4 p.m.

JEFFERSON COUNTY HISTORICAL SOCIETY MUSEUM

228 Washington St., Watertown, 315-782-3491; www.jeffersoncountyhistory.org

After massive renovations, the Historical Society Museum re-opened in the 1892 Port Townsend City Hall building. Exhibits explore Jefferson County's unique forested waterfront history including Native American traditions, maritime heritage and an interactive photograph program.

Admission: adults $5, seniors and military $4, students $3, children under 5 free. Tuesday-Friday 10 a.m.-5 p.m.

ROSWELL P. FLOWER MEMORIAL LIBRARY

229 Washington St., Watertown, 315-788-2352; www.flowermemoriallibrary.org

This Neo-Classic marble building houses murals of local history, French furniture and genealogy exhibits. The library also offers numerous children's programs such as story time and the Snowflake Festival.

Free. June-August, Monday-Thursday 8 a.m.-8 p.m., Friday 8 a.m.-4 p.m.; September-May, Monday-Tuesday, Thursday-Friday 9 a.m.- 8 p.m., Wednesday, Friday-Saturday 9 a.m.- 5 p.m.

SCI-TECH CENTER

154 Stone St., Watertown, 315-788-1340; www.scitechcenter.org

Kids will love the hands-on focus at this science and technology museum. With more than 40 exhibits, including a laser display and discovery boxes, there's plenty to keep everyone busy. Stop into the science store to grab a souvenir on your way out.

Admission: adults $4, Children 3-18 $3, seniors $2, children under 3 free. Tuesday-Thursday 10 a.m.-2 p.m., Friday-Saturday 10 a.m.-4 p.m.

WHERE TO STAY
★★BEST WESTERN CARRIAGE HOUSE INN

300 Washington St., Watertown, 315-782-8000; www.bestwesternwatertownny.com

With amenities you might expect—a fitness center, wireless Internet—and some you might not—an onsite barber shop and salon—this Best Western branch is well situated to explore the Thousand Islands and Black River. Some guest rooms have been updated with microwaves and hot tubs, and all guests receive complimentary coffee each morning.

160 rooms. Restaurant, bar. Fitness center. Pool. Pets accepted. $61-150

★DAYS INN

110 Commerce Park Drive, Watertown, 315-782-2700; www.daysinn.com

Though guest rooms could use a facelift on the décor front, they are spacious and well equipped with microwaves, cable TVs and minibars. The fitness center is cramped, but the indoor pool is a nice bonus.

135 rooms. Restaurant, bar. Business center. Fitness center. Pool. $61-150

WATKINS GLEN

See also Corning, Elmira, Ithaca

Watkins Glen is situated at the southern end of Seneca Lake, where the famous tributary gorge for which it is named emerges in the middle of the town. Several estate wineries offering tours and tasting are located near town on the southern shores of the lake. The International Speedway that opened here in 1956 also draws racing fans and car aficionados.

WHAT TO SEE
FAMOUS BRANDS OUTLET

412 N. Franklin St., Watkins Glen, 607-535-4952; www.famousbrandsoutlet.com

This is a popular spot for finding deals on such brand names as Carhartt, Dockers and Columbia.

Free. Monday-Saturday 9 a.m.-8 p.m., Sunday 10 a.m.-5 p.m.

INTERNATIONAL MOTOR RACING RESEARCH CENTER AT WATKINS GLEN

610 S. Decatur St., Watkins Glen, 607-535-9044; www.racingarchives.org

The center features a wonderful display of all things racing, including cars. The broad collection also showcases books, films, fine art, photographs, documents, magazines, programs and memorabilia with a motor sports theme.

Free. Monday-Saturday 9 a.m.-5 p.m.; also some Sunday race days.

SENECA LAKE WINE TRAIL

Watkins Glen; www.senecalakewine.com

Thirty-six wineries dot the hillsides of Seneca Lake, and each comes complete with its own charm, lake-filled scenery and tasty wines. The region and climate support a variety of different grapes to produce rieslings, chardonnays, cabernet francs and pinot noirs, along with many hybrid blends. Follow Highways 14 or 414 for tastings and tours. Contact the Seneca Lake Wine Trail for more information.

Admission: prices vary. Hours vary.

SENECA LODGE

State Route 329, Watkins Glen, 607-535-2014; www.senecalodge.com

This place is very popular with race fans, many of whom reserve a year in advance. Onsite is the historic Seneca Lodge Restaurant. The bar has NASCAR memorabilia and gets its fair share of pro race mechanics.

Free. Daily.

WATKINS GLEN STATE PARK

Route 14, Watkins Glen, 607-535-4511; www.nysparks.state.ny.us/parks

This park is all about its amazing natural gorge and waterfalls. Water drops more than 400 feet over two miles and a span of 19 waterfalls. Be sure to hit the gorge trail (as long as you have adequate hiking shoes) as it winds along beautiful Glen Creek for more than a mile, under waterfalls and through the Cavern Cascade. There is also an Olympic-sized pool for a dip during the summer. Guided walking tours by certified naturalists are available. If you have the equipment, Watkins Glen also is considered to have some of the best

campgrounds in the country.
Free. Daily.

SPECIAL EVENTS
GRAND PRIX FESTIVAL
Watkins Glen, 607-535-4300; www.lightlink.com/gpfest
Every fall, Watkins Glen transitions from a quiet community to a vintage racing forum with antique race cars buzzing through the streets along part of the original 6.6 mile race circuit. New drivers are inducted into the Drivers Walk of Fame and photograph and memorabilia displays are set up around town. September.

WATKINS GLEN INTERNATIONAL
2790 County Road 16, Watkins Glen, 607-535-2481; www.theglen.com
IMSA and NASCAR Winston Cup races are held here. Tours are also available and let you drive the track (in your own set of wheels) behind a pace car.
Late May-September.

WHERE TO EAT
★★CASTEL GRISCH
3380 County Road 28, Watkins Glen, 607-535-9614; www.castelgrisch.com
Leave the lederhosen at home, but bring your appetite for German fare to this popular local restaurant. Wiener schnitzel is a must here, as is the apple strudel. There is also a wine tasting room open April through December.
Alpine. Lunch, dinner (Friday-Saturday). Outdoor seating. $16-35

★★WILDFLOWER CAFÉ
301 N. Franklin St., Watkins Glen, 607-535-9797; www.roosterfishbrewing.com
A nice treat after a day in Watkins Glen State Park (the restaurant is located near the entrance), this upscale spot serves everything from jambalaya to Philly cheese steaks. The Crooked Rooster Brewpub next door has a fine selection of craft ales on tap.
American. Lunch, dinner. Bar. $16-35

WEST POINT
See also Newburgh
West Point has been of military importance since Revolutionary days when it was one of four points on the mid-Hudson River fortified against the British. In 1778, a great chain was strung across the river to stop British ships and links can still be seen today. The military academy was founded by an act of Congress in 1802. The barracks, academic and administration buildings are closed to visitors, but there is still plenty to explore.

WHAT TO SEE
BATTLE MONUMENT
Thayer and Washington Roads, West Point, 845-938-4011; www.usma.army.mil
One of the most prominent monuments at the academy, this memorial was dedicated in 1897 to the 2,230 officers and men of the Regular Army who

died in action during the Civil War. Nearby are some links from the chain used to block the river from 1778 to 1782.
Free. Daily.

CADET CHAPEL

Ruger Road and Cadet Drive, West Point, 845-938-4011; www.usma.army.mil
On a hill overlooking the campus, this large edifice was constructed entirely in native granite and has Gothic and Medieval influences in its architectural style. The Cadet Chapel organ, dating back to 1911 is now the largest church organ in the world. Don't miss the Sanctuary Window with the inscription "Duty, Honor, Country."
Free. Daily.

MICHIE STADIUM

700 Mills Road, West Point, 845-938-4011
This 42,000-seat stadium sits directly alongside the Hudson River and boasts spectacular views of the waterway and the field from nearly every seat. Home football games are a sight to see.
Admission: prices vary. Hours vary.

WEST POINT MUSEUM

Pershing Center, West Point, 845-938-2638; www.usma.edu/Museum
With exhibits on everything from the evolution of warfare to the storied history of West Point, this museum is generally considered the oldest and largest military museum in the nation. Collections include weapons, artwork, uniforms and propaganda.
Daily10:30 a.m.-4:15 p.m.

WHERE TO STAY
★★THE THAYER HOTEL

674 Thayer Rd., West Point, 845-446-4731, 800-247-5047; www.thethayerhotel.com
Located in the heart of the Hudson Valley and on the grounds of the Academy, this historic hotel is both sprawling and intimate. The granite-and-brick structure was originally built to accommodate military personnel in 1926 and carries the name of one of the Academy's early superintendents, Colonel Sylvanius Thayer. Marble floors, detailed chandeliers, and soaring ceilings outfit the lobby, while guest rooms boast rich wood furnishings and prints of historic military scenes. Ask for a room with a view of the Hudson unless you're more inclined to enjoy a vantage towards the Academy and surroundings hillsides. The onsite restaurant serves a spectacular Sunday brunch.
151 rooms. Restaurant, bar. Fitness center. $151-250

WHERE TO EAT
★★CANTERBURY BROOK INN

331 Main St., Cornwall, 845-534-9658; www.thecanterburybrookinn.com
Exposed wood ceiling beams, brick walls and two massive fireplaces lend a rustic appeal to the interior while the kitchen churns out decidedly Swiss fare. The oven-baked French onion soup and grilled Swiss bratwurst are perfect indulgences on a chilly afternoon. In warmer weather, request to sit on the

terrace to enjoy classic wiener schnitzel alongside the meandering brook. Swiss. Lunch, dinner. Closed Sunday-Monday. Outdoor seating. Bar $16-35

★PAINTER'S
266 Hudson St., Cornwall-on-Hudson, 845-534-2109; www.painters-restaurant.com
The menu is eclectic with influences from Italy to Mexico to Japan, but no matter which culinary route you take, your taste buds will be rewarded with fresh flavors. The signature focaccia with red peppers, garlic, mushrooms and provolone is outstanding as is the sesame tuna with sweet Chinese mustard and wasabi cream.
International. Lunch, dinner, Sunday brunch. Reservations recommended. Outdoor seating. Children's menu. Bar. $16-35

WESTBURY
See also Garden City, Roslyn
On Long Island, Westbury and its surrounds offer opportunities to enjoy the great outdoors, learn about American history, shop for antiques and dine on delicious food, all within an hour of New York City.

WHAT TO SEE
OLD WESTBURY GARDENS
71 Old Westbury Road, Old Westbury, 516-333-0048; www.oldwestburygardens.org
This historic mansion dates back to 1906. The 66-room house features paintings, magnificent furniture and trinkets of all kinds. The gardens have a variety of flora and fauna that change with the seasons. The estate has been featured in such films as The Age of Innocence.
Admission: adults $10, seniors $8, children 7-12 $5, children under 7 free. April, Saturday-Sunday 10 a.m.-5 p.m.; May-October, Wednesday-Monday 10 a.m.-5 p.m. Closed November-March.

WESTBURY MUSIC FAIR
960 Brush Hollow Road, Westbury, 516-334-0800; www.musicfair.com
This concert series offers a unique chance to see performances in a theater-in-the-round style. Most of the stars are from eras past and have included Paul Anka, Ringo Starr, Aaron Neville and Tony Bennett. Schedules vary so check the Web site for updated concert listings.
Prices and showtimes vary.

WHERE TO EAT
★★BENNY'S RISTORANTE
199 Post Ave., Westbury, 516-997-8111; www.bennysristorante.com
If the line that snakes out the door is any indication, this is certainly a popular place with locals. The atmosphere is casual and the owner, Benny, makes you feel at home from the moment you sit down. All of the pasta dishes are winners. If you're looking for a more filling entrée, opt for the almond-crusted branzino or filet mignon "Rossini." Patience is a requirement on weekend nights when chaos is part of the experience.
Italian menu. Lunch (Monday-Friday), dinner. Closed Sunday. Reservations recommended. $36-85

★★GIULIO CESARE RISTORANTE

18 Ellison Ave., Westbury, 516-334-2982

A veteran to the Long Island dining scene, this traditional Italian restaurant shows its age through kitschy décor and brusque service. Nevertheless, the food is fresh and perfectly seasoned with such interests as striped bass alla Livornese and veal Milanese.

Italian menu. Lunch, dinner. Closed Sunday. Bar. $36-85

WHITE PLAINS

See also Brewster, Mount Kisco, Tarrytown, Yonkers

In October 1776, General George Washington outfoxed General Lord Howe here. Howe, with a stronger, fresher force, permitted Washington to retreat to an impregnable position. He never could explain why he had not pursued his overwhelming advantage. Today, White Plains is a popular suburb to New York City.

WHAT TO SEE
MONUMENT

S. Broadway and Mitchell Place, White Plains

The Declaration of Independence was adopted at this site on July 1776, and the State of New York was formally organized.

Free. Daily.

WASHINGTON'S HEADQUARTERS

140 Virginia Road, North White Plains, 914-949-1236; www.westchestergov.com

This 18th century farmhouse once served as Washington's command post during the Battle of White Plains. The converted museum now showcases Revolutionary War relics, colonial artifacts and original furniture used by Washington himself.

Free. Third Sunday of the month, noon-3 p.m.

WHERE TO STAY
★LA QUINTA INN AND SUITES

94 Business Park Drive, Armonk, 914-273-9090; www.lq.com

A fitness center, free wireless Internet access and complimentary breakfast are just some of the amenities at this suburban chain property. Business travelers will like the close proximity to numerous company headquarters including IBM. The Marc Charles Steakhouse downstairs is a notch above your typical hotel restaurant.

179 rooms. Restaurant, bar. Complimentary breakfast. Business center. Fitness center. Pets accepted. $61-150

★★★HILTON RYE TOWN

699 Westchester Ave., Rye Brook, 914-939-6300; www.hilton.com

Spacious and well-appointed guest rooms await at this hotel in suburban Rye Brook. Accommodations feature Hilton's signature Serenity Beds, with plush mattress-toppers and down comforters and pillows, as well as CD players, alarm clock radios with MP3 docks, mini-bars and work desks with lamps. A fitness center and pool help keep guests fit, and three onsite restaurants provide dining options for every palate.

437 rooms. Restaurant, bar. Business center. Fitness center. Pool. Pets accepted. Tennis. $151-250

★★★RENAISSANCE WESTCHESTER HOTEL

80 W. Red Oak Lane, White Plains, 914-694-5400, 800-891-2696; www.marriott.com

Rooms at this hotel offer both comfort and luxury with rich fabrics, down comforters, plush pillows and views of the surrounding countryside. An indoor pool, whirlpool and Jacuzzi, as well as indoor tennis courts, volleyball courts and a fitness center with cardio equipment and free weights offer onsite recreation.

350 rooms. Restaurant, bar. Business center. Fitness center. Pool. Tennis. $151-250

★★★THE RITZ-CARLTON, WESTCHESTER

3 Renaissance Square, White Plains, 914-946-5500; www.ritzcarlton.com

Whether it's to avoid the 24-hour honking of New York City or to get closer to nature with nearby bike trails and forest preserves, you'll find plenty to reasons to extend a stay at this elegant hotel. Guest rooms are sizeable and contemporary with neutral tones and modern amenities including flat-screen TVs and wireless Internet. If you can, opt for a room on the club level, which awards you a personal concierge, decadent treats throughout the day and access to a complimentary business center. No need to go into the city for dinner; just book a table at BLT, where famed chef Laurent Tourondel whips up tasty French bistro fare in a chic urbane setting.

118 rooms. Restaurant, bar. Business center. Fitness center. Pool. Spa. $351 and up

SPA

★★★★THE RITZ-CARLTON SPA, WESTCHESTER

3 Renaissance Square, White Plains, 914-467-5888, 800-241-3333;
www.ritzcarlton.com

This gorgeous spa offers a getaway from New York City. The 10,000-square-foot complex features a gym and indoor rooftop pool, but if you really want to relax, head for one of the four massage rooms. Opt for seasonal signature services, such as summertime's Liquid Gold treatment, which includes a cleanse of lemon and chamomile, a warm wrap of jojoba butter and a massage. Or if you want to put your best face forward when you return home, get the Derma Lift Facial, which uses a skin-lifting massage and marine-based products to brighten the skin. Wrap up your trip to the spa with the half-hour New York Minute manicure—the closest you'll get to the hustle and bustle of the Big Apple at this sanctuary.

WILMINGTON

See also Lake Placid, Saranac Lake

The gateway to Whiteface Mountain Memorial Highway, Wilmington is made-to-order for skiers and lovers of scenic splendor. Only a few miles northeast of Lake Placid, this small town hosted many of the ski events for the 1980 Winter Olympics

WHAT TO SEE
HIGH FALLS GORGE

Route 86, Wilmington, 518-946-2278; www.highfallsgorge.com

Deep ravines cut into the base of Whiteface Mountain by the Ausable River have created spectacular waterfall displays and soaring granite cliffs here. A network of modern bridges and paths run throughout the gorge and let you explore the natural beauty either on foot or by snowshoe (during winter). Admission: adults $10-14, children 4-12 $7-10. May-October, daily 9 a.m.-5 p.m.; November-December, Friday-Tuesday 10 a.m.-4 p.m.; January-March, daily 10 a.m.-4 p.m.

WHITEFACE MOUNTAIN MEMORIAL HIGHWAY

Highway 431, Wilmington, 800-462-6236

For a scenic view without quite as much physical exertion, opt for this five-mile toll road to the top of Whiteface Mountain. The top will reward you with views of the St. Lawrence River, Lake Placid and the verdant hills of Vermont. Free. Daily.

WHITEFACE MOUNTAIN SKI CENTER

Highway 86, Wilmington, 518-946-2223, 877-754-3223; www.whiteface.com

One of the most famous mountains in the region for skiing (though it's only the fifth tallest), this mountain boasts runs more than 2 1/2 miles long with a vertical drop of 3,350 feet. There are also rental facilities, ski schools and a cafeteria. From June to October (weather permitting), the chairlifts are used to transport mountain bikers and hikers to the top. Admission: prices vary. Daily.

WHERE TO STAY
★HUNGRY TROUT MOTOR INN

5239 Route 86, Wilmington, 518-946-2217, 800-766-9137; www.hungrytrout.com

While the inn itself isn't anything special, the location is hard to beat, situated alongside the west branch of the Ausable River and only minutes from Whiteface Mountain. Some rooms have kitchenettes and complimentary picture windows framing the slopes of the mountain come standard with every room. Be sure to bring your lure; the Ausable River offers some of the best fly-fishing in the region.

16 rooms. Closed April, November. Bar. Pets accepted. $61-150

★LEDGE ROCK AT WHITEFACE

5078 NYS Route 86, Wilmington, 800-336-4754; www.ledgerockatwhiteface.com

You can't stay much closer to Whiteface Mountain than this two-story motel. The rooms are basic, but comfortable and some rooms have mountain views. Complimentary cookies and hot cocoa are served in the great room in fall and winter, while you enjoy the large fireplace and pool table. Fishing guides are on-hand during peak season.

18 rooms. Bar. Pets accepted. $61-150

WHERE TO EAT
★WILDERNESS INN II
Highway 86, Wilmington, 518-946-2391
Bedecked in wood paneling and a cozy stone fireplace, this small restaurant is a good stop for hearty American fare. Keep it simple with stuffed pork chops or sliced roast beef. In summer, there is a fantastic patio with views of the mountain.
American. Dinner. Closed Wednesday. Outdoor seating. Children's menu. $16-35

WOODSTOCK
See also Kingston, Saugerties, Shandaken
Woodstock has traditionally been known as an art colony. In 1902, Englishman Ralph Radcliffe Whitehead came from California to set up a home and handicraft community (Byrdcliffe, north of town). The Art Students' League of New York established a summer school here a few years later, and in 1916 Hervey White conceived the Maverick Summer Music Concerts, the oldest chamber concert series in the country. Woodstock was the original site chosen for the famous 1969 Woodstock Music Festival. When the event grew bigger than anyone imagined, it was moved 60 miles southwest to a farmer's field near Bethel, New York. Nevertheless, the festival gave Woodstock much notoriety.

WHAT TO SEE
WOODSTOCK ARTISTS ASSOCIATION GALLERY
28 Tinker St., Woodstock, 845-679-2940; www.woodstockart.org
This gallery has been at the heart of the Woodstock community since 1920. Organized into three spaces, the building showcases constantly changing group exhibits, solo shows and a nationally recognized permanent collection. Many of the works displayed here are by local and regional artists and represent all mediums.
Friday-Saturday noon-6 p.m., Sunday noon-5 p.m.

SPECIAL EVENT
MAVERICK CONCERTS
120 Maverick Road, Woodstock, 845-679-8348; www.maverickconcerts.org
Maverick Concerts, America's oldest continuous summer chamber music festival and winner of the Chamber Music America/ASCAP Award for Adventurous Programming, thrives on the love of great music and the spirit of its unique site in the unspoiled woods.
June-August. Prices and showtimes vary.

WHERE TO EAT
★★BEAR CAFÉ
295A Tinker St., Woodstock, 845-679-5555; www.bearcafe.com
When this cafe says streamside, it means it. The outdoor patio is only a few feet from bubbling Saw Kill stream, and the indoor space is just as charming with wood paneled walls and a large stone fireplace. The authentic American fare is skillfully executed with such standout dishes as Alaskan King salmon with French lentils in a Dijon mustard crust, and a half-pound farm-raised

steak sandwich with hand-cut French fries.

American. Lunch, dinner. Closed Tuesday. Outdoor seating. Bar. $36-85

★★BLUE MOUNTAIN BISTRO

1633 Glasco Turnpike, Woodstock, 845-679-8519; www.bluemountainbistro.com

This family-owned and operated country bistro mixes French flair with Mediterranean flavors to produce quality dishes, including the first tapas bar in the region. It is also situated in a charming, weathered barn with a soaring beamed ceiling and a patio adjacent to the herb garden. The jumbo sea scallops with wild mushroom risotto is a standout.

French, Mediterranean. Dinner. Reservations recommended. Outdoor seating. Bar. $16-35

★★VIOLETTE RESTAURANT & WINE BAR

85 Mill Hill Road, Woodstock, 845-679-5300; www.violettewoodstock.com

Brightly colored mismatched chairs and intimate table settings give a sense of simple elegance to this local favorite where mother-and-son team churn out inventive cuisine including butternut squash crepes and moules steamed in a tomato and basil broth.

American. Lunch, dinner, Sunday brunch. Closed Wednesday. Reservations recommended. Outdoor seating. Bar. $16-35

YONKERS

See also Tarrytown, White Plains

Yonkers, on the New York City border, was originally purchased by Adriaen van der Donck in the early 1600s. His status as a young nobleman from Holland gave him the nickname "DeJonkeer," which led to the metamorphoses of the city's name from The Yonkers Land, until finally, Yonkers.

NEW YORK ★★★★★

WHAT TO SEE

BILL OF RIGHTS MUSEUM

897 S. Columbus Ave., Mount Vernon, 914-667-4116

Exhibits include a working model of an 18th-century printing press and dioramas depicting John Peter Zenger, whose trial and acquittal for seditious libel in 1735 helped establish freedom of the press in America.

Free. Monday-Friday 9 a.m.-5 p.m.

THE HUDSON RIVER MUSEUM OF WESTCHESTER

511 Warburton Ave., Yonkers, 914-963-4550; www.hrm.org

Housed in the 1876 Glenview Mansion, an Eastlake-inspired Hudson River house overlooking the Palisades, the museum showcases a slew of constantly changing exhibits depicting 19th- and 20th-century American art. The Andrus Planetarium runs educational programs on the planets, oceans and stars. There's a great jazz festival held here in summer.

Admission: adults $5, seniors and children $3. Wednesday-Sunday noon-5 p.m., Friday noon-8 p.m.

ST. PAUL'S CHURCH NATIONAL HISTORIC SITE

897 S. Columbus Ave., Mount Vernon, 914-667-4116; www.nps.gov/sapa

This storied church was the setting for historical events that established the basic freedoms outlined in the Bill of Rights. The stone-and-brick Georgian structure was started in 1763 but not completed until after the Revolutionary War. It served not only as a church but also as a meetinghouse and courtroom where Aaron Burr once practiced law.

Free. Monday-Friday 9 a.m.-5 p.m.

INDEX

NEW YORK STATE

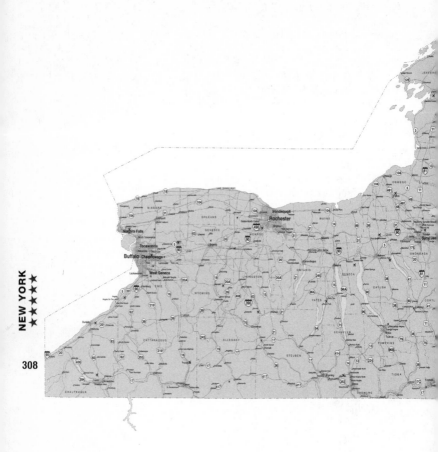

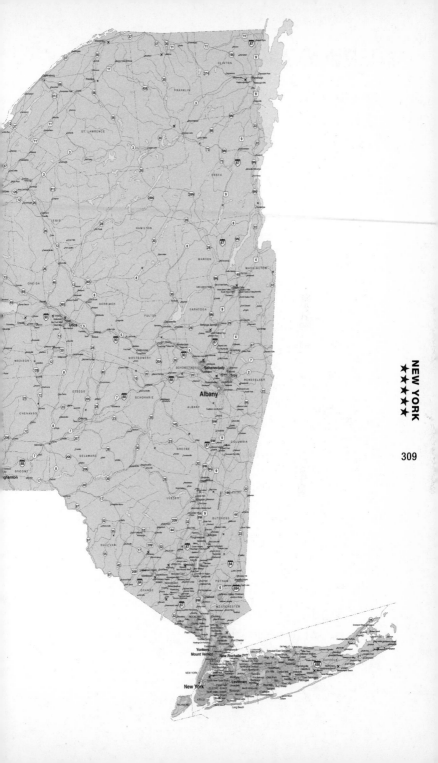

ALBANY

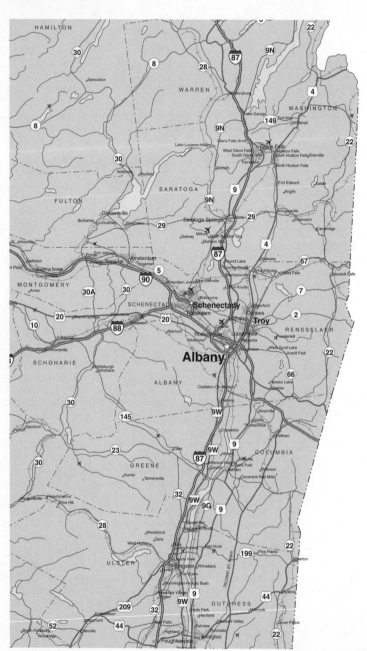

GREATER NEW YORK AREA

NEW YORK
★★★★

311

BUFFALO

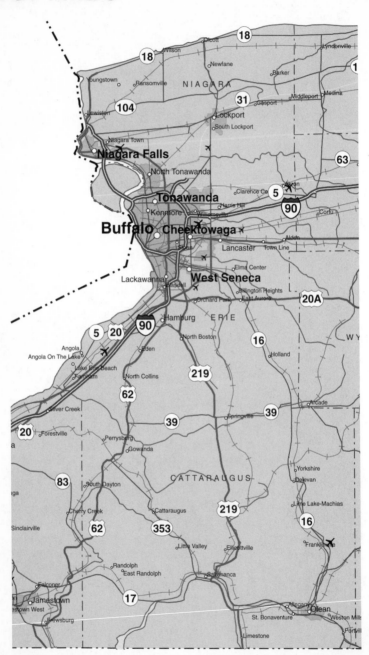

NOTES

NOTES

NOTES

NOTES

NOTES

NOTES